A SUMMARY

OF

BIBLICAL ANTIQUITIES:

FOR THE USE OF

Schools, Bible-Classes and Families.

BY JOHN W. NEVIN, D.D.

Wipf and Stock Publishers
EUGENE, OREGON

ENTERED according to Act of Congress, in the year 1849, by the
AMERICAN SUNDAY-SCHOOL UNION
In the Clerk's Office of the District Court for the Eastern District of Pennsylvania.

Wipf and Stock Publishers
199 West 8th Avenue, Suite 3
Eugene, Oregon 97401

A Summary of Biblical Antiquities
For the Use of Schools, Bible-Classes and Families
By Nevin, John W.
ISBN: 1-59244-374-5
Publication date 10/1/2003
Previously published by American Sunday-School Union, 1849

PREFACE.

The following work was undertaken chiefly with a view of contributing some help to the great cause of Sunday-school education. That something of the kind is much wanted, for the use of common instructors, in the work of such education, cannot be doubted. The books in which such information as it is intended to contain is to be found, are not within the reach of most of those who are called to take upon them this character; and if they were, they are not adapted to answer effectually the want that is felt in the present case. Most of them have been written for the use of such as have far more than common advantages of education and learning, whose business leads them to much reading, and whose minds are trained to diligence and patience in the pursuit of knowledge. Even the few which have been designed for more popular and common use, are such that their advantages can never extend to the great majority of those who read the Bible: they are too large, and, of course, too expensive to be generally procured; they are too diffuse, and too much elevated in style, or darkened with learning, to be generally read or understood. Since the establishment of Sunday-schools, various short sketches of information on some particular points of Jewish Antiquities have been supplied in different publications intended for their use, which have, no doubt, answered a valuable purpose, so far as they extended; but all the advantage which such scattered fragments can secure must manifestly be very limited and imperfect, in comparison with what might be, and ought to be, derived from this quarter of scripture illustration. Evidently, a short, simple, systematic compilation, bringing together, with out technical phrase or learned discussion, the most essential points of the whole subject, in regular order, into small and convenient compass, is the only thing which can adequately meet the necessity that is experienced in this matter.

It is hoped that this present attempt may not be without something of its intended use, in furnishing such a compilation, easy to be procured and easy to be read, for the assistance of teachers. If it should in any measure answer this design, it will accomplish an object of vast usefulness. If, however, the remarks which have already been made are well founded, a work of this kind may be reasonably expected to be yet more extensively useful. As a help to the intelligent reading of the Scriptures, such a compilation, if not greatly defective in its form, is, no doubt, better suited for the use of *all* common readers, than any larger work.

It needs very little reflection, to be convinced of the importance of having some acquaintance with the circumstances, natural and moral, of the time and country in which the Bible was written, in order to read it with understanding. Though an inspired book, its language and style have been wisely conformed to the manner of *men*, for whose use it was designed; of course conformed, in these respects, to the particular manner of the people to whom it was at first directly communicated. Holy men of old spake as they were moved by the Holy Ghost; but they were suffered, at the same time, to speak and write in that style which the general usage of the age, modified by his own peculiar genius and taste, naturally led each one to adopt. Hence, the sacred books of Scripture, like other books, are stamped throughout with the lively impression of the place and period in which they were originally published. It is found not only in the language itself, but in unnumbered references, direct and indirect, to the existing state of things among those who were appointed first to receive them. Historical facts, objects of surrounding nature, the productions of art, with domestic, social, religious, and civil usages, are continually urged before the reader's mind, and noticed as things with which he is supposed to be perfectly familiar. And thus familiar they were to the ancient Jew. But widely different is our situation in this respect. Many hundred years separate us from the times of original revelation. And if Time had left the physical and moral scenery of Israel's ancient land untouched, instead of turning all into a waste, it would still be many hundred miles remote from the spot of our dwelling. With a different climate, we have different feelings; with a different location, different forms of nature around us; with a different education, a widely different manner of life. We are placed, therefore, under a double difficulty, when we come thus circumstanced to read the Bible. We are destitute of the knowledge and feelings of the ancient Jew, and, at the same time, we have notions and views of our own, which we are constantly liable to substitute in their stead. Hence, if no remedy be supplied, we must often be left altogether in the dark, by meeting with terms and images, the objects of which are utterly unknown; and often we shall derive to ourselves an entirely strange and unfounded conception of the writer's meaning, by affixing ideas to other images and terms, such as our habits of thought and speech may suggest, but which are foreign, in no small degree, from the usage of oriental antiquity.

What then is the remedy for this inconvenience? Evidently to seek acquaintance with the time, and the region, and the people, with which the Bible had to do in its first revelation:—as far as possible, become familiar with the history of the Jewish nation, the scenery of Palestine, the religion, government and manners of its ancient wonderful people. To read the Bible, in many parts, with a proper sense of its meaning, we need so much familiarity with these things as to be able to transport our minds away from all around us, and to clothe them, in the midst of Judea itself, with all the moral drapery that hung about the Israelitish spirit ages ago. We need to be conversant with the mountains, the plains and the streams; the beasts of the field and the birds of the air; the labours of the farmer and the habits of the shepherd; we need to walk, in fancy's vivid vision, through the streets of Jerusalem; to mingle with the inmates of the Jewish dwelling; to participate in their seasons of festive joy, and to sympathize with their sorrow in the day of calamity and bereaving death; we need to go up to the temple, to unite in its worship, to behold its solemn rites, and to admire the beautiful grandeur of its scene. True, indeed, *extensive* acquaintance with these things is to be expected only in the scholar; the common reader of the Bible is not favoured with equal opportunity; but is he therefore to content himself with *entire* ignorance? Assuredly not. The fact that such knowledge is wanted now, through the providence of God, to illustrate every page of the Bible, evinces it to be the will of God that *all* should, as far as they have the power, endeavour to acquire it. The same fact must lead every person who loves the Bible diligently to seek it, with every other help that may, under the blessing of the Holy Ghost, contribute to the profitable study of the precious book

TABLE OF CONTENTS.

PART I.

CHAPTER I.

GEOGRAPHY AND CLIMATE.

SECTION 1. *Of the Names and Divisions of the Holy Land* 19
General names, 19. Ancient divisions—Divisions in the time of Christ, 20.

SECT. 2. *Of the general Face of the Country* 21
Mountains, 21. Plains, 23. Deserts, 23. Rivers, 24. Lakes, 25. General advantages, 25.

SECT. 3. *Of Climate* 26
Seasons—Drought, 26. Dew, 26. Rains, 27. Winds—The Simoom, 29.

CHAPTER II.

NATURAL HISTORY.

SECT. 1. *Of Vegetable Productions* 30
I. WILD TREES: The Cedar, 30. The Oak, 31. The Terebinth, 32. The Fir and others—Shittim wood, 33. Gopher wood—Cinnamon, Cassia and Frankincense trees, 34. II. CULTIVATED TREES: The Olive, 35. The Fig tree, 36. The Sycamore—The Pomegranate tree, 37. The Apple tree—The Palm, 39. The Balsam tree—The Almond tree—The Vine, 40. III. PLANTS: Useful Herbs, 42. Weeds, 43. Grain—General fruitfulness in ancient times, 44. Present desolation, 45.

SECT. 2. *Of Animals* 45
I. QUADRUPEDS: Horse, 45. Ox—Ass, 46. Mule, 47. Camel—Sheep, 48. Goat, 49. Dog, 50. Hog—Lion, 51. Unicorn, 52

CONTENTS.

II Birds, 53. III. Water Animals: Whale—Leviathan, 53. Behemoth, 54. IV. Reptiles: Dragon, 54. Serpents, 55. Scorpion, 56. V. Insects: The Bee—The Locust, 56.

CHAPTER III.

DWELLINGS AND HOUSEHOLD ACCOMMODATIONS.

Sect. 1. *Of Dwellings*... 57
    Tents—Houses, 58. Porch—Court, 59. Roof, 60. Materials, 61. Cities—Gates, 62.

Sect. 2. *Of Furniture*... 62
    Carpets—Beds and Seats, 63. Lamp—Pots and Cups—Bottles, 63. Table—Table-couch, 64. Mill, 65. Ovens, 66.

CHAPTER IV.

OCCUPATIONS.

Sect. 1. *Of the Pastoral Life*... 67
    Its origin, 67. Ancient prevalence and dignity, 68. Care of flocks, 69. Wells, 70. Produce—Cheese—Ancient Butter and Wool, 71. Modern Shepherds, 72. Pastoral Imagery, 72.

Sect. 2. *Of Husbandry*.. 73
    The Jews a nation of farmers, 74. Plough, 75. Harrow—Yoke, 76. Ox-goad—Sowing—Harvest, 77. Threshing-floor—Threshing instruments, 78. Winnowing—Vineyards, 80. Vintage—Wine-press—Wine, 81. Emblems, 82. Fruit of the Olive—Oil-press, 83. Oil gardens—Honey, 84.

Sect. 3. *Employments of Handicraft and Trade*........................... 86
    General remarks, 86. Trades little followed before the captivity, held in different esteem afterwards, 87. Commerce—Imports and exports, 88. Measures, Weights and Coins—Measures of length, 89. Hollow Measures, Dry and Liquid, 90. Money in early times, 91. Coins, 92.

Sect. 4. *Of the Learned Professions*.. 93
    Tribe of Levi, 94. Judges—General learning, 95. Prophets, 96. Scribes, 97. Schools, 98.

CHAPTER V.

DRESS, MEALS, SOCIAL INTERCOURSE.

Sect. 1. *Of Dress*.. 98
    Cloth—Colours, 98. Camel's-hair—Sackcloth—The Tunic, 100. The Upper Garment, 101. The Girdle, 102. Sacred Garments—

CONTENTS 11

Sandals and Shoes, 104. The Mitre—The Veil, 105. Hair, 106. The Beard, 107. Ornaments, 108. Wardrobes, 109.

SECT. 2. *Meals and Entertainments*.. 110
Preparation of Food, 110. Time of Meals, 111. Washings—Thanksgiving, 112. Mode of Eating—Social Feasts, 113. Spiritual food, 114.

SECT. 3. *Of Social Intercourse* 116
General remarks, 116. Style of Manners in the East, 117. Salutations, 118. Visits, 119. Formality—Conversation, 121.

CHAPTER VI.

DOMESTIC CUSTOMS AND HABITS.

SECT. 1. *Of the Marriage Relation* 122
Early Marriages, 122. Contract—An espoused Wife, 123. Wedding Customs, 124. The Marriage Supper—Confirmation of Marriage, 125. Spiritual Marriage, 126. Marriage Parables, 127. Polygamy, 130. Divorce, 131.

SECT. 2. *Of the Relation between Parents and Children* 132
Desire of Children—Duty of marrying a childless Brother's widow, 132. Ceremonies relating to Children—Names, 133. Parental Authority—The Birthright, 134. Adoption, 136.

SECT. 3. *Of Slaves*... 136
Character of Slavery among the Jews, 136. The Steward—Slavery among other nations, 137. Branding, 138.

CHAPTER VII.

DISEASES AND FUNERAL CUSTOMS.

SECT. 1. *Of Diseases* 139
Origin of Sickness, 139. Supernatural Diseases—Demoniacal Possessions, 140. Exorcism, 142. The stroke of Heaven under the form of natural fatal Diseases—Some Diseases the channels of God's anger more especially than others, 143. Pestilence or Plague—Leprosy, 144. Sin the leprosy of the soul, 147. Anointing the sick with oil, 148.

SECT. 2. *Customs that attended Death and Burial*.............. 149
Expressions of grief, 149. Embalming, 150. Burial, 151. Sepulchres, 152. Sheol or Hades, 154.

CHAPTER VIII.

MISCELLANEOUS MATTER.

Sect. 1. *Of Writing* 158
Its origin, 158. Ancient Materials for Writing—Books, 159
Letters, 160.

Sect. 2. *Of Music and Dancing* 161
Origin and design of Music, 161. Harp—Psaltery—Organ—Pipe—Horn—Trumpet—Cymbal—Tabret, 162. Sacred Music—Dancing, 163.

Sect. 3. *Of Games and Theatres* 164
Public Shows, 164. Games of Heathen, not Jewish custom—Grecian Games, 165. Object of public Games—Allusions to the Grecian Games in the New Testament, 168. Theatres—Gladiator Shows—Fights with Wild Beasts, 170.

Sect. 4. *Modes of Dividing and Reckoning Time* 171
Days—Hours, 171. Watches—The Week, 173. Months, 175.
The Year, 176. Way of Counting, 177.

CHAPTER IX.

POLITICAL INSTITUTIONS.

Sect. 1. *Patriarchal Government* 178
Its Nature—Origin, 178. History, 179.

Sect. 2. *Ancient Israelitish Government* 182
Its Author—Object, 182. Nature—God its King, 183. Idolatry, 185. Destruction of the Canaanites—Measures to prevent intercourse with Idolaters, 186. Division of the Land, 187. Inheritance, 188. Governments and orders of the individual Tribes, 189. Genealogical Tables, 190. Judges, 191. Tribe of Levi, 192. Kings, 193.

Sect. 3. *Jewish Government after the Captivity* 194
Under the Persians, Greeks and Romans, 194. Centurions—Publicans, 196. Judges—Sanhedrim, 197. Inferior Court, 199. Insurrections, 200. Expectations of the Messiah, 201.

Sect. 4. *Of Kings* 202
Robe—Diadem—Throne—Sceptre—Royal Palace and Table, 203.—Approach to the King, 204. Journeys attended with a splendid retinue—Royal name, 205. Counsellors—Prophets—Recorder—Scribe—High-Priest—Governor of the Palace—King's Companion—Life-guard—Runners, 206. Account of Archelaus, 207.

CONTENTS.

Sect. 5. *Of Punishments* 207
Trials—Trial of our Lord, 207. Design of Punishments—Sin and Trespass Offerings—Fines, 208. Scourging, 209. Confinement, 210. Retaliation—Excommunication, 211. The Blood-avenger. 212. Stoning, 213. Crucifixion, 214.

Sect. 6. *Of Military Affairs* 220
How Armies were raised, 220. David's army, 221. Roman army in Judea—War-chariots, 222. Elephants, 223. DEFENSIVE WEAPONS: Helmet—Breast-plate, 224. Greaves—Girdle—Shield, 225. OFFENSIVE WEAPONS: Sword, 225. Spear—Javelin—Bow and Arrow, 226. Sling—Engines on the walls, 227. Battering-ram—Manner of fighting, 228. Effects of victory—Israelites more humane than other people, 229.

PART II.

CHAPTER I.

GENERAL HISTORY OF RELIGION.

Origin of the Church, 235. Its General Scheme and Relation to the World, 237. Its Unity, 238—and Diversities of Outward Constitution withal, 240. State before the Flood—Call of Abraham, 241. Organization of the Jewish Church—General Plan of the Jewish State; different Sorts of Laws, 242. The Moral Law, 243. Ceremonial Law, 245. Continuance of the Jewish Church all its appointed time, 248. Respect which that Dispensation had to the Gospel, 249. Hope of the Messiah—A General Mistake on this Point, 250. Expectation of Elias, 252. Introduction of the Gospel—Its Conflict with Ancient Prejudices, 254.

CHAPTER II.

THE TABERNACLE.

Origin of the Tabernacle, 256. The Court of the Tabernacle, 258. The Frame and Coverings of the Sacred Tent, 259. The Altar of Burnt-offering, 262. The Brazen Laver, 265. The Golden Candlestick, 266. The Table of Shew-bread, 268. The Altar of Incense, 269. The Ark of the Covenant, 272. The Cherubim, 273. The Shechinah, 275. Meaning of the whole Picture, 276. The Tabernacle in the Wilderness, 279. The Tabernacle in the Land of Canaan, 280.

CHAPTER III.

THE TEMPLE.

Sect. 1. *The Holy City* 282
Origin of Jerusalem—Situation, 282. Mount of Olives, 283 The Garden of Gethsemane—Valley of Hinnom, 284. Siloam, 285. Calvary—First Destruction of the City, 286. Ruin by the Romans—Present State, 287.

Sect. 2. *The First Temple* 288
Preparation for it by David, 288. General Plan, 290. Dedication and Ruin, 293.

Sect. 3. *The Second Temple* 294
Its Building, and Defects, 294. Subsequent Glory of it—Work of Herod, 295. The Court of the Gentiles, 296. Porches, 297. Markets, 299. The Court of the Women, 300. The Court of Israel, 302. The Court of the Priests, 303. The Sanctuary, 304. The Tower of Antonia, 306. Beauty of the Second Temple, 307. Its Final Ruin, 308.

CHAPTER IV.

MINISTERS OF THE TABERNACLE AND TEMPLE.

Sect. 1. *The Levites* 309
Their Separation, 309. Duties—Porters, 310. Musicians, 311 Nethinims, 313.

Sect. 2. *The Priests* 313
Origin of the Priestly Office—Separation of Aaron and his Family, 313. Duties of the Priests, and Qualifications, 314. Division into Courses, 315. Meaning of the Priesthood, 316.

Sect. 3. *The High-Priest* 318
Virtue of his Office—Sacred Dress, 318. Succession, 319. Urim and Thummim, 320. Signification of the High-Priest's Office, 322

CHAPTER V.

SACRIFICES AND OTHER RELIGIOUS OFFERINGS.

Sect 1. *Different Kinds of Sacrificial Offerings in use among the Jews* 323
Sacrifices in use from the Fall, 323. BLOODY OFFERINGS, 324. Four Kinds of them, viz: Burnt Offerings, 225. Sin Offerings,

CONTENTS.

326. Trespass Offerings, 327. Peace Offerings, 328. Covenant Sacrifices, 330. Private and Public Sacrifices, 331. SACRIFICES THAT WERE NOT BLOODY, 332. First-fruits, 335. The First-born, 336. Tithes, 337. Vow-gifts, 339. Half-shekel Tax, 341. Lesson derived from this Subject, 342.

SECT. 2. *Sacrificial Rites*.. 343

Laying of Hands on the Head of the Victim, 343. Slaying of it—Sacredness of Blood, 344. Preparation for the Altar, 345. Waving and Heaving, 346. Fat, 346. Salt, 347. The Sacrificial Pile—Disposal of the Flesh, 348.

SECT. 3. *Meaning and Origin of Sacrifices*............................... 349

Reason cannot account for the Use of Bloody Sacrifices, 349. Their Meaning according to the Bible, 350. Their Origin, 354 The idea of Atonement connected with the Use of them, before as well as after the time of Moses, 355. Sacrifices of Cain and Abel, 356. Acceptance of Sacrifices by Fire—Figurative Sacrifices, 358.

CHAPTER VI.

SACRED TIMES AND SOLEMNITIES.

SECT. 1 *The Daily Service*... 359

Morning and Evening Services, 359. Manner of the Morning Service, 360. The Evening Service, 364. Reverence for the Sanctuary, 364.

SECT. 2. *The Sabbath*.. 366

Its Origin, 366. Character in the Jewish economy, 367. Manner of its Observance, 368.

SECT. 3. *New Moons and Feast of Trumpets*............................ 370

SECT. 4. *The Three Great Festivals*....................................... 372

The Passover, 373. How celebrated in the Time of our Saviour, 374. Paschal Families, 375. Search for Leaven, 375. Slaying of the Lambs, 376. The Supper, 377. The Hagigah, 379. Introduction of the Harvest, 380. Meaning of the Passover, 381. The Feast of Weeks, 382. The Feast of Tabernacles, 382. Ceremonies added to it in later times, 383.

SECT. 5. *The Great Day of Atonement*.................................... 386

Nature of this Solemnity—Manner of its Service, 386. Meaning of it, 388.

SECT. 6. *Sacred Years*... 390

The Sabbatic Year, 390. The Year of Jubilee, 391.

CONTENTS

SECT. 7. *Sacred Seasons of Human Institution* 392
  Annual Fast Days, 392. The Feast of Purim, 393. The Feast of Dedication, 393.

CHAPTER VII.

MEMBERS OF THE JEWISH CHURCH.

Members by Birth, 395. Ceremonial Disqualifications for Sacred Duties, 396. Removal of Uncleanness, 397. The Water of Separation, 397. Its typical import, 398. Proselytes, 399.

CHAPTER VIII.

SYNAGOGUES.

Origin of Synagogues, 400. Plan of Synagogue-Houses, 402. Officers of the Synagogue, 404. The Synagogue Worship, 407. Lessons from the Law and the Prophets, 407. Synagogue Discipline, 411. Pattern of the Synagogue followed in the Constitution of the Christian Church, 413.

CHAPTER IX.

RELIGIOUS SECTS.

SECT. 1. *The Pharisees* 415
  Belief of the Pharisees, 416. Tradition of the Pharisees, 417.

SECT. 2. *The Sadducees* 423
  Origin of the Sect, 423. Doctrines of the Sadducees, 425.

SECT. 3. *The Essenes* 427

SECT. 4. *The Samaritans* 432

APPENDIX 439

BIBLICAL ANTIQUITIES.

PART I.

BIBLICAL ANTIQUITIES.

PART I.

CHAPTER I.
GEOGRAPHY AND CLIMATE.

SECTION I.
NAMES AND DIVISIONS OF THE LAND.

The country in which the Jews anciently lived has been distinguished by different names. It is called, in Scripture, the *Land of Canaan*, because it was first settled by Canaan, the youngest son of Ham, and because his descendants, the *Canaanites*, dwelt in it, till the "measure of their iniquity was full," and God destroyed them, to make room for his own people. It is styled the *Land of Promise*, on account of the promise made to Abraham, that it should be given to his seed for an inheritance, when he himself sojourned there as a stranger in a strange land. From the names of the nation to whom it was given, it is called the *Land of the Hebrews;* the *Land of Israel;* and the *Land of Judah.* Because it was chosen by God as the country in which his true worship should be preserved, and was long honoured with his peculiar presence and care, it is often named, the *Holy Land;* and once, by Hosea, the *Lord's Land.* It is also called *Palestine:* this name is very old, (Ex. xv. 14;) it is the same as *Philistia*, meaning, properly, the *Land of the Philistines;* and then used in a larger sense, for the whole country of Canaan, because the Philistines were so important a people among the nations by whom it was first settled. This last is the most convenient name, and is now become the most common, in speaking of the whole country which the ancient Jews inhabited. It will, therefore, be the one most generally used for that purpose, in the present work.

For many years, the whole land, from the mountains of Lebanon in the north, to the borders of Edom in the south, and from the great Mediterranean Sea on the west, to the mountains of Gilead eastward, remained united under one government. Each of the twelve tribes had its particular portion assigned by lot, in which it dwelt separate from the others; but all together made one people and one nation. On the east side of Jordan, Reuben, Gad, and half of the tribe of Manasseh, had their inheritance: all the others were settled west of that river. But immediately after the death of Solomon, this beautiful union was broken asunder. Two kingdoms occupied the land instead of one. The *Kingdom of Judah* lay to the south, taking in the tribes of Judah and Benjamin. The other ten tribes revolted from the house of David, and formed all the country north of Benjamin, together with that which lay east of Jordan, into a new government. This was called the *Kingdom of Israel*; frequently, by the prophets, *Ephraim*, because that was the principal tribe, and the one in which the capital city of the kingdom stood; and sometimes, from the name of its capital, the whole kingdom was called *Samaria*.

In the time of our Saviour, the land of Palestine was divided into several provinces, under the Roman government. On the west side of Jordan, the northern part, as far down as the lower end of the lake of Gennesareth, was called *Galilee*. Part of this was named *Galilee of the Gentiles*, because it bordered on the land of the heathen; and also *Upper Galilee*, because it lay farthest north and abounded in mountains. The southern part of it was called *Lower Galilee*. It took in all the country directly west of the Gennesareth lake, and was, in general, a rich and fruitful plain. This particular district enjoyed, more than any other, the presence of Jesus Christ, while he was on earth. Hence he was called the *Galilean*, and his disciples are styled *Men of Galilee*. (Acts i. 11.)

South of Galilee lay *Samaria*, so called from the city of that name. It embraced the lower part of what had once been the kingdom of Israel, or the ten tribes. The origin of the name and of the city to which it was first given, is related 1 Kings xvi. 24. The Samaritans were a mixed race, settled in the country after the captivity of the ten tribes.*

South of Samaria was the country of *Judea*. Sometimes this name seems to have been used for the whole land of Palestine, in the time of Christ; but more commonly and properly, only for that part which, before the captivity, had been the kingdom of Judah, including all the country south of

---

* See the history of their rise, in the 17th chapter of the Second Book of Kings.

Samaria. From this account of the situation of each province, it appears, that any person going directly from Galilee to Judea "must needs go through Samaria," (John iv. 4,) because it lay just between the two. That part of Judea which lay farthest south was inhabited principally by descendants of the ancient Edomites. They had settled themselves there while the Jews were in captivity at Babylon, having been driven from their own country, which lay just below, by the violence of war, and finding none to hinder them from taking possession of the land. When the Jews returned, they were, for a long time, too weak to recover their territory out of their hands: the Edomites, or Idumeans, as they were then called, still continued to dwell in the southern border. At length, however, a little more than a hundred years before the coming of Christ, John Hyrcanus, the great Jewish prince, conquered them completely, and compelled them either to leave the country or to embrace the religion of the Jews. They chose to change their religion rather than their place, and, accordingly, from that time, became a part of the Jewish nation. Still, that part of the country in which they lived continued to be called *Idumea*, and the people *Idumeans*, long after. (Mark iii. 8.)

The country *beyond Jordan* was broken up into seven or eight different provinces. As, however, these divisions seem to have been not very clearly defined, and more than once altered, it is not easy to describe exactly their situation: nor is it necessary, since only a part of them are so much as named in the New Testament, and these scarcely more than mentioned. It is enough to know that *Decapolis* was a tract of country lying east of the lake of Gennesareth, and stretching somewhat above it, also, towards the north: that *Iturea* and *Trachonitis*, of which Philip was tetrarch, (Luke iii. 1,) took in the country still farther north, though the lower part of Iturea was probably the same as the upper part of what was called the region of Decapolis; and that *Abilene*, mentioned in the same passage, was the most northern district of all, lying in a valley formed by the mountains of Lebanon, not far westward from Damascus.

SECTION II.

FACE OF THE COUNTRY.

PALESTINE is a mountainous country. Two great ranges seem to run through the whole length of the land; one on the east and the other on the west side of Jordan; not in one regular, unbroken chain but frequently interrupted by valleys, and shooting off in irregular heights, sometimes to one side and sometimes to the other, so as occasionally to leave a considerable plain through the middle of the country. Hence, the same range is called by different names, in different regions. The *Mountains of Gilead* formed the eastern range. The southern part of these mountains was called *Abarim*. From the high summit of one of these, called *Nebo*, Moses surveyed the whole land of Canaan, before he died. The northern part of the same range was named *Bashan*; it was much celebrated for its stately oaks and excellent pastures, where numerous herds of the finest cattle were fed. Hence, there is often allusion made in the Bible to the *oaks of Bashan*, and the strong *bulls of Bashan*, (Psalm xxii. 12, Isa. ii. 13, &c.) This range joins the Mountains of *Lebanon*, on the north, in that part which was anciently called *Hermon*. Lebanon abounded in lofty cedars, in choice fir trees and refreshing springs of water. Its highest summits are covered with continual snow.

Stretching down toward the south, the western range spreads itself, in numerous ridges, all over Galilee of the Gentiles. In lower Galilee, its principal appearance was confined to the western border, near the Great Sea, leaving a great part of the country level, with only here and there a separate height rising on the prospect, such as Mount *Tabor*, where our Saviour is supposed to have been transfigured, or the Mount of *Gilboa*, where Saul was defeated and slain. Several of these heights were frequented by our Saviour. He was accustomed to "go out into a mountain to pray," and sometimes continued there "all night, in prayer to God," (Luke vi. 12;) and on one of them, he preached the remarkable sermon recorded by Matthew in his gospel. (Chaps. v. vi. vii.) The most considerable mountain in this region is *Carmel*, situated on the shore of the Mediterranean Sea. It was exceedingly fruitful, as is intimated by its name, which means, *a vineyard of God*. On the top of this mountain, Elijah the prophet prayed for rain, in the days of Ahab, while his servant went seven times to look for the cloud, till at last it rose like a man's hand over the western sea. (1 Kings xviii. 42—44.) Farther down, toward the south, the same general range was called the *Mountains of Israel*, and the *Mountains of Ephraim*. Among these were Mount Ebal and Mount Gerizim, separated from each other by a small valley, in which stood the ancient city of Shechem, called, in the New Testament, Sychar. The *Mountains of Judah* were the continuance of the range, as it passes southward, through the territory of that tribe, to the ancient heritage of Edom. These mountainous tracts abound with caverns, which are sometimes found of great size. In times of danger from enemies, it was anciently common to seek refuge and shelter in such natural hiding-places. To " enter into the holes of the rocks and into the caves of the earth," was, therefore, an expression that represented a season of distress and dismay. (Isa. ii. 19.) The great caves of Judah afforded no small protection to David, in the time of his cruel persecution by Saul. Robbers, also, were accustomed to conceal themselves in the same sort of retreats; and to this day, the large caverns of Palestine are not unfrequently made, in this way, as they were in the days of our Saviour, *dens of thieves.*

As so great a proportion of the land is covered with mountains and hills, a tract of level country of any extent was regarded with more notice than in countries like our own : hence, every such plain had its distinguishing name. The most noted among them was the *Plain of Jezreel,* or, as it is sometimes called, the *Great Plain.* It reached entirely across the country, from Mount Carmel and the sea to the bottom of lake Gennesareth, about ten miles. It has been the scene of several great battles: there Barak discomfited the mighty army of Sisera, so that " there was not a man left," (Judges iv. 16;) and there, also, king Josiah fell, when he went out and fought in disguise with Necho, king of Egypt. (2 Kings xxiii. 29.) Another plain lay along the Mediterranean Sea, from Mount Carmel to the southern border of Judah. The upper part of this was called *Sharon,* a name that belonged also to two other places. There was also the " region round about Jordan." (Matt. iii. 5.) This was a tract of level country, on the sides of that river, from the lake of Gennesareth to the Dead Sea, about twelve miles broad.

Wildernesses and *Deserts* are frequently mentioned in the Scriptures; but we must not suppose that these always mean desolate regions without inhabitants. The Jews gave the name of desert, or wilderness, to any tract of country that was not cultivated. There were accordingly two kinds of deserts. First, such as we are accustomed to understand by that name in our own age; plains of barren sand, where scarce a fountain of water can be found, and only the most scanty herbage can grow. Such as these are not found in Palestine itself; but, in the neighbouring country of Arabia, have always been well known. The other kind of deserts were mountainous tracts of country, thinly inhabited, and chiefly used for the pasturing of cattle; less fruitful than other parts of the land, but not without considerable growth of different wild productions, with sufficient supply of water. Such were the *wildernesses* of

Judah, mentioned in the history of David, and the "Wilderness of Judea," in which John began to preach, (Matt. iii. 1,) as well as the *deserts* in which he lived "till the day of his showing unto Israel." (Luke i. 80.) One of the most dreary and barren of these deserts lay between the Mount of Olives and the Plains of Jericho, and became a favourite lurking place for thieves or robbers, where they fell upon travellers on the road between Jerusalem and Jericho. (Luke x. 30.) So many robberies were committed there, that it was called the *Bloody Way*. Into some part of this wild region, probably, our Saviour was led by the Spirit, "to be tempted of the devil," after his baptism. (Matt. iv. 1.)

There is only one river in Palestine that deserves the name; this is the Jordan. The other streams that are sometimes called rivers, become important only when they are swelled with floods of rain or melting snow and ice from the mountains. Then they dash and roll along with a great deal of noise and force; but when the drought of summer comes, they sink down into mere brooks, and often are dried up altogether. Hence, Job, because his friends had disappointed his expectation, and brought him only reproach instead of comfort, compares them to such streams: "My brethren have dealt deceitfully as a brook, and as the stream of brooks they pass away; which are blackish by reason of the ice, and wherein the snow is hid; what time they wax warm, they vanish: when it is hot, they are consumed out of their place. The paths of their way are turned aside: they go to nothing and perish." (Job vi. 15—18.)

The *Jordan* runs from Mount Lebanon to the Dead Sea, passing through the lake of Gennesareth in its way. In the spring, when the snows of Lebanon melt, it rises above its common banks: from this circumstance, it has two channels; one far wider than the other, with banks of its own, to hold the water in the time of this flood. It was in the spring, the harvest-time of Palestine, during this swelling of the river, that the Israelites, in the time of Joshua, passed over, at the command of God, into the land of Canaan; when "the waters above stood and rose up upon an heap very far," till the whole nation had gone over the dry channel. (Josh. iii. 15, 16.) The space between the outer and inner bank, on each side, which (except in the spring) remains dry, is grown over with thick bushes and reeds, where wild beasts find a safe hiding place, until the yearly rise of the river compels them to fly; whence the expression, to "come up as a lion from the swellings of Jordan." (Jer. xlix. 19.)

The *lake of Gennesareth*, through which the Jordan flows, called, also, the *Sea of Galilee*, because it lay just east of that country, and the *Sea of Tiberias*, from a city of that name which stood on its shore,) is filled with clear, pure water, excellent to drink, and abounds with different kinds of fish. On account of these advantages, it was a common saying among the Jews, that " God loved that sea more than all other seas in the world." It has its bed in a valley surrounded by lofty and steep hills. Here, the disciples of our Lord pursued their business of fishing: over its beautiful bosom the Redeemer himself often sailed: when its waves were tost with the tempest they heard his voice and were still: and when he willed to walk upon its waters, they bore him up like solid ground.

The *Dead Sea*, called, also, the *Sea of the Plain* and the *Salt Sea*, into which the Jordan empties all its waters, is spread over the ruins of four ancient cities, destroyed for their wickedness, by a miracle from God. (Gen. xix. 24, 25.) It too, like the lake just mentioned, is surrounded with high hills, except on the corner toward Jerusalem, where it is bounded by a barren, scorched plain. Its waters are bitter and nauseous, and more salt than those of the ocean; and the land around it is so filled with salt that it will not produce plants. The whole appearance of the place is dismal, as if the wrath of the Almighty were abiding upon it still.

The land of Palestine is highly praised, in the Scriptures, for its natural advantages. It is described as a "good land and a large, a land flowing with milk and honey." (Ex. iii. 8) " A land of brooks of water, of fountains and depths, that spring out of the valleys and hills; a land of wheat, and barley, and vines, and fig trees, and pomegranates; a land of oil olive and honey;" a land wherein the people should eat bread without scarceness, and lack nothing; whose stones were iron, and out of whose hills they might dig brass. (Deut. viii. 7—9.) No country in the east could boast such a variety of blessings. Egypt alone could compare with it in fruitfulness of soil; but, then, Egypt was never cheered with showers of rain: it was watered only by the yearly overflowing of the river Nile. Egypt, too, was not adorned with mountains and hills; and, of course, could not abound in the same variety of productions. Nothing like the *glory of Lebanon*, or the *excellency of Carmel*, *the cold flowing waters of the rock*, or *the springs of the valleys*, was found in all its extent. Hence, Moses tells the Israelites, that Egypt, with all its advantages, was by no means equal to the land which they were going to inherit. "The land whither thou goest in to possess it, is not as the land of Egypt from which ye came out, where thou sowedst thy seed, and wateredst it with thy foot, as a garden of herbs; but the land whither ye go to possess it, is *a land of hills and valleys, and drinketh water of the rain of heaven.*" (Deut. xi. 10, 11.)

SECTION III.
CLIMATE.

THE weather in Palestine, as in our own country, varies in different places and at different times. The year seems to have been divided, at a very early period, into SIX SEASONS, each consisting of two months. We find them all mentioned in God's promise to Noah, after the flood: "While the earth remaineth, seedtime and harvest and cold and heat and summer and winter shall not cease." (Gen. viii. 22.) These same divisions are found among the Arabs to this day.

HARVEST began some time in the first part of our April, and so ended in the first part of June. During this season, the weather is generally very pleasant: towards the close of it, however, it begins to grow uncomfortable through heat. SUMMER, or the time of fruits, followed the season of harvest, and lasted the next two months. During this time, the heat in that country becomes more and more severe; so that the inhabitants choose to sleep under the open sky, on the roofs of their houses. The HOT SEASON came next, beginning in the middle of August: the early part of this period is excessively warm; but toward the end of it, the weather gradually grew less oppressive.

From the middle of April to the middle of September, it neither rains nor thunders: hence, in the time of Samuel it was considered a miracle, when, in answer to his prayer, it thundered and rained in the time of harvest. (1 Sam. xii. 17.) And hence, the ancient proverb, "As snow in summer, and as rain in harvest, so honour is not seemly for a fool." (Prov. xxvi. 1.) Sometimes, in the beginning of harvest, a cloud is seen in the morning, but as the sun rises, it vanishes away. (Hos. vi. 4.) Afterward, during May, June, July and August, not a solitary cloud appears, and the earth receives no moisture but from the dews of the night. These dews fall far more plentifully there, than any in our part of the world; so that those who are exposed to them become wet to the skin. In Solomon's Song, the Bridegroom says, "my head is filled with dew, and my locks with the drops of the night." Because they are so heavy and so important, they are often mentioned in the Scriptures among th. rich blessings of the country, and the *dew* is everywhere us. 1 as a symbol of the divine goodness. In the morning. he ever, it is speedily dried up, according to the beautiful allusion of Hosea, (vi. 4:) "O Ephraim, what shall I do unto thee? O Judah, what shall I do unto thee? for your goodness is as a morning cloud, and as the early dew it goeth away." The stronger plants, by nourishment received each night from these gentle showers, are enabled to withstand the heat of the day; but all the smaller herbs, unless they grow by some rivulet of water, wither and die. The country is covered with dreariness; the fountains and brooks are in a great measure dried; and the ground becomes so hard, that it often splits open with large clefts. The heat is rendered still more distressing, if the east wind happens to blow for a few days; this is dry and withering, and proves very injurious to the vines and the crops of the field. Hence, it is used as an emblem of great calamity: "Though he be fruitful among his brethren, an east wind shall come, the wind of the Lord shall come up from the wilderness, and his spring shall become dry, and his fountain shall be dried up." (Hos. xiii. 15.)

After the hot season, came SEEDTIME; it lasted from the first part of October to the first part of December. During this season, the weather is various—often misty, cloudy and rainy. The air, at the commencement of this period, is still very warm; as it advances, it becomes continually cooler, till toward the end of it, the snow begins to fall upon the mountains. WINTER was made up of the two following months. In this season, snow frequently falls, but seldom lies a whole day, except on the mountains; thin ice also is formed, which melts as soon as the sun rises to any height; the north winds are chill; thunder, lightning and hail, are frequent, with heavy showers of rain; the roads become difficult to travel, especially among the mountains: whence our Lord told his disciples to pray that their *flight might not be in the winter.* (Matt. xxiv. 20.) The brooks are filled, and streams that were scarcely noticed before, swell into the likeness of rivers, rushing in every direction through the land. The remainder of the year, from the first half of February to the first half of April, was called the COLD SEASON, because, in the beginning of it, the weather is still cold, though it soon grows warm, and, in some places, quite hot. During this time, the rains still continue, with frequent thunder, lightning and hail. From the commencement of it, the earth begins to put forth the appearance of spring; the trees are soon covered with leaves, and the fields with flourishing grain, or flowers of every different hue.

From seedtime to harvest, Palestine is watered with numerous showers of rain. According to the accounts of travellers, a rain of two or three days falls in the early part of October. By this, the ground is prepared for ploughing and sowing; being before so hard, that it could not receive cultivation, and so dry, that seed cast upon it could not possibly grow. A season of clear weather, of about twenty days, follows, which the farmer improves, if he is wise, as his most favourable seedtime. When this is over, the rains return with plentiful fall. These first heavy showers, with which the rainy season commenced after the long drought of summer, were called the *former or early rains*. In like manner, the rain that fell just before harvest, in the spring, was called *the latter rain*, because with it the rainy season ended: it comes about the beginning of April, and was considered necessary, to bring the crops forward to their full perfection. *The early and the latter rain* are mentioned, in Scripture, as the rich blessing of God; since, when these were rendered sure, the period between them being always abundant with showers, the crop of the husbandman could hardly fail to be good. The quantity of rain that falls between seedtime and harvest is very great. Sometimes it descends in torrents, rushing down the hills, and sweeping away even houses and cattle that may fall in the way. To these violent rains our Saviour refers, beautifully and impressively, at the close of his sermon on the mount: "The rains descended, and the floods came, and the winds blew, and beat upon that house, &c." (Matt. vii. 25, 27.)

Through the winter, the weather is extremely various, as it is felt at different times and in different places. On the higher mountains, it is exceedingly cold, while, at the same time, it is found not unfrequently, in the plains, quite warm. Some of the people pass the whole year without fire, though it is considered agreeable, and for more delicate persons, necessary, from December to March. The nights are often severely cold, even after the warmest days. "In the day, says Jacob, the drought consumed me, and the frost by night." (Gen. xxxi. 40.) The snow falls in large flakes, equal in size to a walnut, and has more resemblance to locks of wool than it has in our country. "He giveth snow like wool." (Ps. cxlvii. 16.)

When the sky was red in the evening, it was considered a sign of fair weather on the next day, but if it happened to be so in the morning, it led them to expect rain, as appears from the words of our Saviour, (Matt. xvi. 2, 3:) "When it is evening, ye say, It will be fair weather, for the sky is red; and in the morning, It will be foul weather to-day, for the sky is ed and lowering." A cloud rising from the west also gave warning of rain: "he said to the people, When ye see a cloud rise out of the west, straightway ye say, There cometh a shower, and so it is." (Luke xii. 54.)

WINDS. The east wind was the most injurious. In the summer, as has been said, it was dry and hot; withering, as it passed along, the herbage of the field. (Ps. ciii. 15, 16.) In the winter, it was cold and still without moisture, and left a sickly blight upon the grain wherever its influence fell. It was also particularly dangerous at sea: "Thou breakest the ships of Tarshish with an east wind." (Ps. xlviii. 7.) Every wind coming from any direction between east and north, or east and south, was called an east wind. Such was that tempestuous wind, called Euroclydon, that caused the wreck of the vessel in which Paul was sailing to Rome. (Acts xxvii. 14.) They are still common in that sea, and dreaded by the sailors. The west wind, coming from the sea, generally brought rain. That which came from the north is described by Solomon as *driving away rain*. (Prov. xxv. 23.) And Job tells us that *cold and fair weather are from the north*, (xxxvii. 9, 22 :) while the whirlwind more frequently rose from the south; and the winds from that quarter ordinarily brought heat; though sometimes the southern breezes appear to have been considered agreeable.

THE SIMOOM. There is a wind that blows at times in some countries of the East, of the most terrible character. It comes in a stream from over the burning sands of the desert, bearing poison and death with its course. Its approach is signified by the appearance of distant clouds slightly tinged with red; the sky loses its serenity, and becomes gloomy and alarming. As the current draws nearer, it presents to the eye a hazy aspect, resembling a sheet of smoke, coloured with purple, such as is seen in the rainbow. Happily, its path is never broad, generally measuring less than a hundred feet, and its rapid flight soon carries it over the country, not allowing it to be felt at any one point more than eight or ten minutes. At the same time, it always keeps about two feet above the surface of the ground. Persons, therefore, who see it coming, may save their lives, by throwing themselves instantly flat upon the earth, with their faces downward, and breathing as little as possible till it is past. This is the way commonly practised to avoid its deadly touch. A man would be equally secure if he could place himself about fifteen feet *above* the ground, as the current of the wind is generally not more than twelve feet high. Camels and other animals are instinctively taught, when they perceive its approach, to thrust their heads down and bury their nostrils in the earth Men, however, are often destroyed by its blast. It comes with such amazing rapidity, that it overtakes them on their feet before they are aware, and thus they receive its fatal, suffocating vapour into their lungs. They fall down directly, and lie without motion or life. If one of their limbs is shaken, to arouse them, it falls off; and very soon, the whole body turns black, with mortification spread throughout. It is especially dangerous when it comes in the night. Thousands, it is said, have, in more than one instance, perished in a single night, from its desolating breath. This wind is called, by the Arabs, *Simoom*, and, by the Turks, *Samyel*. It is supposed, by some, that the prophet intended the same, when he compared the coming judgments of God to *a dry wind of the high places in the wilderness*. (Jer. iv. 11.)

CHAPTER II.

NATURAL HISTORY.

SECTION I.

OF VEGETABLE PRODUCTIONS.

Moses describes the land of Palestine, as *a land of wheat, and barley, and vines, and fig-trees, and pomegranates; a land of oil olive and honey;* and the Scriptures abound with allusions to different kinds of trees and plants. Solomon, we are told, left a book on this subject: "He spake of trees, from the cedar of Lebanon, even unto the hyssop that springeth out of the wall: he spake also of beasts, and of fowl, and of creeping things, and of fishes." (1 Kings iv. 33.) If we had this book, we should, no doubt, know all about the different productions of the country in his time; but as it has been long since lost, we must rest satisfied with such general knowledge as can be gathered from the occasional notices found in the Bible, compared with the observations of travellers who have visited the east in modern times.

WILD TREES.

The *Cedar*, to which such frequent allusion is made in Scripture, is a most stately tree. Its roots spread far around below; it rises to a lofty height; its branches reach a great distance out on every side, forming a large and delightful shade,

Cedar Tree.

nd remaining covered with green leaves from one end of the year to the other. Its trunk often becomes exceedingly large, sometimes measuring twelve yards around; the wood is of a beautiful brownish colour, with a pleasant smell; being somewhat bitter, it is not touched by worms, so that it has been known to last in a building two thousand years. The principal growth of cedars was anciently on Mount Lebanon: most of them, however, have since been cut down, so that now only a few can be found, growing amid the snows in the highest part of the mountain. Kings, great men, and proud men, are compared to cedars, on account of their *strength* or their *loftiness;* so also the righteous, on the other hand, in allusion to their *usefulness* and *beauty.* (Ps. xcii. 12.)

Oaks abounded anciently in different parts of Palestine. Those which grew on Bashan were considered peculiarly fine. The broad and refreshing shade which they supplied was particularly grateful in that warm climate. It was common, in early times, to choose such a shade as the most pleasant place for setting up a tent. Under the shadow of the oak, also, idols were often erected by the corrupt, where they resorted from time to time, to engage in their abominable worship; and sometimes whole groves of this venerable tree were thus turned into retreats of impiety and shame, on account of the agreeable and secret shelter which they afforded.

Under the name of oak, in our translation of the Bible, is

Oak Tree.

included, (besides the common tree so called,) the *Terebinth* or *Turpentine* tree which belongs to the east. This is a large evergreen tree, with wide-spreading branches and numerous leaves. If allowed to stand, it is said that it will live a thousand years; and when it dies, its place is soon supplied by a new trunk, rising on the same spot, to equal size, and flourishing to an equal age. It was on account of this lasting character, and because of the single and separate manner in which they often grew, that these trees were sometimes used to designate particular places; and an aged *Terebinth* was spoken of with something of the same sort of distinction as that with which we make mention of a castle or a city Thus we read of the oak by Shechem, the oak in Ophrah, the oak in Jabesh, &c., as being perfectly well known to everybody that had ever been in those places. Several such trees grew in the region of Hebron, where Abraham dwelt a considerable time. Mamre, the brother of Aner and Eschol, was a personage of chief importance ir that district, to whom it especially belonged. Hence, it was called, according to the usage just noticed, the *Oaks*, or *Terebinths of Mamre;* for this seems to be what we are to understand by the *Plains of Mamre*, where the ancient patriarch pitched his tent Under the shade of one of these long-living trees, his simple dwelling stood; and it is said, that the very same tree continued standing till after the time of our Saviour. There might have been one growing on the same spot.

The *Fir tree* grows to a great height, and continues, like the cedar and the terebinth, green all the year. It was anciently used for building and for making furniture. It grew especially on Lebanon and Carmel. Several other kinds of trees grew wild on the mountains; such as the tall, straight *Cypress*, used at times for the making of dumb idols, because its wood refused to rot, and the stately *Pine*, well known in every quarter of the world. On lower grounds, along the mountain foot, or by the sides of the brook or river stream, or over the bosom of the fruitful plain, grew various trees and shrubs of humbler appearance. Among these were the *Linden*, or *Teil tree*, the *Alder*, the *Poplar*, the *Willow*, the *Laurel* and the *Myrtle*. This last is a large shrub, sometimes growing to the size of a small tree, very common in the valleys of Palestine. It is perpetually covered with leaves of the most beautiful green, and in its season, produces a great abundance of rose-like flowers, which delight the eye, and breathe a most fragrant perfume on all the air around.

The *Shittim-wood*, so frequently mentioned in Scripture, does not appear to have grown in the land of Palestine. There is the best reason to believe that it was the wood of the black *Acacia*. This tree flourishes in some parts of Egypt, and abundantly through the deserts of Arabia. It is of the size of a large mulberry tree, with rough bark and spreading branches well supplied with thorns. The wood is hard, tough, and capable of receiving from the hands of the carpenter a very smooth and beautiful polish. It produces flowers of an excellent fragrance. Hence, Isaiah joins the Shittah tree with the myrtle, and others held in esteem for beauty or richness of smell. (Isa. xli. 19.) It was particularly the wood of this tree which was used in the wilderness for making the tabernacle and its furniture. The wilderness of Arabia, in which the whole work was completed, furnishes no other tree at all suited for this use; while the acacia, or shittah, is so admirably fitted for it, by reason of its solid, beautiful and lasting character, that a better could scarcely have been found, if it could have been possible to make choice out of all the trees in the world. The moun tains of Sinai and Horeb might still, as in ancient times, afford an abundant supply of the same timber for such a building.

It is far more difficult to determine what was the *Gopher-wood*, of which the ark was made. Some have imagined that cedar is to be understood under that name; others, that it was the timber of pine; another class conceive that the solid and almost imperishable wood of the cypress is so called; while a still different interpretation supposes that the word Gopher was not intended to signify any particular tree at all, but merely expresses some circumstance in the manner of its use in that building, as *squared* timbers, *planed* wood, or *pitched* wood, as we know the ark was daubed with pitch, within and without. From this confusion of opinions, it appears that nothing satisfactory can be known on this subject.

In Arabia, also, as well as in India, grew the *Cinnamon* tree, and the *Cassia*, that resembles the cinnamon so much; each yields a valuable spice, bearing its name to the most distant countries. There, also, the precious *Frankincense* seems to have been procured. It is a dry gum, of a yellowish white colour, and a strong, fragrant smell, with a warm and biting bitter taste, formed of the sap that flows from some tree which travellers have not yet been able to discover and describe. It takes fire easily, and burns with a bright and strong flame, sending upwards a heavy cloud of aromatic smoke. Every morning and evening, it was thus offered on the golden altar of the holy place, in the sanctuary, representing the prayers of saints, which rise as a most acceptable offering to God, when presented through the Great High Priest, Christ Jesus. (Ps. cxli. 2, Mal. i. 11.) It seems, however, to have signified *especially*, the merits of the Redeemer himself, which rise like grateful perfume with the prayers of his people, and dispose God graciously to hear and answer, and without which, no prayer of sinful man could ever be regarded by the HOLY ONE. (Luke i. 10, Rev. viii. 3, 4.) The *Myrrh*, repeatedly mentioned in Scripture, was another production of Arabia, procured, like the frankincense, from the trunk of some tree that flourishes in that spicy region. This precious gum has an extremely bitter taste, and a strong, though by no means disagreeable, smell. Among the ancients, it formed one article in the composition of the most costly ointments and was used by delicate persons as a perfume, either by scenting their clothes with it, or by carrying it in little caskets in their bosoms. Wine mingled with myrrh,—which Matthew calls *gall*, a word that means any thing exceedingly bitter,—was offered to our Saviour on the cross, to drink, because of its power to take away, in some mea-

BIBLICAL ANTIQUITIES. 35

sure, the sense of pain. Myrrh was much used for embalming the dead, and is mentioned as one of the articles brought by Nicodemus for this purpose, when he came to bury the body of Jesus

CULTIVATED TREES.

Several trees were cultivated with care, on account of their *fruit*, and often became a source of no small profit to the husbandman. Of this class, was the *Olive*. It appears to have been cultivated very early; for we read of *oil* in the time of Jacob. (Gen. xxviii. 18.) This tree grows better in Palestine than in any other country of the east, where it is found. It flourishes with most advantage on land that is barren, mountainous, sandy and dry. Such a soil it finds on the hills just over against Jerusalem on the east, where, accordingly, it has been so common as to give name to the whole tract—the celebrated MOUNT OF OLIVES. The Olive is a handsome tree, with wide spreading branches, and leaves resembling those of the willow, which continue green all the year. Its trunk is

Olive Tree.

somewhat knotty, with smooth bark, and wood of a yellowish colour. It flourishes about two hundred years. The fruit, when it becomes ripe, is black, and pleasant to the taste; nearly all of it is thrown into the *oil-press*. The oil thus procured has always been highly esteemed. The olive has been the emblem of *peace* among all nations; perhaps, because an olive-branch, brought by the dove to Noah in the ark, was the first sign which he received of peace restored between Heaven and earth, after the bursting forth of God's awful wrath in the waters of the flood. It was also the symbol of prosperity of every kind. The oil likewise became the emblem of gladness and joy, and more especially of the cheering grace of the Holy Spirit. There are, also, *Wild-olives* in that country, of no value in themselves, but capable of being grafted into others. (Rom. xi. 17—24.)

The *Fig tree* delights also in dry and sandy soils. It grows, in the east, to a considerable size; not rising altogether straight in its trunk, but often reaching a goodly height, and dividing itself into a great number of branches, well furnished with broad leaves, so as to form a very agreeable shade. It was customary,

Fig Tree.

among the Jews, to rest themselves under its friendly covering (Mic. iv. 4.) Nathanael, it seems, was accustomed to find under the branches of such a tree, a retreat for solemn meditation and prayer. It was a retirement so completely concealed, probably in the midst of a thick cluster of other trees, that he was well persuaded no eye could see him there, except the all-exploring eye of God. (John i. 48—50.) The fruit of the fig tree makes its appearance before the leaves, growing from the trunk and large branches, and not from the smaller shoots, as the fruit of other trees usually does. There are three kinds, ripening at different seasons of the year. 1. The *First-ripe Fig*, which appears in the latter part of March, and becomes ripe toward the end of June; this is the best sort. (Hos. ix. 10, Jer. xxiv. 2.) 2. The *Summer* or *Dry Fig*, which appears about the middle of June, and becomes ripe in August. 3. The *Winter Fig*, which appears in August, and does not ripen till about the end of November. All figs, when ripe, but especially the *first-ripe* sort, fall of themselves. (Nahum iii. 12.) It is common to dry them in the sun, and preserve them in masses; these are called *cakes of figs*. (1 Sam. xxv. 18.) As fig trees begin to sprout toward the end of March, they became a sign of the approach of summer: "Now learn a parable of the fig tree; when his branch is yet tender, and putteth forth leaves, ye know that summer is nigh." (Matt. xxiv. 32.)

The *Sycamore tree*, or *Sycamine*, as it is sometimes called, abounds especially in Egypt, but is also common in the low lands of Palestine. In size and figure, and in the appearance of its leaves, it bears much resemblance to the mulberry tree. Its fruit grows in clusters on little sprigs like grape-stalks, which shoot out directly from the trunk: it resembles the fig; on which account, the tree is sometimes styled the *Egyptian fig tree*. The body of the tree is very large, and it has numerous branches growing out from it, almost in a straight direction. On this account, it is particularly easy to be climbed. On one which stood by the road, Zaccheus climbed, to see the Lord. (Luke xix. 4.) It is always green. The wood, which is of a dark colour, will last a thousand years; on this account, it was much used in building. The fruit is so sweet as to be hurtful to the stomach, and therefore is not eaten, except by the poorer class, who have nothing better. Amos, the prophet, was employed in gathering sycamore fruit; a business that was pretty troublesome; for before it will get ripe, it must all be opened with the nail, or a piece of iron, to let out the milky juice; and this seems to have been his principal work. The tree yields fruit several times through the year, without regard to particular seasons.

The *Pomegranate* tree grows in almost all countries of the east. It does not rise high, and at a little distance from the ground shoots out into a multitude of branches, so as to appear like a large shrub. It bears large, handsome, reddish blossoms, shaped like bells. The fruit which these produce is very beautiful to the eye and pleasant to the taste. It is about the size of a large apple, perfectly round, encircled at the upper part with something resembling a crown, and covered with a rind which is thick and hard, but easily broken. The juice which it affords, is sometimes made into a kind of wine by itself, and sometimes mixed with other wine, to give it more sharpness: mention is made of *the spiced wine of the juice of the pomegranate*. (Song viii. 2.) Artificial pomegranates, made to resemble the natural ones, were esteemed, among the Jews, a considerable ornament; they were hung round the hem of the

Pomegranate Fruit.

high priest's robe, (Ex. xxviii. 33,) and on the net work which covered the tops of the two pillars, Jachin and Boaz, in the temple of Solomon, (1 Kings vii. 18.)

Pomegranate Tree.

Orange and *Lemon* trees are not common in Palestine; but they have been probably brought there from some more eastern country, in later times, as they are not mentioned in the Sacred Volume.

The *Apple tree* is mentioned with peculiar praise: "As the apple tree among the trees of the wood, so is my beloved among the sons; I sat down under his shadow with great delight, and his fruit was sweet to my taste," (Song ii. 3;) but the tree which we are accustomed to call by this name does not thrive well in the east, and bears only indifferent fruit; it is generally agreed, therefore, that the *apple tree* of the Scripture is the same as the *Citron tree.* This is a tree of noble appearance and great size, furnished with beautiful leaves through the whole year, and affording a most delightful shadow. The fruit is very sweet and pleasant, of the colour of gold, extremely fragrant, and proper to refresh such as are weary or faint. Words fitly spoken, Solomon tells us, are *like apples of gold* in pictures of silver. (Prov. xxv. 11.)

The *Palm tree* is not now often found in Palestine: the reason is, because it needs careful and skilful cultivation, which the state of that country has for a long time prevented. It is still very common in other regions of the east, and, as it appears from the Bible, once abounded in Judea. On ancient coins of the Jews, also, the figure of the palm tree is found sometimes stamped, often with a sheaf of wheat and a cluster of grapes, as a symbol of their nation. It rises perfectly straight to a very great height, without any limbs, except near its top, which is crowned with continual green. It grows most commonly in valleys and plains: the finest groves of it, anciently, were found in the neighbourhood of Jordan, especially in the plains of Jericho, which city was, on this account,

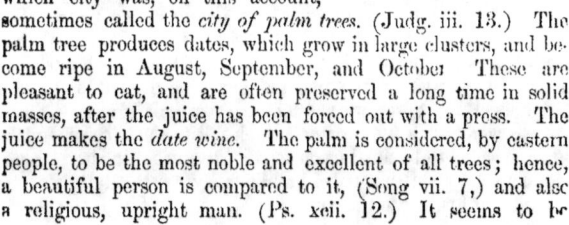

sometimes called the *city of palm trees.* (Judg. iii. 13.) The palm tree produces dates, which grow in large clusters, and become ripe in August, September, and October These are pleasant to eat, and are often preserved a long time in solid masses, after the juice has been forced out with a press. The juice makes the *date wine.* The palm is considered, by eastern people, to be the most noble and excellent of all trees; hence, a beautiful person is compared to it, (Song vii. 7,) and also a religious, upright man. (Ps. xcii. 12.) It seems to be intended, in that beautiful image of the first Psalm: "He shall be like a tree *planted by the rivers of water*, that bringeth forth his fruit in his season; *his leaf also shall not wither.*" It was usual to scatter branches of palm in the way before kings, when they entered, on public occasions, into cities; it was, therefore, a mark of highest honour to the Saviour, when the people "took branches of palm trees and went forth to meet him," (John xii. 13,) and strewed them before him, as he entered into Jerusalem. (Matt. xxi. 8.) In the Grecian games, those who conquered were rewarded, frequently, with a branch of palm: to this there is allusion in the vision of St. John: "I beheld, and lo, a great multitude which no man could number——stood before the throne and the Lamb, clothed with white robes, and *palms in their hands.*" (Rev. vii. 9.) This denotes victory over Satan and sin, crowned with the reward of eternal glory. The likeness of the palm tree was often carved in ornamental work.

The *Balsam* or *Balm tree* also grew formerly in Palestine, though, for want of culture, it is not found there now. It is still raised in some parts of Arabia and Egypt. There are three kinds of it; two growing like shrubs, the other a regular tree. The *balm*, mentioned in the Bible as an article of commerce and a valuable medicine, is made either of the sap of the tree, or of the juice of its fruit. Gardens of balm were, at a very early period, cultivated in the neighbourhood of Jericho and Engedi, and also in Gilead: the balm of Gilead was particularly esteemed. (Gen. xxxvii. 25, Jer. viii. 22.)

The *Almond tree* is the first to blossom in the opening year. It is covered with its snow-white flowers in the latter part of January, and before the end of March displays its ripe fruit. The rod of an almond tree, seen by Jeremiah in vision, denoted, from this circumstance, the rapid approach of God's threatened judgments: "Thou hast well seen; for I will hasten my word to perform it." (Jer. i. 12.)

The *Vine* deserves especial mention. It was, no doubt, cultivated before the flood, as Noah, immediately after coming out of the ark, *planted a vineyard and drank of the wine.* The soil of Palestine was of the best sort for raising it; and hence it became a principal object of attention to the Jewish husbandman. In particular the mountains of Engedi and the valleys of Eshcol and Sorek were celebrated for their grapes. These places were all in the territory which fell to the tribe of Judah. There seems to be an allusion to this advantage, in the blessing pronounced upon that tribe, prophetically, by the dying Jacob: 'Binding his foal to the vine, and his ass's colt unto the choice

Almond Tree.

vine, he washed his garments in wine, and his clothes in the blood of grapes." (Gen. xlix. 11.) The clusters of grapes grow, in that country, at the present day, to the weight of twelve pounds; in ancient times, no doubt, they were often larger. One of these great clusters, from the vale of Eshcol, the spies brought to Moses, as a sample of the fruitfulness of the land, *bearing it between two, on a staff*, that its large grapes might not be bruised together. (Numb. xiii. 23, 24.) Some vines, in growing, ran along the ground; others grew upright of themselves, without any support; while a third sort needed a pole or frame, to assist them in rising, and to bear up their weight. Vineyards were generally planted upon the sides of hills and mountains, toward the south. The Palestine grapes are mostly red or black; whence the common expression, *the blood of grapes*. The vine was sometimes employed to make sceptres for kings. *To sit under a man's own vine and fig tree*, was a phrase signifying a state of prosperity and peace. (Mic. iv. 4.) Our Lord compares himself to a vine: "I am the true vine and my Father is the husbandman. I am the vine; ye are the branches." (John xv. 1, 5.) As the trunk, planted and dressed by the husbandman's care, affords life and nourishment to

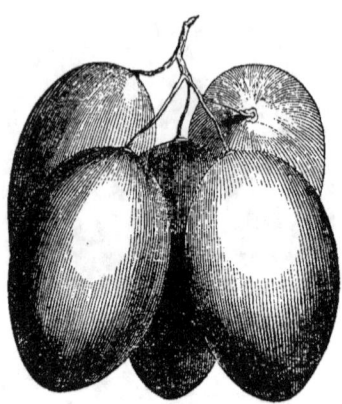

Palestine Grapes.

its branches, and enables them to bring forth clusters of grapes; so is He the source of all spiritual life and strength and fruitfulness, to his people, appointed of God the Father, and sent forth into the world, that he might become such to every one that believeth on his name. The Jewish nation is also compared to a vine, and to a vineyard, to denote the kind care which it had received from God. (Ps. lxxx. 8, Is. v. 1.)

The *Vine of Sodom* grows in the neighbourhood of Jericho, not far from the Dead Sea. It produces grapes of a poisonous kind, bitter as gall. Moses compares the rebellious Israelites to this plant: "Their vine is the vine of Sodom, and of the fields of Gomorrah; their grapes are grapes of gall, and their clusters are bitter." (Deut. xxxii. 32.)

PLANTS.

Of *Plants* belonging to Palestine, there are mentioned in the Bible several of useful or agreeable character, and some of hurtful and unlovely sort. The *Lily* displays uncommon elegance in that country: "Solomon," we are told, "in all his glory, was not arrayed like one of these." (Matt. vi. 29.) Here, too, we may notice the *Rose*, though of a somewhat higher class. A great many kinds of it are found in the east; some of them very remarkable for the richness and beauty of their flowers, and the delightful fragrance which they send forth. The rose of Sharon was particularly fine, in ancient days. (Song ii. 1.) The *Mandrake* is a kind of melon, with pleasant smell and taste. The

Mustard-plant rises from the smallest seed into the likeness of a tree. (Matt. xiii. 32.) It presents a remarkable growth among herbs, in our own country; but in that region rises and spreads its branches to a much greater extent. The *Spikenard* is a much esteemed plant: only an inferior kind of it, however, is found in the region where Palestine lies; the true Spikenard, or Nard, belongs to India, in the more distant east. It grows in large tufts, rising upward like tall grass, and has a strong aromatic smell. An ointment of the most precious kind is made out of it, which anciently was exceedingly prized, and purchased with great expense in different countries. A box of it, containing a pound, was valued, in the time of our Saviour, at more than three hundred pence. So much Mary poured on his head, a short time before his death; *and the house was filled with the odour.* (John xii. 3.) The *Aloe* is a plant with broad prickly leaves, nearly two inches thick, which grows about two feet high. A very bitter gum is procured from it, used as a medicine, and anciently for the embalming of dead bodies. Nicodemus brought a hundred pounds of myrrh and aloes, to embalm the body of the Redeemer. (John xix. 39.) Besides this herb, however, which is found in eastern countries generally, there is a small tree, with beautiful flowers and most fragrant wood, that grows in India under the same name. The *Hyssop* is a small herb, growing on mountainous lands, with bushy stalks about a foot and a half high. The leaves of it have an aromatic smell, and a warm bitter taste. It is found abundantly on the hills near Jerusalem. *Cucumbers* and various kinds of *Melons* were cultivated among the Jews. Egypt, however, produces the finest melons. The *Water melon*, especially, is raised with great advantage, on the banks of the Nile, and furnishes a most agreeable refreshment in the warm climate of that country. Many poor people live on them almost entirely, while they last. The Israelites remembered them in the wilderness, as well as the *Leeks* and the *Onions*, with longing desire. (Numb. xi. 5.) Onions in Egypt are better than they are anywhere else in the world, being sweet and pleasant to the taste, without the hardness which commonly makes them unfit to be eaten. The *Thistle* and the *Nettle*, besides several kinds of thorns and brambles, were common in the fields of the Jewish farmer. He was also troubled with the *Tare*. This tare seems to have been the same weed that is now called *Darnel*, still known in that country, as well as in many others. It often gets among wheat and other grain, after the manner of cockle and other such hurtful plants. The bread made of grain in which much of its seed is found, is very unwholesome; it creates dizziness, drowsiness, and headache. It is all-important, therefore, to separate it from the crop. This, however, cannot well be done while it is growing in the field; because its roots are so connected with those of the wheat, that to pluck up the one would materially injure the other. (Matt. xiii. 24—30.)

The different sorts of grain raised by the Jews, were, *Wheat*, which grows in almost every country; *Millet*, a coarse kind of grain, eaten by the poorer people; *Spelt, Barley, Beans, Lentils, Fitches, Anise* and *Cummin*. The two last were common small herbs: the Pharisees pretended to great religious scrupulosity, by carefully paying tithes of these and other little garden plants, such as *Mint* and *Rue*, while they neglected "the weightier matters of the law, judgment, mercy, and faith." (Matt. xxiii. 23, Luke xi. 42.) *Flax*, also, and *Cotton*, were cultivated. Cotton grows in large pods, either on trees of considerable size, or on shrubs that spring up from the seed, and last only one year. The word *Corn*, in Scripture, is used as a general name for all sorts of grain. Rye and oats do not grow in countries where the climate is so warm: their place is supplied by barley.

From this general survey of its different productions, we may learn how extremely fruitful Palestine must have been, in the days of its ancient prosperity and peace. Every variety of soil had its use; some valuable tree or plant growing better upon it, than upon any other; so that the poorest and the roughest grounds yielded, oftentimes, as much as the fairest and most rich. While the different kinds of grain flourished on the more level and fertile tracts, plantations of the serviceable olive covered the barren and sandy hil's; the low watery soils of clay nourished groves of the tall and beautiful palm; the steepest mountain sides were hung with the rich dark clusters of the vine. By the hand of industry, the naked rocks, on such steep places, were covered with earth, and walls were builded to hinder it from being swept away with the showers. So, from the bottom to the top, might sometimes be seen, rising one above another, plot after plot thus raised by labour and art, where the vine was reared by the husbandman's care, and rewarded his toil with its plentiful fruit. As every family had only a small piece of ground to till, every foot of it that could be improved was cultivated, and no pains were spared to turn it to its best account. Hence, the land had the appearance of a garden, and yielded support to a vast number of inhabitants. The country of Lower Galilee, especially, has been celebrated for its fruitfulness. According to the testimony of Josephus, the Jewish historian, who lived just after the time of Christ, that part of it which bordered on the lake of Gennesareth, where our Lord spent so much of his time, was especially remarkable for the great variety and plenty of its productions; every plant seemed to thrive in it; fruits that naturally grow in different climates were raised with equal ease here; so that it seemed, says that writer, as if God had taken a peculiar delight in that region, and the seasons had rivalled each other in the richness of their gifts.

But when the traveller passes through Palestine now, his eye meets no such scenery of fruitfulness and beauty, over its mountains and plains. Large tracts of the country seem a barren waste; the rich covering of the field is gone, and the hills are stripped of the vine; a thinly scattered people live in comparative poverty and idleness, where once the many thousands of Israel and Judah found plentiful support. The country, for more than a thousand years, has been given up to be wasted by war and crushed by oppression. Its people have been driven away and trampled under foot, by cruel enemies. The whole land is now under the dominion of the Turks, who, instead of encouraging industry, leave it without protection and without profit. The farmer has no motive to plough and sow; his crops would grow up only to be plundered by wandering Arabs; and if he could secure any property, it would only expose him to danger from the avarice of some tyrant officer of the government, determined to seize it all for himself. No wonder, then, that "the fruitful land has been turned into barrenness." It has been done, however, "for the wickedness of them that dwelt therein," and is a wonderful fulfilment of the threatenings of God, delivered even as far back as the time of Moses, (Deut. xxix. 22—28,) and repeated by the prophets that followed after.

SECTION II.

OF ANIMALS.

It would require a volume to describe the different sorts of insects, reptiles, fishes, birds, and beasts, that are found in Palestine. Many of them are found, also, in our own country, and have been known to us all our lives; but many others are peculiar to the east. We can only notice a few which are frequently mentioned in the Bible.

QUADRUPEDS.

The *Horse*. This useful animal is first mentioned in the history of Jacob and Joseph. It was, in their time, found in Egypt, and continued, long after, to be much used in that land

It seems to have lived at first, in its wild state, in some part of Africa, and in the northern regions of Asia. The Jews made no use of horses before the time of Solomon; their country was too hilly for them to be of any service in war, and it was not usual then to use them as beasts of burden or labour in times of peace. Much use of them seems, indeed, to be discouraged in the law of Moses, as it is expressly forbidden for any future king *to multiply horses*. (Deut. xvii. 16.) Joshua also was commanded of God, when he took horses in war, to cut their hamstrings; and the same thing was long after done by David. This was the quickest way of rendering them useless for time to come, as it completely disabled them at once, and soon caused them to die. Solomon carried on a great trade in horses; they were brought in great numbers, in his day, from Egypt. After his time, they were never uncommon in the country. The rider, in those times, had no saddle, but sat merely upon a piece of cloth.

The *Ox*. Cattle of the ox kind are smaller in eastern countries than with us, and have something of a lump on the back, just over the fore-feet. The finest kind were raised in the rich pastures of Bashan, where they became very fat and strong, and sometimes exceedingly fierce. These animals were highly esteemed among the Jews for their usefulness, and seem to have held pretty much the same rank of importance with the farmer that the horse has among us. Bulls and cows were both used to the yoke, and employed to draw the cart and the plough, and tread out the grain when it was gathered to the threshing-floor. A particular law was made by God, that the ox should not be muzzled, or have his mouth bound, when he was engaged in this last employment. (Deut. xxv. 4, 1 Cor. ix. 9, 1 Tim. v. 18.) Besides the *labour* of the animal, however, the cow was valued, as with us, for her milk, which was either drunk in its simple state, or made into cheese of various kinds. Horns are frequently used in the Bible as the sign of strength and power: to have *the horn exalted*, denotes prosperity and triumph, (Ps. lxxxix. 17, 24;) to have it *cut off*, signifies the loss of power. "All the horns of the wicked," says David, "will I cut off; but the horns of the righteous shall be exalted." (Ps. lxxv. 10.) To *lift up the horn*, is to act proudly. Christ is called *a horn of salvation*, because he is *mighty* to redeem to the uttermost all that come unto God by him. (Luke i. 69.)

The *Ass*. In the east, this animal has nothing of the mean character that belongs to it in our country. Asses, there, are not only fit for hard labour, but are, at the same time, active and beautiful in appearance. In early times, they made a large

Ox, Camel and Ass of Syria.

part of the property of the more wealthy: hence, they are always mentioned, in Scripture, in giving an account of the possessions of any of the ancient patriarchs. They were used to carry burdens of every kind, and made to draw in ploughing and hauling. Anciently, princes and great men always rode upon asses; and it seems to have been regarded as a mark of distinction, to be so mounted. As an evidence of the greatness and wealth of one of the Judges, Jair the Gileadite, it is said, "he had thirty sons, that rode upon thirty ass-colts, and they had thirty cities," (Judg. x. 4;) and of another, that he "had forty sons and thirty nephews, that rode on seventy ass-colts." (Judg. xii. 14.) Our Saviour, in fulfilment of a prophecy of Zechariah, (ix. 9,) entered Jerusalem riding upon an ass, amidst the acclamations of a multitude of people. This was the only instance, during his life, in which he assumed any regal pomp; and even this manifestation of himself as a king, was connected with circumstances of deep humiliation. (Matt. xxi. 5.) "Behold thy king cometh unto thee: he is just and having salvation; lowly, and riding on an ass, and upon a colt, the foal of an ass." Moreover, as horses were especially used in times of war, and asses were of most service in days of peace, *to ride upon an ass* represented a meek and peaceful character, and was, therefore, beautifully appropriate for the King of *Salem*—the Prince of *Peace*. The coronation entry of the kings of Israel into Jerusalem, was made upon asses.—Asses in the east are of a flaxen colour, with silvery white along the belly. In their wild state, they are sometimes altogether white; such, in the days of the Judges, were highly esteemed. (Judg. v. 10.) Asses are still used in Egypt for riding: they are very handsome in that country.

Wild asses abound in the east. They are beautiful and very wild; easily taking alarm; and when they fly through the desert, they outstrip every other animal in swiftness of foot. A description of this animal is found in Job. (xxxix. 5—8.) It has power to smell water at a great distance: this is referred to in the description of a great drought. "The wild asses did stand in the high places: they snuffed up the wind like dragons." (Jer. xiv. 6.) Travellers who want to find water, are accustomed to follow them.

The *Mule* was known very early, and considerably used for carrying burdens. They are very sure-footed animals; kings and princes often rode upon them: thus David was carried on a mule kept for his own use, and all his sons rode upon animals of the same kind. Absalom sat on one when he passed under the boughs of a great oak, and was caught by his head among the branches.

The *Camel.* There are two kinds of this animal; one large and strong, with two bunches on the back; the other smaller, and more rapid in its movement, with but one bunch on the back. This last is called the *Dromedary,* or Arabian Camel; it bears heat better than the other. The camel seems to have been formed expressly for the eastern countries; so that we cannot conceive how they could dispense with its services. It carries an immense burden, needs but little food, and can go without water a whole month: all this fits it exactly for bearing merchandise in those regions; where they have often to pass a wide sandy desert without water, in going from one country to another. The camel is sometimes rode upon, as it is common to ride on horses. At other times, two long chairs, like cradles, are fixed over its back, one on each side, or two large basket-like seats are thrown across so as to balance each other. In each of these a traveller may sit at his ease, or even resign himself to sleep without inconvenience. Sometimes a little covered room is fastened on  its back, in which the traveller may carry with him some little furniture, and shut himself, if he please, entirely out of sight. This kind of conveyance is used chiefly by women. Perhaps in something of the sort Rebecca was riding, with the curtains rolled up, when she saw Isaac walking in the field, and *lighted off the camel* to receive him. The *hair* of the camel is woven sometimes into a coarse kind of cloth, used by the poorer people. John the Baptist "had his raiment of camel's hair, with a leathern girdle round his loins." (Matt. iii. 4.) To the Jews, the camel was an unclean animal, not allowed to be used for food; but the Arabs eat its flesh and drink its milk. To pass a *camel through the eye of a needle,* was a proverb, to denote any thing extremely difficult, or impossible. (Matt. xix. 24.)

The *Sheep.* The common kind of this animal, so well known among us, is found in Palestine; but there is in that country a breed something larger, and clothed with finer wool. These are remarkable for having very large, broad tails. Their tails are esteemed a particular delicacy, being of a substance between fat and marrow; they have an excellent richness, and are sometimes used instead of butter. On this account, *the whole rump*, taken off *hard by the back-bone*, was appointed in peace-offerings, to be burnt with the other fat upon the altar, for a sweet savour unto the Lord. (Lev. iii. 9.) Thousands of sheep, in early days, were sometimes owned by one man, ranging the pastures of the wilderness, and continually adding to the wealth of their possessor. They bring forth their young twice in the year, and frequently bear twins. Their flesh is used for food; and their milk supplies a wholesome drink. But they are chiefly valuable for the fine fleeces of wool, which, twice in the year, are shorn from their backs. The sheep in that country become very familiar with the shepherd, and know his voice when he speaks. (John x. 3, 14.) The flocks live both night and day under the open sky, and are only brought into the *sheepfold* at the times of shearing. The sheep is a weak and timid animal, unable to defend itself, without much wisdom, and needing the continual care of a keeper, to be kept from wandering into danger, or losing itself among the mountains. Hence, it is frequently referred to in the figurative language of Scripture, to represent a condition of helplessness or folly: "My people," says God, "have been lost sheep; they have gone from mountain to hill; they have forgotten their resting-place." (Isa. l. 6.) "All we like sheep have gone astray; we have turned every one to his own way." (Isa. liii. 6.) "When he saw the multitudes he was moved with compassion on them, because they fainted, and were scattered abroad, as *sheep having no shepherd*." (Matt. ix. 36.)

The *Goat*. This belonged also to the *flocks* of the shepherd. There are two kinds of this animal, as well as of the last, found in the east: one, our common goat; the other, a somewhat larger race, remarkable for having large, broad ears, that hang down a foot, and sometimes a foot and a half in length. Probably this kind was referred to by Amos, in that verse, "As the shepherd taketh out of the mouth of the lion, two legs or *a piece of an ear*, so, &c." (iii. 12.) The goat yields a considerable quantity of milk, which is very sweet, and has always been esteemed more than any other, in eastern countries. Hence, the promise to the careful and diligent man is, "Thou shalt have goat's milk enough for thy food, for the food of thy household, and for the maintenance of thy maidens." (Prov. xxvii. 27.) The *flesh* of goats, also, is much prized. Their long black-coloured *hair* is made into different kinds of cloth, with which the shepherds frequently cover their tents. The tabernacle was covered with curtains of goat's hair, spun by the women of Israel in the wilderness

50 BIBLICAL ANTIQUITIES.

(Ex. xxxv. 26.) It is still the business of the Arabian women to make such cloths. Some goats have extremely fine hair, out of which stuffs are formed, almost equal to silk in delicacy and beauty. From the *skins* of these animals, it has been common, since the earliest times, to form large *bottles;* the skins of kids are wrought, in some places, by means of smoke, into more convenient and even elegant *flasks.* It was forbidden, by the law of Moses, to "seethe a kid in its mother's milk;" to enforce, perhaps, the general duty of a humane disposition toward animals; and it may be, also, because some practice of this kind was common among the superstitious rites of the heathen.

The *Dog.* At a very early period, as we learn from Job, dogs were trained by shepherds to guard their flocks. (Job xxx

Street Dogs of Syria.

1.) They can be taught to drive the sheep or goats from one place to another, to keep them from straggling or wandering away, and to manage them, in fact, with every kind of care. In their wild condition, however, they are like the wolf, greedy, selfish, impudent, quarrelsome and savage. In the east, there are multitudes of them in this state; they wander about, frequently in troops, hunting for prey, and often attack the strongest and fiercest beasts of the forest. But they do not confine themselves to the wilderness; they choose rather to seek their living in towns and cities. Here they are found in great numbers, ranging the streets by day and by night, and greedily devouring the offal that is cast into the gutters or about the markets. As they are sometimes reduced almost to starvation, they are ready to consume human corpses, and in the night, fall even upon living men. From possessing this character, the dog, where it has not been trained for hunting, or for watching flocks, has long been, in that part of the world, held in great contempt and abhorrence. Hence, in Scripture, wicked men are compared to dogs. (Ps. xxii. 16.) "They return at evening," says David; "they make a noise like a dog, and go round about the city; they wander up and down for meat, and grudge if they be not satisfied." (Ps. lix. 6, 15.) "Give not that which is holy unto the dogs." (Matt. vii. 6.) "Beware of dogs, beware of evil workers." (Phil. iii. 2.) "Without are dogs, and sorcerers," &c. (Rev. xxii. 15.) To call a man a *dog*, is still exceedingly reproachful, as it was in ancient times. (2 Sam. xvi. 9, 2 Kings viii 13.) The Jews, in the time of our Saviour, were accustomed to call the Gentiles by this contemptuous epithet; to which Christ had allusion, when he said to the woman of Canaan, in order to try her faith, "It is not meet to take the children's bread, and to cast it to *the dogs*." (Matt. xv. 26.) In our day, the Mohammedans in that country still use the same language of contempt towards those who differ from them in religion, especially Christians and Jews, styling them *Christian dogs—Jewish dogs*.

Hogs were considered peculiarly unclean by the Jews, and seem not to have been kept in Palestine, at all, in earlier times. They were considered the vilest of all animals, and scarcely named in common speech. The eastern nations generally still abstain from eating pork, as in warm climates its flesh is always unwholesome.

The *Lion* is frequently mentioned in Scripture—the noblest and the boldest beast of the forest. He moves with slow and majestic step along his way, and fears not the face of any living creature. (Prov. xxx. 29, 30.) When angry, he lashes

his sides and the ground with his tail, shakes his shaggy mane, knits his great eyebrows, displays his dreadful tusks, and thrusts out his tongue: when he roars, it is like the sound of distant thunder; and as it echoes through the mountains, all the beasts of th forest tremble. "The lion has roared," says the prophet; "who will not fear?" (Amos iii. 8.) It is said that he roars only when he is in sight of his prey, or striking it down with his mighty paw. Hence, the same prophet says: "Will a lion roar in the forest, when he hath no prey? Will a young lion cry out of his den, if he have taken nothing?" (Amos iii. 4.) Strong men are compared to lions. God is likened to a lion, because, when his anger is kindled against the wicked, who can withstand his power, or who may abide his wrath? Christ is the *Lion of Judah*—dreadful to his enemies, as well as the *Lamb of God* that taketh away the sin of the world. The Devil is a roaring lion, going about and seeking whom he may devour. (1 Pet. v. 8.)

The *Unicorn*. The animal to which this name is applied in the Bible, is represented as a wild ungovernable beast, remarkable for the loftiness either of its stature or of its horns, and perhaps of both; possessed of great strength, and inclined, at times, to exercise it furiously and without mercy, even against man. It is, however, no easy matter to determine which, of all the animals that are now known in the east, has the best claim to be considered the unicorn of Scripture.] Hebrew name carries in its signification merely a reference to that *loftiness* by which it was distinguished, without any other indication of its nature or appearances. In the earliest translation of the Bible into another language, it was called the Unicorn, or the *one-horned* animal. Under this name, the ancients have described a very peculiar beast. It is represented as having the legs and body of a deer, with the head, mane, and tail of a horse, armed with a single straight horn from the middle of its forehead, and presenting altogether a form and appearance of no common elegance. But travellers have not been able to find, in later times, any animal of this sort in eastern countries. Animals with only one horn have indeed been discovered, but none of them suit the description of the ancient unicorn Many learned commentators, however, have been of opinion that the *Rhinoceros* is intended by the unicorn; to which the principal objection is, that this animal is now only found in countries very remote from Judea.

The cow, the deer, the bear, the leopard, the fox, &c., are too well known to need any description: but it deserves to be noticed, that most learned men are now of opinion that the animals caught in such numbers by Samson were not of the species of our fox, but the jackal, of which the number is very great in the east, and who are accustomed to go in large companies.

BIRDS.

We must also omit a particular description of the birds. Among these, we find mentioned in Scripture the *Eagle*, excelling all the rest in strength, boldness, and violence; dwelling alone in the wilderness and on the mountain top, amid the highest branches of the cedar, or soaring, with rapid wing, far above the clouds of heaven, where no bird can follow, (Obad. 4, Jer. xlix. 16, Job xxxix. 27—30;) the *Ostrich*, largest of the winged race, delighting in the sandy desert, where *she leaveth her eggs in the earth, and warmeth them in the sand, forgetting that the foot may crush them;* and over which, with outspread, quivering wing, she runs with speed that scarcely seems to touch the ground, scorning the horse and his rider, (Job xxxix. 13—18, Lam. iv. 3;) the *Stork*, whose *house is in the fir-trees*, (Ps. civ. 17,) or in the summit of some ruined tower, and who *knoweth her appointed time* to move toward the north or the south, as the seasons change, (Jer. viii. 7;) the *Pelican*, inhabiting the marshy places and solitary lakes, (Ps. cii. 6;) the *Raven*, with feathers beautifully black, whose mournful croak is heard from deserted ruins, and who hovers near the field of battle, to feed on the bodies of the slain, (Song v. 11, Isa. xxxiv. 11, Ps. cxlvii. 9, Luke xii. 24;) the *Owl*, fond also of dreary places and scenes of desolation, (Isa. xxxiv. 11, Ps. cii. 6;) the *Hawk*, daring, swift, and delighting in blood; the harmless, fair-eyed *Dove*, (Song i. 15, v. 12;) the noisy, wandering *Crane*, (Jer. viii. 7;) the *Swallow;* the *Partridge;* and the *Sparrow*. The *Peacock* seems to have been brought into Palestine first, in the reign of Solomon; probably from Persia. (1 Kings x. 22.)

WATER ANIMALS.

Only two or three particular kinds of water animals are mentioned in the Bible. The *Whale* is named several times. In the book of Job is described another great water animal, called *Leviathan*. (Job xli.) Many have supposed that the whale was intended by this name, but the description of Job suits the crocodile much better; yet there is reason to believe that huge sea-monsters of several kinds are spoken of, in different places of the Scriptures, under this term. For we read in Isaiah (xxvii. 1) that the Lord "shall punish leviathan the piercing serpent, even (and) leviathan that crooked serpent."

Behemoth.—This is very commonly considered to be another name for the elephant; but there seems much better reason to suppose that it means the *Hippopotamus,* or *River Horse,* which is an amphibious animal, but spends much of his time among the reeds and fens of the Nile, where the trees cover him with their shadow, and the willows of the brook compass him about, according to the description in Job, (xl. 15—24.)

REPTILES.

Among animals of the reptile kind, the *Dragon* is frequently named in Scripture. Under this name, however, different kinds of monsters, belonging either to the dry land or the deep, seem to be understood. Properly, the dragon is the name of a serpent of prodigious size. It is described by the ancients as being very frightful in its appearance, covered with scales of a bright yellow or red colour, with a shining crest, and a swelling on its head, that looks like burning coal. A huge red serpent, of a kind somewhat answering to this description, is still found in the east. It seizes large animals, like the stag or the ox, breaks their bones all to pieces by crushing them with the folds of its body against a tree, and swallows them down whole. It sometimes raises itself up, upright upon its tail, and with amazing strength attacks its prey in this attitude; at other times, its tail is employed in the work of destruction, playing around with a force that is dreadful. Such seems to have been the *Great red Dragon,* which John saw in vision: its "*tail drew* the third part of the stars of heaven, and did cast them to the earth;" and it "*stood* before the woman, to devour her child as soon as it was born." This, we are informed, was "that *old Serpent,* called the Devil, and Satan, who deceiveth the whole world," as long since he deceived our first mother, Eve. (Rev. xii. 3—9.) The silent and desolate wilderness is represented as the chosen haunt of the dragon. Hence, the prophets, in foretelling the utter ruin of great cities, declare, among other frightful circumstances, that they shall become the *habitation of dragons.* (Isa xiii. 22, xxxiv. 13, Jer. ix. 11.) In such cases, we may suppose that the name is used with a general meaning, to signify wild reptiles of different sorts, such as are found lurking among the rubbish of ancient ruins The croco dile is called a dragon; as in that passage where Pharaoh is likened to "the great dragon that lieth in the midst of his rivers, which hath said, My river is mine own; I have made it for myself." (Ezek. xxix. 3.) The *river* intended is the Nile, where the crocodile abounds. *Dragons of the sea* seem to mean various great monsters dwelling in the deep, with which men are little acquainted, and so have commonly only an indefinite notion of their appearance, suggested by imagination rather than by accurate knowledge.

We read in the Bible of the *Fiery Serpent*. It was found in the desert of Arabia, when the Israelites passed through it, on their way to Canaan. They were called *fiery*, on account of their flaming colour, which was represented by the bright *brazen* serpent that Moses lifted up, to be looked at by those who were bitten. We hear again of *flying* fiery serpents. (Isa. xxx. 6.) What we are to understand by this is not altogether clear. There is found at the present day, in some countries, a serpent that darts with great rapidity from the branches of trees, and on this account has received the name of a flying serpent, which some have imagined to be the same that is mentioned in the Bible. Ancient writers, however, have described a different serpent under this name, having a short body spotted with divers colours, and furnished with wings resembling those of a bat, which they tell us was not uncommon in Arabia and some other regions in the east. Modern travellers, it is true, have never met with such an animal: but as its existence in earlier times is asserted by most respectable authority, it seems probable that the winged serpent of Scripture was no other.

The *Cockatrice* is several times mentioned in Scripture, as a serpent of most dangerous kind. It could not be charmed. (Jer. viii. 17.) The *Asp* is another serpent, of small size, whose poison certainly and rapidly produces death, throwing the person that is bitten into a state of drowsiness and fatal sleep. As a sign of the great blessings of Christ's kingdom, about to fill the world in *the last days*, it is said in prophecy, among other things, that "the sucking child shall play on the hole of the asp, and the weaned child shall put his hand upon the cockatrice's den." (Isa. xi. 8.) *Adder* is a name given, in the English translation of the Bible, to more than one kind of venomous snakes. The *Viper* is a well known, deadly, and malignant serpent. It was a great miracle, when Paul shook off such a reptile from his hand, *and felt no harm*. The Pharisees, on account of their wickedness and malice, were called by John, "a generation of vipers." (Matt. iii. 7.)

BIBLICAL ANTIQUITIES.

The *Scorpion* is sometimes joined with the serpent, on account of its poison. It is a most loathsome animal, resembling, in some measure, a lobster or crab. Each scorpion has six or eight eyes. It has, moreover, a tail, and in the end of it, a sting, which it is ready to use upon every object that comes within its reach, darting a cold and dangerous poison into the wound. The little creature is extremely passionate and mischievous, and exceedingly troublesome to man and beast in those countries where it abounds. (Deut. viii. 15, Rev. ix. 5, 6, 10.) What father would give such an animal to a child, when it asked him for an egg? (Luke xi. 12;) and what a security did Christ throw around his disciples, when he gave them power even "to tread upon serpents and scorpions," without harm! (Luke x. 19.)

INSECTS.

The *Bee* was very common anciently, as it still is, in the east. Palestine is represented as abounding with honey. Great quantities of it were laid up by wild bees in the crevices of the rocks, and in the hollows of decayed trees. The *Hornet* is also spoken of in the Bible. God threatened to send it against the enemies of the Israelites in Canaan to drive them out of the land. (Ex. xxiii. 28, Deut. vii. 20.) From Joshua xxiv. 12, we learn that the two kings of the Amorites were actually driven out of their place by this means. We have mention made also of the *Ant*, the *Beetle*, the *Grasshopper*, &c. *Flies* of various sorts, some of which are not known at all in other countries, have always been troublesome in eastern regions. Some of them are very large, and exceedingly vexatious and tormenting to man and beast.

The *Locust.*—There is one insect, out of the many kinds which abound in the east, which deserves a more particular notice. The locust in those countries is very large, about half a foot long, and as thick as a man's finger. It has a head, in form resembling that of a horse, furnished with strong, sharp teeth. With these, it feeds upon every thing that is green, and by reason of its numbers, often becomes one of the most dreadful plagues which a country can suffer. Immense armies of them, reaching several miles in length and breadth, are seen flying through the air, so thick that they darken the light of the sun, like a heavy, black cloud. The sound of their wings is terrible. When they light upon the ground, they cover it over completely They then march forward, in regular order, toward the north, passing in a straight line over every thing that comes in their way, devouring the whole herbage of the field and stripping every tree of its leaves and tender bark. Nothing can stop them: ditches may be dug, but they are directly filled up with their bodies; fires may be kindled, but they move right into them, and by their numbers soon put them out, with little loss to their huge army. The prophet Joel describes them in the second chapter of his book, as a picture of the terrible Assyrian army, which God was about soon to bring upon the land: "The land," says he, "is as the garden of Eden before them, and behind them a desolate wilderness!" It is dreadful enough to be visited with one army of these destructive insects; but this is but a part of the evil: the first swarm is quickly followed by a second, and a third, and sometimes a fourth, which sweep new tracks of desolation through the land, till it is laid utterly waste, as if it had been ravaged with fire. At length, they are borne by the wind into the sea, where they speedily perish; but a new plague frequently follows. Their innumerable carcasses are driven back by the waves upon the shore, where they breed a dreadful putrid stench, that renders the air, for a great distance, extremely unwholesome, and sometimes even gives rise to the Pestilence. So awful was the plague which God brought upon Egypt, when he bid the east wind blow from Arabia, the birth-place of locusts, to bear their countless host upon that guilty land. (Ex. x. 14.) The Mohammedan armies were represented in vision to the apostle John, under a swarm of locusts. (Rev. ix.) These animals are frequently used for food; salted and dried in the smoke, or boiled with a little oil or butter, or toasted before the fire. Some people live on them nearly altogether. Such was the plain fare of John the Baptist in the wilderness: "His meat was *locusts and wild honey.*" (Matt. iii. 4.)

CHAPTER III.

DWELLINGS AND HOUSEHOLD ACCOMMODATIONS.

SECTION I.

DWELLINGS.

In eastern countries, men dwell either in *tents* or in *houses.* Those who lead a wandering life, as the Arabs, prefer the tent, as it may conveniently be carried with them from place to place; and in that warm climate, possesses, as a habitation, al'

the advantages which their rude and simple manners require
In very early times, it seems to have been altogether the most
common kind of dwelling. The life of a shepherd, roving
and unsettled, has always been connected with "living in a
tent." Jabal was the "father of such as dwell in tents and
have cattle," before the flood; and after it, we find Noah in
the same sort of dwelling, as at a later period, Abraham,
Isaac, and Jacob.

Tents are formed by setting up three, seven, or nine poles
as they are smaller or larger, and spreading over them a great
covering of cloth or skin. If more than three poles are used,
the three longest are placed in a row in the middle, and the
others on each side; if there be only three, they are placed in
a single row; then the covering is drawn over them, and
made to slope outward, like the roof of a house, towards the
ground, by means of cords, which are fastened down to the earth
with wooden pins or stakes. (Isa. liv. 2.) The covering is
generally made of that strong black cloth which is formed of
goat's hair. When a number of them are seen at a distance,
pitched together, as they frequently are, in a circle upon some
hill, they have a very beautiful appearance: "I am black,"
says the spouse, "but comely as the tents of Kedar." (Song i.
5.) The larger kind are divided by curtains into two or three
rooms. The bottom of the tent is covered with mats, and
sometimes carpets, on which those who live in them sit. A
small hole, dug in the middle, serves as a fireplace for cooking; and a few vessels of shell or brass, with some goat-skin
bottles and a hand-mill for grinding grain, make up the simple furniture of the eastern shepherd's slender dwelling. The
tents of the great and wealthy, however, are sometimes very
splendid, and supplied with richer accommodations.

Houses rise, as men give up a wandering life, and fix themselves on one spot, to till the ground or to attend to different
kinds of art and science. They had learned to build them
long before the flood, as we may clearly conclude from the
building of the ark. The Jews, after their settlement in Canaan, being chiefly employed in husbandry, dwelt generally
in houses. Their houses, however, were very different, in several respects, from ours; and to understand some passages of
the Bible, we must be acquainted with this difference. The same
general plan of building seems to have continued from the
earliest times to the present day, in the eastern countries.
Let us attend, then, to the account which travellers have given
us of a house, as it is common there; taking for an example
one of the larger and more respectable sort.

The outside of the house presents a square figure, with a flat top and dull appearance, having only a single door in the front side, and one latticed window looking from the upper part. On opening this door, we enter into a square room of moderate size, which is called the *Porch*. On one side of it is fixed a seat for the accommodation of strangers; few persons being allowed to get any farther into the house, except on great festival occasions. Going straight forward through the porch, we open a second door, which brings us into a large open square, right in the centre of the building, called the *Court*. When we raise our eyes upward, in this place, we find that there is nothing over our heads but the sky itself: the only covering which it ever has is a large veil or curtain, sometimes drawn over it by cords, from one side to the other, to keep off the sun, when a large company is to be received. When it rains, the water falls upon the pavement below, which is made of marble or some other solid material, and is carried out by a pipe or trough through the building. It is consi-

Interior court of an Eastern house.

dered a great ornament and luxury to have a fountain in the middle of this pavement, constantly pouring forth its refreshing stream. Around the court, on its four sides, are seen large windows and handsome doors, opening into it from all the rooms of the house. When you come out of these rooms, however, you do not generally step at once upon the pavement, but upon a covered walk, or porch with pillars, (such as we often see in front of our houses,) which goes along each side of the square. If the house has more than one story, the doors of the upper chambers open out upon a gallery or balcony, that runs round above this porch, and has, in front of it, toward the centre of the court, a balustrade, or some kind of railing, to keep people from falling down upon the hard pavement below. A person, in going from one room to another, must always come out of the first room and go into the second by the doors that open into the court; for there is no door or passage leading directly from one to the other, in the inside. On great occasions, such as a marriage, company is always received in the court.

From the square room, called the *Porch*, into which, as we have seen, the front door on the outside opens, a flight of stairs rises to the upper story, and so on to the roof of the house. The roof is flat, covered over with solid earth, or a kind of plaster, made of coals, ashes, stones, and other substances, well pounded together. It is surrounded on the outside with a low wall, and on the inside, round the court, with a breastwork, or railing, like the balustrade of the balcony, to prevent persons from falling either way. (Deut. xxii. 8.) On such roofs, a little grass will sometimes spring up; but it soon withers under the heat of the sun. (Ps. cxxix. 6—8.) The roof has always been much used as a place of agreeable retirement. There it is common to walk in the evening, to enjoy the cool breeze, and there, in summer, persons often sleep under the broad arch of heaven. On such a roof, Rahab concealed the spies with stalks of flax, (Josh. ii. 6;) Samuel talked with Saul, (1 Sam. ix. 25;) David walked at eventide, (2 Sam. xi. 2;) and Peter employed himself in meditation and prayer. (Acts x. 9.) In cities, the roof of one house is joined to another, so that a person may pass along a whole street, sometimes, without coming down. When, therefore, our Saviour said, "Let him that is on the housetop not go down into the house, neither enter therein, to take any thing out of his house," (Mark xiii. 15,) he might mean, that he should pass right along the roofs of the houses, and get to the end of the street, and so out of the city, by the shortest possible way. More probably, however, he meant that he should go directly down the stairs into the *Porch*, and so out by the street door, without turning backward through the *Court*, to any of the chambers, lest even so small a delay should cost him his life. It seems to have been by taking advantage of this close connection of several roofs, that the friends of the man who was sick with the palsy brought him into the presence of Jesus. (Mark ii. 3, 4.) While the Redeemer was preaching in the court of a certain house in Capernaum, they came, carrying the sufferer upon a bed; but the crowd was so great in the house and about the door, that they found it impossible to come near him. They then took the man up, through some neighbouring house, to the top, and thus brought him along till they stood by the inner breastwork of the roof, just over the place where our Saviour was. There they *uncovered the roof;* that is, took away the covering of cloth that was spread over the court to keep off the sun, and *broke up,* or tore away, some part of the balustrade; and so, with cords, let down the bed, whereon the sick man lay, into the midst, right before Him who was able to heal. (Luke v. 19.)

The rich sometimes have two houses; one for summer, and another for winter. (Amos iii. 15.) The former faces the north, to be cool; the latter opens toward the south, to be warm. The rooms are generally large; those in the upper story being fitted up with more elegance than those below. The back part of the house is occupied by the women. An *Upper Chamber*, just over the porch, in the front part of the building, was generally, among the Jews, set apart to lodge strangers. (1 Kings xvii. 19.) When the house had only one story, this room seems to have been raised above it, to the height of a second, with a door opening out upon the roof. (2 Kings iv. 10.) When fire was used, the smoke had no chimney to carry it away; it went out by a hole in the wall, though it is called a chimney in one place. (Hos. xiii. 3.) Windows had no glass, but merely lattice-work.

Houses, in earlier times, seem to have been commonly only one story high, in Palestine; but long before the time of Christ, many of them were much higher, and very splendid; ceiled with cedar, painted with vermilion, and richly adorned with ivory, gold, and precious gems. (Jer. xxii. 14, 1 Kings xxii. 39.) Stone was used for building before the time of Moses, (Lev. xiv. 40,) and always continued common. Timber, too, was much employed. (Isa. ix. 10.) The bricks mentioned in several places, were square pieces of clay, hardened merely by the heat of the sun. The walls of many houses of the more common sort were made of this material, which could seldom last longer than the life of one man. As it was comparatively soft, it was not hard to dig a hole right through it. (Matt. vi. 19; Ezek. xii. 5.) Serpents, also, would occasionally find a hiding-place in it. (Amos v. 19.) Heavy rains injure such walls very much; and if they were not well secured about the foundation, sometimes swept them utterly away: to such a house our Saviour seems to refer: "The rain descended, and the floods came, and the winds blew, and beat upon that house; and it fell: and great was the fall of it." (Matt. vii. 27.) Such frail houses are still common in the east. So many of them are in the city of Damascus, that when a violent rain falls, the streets become like a quagmire, with the clay that is washed from the walls.

In eastern cities, the houses are generally built with very narrow streets between them; not more than four or five feet wide. This is to have them, almost all the time, completely shaded from the oppressive power of the sun. In ancient times, however, as we read, chariots were driven through them; so that some of them must have been much wider. The *Gates* were important places. A considerable space was left unoccupied about them, where markets were held and goods of all sorts exposed to sale, either in tents or under the open sky. (2 Kings vii. 18.) Here, also, was the seat of justice, and the common place of resort, where all matters of law were settled, and public business of every kind transacted. When Abraham bought a field of the sons of Heth, the bargain was made "at the gate of the city." (Gen. xxiii. 10, 18. See also Gen. xxxiv. 20, Ruth iv. 1—10.) Hence, the expressions, "to be crushed in the gate," that is, to be utterly condemned in judgment, (Job v. 4;) "to open the mouth in the gate, to reprove in the gate, to turn aside judgment in the gate," &c. The gates were made very strong; sometimes of iron or brass. *Gates*, then, may be used to signify both strength and wisdom; as when it is said, "The gates of hell shall not prevail against" the church. (Matt. xvi. 18.)

SECTION II.

OF FURNITURE.

LET us next consider the furniture of an eastern house. The floors of the rooms are covered with mats or carpets. In a box beside the wall, are kept some thick, coarse mattresses, which at night are thrown upon the floor and slept upon; the poorer people use skins. Bedsteads and chairs are not seen. It is an easy matter to carry such a bed; as our Saviour commanded the sick man: "Take up thy bed and walk." On two or three sides of the room, there is sometimes seen a raised place, about three feet broad and a foot high, running all along the wall. On this lies, from one end to the other, a stuffed cushion: and here the people sit cross-legged, somewhat after the manner of our tailors when at work, leaning their backs against bolsters that are fixed up along the wall. The seat at the corner is the most comfortable and the most honourable. This raised place, on which it has always been usual to lie, as well as sit, (2 Kings xx. 2,) is called sometimes in Scripture, a *bed*, (Amos iii. 12;) and sometimes, under the same name, appears to be meant a moveable settee, or sofa, of the same height and breadth, furnished with the same conveniences, and used in the same way, for sitting or lying. Such were the "beds of ivory," (Amos vi. 4;) and something of the sort, perhaps, was the "iron bedstead" of Og, king of Bashan. (Deut. iii. 11.)

The bottom of a room in a Jewish house was always perfectly clean. Nobody dreamed of stepping into it with a sandal or shoe on his foot, and tobacco was utterly unknown. Hence, it was very seldom necessary to scrub or sweep. (Matt. xii. 44, Luke xv. 8.)

A *Lamp*, fed with olive oil, and supported on a large candlestick, seems to have been kept burning constantly through the night, in the room where the family slept. Such is still the custom in Egypt, even among the poorest people. Hence, to the ear of a Jew, the phrase, to *put out a man's light*, employed to signify calamity, was more full of meaning than we are apt to conceive. (Job xxi. 17, xviii. 5, 6.) "Whoso curseth his father or his mother, his lamp shall be put out in obscure darkness." (Prov. xx. 20.)

Forms of Lamps.

Pots, plates, and cups of different kinds, sometimes pretty costly, were found in the Jewish dwelling. One of the most useful articles was the goat-skin bottle. It is made by stripping off the

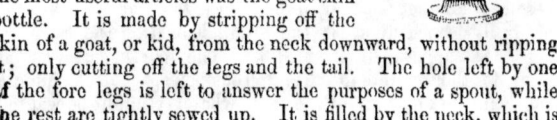

skin of a goat, or kid, from the neck downward, without ripping it; only cutting off the legs and the tail. The hole left by one of the fore legs is left to answer the purposes of a spout, while the rest are tightly sewed up. It is filled by the neck, which is

afterwards tied like the mouth of a sack
Into this vessel is put water, milk, and
wine, which are kept more fresh and
sweet this way, than they can be in any
other. They are used, indeed, to carry
almost every kind of provision. When
they get old, they often break, and often
are mended in different ways. Such
were the "wine bottles, old, and rent,
and bound up," of the cunning Gibeonites, (Josh. ix. 4;) and such bottles our
Saviour had in view, when he said,
"Neither do men put new wine into old
bottles; else the bottles break, and the wine runneth out, and
the bottles perish." (Matt. ix. 17.) The Arabs still use these
bottles, and sometimes form a vessel nearly as large as a hogs-
head, out of an *ox-skin*. Two of these last, filled with water,
and slung over the back of a camel, are of great value to a
company travelling through the desert.

The most ancient table for eating, probably resembled that
which is still common in the east; a circular piece of leather
spread upon the floor, around which those who ate sat with
legs bent and crossed, on cushions or small carpets. So the
brethren of Joseph *sat before him*, when they dined with him
in Egypt. (Gen. xliii. 33.) It seems to have been common,
in very early times, to have separate small tables, placed in a
circle at the social meal, one before each person, as we give
each a separate plate. Every one had his *portion* set on his
own table. After the captivity, the Persian custom of lying
at meals, which came into use also among the Greeks and
Romans, grew fashionable in Palestine. This required a new
kind of table. It was made up of three narrow tables, raised,
like ours, from the ground, and placed together so as to form
a square, with a clear space in the middle, and one end quite
open. Around these three tables, on the outside, were placed
three couches or beds, reaching far enough back to allow a
man's body to be stretched nearly straight across. On these,
the guests lay, in a slanting position, one before the other,
each leaning upon his left arm, with his face turned toward
the table. In this way, the head of one was placed before the
bosom of another, so that, if he turned to speak with him, he
naturally leaned upon it; thus John leaned on the Saviour's
bosom at supper. (John xiii. 23.) The fourth side was left
clear, for the servants to pass into the open space in the middle,
and bring to any part of the table whatever might be wanted.

On one of these table-couches, or beds, Queen Esther was leaning, when Haman fell before her to supplicate mercy. (Esth. vii. 8.) On such a couch, also, the Redeemer lay at meat in the Pharisee's house, when there came a woman "that was a sinner, and stood at his feet behind him, weeping, and began to wash his feet with tears, and did wipe them with the hairs of her head, and kissed his feet, and anointed them with ointment." (Luke vii. 36—38.) She stood on the floor, by the outside of the high couch. In a similar manner, our Lord approached the feet of his disciples, when he rose from supper, took a towel, with a basin of water, and began to wash them and wipe them, one after another, as they lay round the table. (John xiii. 4—12.) Wherever, in the New Testament, we read of *sitting* at meat, we are to remember that it means no other position than this of stretching out the body at full length, with the head and shoulders raised upon the left arm.

A most indispensable article in every house was the *Mill*. We read of fine meal in the time of Abraham; so, before his age, the mill must have been well known. It was made of two circular stones, about the size of our common grindstones, placed one above the other. The lower one was fixed so as not to move, and had a little rise toward the centre, on its upper part; the upper one was hollowed out on its lower side, to fit this rise, and had a wooden handle fixed above, to turn it round, with a hole through the middle to receive the grain. This mill was used day after day, as regularly as our coffeemill; for as bread in that country will continue good only a short time, it became the universal custom to grind fresh flour and bake every day, except the Sabbath. It was the business of maid servants to grind, and so considered a degrading employment for a man, (Judg. xvi. 21,) or for a lady of rank. (Isa. xlvii. 2.) Sometimes one turned the mill alone: but frequently two were employed together to make the work lighter. In the latter case, they sate one on each side, thrusting the handle round continually from one to the other. Thus our Saviour speaks of "two women grinding at the mill." (Matt. xxiv. 41.) As the mill was so essential to every family, it was forbidden to take the nether or the upper stone for a pledge. (Deut. xxiv. 6.) If, in the days of her glory, we had walked along the streets of Jerusalem about the twilight of evening, or the dawn of morning, when the noise of grinding came upon the ear from every quarter, we should better understand the image of desolation which the prophet presented, when he foretold that God would take away from the city "the voice of the bridegroom and the bride, *the sound of the millstones*, and the light of the candle." (Jer. xxv. 10.) These handmills are still used all over the East.

Ovens were of different sorts. A common fashion was to make them of stone or brick, covered over with mortar, something in the shape of a large pitcher. Fire was put in the inside, and the dough spread, like a thin paste, over the outside; it was baked in less than a minute. Another oven was a round hole dug in the earth, and paved at the bottom with stones: after it was heated, the fire was taken away, the cakes placed upon the stones, and the mouth shut up. Because other fuel was often scarce, it was common, (as it still is in that quarter of the world,) to heat ovens with light brushwood, the prunings of vines, stubble, and such materials. Dried grass often answered the purpose: "If God," said the Saviour, in his sermon on the mount, "so clothe the grass of the field, which to-day is, and to-morrow *is cast into the oven*, shall he not much more clothe you, O ye of little faith?" (Matt. vi. 30.) The dung of animals, such as horses, camels, and cows, thoroughly dried, was employed in the same manner. In many places of the east, at the present time, it forms the most general supply of fuel for all purposes of cooking or baking, and is laid up and kept in large stacks, with much care, for standing family use. It is bought and sold, also, by cart-loads, as wood is in other countries. (Ezek. iv. 15.) Cakes were often baked in the ashes, (Gen. xviii. 6,) and sometimes on pans or plates of iron, placed over the fire. (Lev. ii 5.)

CHAPTER IV.

OCCUPATIONS.

SECTION I.

OF THE PASTORAL LIFE.

Its origin. The life of a shepherd had, in early times, much to recommend it to the choice of men. It was attended only with light labour, and afforded, generally, a sure prospect of riches and independence. While the human race continued

comparatively few in number, vast tracts of ground lay in every direction, without cultivation, and without owner, covered with the richest pastures. The shepherd had but to withdraw himself from the more thickly settled communities, when he found, without expense, free range for his flocks and his herds, however vast their number; and when the grass began to fail around him in one place, it was an easy matter to gather up his tent and move with all his substance to some other spot still fresh with the wild abundance of nature. He had no home or family to leave behind, in his wanderings; his dwelling-place, with all its numerous household, followed the steps of his flock; and for him to wander or to rest, was to be alike at home.

ITS PREVALENCE. Accordingly, in the eastern part of the world, this manner of life found great numbers to embrace it, in the first ages of time. Before the flood, Abel was *a keeper of sheep*, and Jabal "was the father of such as dwell in tents *and have cattle.*" After that great event, we read that the illustrious patriarchs of the Jewish nation, Abraham, Isaac, and Jacob, with all his sons, pursued the same business. These were shepherds of the highest rank, exceedingly rich in silver, and gold, and flocks of every kind, (Gen. xiii. 2, 5,) and surrounded with a household of several hundred servants. (Gen xiv. 14.) Each was a prince in the midst of his great family, perfectly independent; making war, and making treaties of peace, with states and tribes around him, by his own sovereign authority. Such a shepherd was Job, also, " the greatest of all the men of the east," in his time. By reason of the dignity and power which belonged to the prince-like shepherds of ancient times, as well as on account of the tender care with which they governed their flocks, it became customary to give the title to rulers and kings. God himself is frequently styled a shepherd, and his people compared to a flock under his almighty protection.

In Egypt, the Israelites devoted themselves as a people to the employment of their fathers. And even after their settlement in the land of promise, although husbandry became the national business, many still clung to this early manner of life. That part of the country which lay east of the Jordan afforded peculiar advantages to those who made such a choice. On this account, the children of Reuben and Gad, because " they had a very great multitude of cattle," requested to have it for their inheritance. (Numb. xxxii. 1—5.) The mountainous tracts of Gilead and Bashan abounded with the finest pastures, and beyond their extensive range lay, far and wide outspread, the wilderness of Arabia; which, though in general sandy and barren, had yet scattered over it some fertile spots, rising like islands on the dreary ocean, and inviting the shepherd to wander with his flocks over the unoccupied waste. All this, except the territories of Ammon toward the north, and Moab toward the south, belonged properly to the Israelites, (Gen. xv. 18;) and we read that the shepherds of Reuben did, in the days of Saul, when their herds were greatly multiplied in the land of Gilead, destroy four Arabian nations who opposed their way, and dwelt in tents far east of the mountains, toward the great river Euphrates. (1 Chron. v. 9, 10, 18—22.) It was not altogether uncommon to pursue the same kind of life on the other side of Jordan, especially among the hills of Ephraim and Judah, as we may see in the history of David. The business, however, could not be conducted on the same great scale, as little of the land could be spared from the labour of the farmer. In the days of our Saviour, shepherds were still found, watching their flocks, in the land of Judea. (Luke ii. 8.) The nations who dwelt to the south and south-east of the land of Canaan, were made up, in a great measure, of unsettled herdsmen and shepherds. Such were the Amalekites, the Ishmaelites, and Midianites. They owned, indeed, some villages and towns, and were confined in some measure to particular regions of the broad uncultivated wilderness; but they had no fixed boundaries; whole families and tribes wandered with their flocks from place to place, as inclination led, and thus were often found far asunder from the body of their nation, or even surrounded, at times, with the tents and possessions of a different people. Thus the Kenites were found within the borders of Amalek, when Saul came to destroy that devoted nation. (1 Sam. xv. 6.) Even the country of Edom, though it had much cultivated land and several large cities, seems to have consisted, in a great part, of wild, unsettled wastes, thus occupied with wandering hordes of such as dwell in tents and are employed with the care of cattle.

CARE OF FLOCKS. The flocks were tended by servants; also by the sons, and frequently by the daughters of the owner, who himself was often employed in the same service. In the summer, they generally moved toward the north, or occupied the loftier parts of the mountains; in the winter, they returned to the south, or sought a favourable retreat in the valleys. A shepherd was exposed to all the changes of the season, as the flock required to be watched by day and by night under the open sky. Thus Jacob described his service: "In the day the drought consumed me, and the frost by night; and my sleep departed from mine eyes." So, also, the shepherds were watching their flocks *by night*, when the angel of the Lord came down with the glad tidings of a Saviour's birth. The flocks did not, however, give so much trouble as we might imagine such vast numbers would. They grew familiar with the rules of order, and learned to conform themselves to the wishes of their keeper, on the slightest notice. They became acquainted with his voice, and when called by its sound, immediately gathered around him. It was even common to give every individual of the flock its own name, to which it learned to attend, as horses and dogs are accustomed to do among us. If the keeper's voice was at any time not heeded, or could not reach some straggling party, he had but to tell his dog, who was almost wise enough to manage a flock by himself, and immediately he was seen bounding over the distance, and rapidly restoring all to obedience and order. When he wanted to move from one place to another, he called them all together, and marched before them, with his staff in his hand, and his dog by his side, like a general at the head of his army. Such is the beautiful discipline which still is often seen in the flocks of eastern shepherds. With a knowledge of these circumstances, we can better understand the language of our Saviour, in his beautiful parable of the Shepherd and his flock: "The sheep hear his voice; and he calleth his own sheep by name, and leadeth them out. And when he putteth forth his own sheep, he goeth before them, and the sheep follow him; for they know his voice. And a stranger will they not follow, but will flee from him; for they know not the voice of strangers." (John x. 3—5.)

It was the business of the shepherd to protect his flock from harm, for which purpose he generally carried a sling or bow; to lead them where sufficient pasture might be found; and to take care that they were well supplied with water. (Ps. xxiii 1—4.) The last thing was not, generally, in those regions which were traversed by shepherds, a very easy matter. The stream, or living fountain, were seldom to be found. It was necessary to dig wells; and as the flocks had to be led to different pasturing places, sometimes far apart, it was necessary to dig several wells. A shepherd who managed his business right, would have a regular round of places, with a well of water at each, which he might visit in succession every year. Thus we read of Abraham and Isaac digging one well after another. It is easy to see, that where water was so scarce, while for the support of large herds and flocks so much was wanted, a well became a most valuable part of property. (Gen. xxvi. 15—22, 32, 33, Numb. xx. 17—19.) Hence, they were carefully covered and concealed, as far as possible, from view, that others might not steal away the water; another reason for covering them, was to keep them from being filled up with sand, as it rolled over them before the wind. Sometimes, several shepherds had a well in common. (Gen. xxix. 2, 3.) It was a cruel act to stop up the wells of any people, as it was common for enemies to do: it was to shepherds as bad as the burning of houses in a country like ours. The flocks were watered twice in the day; at noon and about sundown. It was a laborious business to draw water enough for so great a

multitude. The wells were generally very deep; as was that one of Jacob, where our Saviour talked with the woman of Samaria. (John iv. 11.) From the value of water, in places where it was thus scarce and difficult to be procured, it became a common emblem of rich blessings of any sort, and especially of spiritual favour; so that God himself is called a "fountain of living waters." (Jer. ii. 13, xvii. 13.)

PRODUCE.—From his flocks, the shepherd was supplied, as we have already seen, with almost all the comforts of his life. Except a little grain and a few poles, he needed nothing for food, or for raiment, or for dwelling, which they could not furnish. His table was crowned, as often as he chose, with flesh of the best kind; which, however, in those warm countries, was not often used, except on great festivals, or to entertain strangers; while every day, abundance of milk and cheese gave relish to his simple meal. The *butter* mentioned in the Bible, was not, however, like ours; it was something that could be drunk, as Jael is said to have offered it to Sisera, in a lordly dish, when he asked for drink. (Judg. v. 25.) Perhaps it was some preparation of cream. We read of "*floods and brooks* of honey and butter;" and of *washing* a man's steps in it. (Job xx. 17, xxix. 6.) Every *Sheep-shearing*, especially, added to the wealth of the master of the flock. It was always a great occasion. The sheep were all gathered into large folds; a great company of shearers were collected to the place; an unusual preparation of food took place; and the whole season, which generally lasted several days, was turned into a complete festival. (2 Sam. xiii. 23.) By selling continually their cattle and various kinds of produce to the neighbouring cities, the shepherds often became very rich in silver and gold, as well as in their flocks and herds; for as it was not uncommon for them to farm for themselves a piece of land, sufficient to supply them with grain, they supported their great households almost without expense, and reaped a clear profit from every thing they sold.

MODERN SHEPHERDS.—The east, as we have already hinted, still abounds with shepherds; and much light is thrown upon those parts of Scripture which relate to the circumstances of early pastoral life, by an acquaintance with the manners and customs of these wandering tent-dwellers, as they exist in our own day. The same vast regions of uncultivated country, over which, in ancient times, so many scattered families travelled with their numerous flocks and herds, are now found occupied with various tribes of their posterity, equally unsettled and equally free. Through the deserts of Arabia and Syria, from the banks of the Nile to the ancient stream of Euphrates, and far beyond, toward the rising sun, they are found, ranging from one pasturing place to another, and scorning every restraint of civilized fashion or power. The master of each family is a chieftain, or prince, surrounded oftentimes with many hundred dependants and servants. Many of them are exceedingly rich, covering the whole country for miles, as they pass along, with immense droves of camels, oxen, cows, asses, goats, and sheep; and possessing, at the same time, treasures of silver and gold. No doubt, the patriarchal shepherds of the Bible resembled some of them very much, in their wealth, and power, and manner of life. But *they* were blessed with a knowledge of the true God, and their tents were hallowed with the pure spirit of devotion, while the blackness of Mohammedan error reigns in the families of *these*. We may be certain, therefore, that in all those circumstances of character which only can give true ornament or dignity to life, whether found in the tent or the palace, the latter come far short of showing forth any true representation of the former.

PASTORAL IMAGERY.—We have said that God is often compared, in Scripture, to a shepherd. Under the same image the Lord Jesus Christ beautifully and expressively describes his relation to the church; and never was application more happy and complete. The sheep of his flock were once scattered upon the mountains, without shepherd and without understanding, going continually astray, weary and faint from scantiness of pasture and distressing want of water; exposed to spoil from the arm of the prowling robber, and hunted and torn by the hungry wild beast of the forest. He saw and pitied. He left the glorious splendour of his Father's house, to follow and gather to himself the miserable wanderers. His voice was heard upon the hills, calling them to return and feed under his care. As they listened and came, he builded for them a large and secure fold, and led them forth, day by day, to fields of the richest pasture, and by quiet streams of ever-running water. His kind and tender care was constantly employed for their good; he strengthened the weak and cherished the sick; leading with gentleness such as were with young, and gathering the lambs with his arm, to carry them fondly in his bosom. And when the hour of thickest danger came, and all the rage of the enemy threatened to devour and destroy the entire flock at once, he shrunk not from their defence, though the conflict was dreadful beyond all expression. He met the danger in his single strength, and firmly *laid down his life for the sheep!* But in dying, he overcame, and wrought a deliverance for his sheep, which no power of the enemy can ever destroy. And now, though unseen by mortal eyes, he is still present with the flock, watching over it with the same tender care, conducting its steps by the pastures and waters of life, and shielding its path from the prowling wolf and '*the roaring lion.*' To secure its welfare, he has appointed, under himself, many servants to oversee and tend its different parts. These he has commanded, with awful solemnity, to be faithful *Pastors*, or shepherds, and to feed his flock with diligence and care; they act at all times under his eye, and must render a strict account of their ministry, when He, "the Chief Shepherd," shall finally appear. (Matt. ix. 36. 1 Pet. ii. 25, Isa. xl. 11, Ps. xxiii., John x., Jer. xxiii. 3, 4 Acts xx. 28, 1 Pet. v. 2—4.)

SECTION II.

OF HUSBANDRY.

ADAM began to cultivate the ground directly after his creation: it was his business, with light and pleasant labour, to dress and keep the garden, ere yet sin had blasted its original beauty. After the fall, the earth, pressed under the weight of the Almighty's curse, no longer yielded of her own accord the necessary fruits of life. Labour became indispensable, and, at the same time, severe. Since that time it has been, more or less, in every age and in every nation, an occupation of men to till the soil, and draw from its bosom the means of subsistence and comfort.

Many nations, however, while they could not neglect the business altogether, have made it a matter of comparatively small attention; rather choosing, from the situation of their countries or the disposition of their people, to secure to themselves the blessings of life, by giving their time and care chiefly to some other pursuit. But the Israelites, after their settlement in Canaan, were almost entirely a nation of farmers. A small portion on the eastern side of the Jordan, as we have seen, were principally occupied with the care of flocks and herds; but the great body of the people spent their time, almost exclusively, in cultivating the land. By the direction of God, each tribe had its own particular province, and every family in that tribe its own plantation, clearly marked out from all the rest. No family could entirely lose its plantation; for it never could be sold for any longer time than to the year of Jubilee. Thus, while the daughters of any house, when they married, were moved away to the inheritance of some other family, the sons, to the latest generation, continued on the same estate. In this way, no one man could ever buy up large tracts of country for himself, so as to leave multitudes without property of their own, and so without the strongest inducement to diligence. Every individual knew, that whatever labour or care he bestowed upon his farm, it could never be utterly lost to his family, and thus was animated to spare no pains in its cultivation. And as the portion which fell to each, where *all* were entitled to share, was necessarily small, it was managed with the more skilful art; from which it came to pass, that the whole face of the country presented an appearance of the highest cultivation, so that probably no country that was ever seen, could compare, in this respect, with the land of Palestine in those days.

We have already considered the different productions of this country, which claimed, in ancient times, the attention of the Jewish farmer. It remains to notice his various methods of labour, as employed at different seasons, in the several departments of his care.

THE FIELD.

To prepare the ground for sowing, immediately after the first short season of rain in the fall, he set himself to break it up with the plough. His *plough*, however, was a trifling thing, in comparison with one of ours. It was probably much like the ploughs that are used at the present day in eastern countries. One of those is often so light, that a man can lift it with

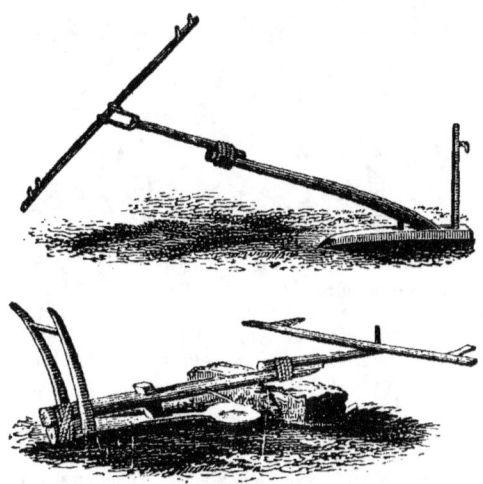

one hand; and when it passes over the ground, it leaves only a moderate *scratch* behind, instead of the deep, broad furrow which *we* are accustomed to see. The *ploughshare* is a piece of iron, somewhat broad, but not large, fixed to the end of a shaft that lies flat. Two handles, and sometimes only one, standing nearly upright from this shaft, prepare it to be guided by the ploughman's hand; while a pole of sufficient length, rudely fastened to the bottom, near the handles, and slanting upward to the proper height, answers the purpose of a beam, to which is fixed the common yoke for drawing. The *share* has a good deal of likeness to the short sword that was anciently used, and might easily be beaten into such an instrument. It was not uncommon, once, to change one into the other, as we may learn from the language of the prophet: "Beat your ploughshares into swords, and your pruning hooks into spears." (Joel iii. 10. See also Isa. ii. 4.) With such a light, unsteady plough, the ploughman needs the greatest caution and care to keep it in the ground, or to make a straight furrow; he must be continually bending over and pressing upon it, so as to giv

n stet liness and weight. For a man, therefore, who undertook to manage a Jewish plough, to turn his head behind him, was even more imprudent and foolish than the same thing is with us. To this our Saviour refers; "No man, having put his hand to the plough and looking back, is fit for the kingdom of heaven." (Luke ix. 62.)

The ground was levelled with a *harrow* still more rude. It seems to have been generally a mere heavy clump of wood, drawn over the field, to *make plain the face of it*, before the seed was sown, (Isa. xxviii. 24, 25;) or sometimes, perhaps, a wicker-drag, or a large rough piece of brushwood, to cover the grain; this, however, was, in most cases, probably done by ploughing it over with a cross furrow.

Bulls and cows, he-asses and she-asses, were the common beasts of labour. If a bull became wild and hard to manage, a hole was bored through his nostrils, and a ring of iron, or

twisted cord, fixed in it; to this was fastened a rope, by which it could be so pulled and twisted, as to stop the animal's breath almost entirely, and so render the most furious quite orderly. By this same contrivance, it was common to manage camels, and even elephants and lions, when they took them alive. To this practice the Lord alludes, in his address to the Assyrian king: "Because thy rage against me and thy tumult is come up into mine ears, therefore I will put *my hook in thy nose*, and my bridle in thy lips, and I will turn thee back by the way by which thou camest." (2 Kings

xix. 28.) So also in that grand description of leviathan, it is asked: "Canst thou put an *hook* into his nose?" to intimate that no art can manage his strength. (Job xli. 2, Ezek. xxxviii. 4.) Both ox and ass worked under a yoke fixed over their necks, and tied with ropes to the beam. It was not lawful, however, to couple one with the other, under the same yoke; not only because they were animals of unequal strength and different habits, and because every such connection is unnatural and unpleasant, but also to make sacred distinction between the *clean* and the *unclean*, as the ox stood chief among beasts of the former class, and the ass among those of the latter. The yoke is a natural symbol of authority and power; and to carry it, denotes subjection and obedience. The Saviour invites us to take upon us his yoke, because it is easy. (Matt. xi. 29, 30.) Sin fastens on the neck a heavy yoke of pain and sorrow. (Lam. i. 14.) To "break the yoke," means, to burst loose from authority and cast off all submission, (Jer. v. 5 ;) when done for any one by another, it is deliverance from oppression and bondage. (Isa. ix. 4, lviii. 6.) The ploughman was furnished with a pole, seven or eight feet long, armed at one end with a flat piece of iron for cleaning the plough, and at the other, with a spike for spurring his beasts. This was called the *ox-goad*. It was sometimes used in war for a spear, and made, when skilfully handled, a very good weapon. With such an instrument in his hand, Shamgar made his bold attack on the Philistines, and six hundred fell dead on the spot. (Judg. iii. 31.)

It was common to begin to sow toward the end of October. it was not, however, too late to sow wheat in December; while January, and even February, was soon enough for the barley. There was no frost to hinder ploughing, through the whole winter. It was desirable, however, to get as well on in the business as possible, during that period of fair weather which always followed the first few days of rain in the fall; for, after it was over, the labour of the farmer was continually exposed to interruption from the showers of rain which fall so abundantly, as we have already seen, from that time to the season of harvest.

The grain became ripe very soon after the *latter rains* were over. On the second day of the Passover, which, as we shall hereafter see, came considerably sooner in some years than in others, a barley sheaf was presented as an offering of the first fruits of the harvest, at the altar of God. After this, the business of reaping began; first, the barley was cut; then the wheat and other kinds of grain. The time of harvest lasted seven weeks, from the Passover until Pentecost, which came, generally, not far from the beginning of June. It was a joyful season. The

master was seen in his field in the midst of his servants and
children, as they pursued their work with cheerful and contented diligence. Age and youth united their hands in the
busy occupation, and even maidens came forth to the field, and
lent their assistance in the general work. On every side, the
movement of industry was displayed, as the reaper plied the
sickle, or the binder's bosom was filled with the new-made sheaf;
while the song of gladness, as it frequently rose from the
scene, carried in its simple melody an assurance of satisfaction,
which the music of palaces failed to express. (Ps. cxxix. 7, Isa.
ix. 3.) What a beautiful picture does the harvest field of Boaz
present, as it is described in the second chapter of Ruth! The
Jewish farmer was not allowed to forget the poor in this season
of joyful labour: "When ye reap the harvest of your land,"
said the Almighty, "thou shalt not wholly reap the *corners* of
thy land: neither shalt thou gather the *gleanings* of thy harvest; thou shalt leave them for the poor and the stranger; I
am the Lord thy God." (Lev. xix. 9, 10.)

The grain was next carried to the *Threshing-floor*, on beasts
of burden, or in wagons. All *wagons*, in those days, moved
upon *two* wheels only, like our carts: frequently, however,
they had beds of considerable size. The threshing-floor was
in the field itself, on the top of some rising ground, where it
might be most open on all sides to the wind. It had neither
covering or walls; and was, in fact nothing more than a sufficient space of ground, levelled with a great roller, and beaten
so as to become completely hard. Here, the sheaves were
thrown together in a loose heap, ready for threshing. To beat
out the lighter kinds of grain, a flail or cudgel was employed;
for crops of the heavier sort, such as wheat and barley, the
common methods were the feet of oxen or the threshing
machine. The ox was used to tread out grain very early.
(Deut. xxv. 4.)

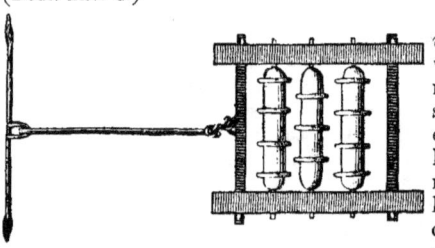

The *Threshing Instrument*
was not always
made in the
same way in
every particular; the general form,
however, was
commonly the
same. Imagine
four stout pieces of timber joined together in a square frame,

and three or four heavy rollers, with axles at each end, reaching across and turning in its opposite sides; suppose each of these rollers to have round it three iron wheels, cut into sharp teeth, like a saw, or to be armed with thick pieces of the same metal,  standing out six inches all over its surface; then fancy a body of some sort raised over this frame, with a seat for a man to sit upon and ride, and you will form a pretty correct notion of this powerful machine. Mounted on his seat, with a yoke of

oxen before him, the driver directed it round the floor. The rollers, as they turned heavily along, crushed and broke all before them. The front part of the machine was turned upward, like the runners of a sled or sleigh, so as to pass along without becoming choked with the straw.

The *Cart*, which Isaiah says was used in threshing, was only some particular form of this instrument. (Isa. xxviii. 27, 28.) Threshing with such a machine presented a very impressive image of destruction and slaughter; and, accordingly, we find it several times introduced in the figurative style of Scripture, to express the severest judgments of God, or the most cruel violence of war. (Hab. iii. 12, Amos i. 3.)

The next business was to *winnow* the grain, or separate it from the straw and chaff. This was done by throwing it up before the wind, with a fork or shovel. The straw, by the force of the threshing instrument, was so cut up and broken into small pieces, that it readily flew off some distance with the chaff. The grain was then cleared of heavier substances, such as lumps of earth, with a sieve. It was because wind was so necessary in this business, that the threshing floor was always on a high place, like that of Araunah, the Jebusite. But to assist in driving away the straw and chaff, it was common to use also a fan. (Isa. xxx. 24.) To purge the heap thoroughly, it was necessary to expose it to the wind more than once. As threshing is used figuratively for severe destruction, so is winnowing for the scattering of a vanquished people: "Behold," says God to his church, "I will make thee a new sharp threshing instrument, having teeth; thou shalt thresh the mountains, and beat them small, and shalt make the hills as chaff. Thou shalt fan them, and the wind shall carry them away, and the whirlwind shall scatter them!" Isa. xli. 15, 16.) The same image is employed, also, fearfully to represent the separation of the wicked from the righteous, and their utter desolation before the wrath of the Almighty. They shall be "as the chaff that is driven with the whirlwind out of the floor;" "as stubble before the wind, and as chaff that the storm carrieth away." (Hos xiii. 3, Job xxi. 18, Ps. i. 4.) And as it was also common to set fire to the chaff, as it lay mingled with the more broken and useless parts of the straw in a neighbouring pile, the image became more terrible still. (Isa. v. 24.) Thus, the righteous judgment which Christ will execute upon the ungodly, is represented by John the Baptist: "His fan is in his hand, and he will throughly purge his floor, and gather his wheat into the garner; but he will burn up the chaff with unquenchable fire. (Matt. iii. 12.) The straw that was less broken was carefully laid up for the use of cattle.

CARE OF THE VINE.

The cultivation of the vine formed another most important part of Jewish husbandry. *Vineyards*, as we have already seen, were generally planted on the sides of hills and mountains. Much labour was employed to prepare the ground. The stones were carefully gathered out; the rock was often covered over with soil, piled up so as to make a broad platform on the sloping height; the whole was surrounded with a hedge or wall; the ground was carefully dug, and set with plants of the choicest kind; a press was sunk for making wine; a tower was raised, in which all the tools and other articles necessary for the labourers might be kept, and where one or more watchmen might always stay to guard the enclosure from thieves and wild animals, especially foxes, which were very troublesome. (Song ii. 15.) These towers seem to have been sometimes built with much elegance, and fitted up with expensive care, as places of pleasure as well as mere use, where the rich owner might occasionally resort with his friends, to enjoy, for a few days, its agreeable retreat. God compares his care of the Jewish nation to the care which the husbandman was accustomed to bestow on his vineyard. (Isa. v. 1, 2, Ps. lxxx. 9—13.) Our Saviour uses the same image: "There was a certain householder which planted a vineyard, and hedged it round about, and digged a wine press in it, and built a tower, and let it out to husbandmen, and went into a far country," &c. (Matt. xxi. 33.) The vines were pruned several times a year, with an instrument made for the purpose, and called the *Pruning-hook*.

The vintage, or season for gathering grapes, began early in the fall, about the middle of September, and generally lasted about two months. It was a time of even more gladness than harvest. With songs and shoutings that sounded all over the hills, the labourers proceeded in their work; gathering the great clusters into baskets, and bearing them to the *Wine-press*. This was commonly dug, like a vat, into the ground, and secured over the bottom and round the sides, with stone-work, plastered so as to hold the juice; frequently, it was hewed in a solid rock. It consisted of two separate parts or vats close together; one of which was sunk considerably lower than the other. The grapes were thrown into the upper vat, where they were trodden completely, by the feet of five or six men, and the juice, as it was pressed out, ran through a small grated opening in the side, close by the bottom, down into the lower one. The treaders sung, and shouted, and jumped; and all their garments became thoroughly stained with the red blood of the grapes. (Jer. xxv. 30, xlviii. 32, 33.)

Out of the juice was made *Wine* and *Vinegar*. The new wine was commonly put into new goat-skin bottles, with the hairy side turned inwards. (Job xxxii. 19, Matt. ix. 17.) It became better the longer it was kept, when the dregs all settled to the bottom. (Isa. xxv. 6.) Besides the vinegar which is usual among us, and to which Solomon refers in one of his proverbs, (Prov. x. 26,) there was a sort of weak wine, used very commonly by labourers, which was called by t

same name. Such was that vinegar which the workmen of Boaz used in his harvest field. (Ruth ii. 14.) This was a common drink also among the Roman soldiers, and seems to have been that *vinegar* which one of them presented in a sponge to our Saviour, when he hung upon the cross. (Matt. xxvii. 48.) The "vinegar mingled with gall," which had been before offered to him, (v. 34,) and which Mark calls "wine mingled with myrrh," was a preparation of wine mixed with this bitter substance, and frequently given to criminals doomed to suffer death, in order to stupify their feeling, and so take away the sense of pain. Our Lord refused the cup; he would not consent, in the deepest agony of his suffering, to taste a drink that could bring relief only as it deranged and blunted the natural powers of the soul. What a lesson for those who, in times of sorrow, betake themselves to strong drink! What a lesson for those who deliberately sacrifice reason and sense for the brutal pleasure of intemperance, without even this wretched plea!

The treading of the wine-press is used figuratively to denote vengeance and wrath, displayed in the terrible destruction of enemies. Thus the Redeemer is represented as trampling upon the enemies of his people: "Who is this," the prophet inquires, as he saw, in vision, one coming toward him in triumph, from the south: "Who is this that cometh from Edom, with dyed garments from Bozrah? this that is glorious in his apparel, travelling in the greatness of his strength?" An answer returns: "I that speak in righteousness, mighty to save." The prophet again asks: "Wherefore art thou red in thine apparel, and thy garments like him that treadeth in the wine-vat?" The reply comes: "I have trodden the wine-press alone; and of the people there was none with me: for I will tread them in mine anger, and trample them in my fury; and their blood shall be sprinkled upon my garments, and I will stain all my raiment." (Isa. lxiii. 1—3.) The same figure is employed in the book of Revelation. (Rev. xiv. 18.) The wrath of God is compared also to a cup of strong wine, on account of its overwhelming effects. Such wine was deeply red; and oftentimes, to render it still more powerful, it was mixed with different spices. "In the hand of the Lord," says the Psalmist, "there is a cup, and the wine is red; it is full of mixture; and he poureth out of the same: but the dregs thereof, all the wicked of the earth shall wring them out and drink them." (Ps. lxxv. 8.)

Grapes were sometimes dried in the sun, and preserved in masses or cakes, like figs. These were the *clusters*, or *bunches of raisins*, which Abigail presented to David on one occasion, and Ziba on another. (1 Sam. xxv. 18, 2 Sam. xvi. 1.) The Jews were not allowed to gather the fruit of their vines, or of any other tree, until the fifth year after it began to bear. (Lev. xix. 23—25.)

CARE OF FRUIT TREES.

The Olive also yielded a rich reward to the husbandman's care. The fruit was sometimes beaten off the tree with a long stick or pole, and at other times shaken. It was not allowed to go over the boughs a second time; the few olives that still clung to the tree were to be left for the poor, as were the grapes that were passed over in the vintage. (Deut. xxiv. 20, 21.) The gleaning of olives and grapes is used to represent a sweeping judgment of God, that leaves scarcely any thing behind. (Isa. xvii. 6, xxiv. 13.) Olives were trodden in a press of a particular kind, as well as grapes. The word *Gethsemane* means an *oil-press;* no doubt, because such a press, and perhaps more than one, was much used there, for making oil from the fruit that grew so plentifully around, upon the *Mount of Olives.* The oil was very valuable; answering, in a great degree, among the Jews, the same purposes that butter does with s, and, at the same time, supplying them with light in their lamps. Sometimes, the fruit was plucked before it was ripe, and instead of being cast into the press, was only beaten and squeezed. The oil obtained in this way was the best, and was called *beaten oil;* the sacred lamp in the Sanctuary was always fed with such. (Ex. xxvii. 20.) The best kind of oil was also mixed with spices and used for *ointment;* all the rest was employed, in various ways, for food, or for common lamps. To "dip the foot in oil," is an expression that signifies to possess a rich and fruitful inheritance. (Deut. xxxiii. 24.) Oil, as has been already said, was a common emblem for gladness, and grace of every kind.

Of other fruits, it is not necessary to speak particularly, though several of them were highly valuable. Their character and use have been already briefly noticed, in our account of trees. The Jews were very fond of gardens, and employed, frequently, a great deal of care, to make them not only profitable, but also beautiful and pleasant. In that warm country, it is peculiarly agreeable to have such retreats, provided with every thing that can gratify and refresh. Shadowy walks, overhung with fruits of richest fragrance; delightful arbours, deeply hid within the cool and silent bosom of some grove planted with fair and stately trees; streamlets of water, sent forth from a constant source, and winding their way in every direction over the whole scene of fruitfulness and beauty: these are luxuries so agreeable to eastern taste, that the rich cannot consent to be entirely without them, if they can be secured by any expense of labour or art. It was common, in ancient times, to build sepulchres in gardens, for the burial of the dead. Thus Manasseh, we are told, was buried in the garden of his own house. (2 Kings xxi. 18.) So also in the place where our Saviour was crucified, "there was a garden, and in the garden a *new sepulchre,*" in which his body was laid. (John xix. 41.)

HONEY.

Bees formed another object of care with the Jewish farmers They abounded in their country from the earliest times; so that it was called, by way of description, "a land flowing with milk and honey." These little animals often laid up their stores in hollow trees, or in the clefts of the rocks, (Ps. lxxxi. 16;) but more commonly, we may suppose, in hives, as with us. Honey was very much used at home, but made in such great quantities that it was also carried away to supply other countries, especially in traffic with the Tyrians. (Ezek. xxvii. 17.)

Butter or cream, and honey, were esteemed a great delicacy, and it was a sign of plenty in the land, when this kind of food abounded. Such seems to have been the meaning of that promise to Ahaz, that before the child that was soon to be born should be old enough to know good from evil, the country should be delivered from her enemies, and such prosperity restored, that butter and honey would be his common food. (Isa. vii. 15, 16.) The same taste still continues in eastern countries: cream and honey are accounted, especially among the Arabs, the richest luxury of the breakfast table. There was also a kind of *wild honey*, not uncommon in that region. It was not made by bees, but collected from other little insects upon the leaves of certain trees, so as to drop down quite plentifully; sometimes all over the ground. Such was the honey which Jonathan tasted in the wood; the *honeycomb* into which he is said to have dipped his rod, was merely a collection of this wild substance. (1 Sam. xiv. 25—27.) The honey which John the Baptist used for food in the wilderness, might have been, at least in part, of this sort; though it is probable he found there much honey of the common kind, as to this day very considerable quantities are laid up among the rocks, through that same region of country: this might very properly be called *wild honey*, as well as the other. (Matt. iii. 4.)

The Gleaners.

SECTION III.

EMPLOYMENTS OF HANDICRAFT, TRADE, &C.

Agriculture, as has been said, was the main business of the whole Jewish nation. It was rendered, by the very constitution of the state, the necessary occupation of the great mass of the people. Hence, there were not with them, as with us, large classes of men employed altogether in the different mechanic arts, or in the business of commerce. Tradesmen and merchants, who make up so respectable a portion of the community in our country, were, for a long time, of almost no account in theirs; and, in fact, could not be said to have been known at all, as distinct, regular orders, in the system of society. This state of things underwent a little alteration, after the time of Solomon. Tradesmen grew more numerous, and began to form, in some measure, a separate class of citizens. Commerce also with foreign nations became, in some degree, and especially at two or three different periods, an object of attention. It was not, however, until the time of the captivity, that the character of society was very materially changed. After that event, a great number of Jews became merchants, and travelled, for the purposes of traffic, into all countries. It grew common, also, to learn particular trades; and hence, we find them frequently mentioned in the New Testament.

It may be asked, how the inhabitants of the cities were employed in those times, when we suppose merchants and tradesmen to have been so few in the land. The answer is, that cities then were generally very small, and pretty much filled with husbandmen. Their small farms lay scattered over the country round, and their chief care was to attend to thier cultivation. (Judg. xix. 15, 16.) Several of them belonged to the Levites, who had their particular employment in another way. Some of the larger ones, only, discovered something of the mercantile character; while a *few* artists might possibly be found in many, if not all. This, however, was not enough to give any importance to either kind of occupation, as forming a distinct profession in society.

Among the earlier Jews, a great many articles that we are in the habit of getting made for us by different tradesmen, were manufactured in every man's own family, as they were wanted. The women spun and wove, besides doing every sort of needle-work; thus clothing was made for the whole family. And as it was common to wear on the head only a mitre of cloth, and on the feet only a pair of simple sandals, the whole dress could be very easily provided, without the smallest assistance from abroad. Thus nobody wanted a *weaver*, a *tailor*, a *hatter*, or a *shoemaker*. A good housewife, with *us*, will dispense with the services of a *baker;* but, among *them*, the very worst could look no further than her kitchen for a *miller*. The common tools, also, that were wanted in farming, and most of the common articles of furniture in their houses, were so simple, that a man of usual ingenuity would not often think of betaking himself to the skill of another to have them made. Still, there were always some things that needed more than common art; and, accordingly, the country was never entirely without men who employed themselves in a few of the more difficult trades. There were carpenters, hewers of stone, and various workmen in gold, silver, brass, and iron The building of the tabernacle in the wilderness, needed some such artists of considerable skill. At that time, however, there was probably a greater proportion of them among the people than afterwards; as, no doubt, the service of many had been employed in this way in Egypt; which country had already made very great progress in the knowledge of various arts. After their settlement in Canaan, there was comparatively little demand for superior skill. The artists, accordingly, seem to have held no very high character for ability in their several trades. Many of them, probably, only turned their attention occasionally to such business, while a great part of their time was spent in other pursuits. Hence, when the temple was to be built, it was thought necessary to procure masons and carpenters from Hiram, king of Tyre. (1 Chron. xiv. 1.)

During the captivity, many of the Jews found themselves, in a great measure shut out from their old manner of life, and so were compelled to apply themselves to arts and merchandise. And as, ever after, their condition was less settled than before, and very many of them were continually scattered among different nations, it became more and more fashionable to learn trades, as the best means of supporting themselves in all circumstances; so that, at last, it came to be a doctrine of their wise men, that all parents were bound to teach their children some kind of handicraft, whether they expected them ever to use it or not. Accordingly, we find in the New Testament, that Joseph was a carpenter, and that our Saviour worked at the same trade. So Paul, also, was by trade a tent-maker, though his birth and education were such that he did not probably suppose, when he learned the business, that he should ever be called upon to employ his skill in this way for a support; but when he was taught to count all things but loss for Christ, and went forth from city to city, persecuted and poor, this humble employment was turned to most serviceable account.

Commerce with foreign nations was not forbidden by the law of Moses; but, at the same time, it was not encouraged in the smallest degree. The reason of this was, that the Jews might be kept as far as possible from mingling with other nations, so as to avoid the danger of falling into their idolatries, and to remain a completely separate people, until the wise purposes of God should be answered. Traffic among themselves, of course, was carried on, upon a small scale, from the earliest times. Hence, we hear from the first, of *weights* and *measures*. Solomon ventured to go far beyond this limited usage of trade. He carried on a traffic with Egypt, for horses; and sent forth a number of vessels, by the way of the Red Sea, to the distant countries of Ophir and Tarshish, which brought him in amazing wealth. After his time, the Jews seem, till their captivity, to have kept up some trade with other people, though it fell far short of what was carried on while he governed the nation.

Wheat, honey, oil, and balm, are mentioned, as articles that were carried out of the country, in traffic with other nations. (Ezek. xxvii. 17.) No doubt, the wine, also, which it yielded so abundantly, of the best quality, was to some considerable extent turned into profit, in the same way. (2 Chron. ii. 10, 15.) In return for these and other commodities, a variety of foreign productions were introduced into the land. In the days of David and Solomon, the principal materials for the building of the temple were thus brought from the kingdom of Tyre. We read, that for this purpose, cedar and fir and almug trees were hewed on Lebanon, and floated on great rafts to Joppa. (2 Chron. ii. 8, 16.) Part of the mountains called Lebanon belonged to Palestine itself; but it seems that the most valuable timber of the kinds just mentioned, grew on that part of their long range which fell within the territories of Hiram, the Tyrian king. What the *Almug*, or *Algum* trees were, cannot now be known. Vast quantities of gold, silver, brass, iron, and all manner of precious stones, were collected by David from different quarters. From Ophir and Tarshish, the ships of Solomon brought gold, silver, precious stones, almug wood, ivory, apes and peacocks. The commerce with Egypt brought in a large supply of horses and linen yarn; while great companies of camels came, time after time, loaded with every fragrant spice, from the farthest regions of Arabia—such as cinnamon, cassia, frankincense, and myrrh. So plentiful was the introduction of foreign treasures of every sort into the country, in the days of this prosperous monarch, that he is said to have made "silver to be in Jerusalem as stones, and cedars as the sycamore trees that were in the vale, for abundance."

It would be very desirable, in reading the Scriptures, to have a correct acquaintance with the systems of *measures*, *weights* and *coins* which regulated, in different ages, the ancient traffic of the east. On this point, however, our knowledge never can be very complete or satisfactory. These matters have ever been subject to gradual alteration and change, and antiquity has left us but few notices that can help us to determine any thing more than mere names. Models, indeed, of the different weights and measures, as they were fixed in the time of Moses, were laid up in the tabernacle, and afterwards in the temple, to be kept as perpetual standards, under the care of the priests. But all these were destroyed when the temple was burnt the first time; and after that period, the whole ancient system was either entirely given up, or at least in a great measure modelled anew, from the systems of other nations. Thus the most ancient weights and measures mentioned in the Old Testament, are left to be determined from the mere slight notices of Scripture itself. Those mentioned in the New Testament are not attended with so great difficulty, though by no means free, in every case, from uncertainty of similar sort.

MEASURES OF LENGTH were, at first, taken from various parts of the human body. So far, then, as we can determine these parts, we may make a probable guess about the length of the measures: yet it will be *only* probable; because, such measures, though suggested at first by the parts from which they are named, become sometimes gradually settled into lengths that vary considerably from their original natural standards. Measures of this sort were the Digit, the Palm, the Span, and the Cubit.

A *Digit* was the breadth of a man's finger or thumb. A *Palm*, called commonly a *hand-breadth*, was equal to four finger-breadths or digits. A *Span* was equal to the distance between the top of the thumb and the top of the little finger, when they were stretched as far as possible apart; it was as much as three hand-breadths. A *Cubit* was, as one opinion supposes, the distance between the elbow and the wrist of a man's arm; according to another, it was the length of the whole arm, or, at least, from the elbow to the knuckles. It is plain that *two* cubits are mentioned in Scripture, one longer than the other, as much as a hand-breadth; the great difficulty is, however, to determine which of these is the oldest and most common. (Ezek. xl. 5.) It has been, nevertheless pretty generally agreed to reckon a cubit about a foot and a half of our measure, so as to consider four of them equal to the common height of a man. Ezekiel mentions a measure called a *reed:* it was equal to six cubits of the longer kind.

In later times, other measures were introduced. The *Furlong* was borrowed from the Greeks: it was one hundred and twenty-five paces in length, equal to the eighth part of a Roman mile. This *Mile*, which is the one intended in the New Testament, being equal to eight furlongs, was, of course, made up of one thousand paces, and was about one hundred and fifty yards shorter than a common English mile. A *Sabbath-day's journey* was about seven furlongs; that is, a little less than a mile. This was a measure invented by the Jews, to determine precisely how far a man might go on the Lord's day, without breaking the commandment. (Ex. xvi. 29.)

HOLLOW MEASURES were of two kinds, as they were used for liquids or for dry articles. Sometimes, however, the same measure was used for both, as we use the gallon and quart. For dry articles, the common measures, in early times, were the Cab, the Omer, the Seah, the Ephah, and the Homer; for liquids, the Hin, the Log, the Bath, and the Homer, seem to have been the most important in use.

The *Cab* was one of the smallest measures, though it is thought by some to have held more than our quart. The *Omer*, we are told, was the tenth part of an ephah, and must, therefore, have contained a little more than five pints. An omer of manna was the allowance of daily food to each Israelite, in the wilderness. The *Seah* held somewhat more than our peck, and was the third part of an ephah. It is called, in our translation of the Bible, simply a *measure;* thus Sarah is requested by Abraham to take three *measures* of fine meal and knead it, (Gen. xviii. 6;) in which passage this particular kind of measure is mentioned in the original. The same measure is to be understood in Matt. xiii. 33, and Luke xiii. 21. The *Ephah* contained three seahs, or about three pecks and three pints of our measure. We are told that it was equal to ten omers. (Ex. xvi. 36.) The *Homer* held ten ephahs, or about eight of our bushels. It was the largest dry measure. The Greek *measure*, mentioned in Rev. vi. 6, held only a quart.

Measures for liquids seem to have been rated, at first, by the number of egg-shell quantities which they could hold

The smallest was perhaps sufficient to contain but one or two such quantities. A *Log* held six egg-shells full. A *Hin* was equal to twelve logs, or as much as seventy-two times the quantity of a single shell. This would be about five quarts of our measure. A *Bath* was equal to six hins, or seven and a half of our gallons. The *Homer*, accordingly, which was used for liquid as well as for dry articles, contained ten baths as well as ten ephahs, and was, of course, something larger than one of our hogsheads. We are to remember that the capacities of all these ancient hollow measures are determined only according to probability. There is by far too little information on the subject to settle the matter, in any case, with precise and solid certainty.

In the times of the New Testament, a *Bushel* was in use. It was the Roman bushel, which contained only a peck in English measure. The *Firkin*, mentioned in the account of our Saviour's first miracle, was a Greek measure, and held about as much as the ancient bath, or ephah; that is, seven and a half gallons. (John ii. 6.)

WEIGHTS.—It was a long time before men began to coin money, as is common now. Gold and silver were very early used in selling and buying; but they were always *weighed*, like other articles of traffic; so that every piece, whatever its shape might be, was valued just according to its purity and its weight in the balance. In this way, we read that Abraham *weighed* the silver which he paid for the field of Machpelah. (Gen. xxiii. 16.) While this method continued, it was common for such as were employed in traffic of any kind, to carry with them a pair of balances, and different weights, in a sort of pouch or bag. These weights were generally stones. Hence, the meaning of those laws which forbid divers weights in the bag, or unjust balances, becomes clear. (Lev. xix. 36, Deut. xxv. 13, 15, Prov. xvi. 11.) Wicked men sometimes carried a different set of weights with them: one class was too light, and with these they sold; the other, too heavy, and with these they bought; thus defrauding others in all their dealings. "Shall I count them pure," the Almighty says of such, "with the wicked balances, and with the bag of deceitful weights?" (Mic. vi. 11.)

From this early manner of using silver and gold, we find that all the terms used in the Old Testament to signify the value of different sums of money, are merely the names of common weights. The most important of these weights was the *Shekel*. The name itself signifies simply *a weight*; which shows that it was very ancient and very much in use. We are not able to know exactly what was its weight before the captivity; for, although the same name was continued long after, even down to the time of Christ, there is much reason to believe that the shekel of early times weighed less than the later one. This last weighed nearly half an ounce; the other, therefore, was probably a good deal under that weight. There was, besides the common shekel, a royal one, called "the king's shekel," which seems to have been considerably smaller than the other. A *Gerah* was the twentieth part of a shekel. (Ex. xxx. 13.) There was also a weight called the *Bekah*, or half-shekel. A *Pound* is supposed to have been equal to sixty shekels, and a *Talent*, to three thousand. By these different weights, both silver and gold were counted, and so valued according to their purity and their scarcity, as it was greater or less at different times. A shekel of silver, according to the later estimation of that weight among the Jews, would be about equal in value to our half-dollars; and so, before the captivity, must have been, in all probability, considerably below that rate.

Coins.—After the captivity, the Jews became acquainted with *coins*, or stamped money. The most ancient coin of which we have any knowledge, was the *Darick*, a Persian coin, stamped by royal authority: the *Drams* mentioned in Ezra and Nehemiah, were this kind of money. The Jews began to coin money for themselves, in the time of the Maccabees, not quite one hundred and fifty years before Christ. A Greek coin, called a *Stater*, was then in common use, and was supposed to be about equal in weight to the early shekel. Accordingly, when the Jews struck off their coin, called after the ancient weight, the *Shekel*, it was made just as heavy as the stater, though, as we have said, it is most probable that the old shekel was considerably lighter. The new shekels were coined both in silver and in gold, and some of them remain to this day. The "*piece of money*," which Peter found in the mouth of a fish, was one of the staters mentioned above, equal in value to a shekel of that time, and so just enough to pay the tribute money for two persons. (Matt. xvii. 27, Ex. xxx 13.) The fourth part of a stater was equal to a *Drachma*, among the Grecian, and to a *Denarius*, or penny, among the Roman coins. This last, in the time of our Saviour, had stamped upon it the head of Cæsar. (Matt. xxii. 20.) In value, it was about twelve and a half cents of our money. The Roman *Farthing* was in value one-tenth of their penny; and not quite equal to one cent and a half among us. It was used to signify the smallest value, as the price of a couple of sparrows. (Matt. x. 29.) A smaller piece of money, equal only to a fourth part of the last, is sometimes mentioned under the same name. (Matt. v. 26.) The smallest of all was the *Mite*, two of them being equal but to one farthing of the least kind: this was the widow's offering. (Mark xii. 42.)

Silver and gold, anciently, were far more scarce than they are now: and, of course, the same weight would be far more valuable. This ought to be remembered, in reading the Scriptures.

SECTION IV.

LEARNED PROFESSIONS.

Besides those who find employment in such active pursuits as have been already mentioned, there is, in our country, a considerable class of men, whose lives are spent more or less in *study*, or in the practice of what are called learned professions. There are many interests of society that cannot be rightly secured, without the direction of knowledge and

Jewish Scribe.

education, such as persons engaged in the common occupations of labour and business can never be expected to acquire. It is necessary, therefore, that some should devote their whole time and attention to the cultivation of such knowledge, for the benefit of the rest. Hence arise various orders of men, whose business it is to watch over the interests of morality and religion, to conduct the affairs of government, to explain the principles of law and justice, to practise the healing art in the continual care of life and health, or to direct and superintend the great concern of general education, through all its stages, from the lowest up to the highest improvement. It is natural to inquire how far, and under what form, such professional employments were found among the Jews. Who in this nation of farmers, were the Ministers of religion, the Judges, the Lawyers, the Physicians, and the Schoolmasters?

In early times, nearly all these orders of men, as far as such orders were distinctly acknowledged in society, were found in the single tribe of Levi. The tribe of Simeon are also said by the Jews to have been much employed as schoolmasters, on account of the scantiness and scattered situation of their inheritance. The tribe of Levi, by the law of Moses, had no inheritance among the others, in the division of the land. It was chosen from among the rest, especially for the service of the sanctuary, and was to be supported entirely by contributions from the whole nation. To this tribe belonged the family of the Priests, and the whole care of the tabernacle and temple was committed exclusively to its members. Their business, however, was by no means confined to the temple. They instructed the people in the knowledge of the law, throughout the land; not indeed by preaching week after week, as our ministers now do, but by scattering themselves in different posts over the whole country; by writing and circulating copies of the Scriptures; by explaining their meaning as they had opportunity, or were consulted by those around them; and by educating the young. At the end of every seven years, they were bound to read over the whole law, in the hearing of all the people, (Deut. xxxi. 10—13;) and it was their duty to be ready at all other times, by its diligent study, to answer the inquiries which others might make on the subject of religion. In those times, when printing was altogether unknown, copies of the sacred volume were necessarily scarce, and hard to be procured. It was, therefore, a most important service which the Levites rendered to society, by writing such copies in the most correct manner, and thus securing the truth of God to the people. There were, probably, but

BIBLICAL ANTIQUITIES.

lew, besides this tribe, who were able to write, as there was but little occasion, in the manners of that age, for them to study the art. Hence, not only the sacred records, but all other kinds of writing, naturally fell to the care of the Levites, among whom, at least a considerable portion were always skilful in the use of the pen. In this way, they came to be of great importance in the business of government, as secretaries, and keepers of the Genealogical Tables. Those of them who were chiefly employed in writing were called *Scribes*. (2 Chron. xxxiv. 13.)

The same tribe furnished the regular Judges of the nation. The extraordinary officers under that name, whom God raised up at different times, to deliver and govern the country, were taken, indeed, without regard to any such distinction. But it was expressly provided, that the common and established administration of justice should be under the care of this tribe. The priests, the sons of Levi, were the supreme judges of the land, by whose word "every controversy and every stroke" were to be tried. (Deut. xxi. 5, Ezek. xliv. 24.) So, also, the inferior judges, appointed for all the cities through the country, seem generally to have been Levites. Thus we read of six thousand who were "officers and judges," in the days of David. (1 Chron. xxiii. 4.) As the only law of the land was the law of God's word, and their whole character required from them the continual and diligent study of that law, it was to be expected that they would be better qualified than others to explain it in judgment, and so, of course, most suitable to be intrusted with that care.

We must suppose, too, that the chief attention which learning of any kind received in the nation, came from this same tribe. The Levites had leisure and opportunity far more than others, and their minds were necessarily more turned to study and science. It is probable, therefore, that the learning of the country was pretty generally confined to their body.

We have no reason, indeed, to believe that the various sciences of the times were pursued, even among the Levites, to any very great extent; except, perhaps, in the days of David and Solomon: yet, that some attention was bestowed on most, if not all, is manifest from several occasional notices of such kinds of knowledge, which may be gathered from the Scriptures. We read of Physicians, and of healing diseases; the science of *Medicine*, therefore, was in some measure studied and understood; and there was a class of men, though it was probably very small, whose business it was to practise this important art. We discover, also, some acquaintance with *Arith-*

metic, Surveying, Geography, and *Astronomy. Mathematical* knowledge, too, to some extent, was necessary in certain employments, which were common among them. But it was especially to the care of history, and genealogical annals, and to the science of morals, that the national taste was turned. It never was the design of the Almighty Governor, who had separated them to himself out of all the nations of the earth, that they should stand eminently distinguished in the world for profound and rare learning of mere human kind. Their wisdom, as well as their glory, was to spring from the simple power of heavenly truth, that its excellency might be of God, and not of man. It was left, therefore, for other kingdoms to explore the deep recesses of science, and make full experiment how far mere unassisted knowledge, such as men are most apt to admire, could secure the true happiness and dignity of life. Babylon and Egypt vied with each other in the variety and depth of their learning. The whole world was filled with the reputation of each. Wise men travelled many hundred miles, from distant regions, to listen to the wisdom of their philosophers, and enrich themselves from their treasures of knowledge. "To be learned in all the wisdom of the Egyptians," as Moses is said to have been, was to stand on the highest summit of science. (Acts vii. 22.) But after all, how empty was the pride of these countries, in comparison with the excellency of Israel and Judah! Babylon bowed down in adoration before the sun and the moon, and the whole starry host of heaven, and worshipped idol gods of stone and wood. Egypt sunk lower still, and abased her wisdom in the worship of bulls and goats and cats, and reptiles of vilest kind: yea, her very leeks and onions were changed into gods. Thus, "in the wisdom of God, the world by its wisdom knew not God," and fell into every abominable vice; while, without any remarkable advantages of science, the nation of the Jews retained the truest knowledge of the Holy One, and the soundest principles of morality; such knowledge and such principles as, to this day, cannot be convicted of error. How could this wonderful difference be, except by the force of instruction more than human? The word of God, though it had little show of wisdom in the eyes of the world, was full of light and power. While they attended to its truth, the Jews were, in all their simplicity, wiser far than the wisest nations of earth.

The *Prophets* formed a very small class of society, but one of principal importance, not only so far as religion was concerned, but also, by reason of their continual connection with the affairs of government, as advisers and reprovers of those

BIBLICAL ANTIQUITIES.

who managed them. They were not confined to any particular tribe, nor admitted to their office by birth, but raised up for their business from different families. They had, of course, much influence through the nation, as they were the extraordinary ministers of God, and proclaimed his will in the messages which they delivered. As early as the time of Samuel, schools were established for the preparatory education of such young men as sought this sacred dignity. They were here instructed, under the care of some aged prophet, in those things which might fit them in the best manner to discharge the duties of the office, should God be pleased to bestow upon them the spirit of prophecy in time to come. The students in these schools were called *Sons of the Prophets*, and their teachers were styled *Fathers*. (2 Kings ii. 3, 5, 7, 12, 15.)

The name of *Scribe* was first given to such as excelled in the use of the pen; but because these were generally distinguished likewise in other branches of knowledge, it came, in time, to mean simply *a learned man*. And as the chief part of learning, among the Jews, was concerned with the sacred books of Scripture, the word signified especially *one who was skilled in the law of God;* one whose business it was, not merely to provide correct copies of its volume, but also to explain its meaning. Thus Ezra is called "a ready scribe of the law of Moses." (Ez. vii. 6.) In the time of our Saviour, the *Scribes* formed quite a considerable class in society. Many of them belonged to the Sanhedrim, or chief council, and are, therefore, frequently mentioned in the New Testament, with the *Elders* and *Chief-Priests*. The *Doctors of the Law*, and the *Lawyers*, of whom we hear, were only the same class of persons under different names, (Luke v. 17, x. 25;) these names they received from their business of teaching and interpreting the Law. Their opinion on this subject had great weight among the people. They were said to "sit in Moses' seat," because they undertook to explain the whole meaning of Moses and the other sacred writers, (Matt. xxiii. 2;) and were, accordingly, consulted in all cases of doubt or uncertainty, about the truth of Scripture. (Matt. ii. 4.) Hence we learn the meaning of those questions: "Why then say the *Scribes* that Elias must first come?" and "How say the *Scribes* that Christ is the son of David?" (Matt xvii. 10, Mark xii. 35.) Our Saviour applies the same word to a well-instructed minister of the gospel: "Every scribe which is instructed unto the kingdom of heaven, is like unto a man that is a householder, which bringeth forth out of his treasure things new and old." (Matt. xiii. 52.)

It was common to address these wise men by the honorary

title of *Rabbi*, which means *Great*, or *Master*. This title was introduced not long before the time of our Saviour, as was also the still higher one, *Rabboni*, which is to say *Master* with more emphasis, or rather, *My great Master*. (John xx. 16.) In the Jewish schools of learning, the title of Rabboni was never bestowed on more than seven persons, who were all peculiarly distinguished for their rank and wisdom. The name of Rabbi was given to every one who went through a regular course of education, under the instruction of some wise doctor of the law, and was judged fit to become the teacher of others. Celebrated doctors were resorted to frequently, by a number of scholars. These listened with the profoundest attention to their words, and treated them with the most respectful reverence. It seems to have been common for them to take their seats much lower than their master, placing themselves before him, around his feet. So Paul, we are told, was brought up, or educated, at the feet of Gamaliel, who was the most learned and honourable doctor of that age. (Acts xxii. 3.) Teachers were sometimes, according to a most ancient custom already noticed, called *Fathers*, and their scholars, or *disciples*, styled their *sons*, or *children*. The exhortation to "call no man Father upon earth," had respect to this use of the term, and means that it is not proper to give ourselves up to the authority of any leader or head of a sect, or to depend on any mere human teacher as an unerring guide in matters of religion and truth, as the Jewish disciples did toward their masters. (Matt. xxiii. 9.) The usage mentioned is also referred to in that question put to the Pharisees: "If I by Beelzebub cast out devils, by whom do your *children* (or disciples) cast them out?" (Matt. xii. 27.)

CHAPTER V.

DRESS, MEALS, AND SOCIAL INTERCOURSE

SECTION I.

OF DRESS.

THE art of making cloth is very ancient: no doubt, long before the flood, spinning and weaving of some sort were known. The first covering which our original parents used, was formed from leaves of the fig tree. God afterward instructed them to employ for this end the skins of animals. Soon, it is probable, they learned to manufacture the long hair of some beasts into a rude kind of cloth, and then gradually brought the discovery to greater degrees of perfection, by the use of wool, cotton, and flax. In the time of Abraham, the art seems to have been well understood.

Spinning and weaving were the business of women. Thus in the wilderness, as we are told, "all the women that were wise hearted did spin with their hands, and brought what they had spun, both of blue and of purple, of scarlet and of fine linen," for the service of the sacred tabernacle which was to be built. Very early, also, they carried the art of embroidery and ornamental needle-work to a very considerable degree of perfection. (Judg. v. 30.) The art of *colouring* cloth was also well understood. Sometimes a most splendid *white* was imparted to it, by a peculiar skill of the fullers. This colour was preferred to every other on festival days. On such ocacsions, the rich and noble robed themselves in garments of white cotton. It was also customary to be clothed in white as a mark of honour, (Esth. viii. 15;) and the colour has always been a natural emblem of purity and joy. In allusion to these ideas, our Saviour promises his people, that they "shall be clothed in white raiment," and "walk with him in white," in his heavenly kingdom. (Rev. iii. 4, 5.) Angels always appeared in white; and when our Redeemer was transfigured, on the mount, into some resemblance of the glory of heaven, his raiment became "exceeding white as snow; so as *no fuller* on earth can white them." (Mark ix. 3.) Kings and princes, when they appeared in state, were generally arrayed in *purple*. This was a very bright colour, supplied from the blood of a certain shell-fish, as it was found in a single white vein near the animal's throat. By reason of its great scarcity, it was considered more precious than gold. The rich man in the gospel, whose awful end the Saviour describes, "was clothed in purple." The *scarlet* colour was also much esteemed. It was taken from certain insects, or their eggs, found on a particular kind of oak. The same colour is sometimes called *crimson*. This also was worn as a mark of royalty and power. In cruel mockery and insult, the Roman soldiers put a *crown* of thorns upon the head of our Redeemer, and a reed in his right hand, to represent a *sceptre*, and arrayed him in a *scarlet robe*, as if they would honour him like a king, bowing the knee before him and crying, Hail, king of the Jews! (Matt. xxvii. 28, 29.) Mark and John called the robe a *purple* one, because that name was used in a general sense, for any bright red colour and often, especially, was applied to a *royal* robe of such a hue, inasmuch as it was itself, by way of distinction, the royal colour.

While the rich adorned themselves with every costly material, the lower ranks contented themselves with clothing of the plainest and cheapest kind. Even coarse hair-cloth was not entirely laid aside, long after the general use of wool and flax. Cloth, as we have already seen, was frequently made from the hair of goats and camels, for the covering of tents. As late as the days of our Saviour, we hear of some such cloth used for garments: John the Baptist, it is said, " had his raiment of camel's hair." Elijah, whom John resembled so much, seems in his day to have worn the same kind of stuff. He is described as " a hairy man, girt with a girdle of leather about his loins;" that is, one dressed in hair, or hair-cloth, after the same style in which the Baptist appeared. (2 Kings i. 8.) We have reason to believe, indeed, that anciently it was very common for prophets to be clothed in such raiment, as we learn from one place, that false prophets were in the habit of wearing " a rough garment to deceive." (Zech. xiii. 4.) John came, therefore, in this respect, precisely in the severe and self-denying fashion of an ancient prophet; for such in fact he was, a greater than whom never before had been. The *soft clothing* of king's houses formed a great contrast with the rugged apparel of this holy man. (Matt. xi. 8.) This same sort of cloth was put on by such as were deeply afflicted, or wanted to express great sorrow; for the *Sackcloth* of which we hear on such occasions, was nothing else. It was formed into a garment like a sack, with merely holes for the arms, which was thrown over the mourner, and reached down below the knees. In this dress, the afflicted individual frequently sat down in the midst of ashes, having the head all covered over with the same. As this cloth was made most commonly out of goat's hair, it was, of course, of a dark or a black colour; hence those images of covering the heavens " with blackness and *sackcloth*," and of the sun becoming " black as *sackcloth of hair*." (Isa. l. 3, Rev. vi. 12.)

THE TUNIC.—The most simple, and probably the most ancient garment, was the *Tunic*. This was worn next to the skin, and fitted tolerably close round the body. It had arm-holes, and sometimes sleeves, and reached down, like a long shirt, below the knees. It was commonly made of linen, though frequently, also, of other cloth. Round the waist it was bound with a girdle. When a man had nothing round him but this under garment, it was common to say he was *naked*. Thus we are told that Isaiah walked *naked* and barefoot; Saul prophesied *naked* before Samuel; Peter was *naked* in the ship. (Isa. xx. 2—4, 1 Sam. xix. 24, John xxi. 7.) In time, the tunic grew to be larger and longer, hanging more loosely round the body, and reaching as low down as the ankles; so that, in later ages, a shirt of wool was sometimes worn under it. In the English Bible, it is called a *coat*. That which our Saviour wore, " was without seam, woven from the top throughout." (John xix. 23.)

THE UPPER GARMENT.—The garment immediately over the tunic was merely a piece of cloth, nearly square, and several feet in length and breadth. This was wrapped round the body or tied over the shoulders. The two corners, which were drawn over the shoulders and hung down in front, were called its *skirts*, or *wings*. It was so large and loose that it was often used for carrying burdens; as when it is said, one found in the fields a wild vine, and gathered his *lap full* of its fruit. (2 Kings iv. 39.) So, also, the Israelites carried their kneading troughs, when they went out of Egypt, " bound up in their clothes, upon their shoulders," (Ex. xii. 34;) and when we read in the New Testament of "good measure, given into the *bosom*," we should think of the large fold of such a garment, gathered round the breast. (Luke vi. 38.) The common people wrapped themselves, at night, in this blanket-like covering, and wanted no other for sleeping. On this account, it was unlawful to keep it as a pledge after sun set : " If thou at all take thy neighbour's raiment to pledge, thou shalt deliver it unto him by that the sun goeth down; for that is his covering only; it is raiment for the skin : wherein shall he sleep?" (Ex. xxii. 26, 27.) Hence, in the description of oppressive rich men, it is said, "They cause the naked to lodge without clothing, that they have no covering in the cold." (Job xxiv. 7.)

Upon the four corners of this garment, the law required that there should be fringes, together with a blue riband, to remind the people of all the command ments of the Lord their God. (Num. xv. 38.) That they might be noticed of men, the Pharisees were accustomed to have these religious signs remarkably large: "They made broad their phylacteries, and enlarged the *borders of their garments.*" (Matt. xxiii. 5.) In our translation of the Scriptures, this article of dress is called a *cloak*, or simply a *garment*, and sometimes an *upper garment.* Such were the garments which the people spread in the way before our Lord, as he entered into Jerusalem. (Matt. xxi. 8.) It was common to lay it aside, when persons engaged in labour or exercise that needed much activity, as it served only to hinder them: this was done by our Saviour, when he washed the feet of his disciples, and by Peter, when he was employed in fishing. (John xiii. 4, xxi. 7.) It was in this way, also, that king David *uncovered* himself, when he "danced before the Lord with all his might," girded merely with a linen ephod. (2 Sam. vi. 14, 20.) The custom may explain that exhortation of our Lord: "Neither let him which is in the field return back to take his clothes." (Matt. xxiv. 18.)

THE GIRDLE.—To remedy the inconvenience which arose from the loose nature of their principal garments, the *Girdle* became a most important and necessary part of dress. There were two sorts of girdles: the one, a plain and simple band of

leather, about six inches broad, fastened round the body with clasps; the other, more costly, wrought out of finer materials, such as cotton or flax, not quite so wide, and sometimes long enough to encircle the wearer two or three times. It was common, when in the house or unemployed, to lay the girdle aside; but when business of an active kind was to be done, it was all-important that it should be put on, or drawn tight round the loins, if it were only slackly fastened; otherwise, a man's limbs would be much hindered with the loose drapery of his dress, and if he wore his upper garment, it would almost necessarily fall off every minute. Hence, the common phrase *to gird up the loins*, means to get ready for action; and, so familiar was its usage in this sense, that it came to be applied even to the mind, or soul, where it could mean nothing else than to cast off negligence and sloth, and summon the spirit to an attitude of firm resolution, or readiness for the discharge of duty. Thus the Almighty calls upon Job: "Gird up now thy loins like a

BIBLICAL ANTIQUITIES.   103

man, for I will demand of thee, and answer thou me." (Job xxxviii. 3.) And so our Saviour exhorts us all to have our loins girded about, and our lights burning, that we may be ready for his coming. (Luke xii. 35.) The image is still more bold in another place: "Gird up the *loins of your mind*, be sober, and hope to the end." (1 Pet. i. 13.) It was especially necessary for every soldier to wear a girdle, and to gird himself well when he entered into battle. Hence, the Christian, who is often compared to a soldier, is required to "have his loins girt about with truth;" that is, with sincerity and soundness in religion: without this girdle, he can have no security or success in his warfare. (Eph. vi. 14.) To gird the loins, signifies also to strengthen, as it always gave more freedom for the use of strength, and was the sign for calling it into action: so, on the other hand, to loose the girdle means to take away strength and power. Thus God girded Cyrus, and loosed the loins of kings before him. (Isa. xlv. 1, 5.) So Jehovah himself is girded with strength. (Ps. xciii. 1.) The girdle was used also for carrying money and other small articles. For this purpose, it was folded double and sewed along the edges, like a long flat purse. It was a very safe and convenient place to put every thing that we are in the habit of crowding into our various pockets. Such were the purses into which the apostles were not allowed to put gold, silver, or brass, when sent out to preach. (Matt. x. 9.) When a sword was carried, it was fastened to the same belt. Secretaries, and writers of every kind, were accustomed to have an ink-horn fixed upon it. (Ezek. ix. 2.)

It seems to have been common to keep two girdles; one for the tunic, and the other for the upper garment. The first was more habitually worn, whenever a man went out; the other was often dispensed with, either because the arms were at leisure to take care of the outer piece of clothing, or because it was laid aside entirely. Thus when Peter was awakened by the angel in prison, he was commanded first to gird himself, and then to cast his upper garment round him, without any mention of a second girdle. (Acts xii. 8.) At other times, however, this also was called into service; or, perhaps, in such cases, the girdle of the tunic was merely unclasped, and bound round the outside, so as to secure both garments together.

Some other peculiar kinds of clothing were worn at certain periods by some individuals. The rich and fashionable appeared not only in robes of finer quality than common, but also occasionally put on garments of different name and form, which belonged not to the general usage of the country. Sometimes, too, the aged or infirm needed, in winter, other articles of dress; and in later times, it was not uncommon to find in the land, various fashions of foreign apparel, introduced by strangers from other nations. The Jews, however, were not, in common, much disposed to alter, in this matter or in any other, the ancient customs of their country.

SACRED GARMENTS.—The garments of the priests were particularly determined by God himself. Under the tunic, or coat, they were required to wear a pair of linen breeches. (Ex. xxviii. 42.) And over it, the High-Priest was clad with the sacred *robe* and an *ephod.* The robe was like a long shirt, having no sleeves, but only holes for the arms, with small handsome binding round the opening for the neck. It reached down to the ankles, and upon the hem of its lower part were seventy-two little golden bells, with pomegranates of needle work between them, round about. These were for causing a sound when he went into the holy place, and when he came out, lest he should die. The ephod consisted of two parts, one of which was hung over the back, and the other over the breast; both pieces being united by a clasp or buckle on each shoulder, and secured by a "curious girdle, round about, under the arms." (Ex. xxviii.) Garments, exactly like those of the High-Priest, for materials, colour, and form, might not be worn by any other person; nor was he himself allowed to wear them, except in the solemn service of his office. Still, articles of dress resembling the sacred robe and ephod, and called by the same names, were sometimes used by others. (1 Chron. xv. 27.)

SANDALS.—*Sandals* were generally used for the feet. The *sandal* was a mere sole of wood or hide, covering the bottom

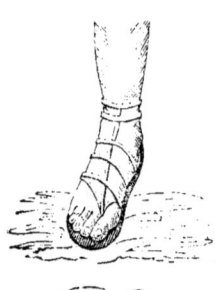

of the foot, and fastened with leather thongs, or straps. When any person was about to enter into a house, it was customary always to take them off, and go in with bare feet. To unloose the thongs on such occasions, and to tie them again when the sandals were to be put on, was the business of the lowest servants. Thus John the Baptist, to express how little notice he deserved, in comparison with Him whose way he came to prepare, exclaimed in his preaching: "There cometh one mightier than I, after me, the latchet of whose shoes I am not worthy to stoop down and unloose.' (Mark

i. 7.) As no stockings were worn, the feet became, of course, dusty and soiled : it was common, therefore, when coming into a house, to have them immediately washed. In receiving a guest, one of the first acts of politeness and kindness was to supply him with water for this purpose. So in the earliest times, we find, in the hospitality of Abraham and others, this circumstance repeatedly mentioned. In his entertainment of the angels, the venerable patriarch proposed this refreshment at once. "Let a little water, I pray you, be fetched, and wash your feet, and rest yourselves under this tree." We see the same thing in Laban's house, and afterward in Joseph's house. (Gen. xxiv. 32, xliii. 24.) The same custom continued to the latest times of the nation. Our Saviour referred to it in his reproof of the Pharisee Simon: "I entered into thine house; thou gavest me no water for my feet." (Luke vii. 44.) It was a business of servants to wash the feet of others, as well as to unloose their sandals; and hence our Lord did it for his disciples, to teach them a lesson of humility and kindness toward each other, though Peter thought such condescension too great to be allowed. (John xiii. 1—16.) As it was utterly contrary to decency and good manners to wear sandals in a house, as much so as among us it is to keep a hat on the head in a parlour, so it came to be considered an expression of reverence toward God, to pull them off on sacred ground, or when drawing near to the Almighty in acts of worship. (Ex. iii. 5, Josh. v. 15.) On this account, the priests were accustomed to attend to all the service of the sanctuary with their feet bare, though the law said nothing on the subject; and much injury to health arose, at times, from standing thus exposed on the cold, damp pavement.

In later ages, shoes of a certain kind, reaching up round the ankle, came to be used. These were considered, however, as more proper for women than for men. Fashionable ladies sometimes wore them, made with much ornament and expense. The mass of the people used only sandals; and these are almost always to be understood, when we read of *shoes* in the English Bible.

THE MITRE.—The covering for the head was formed of cloth, fitted round it frequently with several folds and in various forms, as it was worn by different classes of persons. It was called a *mitre*, or a *bonnet*. The mitres of the priests were higher than common. Princes also wore them high. In later times, very elegant and costly head-dresses came into fashion, especially among the women.

THE VEIL.—The veil was an important article in the dress of women. In very early times, indeed, it does not appear that it was considered by any means essential that every respectable female should wear such a covering, even in the presence of strangers; as we may learn from the history of Sarah and Rebecca and Rachel. But in later ages it was deemed altogether improper for a woman of any rank in life to be seen in public without a veil. The apostle Paul, in his first epistle to the Corinthian church, reproved the notion that in Christian assemblies this usage of the times might be neglected (1 Cor. xi. 13—16.) Veils were of different kinds: sometimes, made to cover the whole person, from head to foot; sometimes, concealing merely the face and breast; and at other times, hanging downward in front only from the nose or the eyes; while a fourth sort, starting like a cap from the bottom of the forehead, spread over the top of the head, and fell down some distance behind. The veil was the chief distinction between the dress of a woman and that of a man. In other respects the difference was small: the garments of females were generally of a somewhat finer quality, and of a greater length, than those of men; but as to general form and fashion, appear to have resembled them altogether. In the management of the hair, however, and in the use of ornaments and trinkets, there was, of course, as we shall immediately see, a very considerable difference.

THE HAIR.—The hair of the Jews, as is the case in eastern countries generally, was almost universally of a black colour. By the men, it was always worn short, except sometimes, perhaps, by delicate and vain persons like Absalom, or by such as were under the Nazarite vow. (Numb. vi. 5.) It was common to anoint the hair, especially on festival occasions. The liquid ointment used for this purpose was made out of the best oil of olives, mixed with spices. (Ps. xxiii. 5, Luke vii. 46.) In

conformity with this custom, Mary poured ointment on our Saviour's head, as he sat at meat in the house of Simon the leper; but to show her very great regard for his person, she used ointment far more costly than the common kind—"ointment of spikenard, very precious." (Mark xiv. 3.) At the same time, to express still more affection and profound respect, she anointed also his feet, and wiped them with the hair of her head. (John xii 3.) Females, as in all other countries, wore their hair long. The apostle Paul teaches us that this usage ought never to be abandoned : "Doth not even nature itself teach you, that if a man have long hair, it is a shame unto him? But if a woman have long hair, it is a glory to her; for her hair is given her for a covering." (1 Cor. xi. 14, 15.) The same apostle, however, was altogether opposed to the fashion of dressing up this simple ornament with an artificial glory of braided tresses and gold and costly gems : on this subject, Peter also thought it proper to leave his inspired admonition. (1 Tim. ii. 9, 1 Pet. iii. 3.) Such vain decorations were very common among the Jewish ladies.

THE BEARD.—Among the men, much more importance was attached to the beard. Ancient nations generally agreed in opinion on this subject. In their estimation, a long, heavy beard, hanging down over the breast, was an ornament of peculiar excellency, and added no little to the dignity and respectability of any man's person. To show any contempt towards it, by plucking it, or catching hold of it, or touching it without good reason, was a most grievous insult; such as, in modern times, a man of honour, according to the worldly meaning of the phrase, would consider abundant cause for a challenge and a duel forthwith. Nobody was allowed to touch it, except for the purpose of respectfully and affectionately kissing it, as intimate friends were accustomed to do, when they met. It was, therefore, most base deceit, when Joab "took Amasa by the beard, with the right hand, to kiss him," (or to kiss *it*,) and then smote him with a sword, in the very act of feigned friendship. (2 Sam. xx. 9.) To shave off half the beard, as Hanun did to the messengers of David, was a provocation of the most insolent and outrageous kind; and such a disgrace did these unhappy men feel it to be, that they could not bear to show their faces in Jerusalem, till a new growth of hair had covered the nakedness of their chins. (2 Sam. x. 4, 5.) To express great grief, however, it was common to tear out part of the beard, and sometimes to cut it off; at other times, sorrow was signified by neglecting to trim and dress it, and letting it grow without any care. (2 Sam. xix. 24.) In the East, the same notions about the beard still continue. The Arabians consider it more disgraceful to have it cut off, than it is with us to be publicly whipped. They admire and envy those who have fine beards. "Pray, do but see," they cry, "that beard; the very sight of it would persuade any one that he to whom it belongs is an honest man!" "For shame of your beard!" they exclaim, when they would reprove a person for acting or speaking wrong. It is a common form of

oath: "By your beard;" or, "By the life of your beard."
And to express the best wishes for another's welfare, they want
no more significant phrase than "May God preserve your
blessed beard!" This comprehends every thing.

ORNAMENTS.—A Jewish gentleman frequently carried a
staff for ornament. He also wore a seal, hung from his neck
over the breast, with his name engraven upon it, and sometimes,
on a finger of his right hand, there was seen a handsome ring.
(Luke xv. 22, James ii. 2.) In the time of our Saviour, the

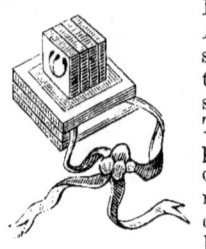

Pharisees wore, for religious show, broad
Phylacteries. These were merely four
small strips of parchment, with a verse or
two of the law written on each, carefully
secured in a little case, or bag of leather.
They were worn especially at times of
prayer; one upon the forehead and another upon the left wrist. It was a common opinion, that they had the power
of charms, to protect the wearer from
harm, or, at least, from all the malice
of evil spirits. The custom arose from a wrong interpretation of the command: "Thou shalt bind them for a sign upon
thy hands, and they shall be as frontlets between thine eyes."
(Deut. vi. 8.) The later Jews imagined these things were to
be done literally.

Time would fail us to tell of all the various ornaments which
the ladies contrived, to decorate their persons and attract admiration: the "beautiful crowns for the head;" the costly gems,

or rings of silver and gold, that hung
from the ears and glittered on the nose;
the "rows of jewels" for the cheeks; the
necklaces of pearl, emerald, or golden
chain-work, that fell far down over the
bosom; the bracelets for the arms; the
rings for the fingers; and the tinkling
ornaments for the feet. (Isa. iii. 18—24,
Ezek. xvi. 10—13, Song i. 10.) With all this finery to
arrange and contemplate, a *Mirror* became absolutely necessary. But in those days, there was no glass; and, of course,
looking-glasses like ours were unknown. Mirrors were made
of molten brass, polished so as to reflect a tolerably clear
image. They were not hung up in chambers, as with us, but
fitted with a neat handle, and carried in the hand, or else hung
upon the girdle, or by a chain from the neck. As they were
made small, they were not much more inconvenient than a

heavy fan. Such were the "women's looking-glasses," which were used in the wilderness for making the brazen laver. (Ex xxxviii. 8.) In later times, they were frequently made of steel. The apostle compares the knowledge of heavenly things which may be gained on earth, to the faint images which these imperfect mirrors reflected: "Now we see through a glass (or by means of a mirror) darkly; but then face to face." (1 Cor. xiii. 12.) It was considered a great ornament to have the eyelids tinged with a deep black stain. The material used for this purpose, down to the present day, in eastern countries, is a rich lead ore, pounded into powder extremely fine. When it is to be used, a small instrument, about the thickness of a quill, is dipped into it, and then drawn through the eyelids, over the ball of the eye. This is probably what is meant by *rending the face with paint.* (Jer. iv. 30.) Such a jetty black colour on the lids sets off the whiteness of the eye to much advantage, and at the same time causes it to appear larger and more expressive. It makes the lashes also, in appearance, long and beautiful. To give grace and dignity to the eye brows, they were probably painted too. According to the fashionable style of the times, Jezebel painted her face, when she dressed herself for the coming of Jehu. (2 Kings ix. 30.)

WARDROBES.—From the general character of the Jewish dress, loose and large, we may easily perceive that the apparel of one person might, without any inconvenience, be worn by another. With us, it is a rare thing if one man's suit of clothes will so exactly fit another that he can wear them without some awkward appearance; but with the Jews, it mattered little for whom a suit was first made: it might pass to a dozen of owners without the smallest trouble. There was no difficulty of this sort, therefore, in the way, when Rebecca wanted to clothe her favourite son in the "goodly raiment of Esau," or when Jonathan stripped himself of his robe and garments, and put them on his friend David. (Gen. xxvii. 15, 1 Sam. xviii. 4.) From this circumstance, it came to pass that the rich frequently supplied themselves with a great many changes of raiment; so that no inconsiderable portion of their property was found in their great wardrobes. These garments they never expected to use themselves; but they served, like some men's fine libraries of untarnished books, to display their wealth and taste; and then, while they occasionally made presents out of them to their friends, they might hand them down to their children and heirs, from generation to generation, with all their original value. There was no danger of any new fashion coming forward and spoiling the inheritance, by throwing a whimsical strangeness over its ancient dresses, as must inevitably take place in our country; the eastern manners never allowed such fantastic changes. To this custom of multiplying garments, as one way of laying up treasures, our Lord refers, in that admonition: "Lay not up for yourselves treasures on earth, where *moth* and rust doth corrupt." (Matt. vi. 19.) So also the apostle James: "Go to, now, ye rich men; weep and howl for your miseries that shall come upon you: your gold and silver is cankered; your *garments are moth-eaten.*" (James v. 2, 3. See also Acts xx. 33.) Job describes such also in his day: they "heap up silver as the dust, and prepare raiment as the clay." (Job xxvii. 16.) Princes and great men were accustomed to give a change of raiment to those whom they wished to honour. Thus Joseph gave changes of raiment to all his brothers, and to Benjamin no less than five. (Gen. xlv 22. See also Esth. viii. 15.) It was not uncommon for kings or wealthy noblemen, when they made a feast, to furnish every guest with a suitable garment for the occasion. It was thus Joseph treated his brethren. Especially was this the case at marriage festivals. (Matt. xxii. 11, 12.) Not immediately to put on a garment thus presented, was great disrespect to the master of the house.

SECTION II.

MEALS AND ENTERTAINMENTS.

Having attended to the general manner in which the Jews were accustomed to provide for the *dress* and *ornament* of the body, let us next consider their peculiar usages in the matter of supplying it with the *refreshment of food*.

In the chapter on dwellings, we have already given a short account of the utensils most important to be noticed, which were used for the preparation of food and the convenience of eating. The mill, the oven, the table, and the couches, have been described; we need not, therefore, say any thing about them in this place. Nor is it necessary to enter into a detail of the several modes of cookery; a single glance into the kitchen will be quite enough. Vegetables and flesh were prepared there in various ways, but still the general methods of rendering them fit for the table did not differ materially from those which are now common. Baking, boiling, roasting, and frying, were all employed to give variety to the social feast, as they continually are among ourselves; only, in our age and country, we are fur nished, by the improvements of art, with greater conveniences for the several purposes than were enjoyed in those days. As it was not easy, in that country, to keep flesh any time without its being spoiled, it was common to cook at once the whole of an animal, immediately after it was killed. Thus Abraham dressed for his three guests an entire calf, and set it before them.

The Jews, in the time of our Saviour, were not in the habit of sitting down at a breakfast table early in the morning, as is common with us. It was not considered proper to take a regular meal till after the public prayers of the morning were over. This was not till about ten o'clock in the forenoon. On Sabbaths and sacred feast-days, it was the custom not to taste a particle of solid food or drink before that time; and if, on other days, any thing was eaten, it was only some small refreshment of the lightest kind. So on the day of Pentecost, when the disciples were charged with drunkenness, Peter considered it a completely satisfactory reply, that it was then but the third hour of the day, or nine o'clock in the morning; an hour, at least, before the time when any person thought of tasting wine. (Acts ii. 15.)* Between ten and eleven o'clock of our time, dinner was taken. It was, however, but a slight meal, made up chiefly of fruit, milk, cheese, and such simple articles of food. The most important meal was supper; for, through the middle of the day, in their warm climate, there was generally little inclination to indulge in the pleasures of the table. Accordingly, we find that great entertainments and feasts were always provided in the evening; they were *Suppers*. Thus we are told, that "Herod on his birth-day made a *supper* to his lords, high captains, and chief estates of Galilee." (Mark vi. 21.) When Jesus visited Lazarus and his sisters, "they made him a *supper*." (John xii. 2.) So in the parable, "a certain man made a great *supper*." (Luke xiv. 16.) A *supper* was of the same importance among the Jews, that a *dinner* is among us; the most notable meal, at which (however slight might be the preparation for other meals) some substantial provision was expected. Whenever, therefore, it was wanted to provide for the table with more than common liberality, by way of self-indulgence or kindness to others, the time naturally selected for the purpose was the evening, and the manner of entertainment, a supper. Hence, such occasions as with us call for special dinners, were honoured among them with special suppers. In conformity with the custom of the

---

* See the Jewish manner of reckoning hours, in the eighth chapter of this volume.

nation, the sacred feast of the Passover was celebrated in the evening. And because it was during the celebration of one of these religious suppers, that our Lord instituted the second Christian sacrament, which was to come in the room of that ancient ordinance, this, also, has ever since been called the Lord's *Supper*, although it is now very properly taken at an entirely different time.

Before every meal, it was customary to wash the hands, as well as after eating. Thus we are informed by the sacred writer: "The Pharisees and all the Jews, except they wash their hands oft, eat not, holding the tradition of the elders." (Mark vii. 3, 4.) So great was the stress laid upon this ceremony, that they found much fault with the disciples of our Saviour, when they observed them neglecting it: "Why do thy disciples transgress the tradition of the elders? for they wash not their hands when they eat bread." (Matt. xv. 2.) As these washings (as well as others which they employed superstitiously, for the purification of cups, pots, brazen vessels, tables, and such things) were so continually called for, it was common to have vessels always standing in a convenient place, with water in them, which might be drawn out and used in this way, whenever wanted. Such were the six large water-pots of stone that stood in the house where our Saviour attended the marriage in Cana of Galilee: they were set there, we are told, *after the manner of the purifying of the Jews;* that is, according to the plan common among the Jews, for convenience of washing. (John ii. 6.) One good reason for washing before and after meals, was, that they used their hands altogether in taking their victuals: cleanliness, in such a case, could not well be too carefully observed. But when the custom was turned into a superstitious obligation, and insisted upon as a solemn matter of conscience and religious duty, it became an ignorant, childish, and unlawful tradition. In washing, water was sometimes poured lightly over the hands, and at other times the hands were dipped into it.

Before and after each meal, a short prayer or tribute of thanks was offered up to God. This was, no doubt, a sacred custom, handed down from the earliest times. Our Saviour always taught his disciples the duty of looking up, with such an act of worship, to the great Author of every good gift, by his own example. When he fed the multitudes by miracle, he first lifted up his eyes to heaven, and blessed and gave thanks. (Matt xiv. 19, xv. 36.) The apostle refers to the same duty, and teaches us that every meal is unsanctified where God is not heartily and humbly remembered: "Every creature of God is

Offering Thanks.

good, and nothing to be refused, if it be received with thanksgiving; for it is sanctified by the word of God and prayer." (1 Tim. iv. 4, 5.)

Knives and forks were not used in eating. The meat was carved into pieces of convenient size, beforehand. Every person helped himself with his right hand. In early times, each had his own portion separate from the rest, as we may see in the account which is given of the entertainment of Joseph's brethren in Egypt; but at a later period, it became customary to eat from common dishes. When food of a liquid sort, like broth, was on the table, each person broke his bread into morsels, and dipped it, with his fingers, into the dish. (Ruth ii. 14.) Such was the *sop* which our Lord dipped and handed to Judas. (John xiii. 26.) Drink was handed to each, in separate bowls, or cups; hence, a man's *cup* is used figuratively to mean his lot or destiny. (Ps. xi. 6, xxiii. 5.) The Saviour's *cup* was the awful wrath of the Almighty which he drank in the room of guilty men. (Matt. xxvi. 39.)

Social feasts were common from the earliest times. By the law of Moses, every farmer was required to use a considerable portion of the fruits of his land, each year, in this way. The tithe, or a tenth part of his corn and his wine and his oil, with the firstlings of his flocks and his herds, after a like portion had been set apart for the Levites, were to be consecrated to God, and eaten in a sacred feast before Him, with thankfulness and joy. In this feast, servants and strangers, and or plans and widows, and the Levite without inheritance in the land, were to be made free partakers: "Thou must eat them before the Lord thy God, in the place which the Lord thy God shall choose; thou, and thy son, and thy daughter, and thy man-servant, and thy maid-servant, and the Levite that is within thy gates: and thou shalt rejoice before the Lord thy God, in all that thou puttest thine hand unto." (Deut. xii. 17, 18, xiv. 22—29.) These were properly *religious* festivals, excellently adapted to promote a grateful sense of God's favours, and to diffuse the kindly feeling of friendship through all the various classes of society. But besides these, it was usual, as in every country of the world, to make other feasts; as on occasions of domestic joy, such as a marriage or a birth-day, or for the sake of showing respect to friends and cherishing social intercourse, or merely to gratify the spirit of worldly pride by a vain parade of kindness and hospitality. At such times, the guests were invited by servants to come at the appointed season. When they arrived, they were received with the greatest attention. They were arranged around the table, by the master of the house, who generally took care to place such as he considered the most honourable of the company, in what were accounted the chief seats. The table was supplied in the most plentiful manner. Servants stood ready to attend to the slightest wish, and to see continually that every guest was properly supplied. All proceeded under the eye and direction of the *Governor of the feast*. (John ii. 8.) This was one of the company, appointed to overlook the rest, to preserve harmony and good humour, to see that the servants attended to their business, and to regulate the whole service of the table. While the guests were surrounding the table, it seems not to have been uncommon for servants, by order of the master, to anoint their heads with rich ointment, (Luke vii. 46;) and sometimes, perhaps, to regale them by burning frankincense, or other aromatic substances in the room.

Our Lord, in his parable of the marriage of the king's son, introduces several circumstances from the customs of the great feasts which were common in that age. (Matt. xxii. 1—14.) On another occasion, also, he uttered a parable of a similar kind, while he was reclining at table in the house of one of the chief Pharisees. (Luke xiv. 16—24.) It was at the same entertainment, that he reproved the lawyers and Pharisees, "when he marked how they chose out the chief rooms," or places at the table, and recommended to them a contrary method, of modesty and humility.

SPIRITUAL FOOD.—As spiritual and heavenly things can be

represented in the language of earth, only by the help of images of an earthly and sensible kind, it has always been common, among other forms of describing them, to borrow much for the purpose from the character and circumstances of that refreshment and support which our bodies receive from food. As the body is nourished by its appointed food, so the soul, because its welfare and improvement are made to depend on knowledge adapted to its nature, and on the continual communication to it of God's grace, is said to *be fed* by them, and thus to *grow* and *become strong;* while, on the other hand, by being deprived of them, it becomes *lean, empty, languishing,* and *dead.* So, also, all that is necessary to make it thus thrive and grow, is called its *food*, its *bread,* and its *drink.* Such imagery is known to some extent among all people, because it is exceedingly natural; but among the Jews, it was drawn forth in its most unlimited form. Not merely is the soul represented as having its food by which it is supported and strengthened, but this food is served up for its entertainment with all the variety and preparation of a feast. It is not only refreshed with *water,* of which God himself is the great and inexhaustible FOUNTAIN, but supplied, if obedient to the heavenly invitation, with abundance of *milk* and of richest *wine.* A table is spread for its use; provisions of the most excellent sort are prepared with the greatest profusion; and it is called upon to satisfy its hunger without restraint. "Wisdom," says Solomon, "hath builded her house; she hath hewn out her seven pillars; she hath killed her beasts; she hath mingled her wine; she hath also furnished her table. She hath sent forth her maidens; she crieth upon the highest places of the city, Whoso is simple, let him turn in hither! as for him that wanteth understanding, she saith to him, Come, eat of my bread, and drink of the wine which I have mingled." (Prov. ix. 1—5.) In similar style, Isaiah more than once sets forth the rich fulness of spiritual blessings which God is ready to bestow upon his people. "In this mountain shall the Lord of hosts make unto all people a feast of fat things, a feast of wines on the lees; of fat things full of marrow, of wines on the lees well refined." (Isa. xxv. 6.) "Ho, every one that thirsteth! come ye to the waters. And he that hath no money! come, ye; buy and eat. Yea, come; buy WINE and MILK without money and without price." (Isa. lv. 1.)

But it became common to extend the image still farther. The whole richness of that enjoyment which awaits the righteous in the world to come was often spoken of under this same representation. In the house of their heavenly Father, his happy children were represented as ever encircling his table, richly spread with the provisions of life, and finding in its social banquet all fulness of enjoyment without interruption, in his presence. Hence that expression: "Blessed is he that shall eat bread in the kingdom of God!" (Luke xiv. 15.) And hence, also, it would seem, the phrase, "*To lie in Abraham's bosom,*" is used to express the same idea of heavenly felicity. (Luke xvi. 22, 23, compared with John xiii. 23.) There is allusion to the image under consideration, also, in the Saviour's threatening declaration to the Jews, who supposed *themselves* to be exclusively the children of the kingdom—the peculiar family of God, while the Gentiles were entirely outcast from his favour: "There shall be weeping and gnashing of teeth, when ye shall see Abraham, and Isaac, and Jacob, and all the prophets, in the kingdom of God, and you yourselves thrust out: and they shall come from the east, and from the west, and from the north, and from the south, and shall *sit down* (or *recline,* as at table) in the kingdom of God." (Luke xiii. 28, 29.) So in like manner, in that most glorious promise to the disciples at the last supper: "I appoint unto you a kingdom, as my Father hath appointed unto me; that ye may *eat and drink at my table,* in my kingdom, and sit on thrones, judging the twelve tribes of Israel." (Luke xxii. 29, 30.) On the same solemn occasion, when the Redeemer took the cup, and gave thanks, and handed it to the twelve, in the institution of the Lord's Supper, he added these words: "I say unto you, I will not drink henceforth of this fruit of the vine, until that day when I *drink it new with you in my Father's kingdom.*" (Matt. xxvi. 29.) By this figurative declaration, he intimated that he was very shortly to leave this earthly state, and directed the sorrowful minds of his followers to that infinite blessedness which was to be enjoyed in heaven, where they were all quickly to be re-united.

SECTION III.

OF SOCIAL INTERCOURSE.

In every country, there are certain forms of conduct and speech, by which men regulate their intercourse, and which, by the authority of long custom, are rendered, in a great measure, incapable of change. These are widely different, in different nations and regions, because they have taken their rise, in all cases, from fancy rather than reason, and have all been modified by a hundred accidental circumstances in their progress of refinement. Hence, too, the manners of one people have always some appearance of ridiculous folly, in the eyes of another, so far as they are found to be different. Education and use render us blind to the absurdity of our own, while those of other countries, presenting themselves to our calm consideration without any such advantage, strike us at once with a sense of their true character. The truth is, no country has a system of manners free from folly. Was the moral nature of man without derangement, it would of itself teach him true politeness, which would be the same politeness in all countries. But while selfishness and pride continue to be the reigning principles of the human character, this cannot be expected. Every system, therefore, which he devises and puts in practice, can only be a very rude imitation of what he imagines a rightly constituted mind would adopt, and which he himself is driven to find out from necessity and self-love, rather than from good will to others. Where the conception, however, is necessarily so defective, and the imitation of that conception so artificial, the result cannot be otherwise than ridiculous. Still, the imitation under any form is better than nothing at all; and inasmuch as what is true and perfect cannot be hoped for, it becomes us to esteem its resemblance, in whatever country we are found, as a real benefit to society. At the same time, we should not judge that which prevails among other people to be vastly more unreasonable than our own; it accomplishes the same end, and may be, after all, substantially as good and proper.

The forms of politeness and civility, in eastern countries, have always been far more extravagant in their appearance, than any to which we are accustomed. The most common expressions of good will, as they prevail there, would to us seem ridiculous and excessive. The ordinary salutations that pass between friends or acquaintances when they meet, are lengthened out in long and formal ceremony, with the strongest gestures and the warmest professions of regard. To show peculiar respect, it is common to bow the body downward almost to the ground, or to fall entirely prostrate on the earth. We have, in the Bible, repeated intimations of similar manners among the Jews; tempered, indeed, and dignified, in many instances, by the seriousness of religion, but still wearing an aspect peculiar to the east. Thus, in the earliest times, we read that the pious Abraham showed respect to strangers, bowing himself before them low to the ground. (Gen. xviii. 2, xxiii. 7, 12.) And afterward, down to the time of our Saviour, we find in all the course of sacred history, notices of the same fashion. In the parable of the two debtors who could not pay, we are told of them both, that they fell down at the feet of their creditors, when they implored their forbearance. In these cases, it is true, this humble attitude was prompted by great and peculiar distress; but still it would not have been assumed, unless the custom of the times had given it sanction, in the practice of those who wanted to show extreme respect to their superiors (Matt. xviii. 26, 29.) It seems to have been common to show different degrees of respect to different persons, according to their rank and importance, by bending the body in a greater or less measure.  Simply to bow down the head, was an expression of mere common civility, that marked no particular regard : to curve the body low down, signified a considerable degree of reverence : to throw it entirely down, with the face upon the ground, was an act of the greatest homage. As the attitude, in some of these cases, was similar to that which it was common to assume in the worship of Almighty God, the same term was sometimes used to express both actions. Hence in the language of Scripture, to *worship* another, sometimes means merely to show him the greatest respect, by an act of the most profound obeisance.

Among the Jews, the common phrases of salutation at meeting friends, and those which were used in parting from them, were of a religious character, expressing prayers for the blessing of God on those to whom they were spoken. "Be thou blessed of Jehovah ;" "The blessing of Jehovah be upon thee ;" "God be with thee." Such were usual forms in the most ancient times. A still more universal expression was, "Peace be with you ;" and this is the general salutation in eastern countries, to this day. Thus our Saviour saluted his disciples, when he presented himself among them after his resurrection. When uttered by his lips, the words had real and rich signification, widely different from their empty value, as they were commonly used in the ceremonies of a frivolous world. To this difference he himself directed the attention of his afflicted followers, when he was about to be taken from them by death : "Peace I leave with you, *My* peace I give unto you: not as the *world* giveth, give I unto you."

At the present day, eastern salutations take up a considerable time. When an Arab meets his friend, he begins, while he is yet some distance from him, to make gestures that may express his very great satisfaction in seeing him. When he comes up to him, he grasps him by the right hand, and then brings back his own hand to his lips, in token of respect. He next proceeds to place his hand gently under the long beard of the other, and honours it with an affectionate kiss. He inquires particularly, again and again, concerning his health and the health of his family; and repeats, over and over, the best wishes for his prosperity and peace, giving thanks to God that he is permitted once more to behold his face. All this round of gestures and words is, of course, gone over by the friend too, with like formality. But they are not generally satisfied with a single exchange of the sort; they sometimes repeat as often as ten times, the whole tiresome ceremony, with little or no variation. Some such tedious modes of salutation were common also of old; so that a man might suffer very material delay in travelling, if he chanced to meet several acquaintances, and should undertake to salute each according to the custom of the country. On this account, when Elisha sent his servant Gehazi, in great haste, to the Shunamite's house, he said to him: "If thou meet any man, salute him not; and if any salute thee, answer him not again." (2 Kings iv. 29.) So, when our Lord sent forth his seventy disciples, among other instructions, he bade them "salute no man by the way;" meaning, that their work was too important to allow such a waste of time in the exchange of mere unmeaning ceremonies. (Luke x. 4.) We have presented to us, in the meeting of Jacob and Esau, a form of salutation which may give us some notion of the manners of their early age in this respect. Few instances, however, could equal that, in the genuine and affecting interest which it displayed, and we may well suppose, that in common cases, where there was less of friendly feeling, there was, at the same time, more attention to formal ceremony. On that occasion, Jacob, we are told, " bowed himself to the ground *seven times,* until he came near to his brother; and Esau ran to meet him, and embraced him, and fell on his neck, and kissed him: *and they wept.*" (Gen. xxxiii. 3, 4.)

When one person made a visit to another, especially if it was to one of high rank in society, it was customary to carry with him some kind of a present. In the earliest times, it is probable that it was principally in this way kings and rulers received their tribute from the people; each one brought, whenever he came into their presence, some gift of greater or less value, as a free expression of his homage. Afterwards, by the power of custom, it came to be considered a matter of course, that no person might visit one in authority over him, without such an offering by way of introduction and recommendation Gradually, the same way of showing respect grew to be fashionable toward any other great man. (Gen. xliii. 11.) When Saul was made king, there were certain persons who "despised him, and *brought him no presents.*" (1 Sam. x. 27.) God reproves the Jews for their unsound offerings, by applying the case to such approaches toward an earthly ruler: "Offer it now unto thy governor; will he be pleased with thee, or accept thy person?" (Mal. i. 8.) From the notion of respect which such gifts carried in the minds of all, and which led to the general practice of offering them to all distinguished persons, it became an established custom to bring them also to prophets, when they were visited for direction and advice. Hence, when it was proposed to Saul by his servant, to visit Samuel, on a certain occasion of perplexity, he considered it out of the question, for want of some gift to appear in a respectful and becoming manner: "Behold," said he, "if we go, what shall we bring the man? for the bread is spent in our vessels, and there is not a present to bring to the man of God. What have we? And the servant answered, Behold I have here at hand, the fourth part of a shekel of silver; that will I give to the man of God." (1 Sam. ix. 7, 8.) From the extreme smallness of the present here considered sufficient, it is plain that the common offerings which the prophets received, were not of any importance as to real value, but were simply meant to express respect, and could not be omitted, according to the usage of the times, without an appearance of rude indifference to the dignity of their character. In the opinion of Saul, a small portion of bread would have been enough, and he was satisfied with the quarter of a shekel, though it was not equal in value to twelve and a half cents. Sometimes, however, princes and great men made them quite magnificent presents. In some instances, they refused to take such offerings, lest they should seem to be actuated by a worldly spirit. It was common, in making presents of any value, to bring them with much parade and show. Thus Hazael, when he went to meet Elisha, took with him a present of every good thing of Damascus, piled with great display on the backs of *forty* camels; though we have no reason to suppose that any thing like that number of these animals was really necessary to carry it; otherwise, the gift would have been altogether enormous. In eastern countries, the custom of making presents when visits are performed, is still universally common. To neglect such a tribute of respect, particularly toward one of more than equal rank, is gross rudeness, and cannot fail to meet with marked disapprobation. These gifts are oftentimes carried with great pomp, and so arranged as to make the greatest possible appearance of magnificence and worth; half a dozen horses being employed to carry what might, without much inconvenience, be borne by one. In conformity with the ancient usage of bringing gifts to kings and princes, as tokens of respect and homage, the wise men who came from the east to worship Him that was "born King of the Jews," came not with empty hands: "When they had opened their treasures, they presented unto him gifts—gold, and frankincense, and myrrh." (Matt. ii. 11.)

In the entertainment of guests, much attention and much formality have always distinguished the eastern manners. The most scrupulous regard to the established forms of dignity and respect is constantly observed. The particular seat which a man occupies in the room, and the particular posture of his body while he sits, are not matters of indifference; there is a law of long-established power to determine both. The seat at the corner of the room is most honourable, and is given to visiters by way of distinction. When an individual sits in the presence of a superior, he shows his respect by sitting completely upon his heels. To anoint the head, regale with burnt perfume, and sprinkle with scented water, are various methods of displaying regard.

Conversation, in these countries, is generally reserved and grave. The people are little disposed to indulge themselves with that free and unrestrained liberty in this matter, that is common among us. They seem to feel, that in a multitude of words there wanteth not vanity; and that in the mere talk of the lips, there is not often much profit. It is not with them, as in some other countries, a principle that much silence in company is unlovely, or impolite, or that it is better to talk nonsense for the sake of social intercourse, than to sit with sealed lips when a person has nothing to say: their words are commonly few and formal, and uttered only when they imagine it may be done with dignity, either in the way of compliment or occasional general remark. In ancient times, there appears to have been more disposition for social conversation. Still we find among the Jews, as they are presented to us in the Bible, a considerable degree of the same character in this respect. Their conversation was marked with gravity and moderation, much more than is common in our ordinary intercourse, and words were expected to have meaning, when they claimed attention from others. Hence it came to pass, that when a man undertook to utter his sentiments, they were often expressed in a formal, sententious strain, and if continued any time, took the appearance of a dignified and regular speech. There is even some room to imagine that the phrase, *to open the mouth,* so commonly made use of to express a commencement of speech, may have had its rise, in some measure, from the general rareness of the thing, and the idea of importance that was attached to such an undertaking. Among *us*, at any rate, it is generally so incessantly open when there is opportunity to speak, and too generally open to so little valuable purpose, that such an expression would seem to have no great propriety.

The common form of assent in conversation was, *Thou hast said,* or *Thou sayest;* meaning, Thou art right; It is as thou hast said. (Matt. xxvi. 64, John xviii. 37.)

In cities, as we have already seen, the common place of general resort was at the Gate. Here there was a convenient space left free for the purpose, and fitted up with seats for the accommodation of the people. Those who were at leisure, and wished to find some interest for their idle moments, were accustomed to take their seat in this place, and occupy themselves either with looking at what was going on around, or in occasional conversation with others on the general affairs of the day.

CHAPTER VI.

DOMESTIC CUSTOMS AND HABITS.

SECTION I.

OF THE MARRIAGE RELATION.

MARRIAGE has always been considered, among the Jews, peculiarly honourable. Their doctrine on this subject has been, that it is unbecoming and unlawful for any person, of proper age, to continue in a single state. With them, to live without a family, and to die without posterity, could never be altogether without reproach. Hence, their marriages have generally been early. At the age of twenty, at farthest, every young person, according to them, ought to be married. At that age, the obligation to take a companion became most serious and indispensable; and it was considered much more respectable and praiseworthy to attend to the duty a good while sooner.

It was common, from the earliest times, for a father to choose wives for his sons, and husbands for his daughters. Thus Abraham sent his servant to procure a wife for his son

Isaac, without consulting *him* particularly on the matter at all; and so, when Samson wanted to marry a particular woman, he applied to his father to get her for him as a wife, as the proper way of accomplishing his desire. (Judg. xiv. 1—4.) In some other cases, however, the matter, in relation to sons, seems to have been left altogether to their own discretion. In the first ages, not only her parents, but her brothers also, had authority in the disposal of a female in marriage, as we see in the instances of Rebecca and Dinah. Instead of receiving any property along with his wife, when he married, a man was expected to pay a considerable price, according to his ability, for the woman herself. Gifts were oftentimes to be made to her brothers, and the father was to receive a settled dowry. In this way, an agreement or contract of marriage was made, without any consultation whatever with the intended bride. After this agreement, however, at least in later ages, the damsel was brought into the presence of her suitor, and a formal covenant, or engagement to become man and wife at some future time, was entered into by both, before witnesses; this was called *espousing*, or *betrothing*. Thus Shechem made a bargain with Jacob and his sons: "Let me find grace in your eyes, and what ye shall say unto me, I will give. Ask me never so much dowry and gift, and I will give according as ye shall say unto me; but give me the damsel to wife." (Gen. xxxiv. 11, 12.) When a young man was not able to purchase a woman with money, he might, if her friends consented, pay for her by a longer or shorter term of service. So Jacob served seven years for each of his two wives. Sometimes a wife was given as a reward of bravery. (Josh. xv. 16, 1 Sam. xviii. 25.) The same custom of purchasing wives is still common in the East; so that it is accounted, in some places, quite a fortune for a father to have many daughters, on account of the wealth which they will bring into his house by their several marriage-dowries. Frequently, however, the presents which the bridegroom makes in this way, are laid out in clothes and furniture for the bride, and so, restored, in some measure, to the giver. Perhaps, in the later times of the Jewish nation, something of the same kind was common.

There was generally an interval of ten or twelve months, and sometimes considerably more, between the time of making the marriage contract, or the day of espousals, and the marriage itself. Thus we read that Samson first went down to Timnath with his parents, and talked with the woman whom he wished for a wife, and "she pleased him well." This was the time of espousals, but it was not till *after a time*, that he "returned to take her" by actual marriage. (Judg. xiv. 7, 8.) During all this interval, however, while the bride continued still in her father's house, she was considered and spoken of as the lawful wife of the man to whom she was betrothed; so that the bridegroom could not destroy their engagement, if he became unwilling to marry her, without giving her a bill of divorce, in the same manner as if she had been fully wedded; and so, on the other hand, if she proved unfaithful to her espoused husband, she was punished as an adulteress. It was between the time of her espousals and her actual marriage, that the Virgin Mary, by the power of the Holy Ghost, conceived in her womb the Redeemer of the world. On this occasion, Joseph had power, as her betrothed husband, to make her a *public example*, by causing her to be stoned according to the law; but, at the same time, he was at liberty to give her a bill of divorce and dismiss her privately. Accordingly, though he considered it his duty to give up his intended marriage, he had too much regard for her reputation, and too much confidence, we may suppose, in her own account of the miracle of her conception, to expose her before the world; and so had concluded to adopt the other course, when the angel relieved his anxiety by commanding him to take her without hesitation. (Matt. i. 18—20.)

When the time of marriage arrived, the bride prepared herself for the occasion with the utmost care. She was adorned by her attendants with all the elegance which the taste of the times rendered fashionable; and to complete her joyful appearance, the bridal crown was placed upon her head. The bridegroom presented himself at her father's house, attended with a number of young men of his own age. The wedding festival frequently lasted seven days, as we may see in the case of Samson, and in that of Jacob at a much earlier period. During this time, the bridegroom and his companions entertained themselves, in various ways, in one part of the house; while the bride was engaged with a like company of her young female friends, in another. It was not considered proper on such occasions, or on any other, for young persons of both sexes to mingle together in the festive circle, or even so much as to eat at the same table. In the account of Samson's wedding, we find that one method of giving life to the intercourse of the young men, was to propose riddles, and exercise their ingenuity in explaining them. The companions of the bridegroom were sometimes called the *children*, or *sons, of the bride-chamber*. On the last day, the bride was conducted to the house of the bridegroom's father. The procession generally set off in the evening, with much ceremony and pomp. The bridegroom was richly clothed with a marriage robe and crown, and the bride was covered with a veil from head to foot. The companions of each attended them with songs and the music of instruments; not in promiscuous assemblage, but each company by itself; while the virgins, according to the custom of the times, were all provided with veils, not indeed so large and thick as that which hung over the bride, but abundantly sufficient to conceal their faces from all around. The way, as they went along, was lighted with numerous torches In the mean time, another company was waiting at the bridegroom's house, ready, at the first notice of their approach, to go forth and meet them. These seem generally to have been young female relations or friends of the bridegroom's family, called in at this time, by a particular invitation, to grace the occasion with their presence. Adorned with robes of gladness and joy, they went forth with lamps or torches in their hands, and welcomed the procession with the customary salutations. They then joined themselves to the marriage train, and the whole company moved forward to the house. There an entertainment was provided for their reception, and the remainder of the evening was spent in a cheerful participation of the Marriage Supper, with such social merriment as suited the joyous occasion. None were admitted to this entertainment, beside the particular number who were selected to attend the wedding; and as the regular and proper time for their entrance into the house was when the bridegroom went in with his bride, the doors were then closed, and no other guest was expected to come in. Such appear to have been the general ceremonies which attended the celebration of a marriage. No doubt, however, among different ranks, and in different ages of the nation, the particular forms and fashions were often considerably different.

In modern times, the Jews have a regular, formal marriage rite, by which the union is solemnly ratified. The parties stand under a canopy, each covered with a black veil; some grave person takes a cup of wine, pronounces a short blessing, and hands it to be tasted by both; the bridegroom puts a ring on the finger of his bride, saying, "By this ring thou art my spouse, according to the custom of Moses and the children of Israel:" the marriage contract is then read, and given to the bride's relations; another cup of wine is brought and blessed six times, when the married couple taste it, and pour the rest out in token of cheerfulness; and to conclude all, the husband dashes the cup itself against the wall, and breaks it all to pieces, in memory of the sad destruction of their once glorious

Temple. But there seems to have been, anciently, very little form of this kind. In very early times, the only ceremony by which the union was confirmed, was a solemn blessing, pronounced by the nearest relations, on the parties who agreed in their presence to become husband and wife; and this was rather a mere circumstance established by pious custom, than a rite by which the marriage itself was performed. (Gen. xxiv 60.) The manner of marriage was of this simple kind, in the days of Ruth. Boaz merely declared in presence of the elders assembled at the gate, that he had resolved to take the daughter of Naomi to be his wife; "and all the people that were in the gate, and all the elders said, We are witnesses. The Lord make the woman that is come into thine house, like Rachel and like Leah, which two did build the house of Israel; and do thou worthily in Ephratah, and be famous in Bethlehem." So Boaz, we are told, "took Ruth, and she became his wife." (Ruth iv. 11, 13.) Before the time of Christ, it became customary to have some little more ceremony: still, it seems that the marriage connection was supposed to be formed, rather by the whole celebration of the wedding together, as a mutual public agreement in the presence of the friends of both parties, than by any one particular rite.

SPIRITUAL MARRIAGE.—As no relation on earth is more intimate and tender than that which is formed by marriage, our blessed Lord, who was accustomed to employ every strong image which the world could furnish, to express his close union with the church of his redeemed people, and his most affectionate concern for their welfare, has, in his holy word, made much use of this connection, among others, for that purpose. The church is his bride and his spouse; and as the bridegroom rejoices over his beloved in the day of marriage, and as the kindest husband cherishes the wife of his bosom, so he delights in his people, and so he keeps them with continual care. The apostle, speaking of this spiritual marriage, in one place calls it *a great mystery;* whereby, as in common marriages, a man and his wife become, according to the original institution of God, *one flesh*, and so the people of Christ are made, as it were, "members of his body, of his flesh, and of his bones." (Eph. v. 23—33.) This way of representing the union between God and his church was used long before the time of Christ. The inspired writers of the Old Testament were familiar with the image. To encourage Zion, the prophet exclaims: "Thy Maker is thy husband; the Lord of Hosts is his name!" "As the bridegroom rejoiceth over the bride, so shall thy God rejoice over thee!" (Isa. liv. 5, lxii. 5. See also Jer ii 2,

Ezek xvi. 8—14.) Hence, in conformity with the same image, nothing is more common in the language of the ancient prophets, than to represent the impiety and idolatry of the Jewish church as adultery, and unfaithfulness to the solemn vows of marriage.

Sometimes, under this image of a marriage union, the relation between God, or Christ, and his *whole professing* church, as a separate society on earth, is represented; at other times, it is employed to shadow forth the far higher and more glorious connection which exists between Him and the *true spiritual* church, made up only of real believers, of which the other is but the outward, and too often, to a great extent, the empty sign. This mysterious and sacred union, whereby the Messiah becomes one with the whole body of his true redeemed people, is beautifully celebrated under the allegory of a royal marriage, in the forty-fifth Psalm. The Bridegroom and bride, magnificently described in that inspired song, were always understood, long before Christ came into the world, to mean the promised Redeemer and his church; and, accordingly, the apostle Paul expressly teaches us that the character of the first belongs only to the Son of God. (Heb. i. 8, 9.) The same allegory is still more fully presented in another whole book of the Old Testament Scriptures. The Song of Solomon is a poem framed altogether in conformity with the solemnity of a real marriage. The bridegroom and bride, and their companions, are all introduced, in regular and animated dialogue; and the whole language and imagery of the piece have immediate respect to the circumstances of an actual marriage scene. From the earliest times, however, the Song has been considered mystically descriptive of a far more exalted love, and a far more intimate union, than any of a mere earthly kind. King Solomon, whom it presents to our view, arrayed in his festival robes, and wearing the "crown wherewith his mother crowned him in the day of his espousals, and in the day of the gladness of his heart," is the humble type of a far more illustrious, even a heavenly Bridegroom. His spouse, "fairest among women," and adorned with all the magnificence of a *Prince's daughter*, represents an exceedingly more glorious bride—the Church of God, *purchased with his own blood*, and rendered comely beyond expression, with the beauty of holiness and the garments of grace, supplied by his own Spirit. This is the bride, *the Lamb's wife*, of whom the apostle speaks in the book of Revelation; and who, as he tells us, is the holy city, the new Jerusalem, that is, the redeemed church of Christ. (Rev. xxi. 2, 9, 10, xxii. 17.) In the vision of prophecy, the inspired discipie is carried far along the distance of many hundred years, to the remotest end of time. Scenes of trial and distress rise upon his view one after another, in long and melancholy succession; and while the church is still upheld, and gradually advances onward to greater importance in the world, it is, nevertheless, surrounded on every side with frightful forms of darkness, and met at every step with rising shapes of difficulty and danger; so as to seem, at times, just ready to be overwhelmed with their power. All this, however, is but the course of preparation for her day of triumph and joy. In the end, a voice is heard, like the sound of many waters and of mightiest thunders: "Hallelujah! for the Lord God omnipotent reigneth! Let us be glad, and rejoice, and give honour to Him; for the marriage of the Lamb is come, and his wife hath made herself ready. And to her," says the sacred writer, "was granted that she should be arrayed in fine linen, clean and white; for the fine linen is the righteousness of the saints." Then said the angel to the holy man: "Write, Blessed are they which are called unto the *marriage supper* of the Lamb!" (Rev. xix. 6—9.)

After this brief consideration of the frequent use which is made of the image in question, in other parts of Scripture, we are better prepared to perceive the beauty and force of several allusions which are made to it in the Gospels. John the Baptist distinguishes Christ by the title of the Bridegroom; no doubt, with reference to that spiritual relation to his church, which, under the image of a marriage, was so familiar to readers of the Jewish Scriptures, and which every serious Jew well understood could be properly ascribed to no other but the Messiah of God, who was to come into the world. He styles himself the Bridegroom's friend, to intimate that he acted in his work but as the humble minister of Christ, and found his own joy in the advancement of his Master's glory. (John iii. 29.) Our Saviour, in another place, represents himself under the same character, and his disciples are, at the same time, called the children of the bride-chamber, or companions of the bridegroom. (Matt. ix. 15.) In the parable of the marriage of the king's son, we have again presented to us the *mystical allegory* of the Old Testament, already noticed, rather than a mere illustration of one particular point by *comparison* with the ceremonies of a great wedding. The King's Son is no other than the Messiah himself, the spiritual Bridegroom of Solomon's Song, whose Father is the King of kings, the everlasting God. To the marriage festival, so long foretold in their own prophecies, the Jews were first invited. But they refused to come as a nation. They put far from them the blessings of the gospel. In anger, God has sent forth his armies to burn up their city, and to scatter them, with great destruction, among all the nations of the earth, as they are found to this day. Then the invitation went forth to the long-neglected and despised Gentiles, who were sunk in the lowest degradation of ignorance and idolatry. To them the call has been sounding ever since, and many have been compelled, by its heavenly persuasion, to attend and come; while many others, alas, have repeated, as multitudes are still repeating, the miserable folly of the Jews, turning a deaf ear to the sound of kindness, till fear came like desolation from the Almighty; and destruction, as a whirlwind, big with the wrath of Jehovah, swept them away. But "when the king came in to see the guests, he saw there a man which had not on a wedding garment." In great houses, festival garments were always kept ready for such an occasion, and furnished freely

for all the guests. It was, therefore, a most offensive disrespect to the master, for any guest to neglect clothing himself with one immediately. When the king asked for an explanation, the man was speechless. "Then said the king to the servants, Bind him hand and foot, and take him away, and cast him into outer darkness." All this strongly represents the danger of trifling with God, by a mere show of complying with the call of the gospel, while the simple terms of salvation are neglected. To sit down at the marriage supper of the Lamb and his bride, we must each one be arrayed in the robe of righteousness, which he himself has provided, at vast expense, for every guest. Whosoever may come forward, to be a partaker in the spiritual feast without this robe, will as surely be covered with speechless confusion, and thrust out into eternal darkness. To be forcibly cast out with shame, from the joyous assembly and the brilliantly lighted room of a royal marriage festival, into the comfortless and lonely gloom of night, outside of the house, would be an exceeding mortification; but this furnishes only a feeble representation of the horror that must seize the soul, when it is driven from the presence of God in anger, and shut out far from his peaceful kingdom, in the deepest night of death and hell. Ah, *there* indeed "shall be weeping and gnashing of teeth!" (Matt. xxii. 1—14.) The danger of failing to secure the blessing of Heaven, through negligence and sloth, is most strikingly displayed in another marriage parable. Five of ten virgins who were assembled at the bridegroom's house, to go forth and meet him with lights, when he should come home in the night with his wedding procession, were so foolish as to take no oil with them in their vessels. At midnight, while they all slept, there was a cry made: "Behold the bridegroom cometh; go ye out to meet him." Then these virgins had no oil, and were compelled, at that late hour, to go and buy. But while they were away, the bridegroom came, "and they that were ready, went in with him to the marriage; *and the door was shut.*" When the foolish virgins returned, they could find no admission to the joyful company within. "Watch, therefore," is the language of the Saviour, "for ye know neither the day nor the hour wherein the Son of man cometh." (Matt. xxv. 1—13.) Blessed are they which are called unto the marriage supper of the Lamb!

POLYGAMY.—God, in the beginning, made only one man and one woman, and thus showed his will, that no man should ever have more than one wife at the same time. (Matt. xix. 4.) Very early, however, this excellent appointment was transgressed. Lamech, long before the flood, had two wives; and afterward it became so common that even pious men, like Abraham and Jacob, fell into the evil. Among the Jews, it was very fashionable, in the time of Moses, to have more than one wife, and continued so, at least in the higher ranks of society, long after. Before the time of our Saviour, however, it seems to have become far less common. The law of Moses suffered it, on account of the hardness of heart which was found among the people. The frown of God, however, was displayed against it, in the dispensations of his righteous providence. How was the comfort of Abraham's house disturbed by his unhappy marriage with Hagar! and how were the years of Jacob afflicted with the bitter jealousy of his wives, and the ungodly conduct of his sons! What a heavy cloud of sorrow hung upon the family of David, from the same source! And what shall we say of Solomon, with his thousand women? They "turned away his heart" from the Lord, so that his most illustrious life was covered, toward its close, with a dreadful darkness of guilt; and a fearful mystery is left to rest, in the word of God, over all his latter end! The *Concubines*, mentioned in the Bible, were true wives, as really married as any others; only they were persons of lower condition than the principal wives, frequently mere servants in the house, and so were married with much less ceremony. Their children were not always placed on an equal footing with those of other wives in the inheritance of their father's property.—Polygamy still exists in eastern countries to an awful extent, and is the source of unnumbered evils.

DIVORCE.—The Jews, from the earliest times, exercised a very arbitrary power over their wives. Divorces were frequent, and often for slight offences. God always regarded such conduct with displeasure. (Mic. ii. 9, Mal. ii. 14—16.) Still, it was not expressly determined by the law of Moses, to what cases the power of the husband should be restrained in this matter. The husband was left to decide for himself, whether a sufficient occasion for separation was found in his wife: and was only required, if he resolved to send her away, to give her a *Bill of divorce*. (Deut. xxiv. 1—4.) Before the time of our Saviour, the Jewish doctors became completely divided in opinion about what should be considered a just cause for divorce. One class maintained, that, according to the true meaning of the words of the law just referred to, no reason, except adultery, was sufficient; while another asserted that the law allowed a man to put away his wife for any matter of displeasure whatever, even the most insignificant. This latter sentiment seems to have prevailed most generally through the mass of the nation, if we may judge from the licentious practice in this point, which was everywhere common. To tempt our Lord, the Pharisees proposed to him this much disputed question: "Is it lawful," they said, "for a man to put away his wife *for every cause?*" Jesus placed before them the original divine institution of marriage, and then pronounced, "What God hath joined together, let no man put asunder." Why then, it was asked, did Moses allow it? Jesus answered: "Moses, because of the hardness of your hearts, suffered you to put away your wives; but from the beginning it was not so." (Matt. xix. 3—9.) The law of Moses in this case, as in some others, only attempted to regulate, with an imperfect remedy, the evil, which the obstinacy of national feeling would not allow to be at once repressed by a positive statute. This, however, was a provision of mere *civil government*, and did, by no means, as many of the Jews thought, establish a rule of *religion*, which might satisfy a man's conscience in the presence of God. Our Lord allowed but one sufficient cause for divorce. (Matt. v. 32.)—Not only was it common for *men* to put away their wives, but, in the latter period of the nation, *women* not unfrequently divorced their husbands. One of Herod's sisters took this step; and his grand-daughter Herodias set a similar example. She first married her uncle Philip; after some time, she separated herself from him, and married his brother, Herod the tetrarch. (Matt. xiv. 3.) Drusilla, the sister of Agrippa, put away, in like manner, her first husband, to marry Felix. (Acts xxiv. 24.)

SECTION II.

OF THE RELATION BETWEEN PARENTS AND CHILDREN.

From the most ancient times it was counted, among the people of the east, a great misfortune, and, in some measure, a reproach, to be childless. It was the honour of families to have their names handed down in a long succession of sons, from age to age, to the remotest generations. It became, therefore, a matter of highest interest, with every new representative of the house, that its genealogy should not be stopped in his person, and thus the shame of disappointing the hope of all his ancestors be brought down upon his single head. On this account, it was disgraceful to continue in an unmarried state; and as life has no security, it was counted unsafe to delay marriage any time, lest death should cut off the privilege of posterity: hence, fathers were anxious to have their children married early. From the common feeling on this subject, arose also that strange custom which required a man's nearest male relation to marry his wife, in case he himself died without children. This custom had existed, with authority that could not be disregarded, a long time before the age of Moses; as we learn from the history of Judah's sons. (Gen. xxxviii. 8—12.) In the law of Moses, it was made a regular statute of the Jewish government. To prevent, however, its unhappy effect in particular instances, where a great unwillingness to marry a brother's widow might be felt, a method of avoiding the connection was appointed, accompanied, indeed, with some disgrace, but, withal, rendering the rule extremely mild, in comparison with its old form of inflexible rigour. The whole design of this regulation was to raise up a succession for the man who died childless, "that his name might not be put out of Israel." (Deut. xxv. 5—10.) Where the desire of having offspring was so strong, it is easy to perceive that barrenness in the married state would be considered a most afflicting calamity. We have repeated illustrations of this in the history of the Bible. In such cases, it was sometimes, at least in the earliest ages, thought expedient by wives to give their maids, as concubines, to their husbands, and then adopt their children as their own. Thus Sarah, Rachel, and Leah too, consented to act. The prophets often refer to this strong national feeling in their figurative pictures of prosperity or desolation. (Isa. xlix. 17—23, liv. 1—4, xlvii. 9.) In allusion to the same feeling, our Saviour says, in predicting a time of dreadful calamity, " Behold, the days are coming, in the which they shall say, Blessed are the barren, and the wombs that never bare, and the paps which never gave suck !" (Luke xxiii. 29.) What a season of distress would such language represent to the ears and feelings of a Jew !

For an account of the ceremonial observances which the law required after the birth of a son or a daughter, read the twelfth chapter of Leviticus. It was an evidence of much poverty in the circumstances of Joseph and Mary that they could bring to the temple, for an offering of purification, only "a pair of turtle-doves or two young pigeons." (Luke ii. 22—24.) At the end of eight days, every son was to be dedicated to God by the right of circumcision. (Gen. xvii. 10—14.) In later times, at least, it became common to give the child its name at the same time as is now the general practice in Christian countries when infants are baptized. (Luke i. 59, ii. 21.) Names, among the Jews, were never without meaning. It was not uncommon for a person, as he advanced in life, to change his first name, or to receive a new one in addition to it. Kings and princes frequently changed the names of those whom they raised to honour and power in their governments. (Gen. xli. 45, 2 Kings xxiii. 34, xxiv. 17.) There was probably some allusion to this custom, when God, as an expression of his favour, gave new names to Abram and Jacob. In the later ages of the nation, when the Jews were compelled to mingle more with other people, and other languages began to creep into the room of the ancient Hebrew, it was very common to be called by different names; one Hebrew, and another Greek or Latin. Sometimes, both of such names signified the same thing; the one being a mere translation of the other: so *Cephas* and *Peter*—the name given to Simon by our Lord Jesus Christ—equally mean a rock or stone. (John i. 42, Matt. xvi. 18.) In the New Testament, we find almost all the Old Testament names that are mentioned, somewhat altered; thus we have *Esaias* for Isaiah, *Elias* for Elijah, and many other such changes, as may be seen in the list of names in the first chapter of Matthew, and also in the third chapter of Luke. These, however, were not intended to be *new* names, of any sort; they are merely the old Hebrew names written as they were usually pronounced by those who spoke Greek according to the smooth and soft style of the Greek language. In translating the Greek Testament into English, these forms have crept into our language too: though it certainly had as much right as the Greek to change them into conformity with its own pronunciation, according to the forms in which it seemed best to express the original Hebrew names themselves.

The authority of a Jewish father, in his family, was very great. We have seen already how absolute it was in providing for the marriage of a son or daughter. When a daughter married, she passed entirely into another family, unless she happened to have no brother, in which case she became heiress of her father's estate. (Numb. xxvii. 1—9.) A son continued to live, after marriage, in his father's house; and while he did so, the father's authority still rested upon him with full weight; and, at the same time, upon the daughter-in-law, with all their children. The whole Scriptures inculcated on children, in the most solemn manner, the duty of affectionate respect and kindness toward their parents, as long as they live. The law required parents, on the other hand, to train up their children, with the most unceasing diligence, in the knowledge of religion and in the fear of God. (Deut. vi. 7, xi. 19.) The gospel has enforced the same duty, with repeated admonitions. What a fearful account must many parents who bear the Christian name, render for their sad neglect of this matter! Can the obligation on such be less than that, which, in the passages referred to above, God laid, with so much solemnity, upon the ancient Jews? "To whomsoever much is given, of him shall be much required!"

THE BIRTHRIGHT.—The *first-born* son inherited peculiar privileges. He received a double portion of his father's estate. (Deut. xxi. 17.) He possessed some authority, similar to that of the father, over his younger brethren; at least when the father was taken away; and was regarded with some peculiar respect, as the principal representative of the family. In the family of Jacob, as the first privilege was given to Joseph, so this second one was secured to Judah, because Reuben had rendered himself unworthy of his natural right, by gross sin. (1 Chron. v. 1, 2.) Before the giving of the law, advantages of a kind yet far more important belonged to the birthright. The oldest son seems to have enjoyed a *religious* pre-eminence over the rest of the children, as well as a mere worldly superiority. The father of every family was its proper priest, whose business it was to offer sacrifice to God, in behalf of his whole house, as Job was accustomed to do. In case of his absence or death, this important office, we have reason to believe, fell to the care of the first-born son. It appears, moreover, that God, in the natural order of his providence and grace, distributed his benefits not without some regard to this distinction of birth; appointing an inseparable connection between them and the father's peculiar solemn *blessing*, while, in the established order of things, this blessing came to be considered the proper right of the first-born. Such, at least, was the method which the Divine wisdom respected as regular, in the case of Esau and Reuben. By virtue of their birthright, they were authorized to expect a large measure of the rich BLESSING pronounced on Abraham, to rest on each of themselves, and to be handed down continually in the line of their posterity, till it should, at last, be crowned with the accomplishment of the Great Promise—the appearance of that *Seed* in whom all the nations of the earth were to be blessed. Reuben lost his natural advantage in this respect by shameful wickedness; as before, Esau had sold his for a morsel of bread; thus profanely despising the rich spiritual blessings with which it was connected. The latter sought the blessing afterwards, "carefully, with tears;" but he "found no place of repentance," (or change,) —no possibility of altering what was done, by a change in his father. (Heb. xii. 17.) The right of the priesthood was given, by the law, to the tribe of Levi, and the religious superiority of the first-born seems to have continued no longer. (Numb. iii. 12—18.) It is easy to see, from what has been said, how the term *first-born* came to be used figuratively, to signify a character of highest dignity, or to denote any thing of principal importance in its kind. "The first-born of the poor" are those who are pressed with exceeding poverty. (Isa. xiv. 30.) "The first-born of death," is a death of uncommon cruelty. (Job xviii. 13.) So, to express the dignity of the saints, they are called "the church of the first-born." (Heb. xii. 23.) Christ is styled the First-born of God, (Ps. lxxxix. 27,

Heb. i. 6;) also the "first-born of every creature," as being before all things—the Beginning and Head of creation, (Col i. 15;) again, the "first-begotten from the dead," as being the Beginning of the resurrection, and the Head of the whole family of believers, who are yet to rise. (Rev. i. 5.)

ADOPTION.—The practice of adopting sons has prevailed to some extent in every age, among different nations. By this act, an entire stranger by birth might be received into a man's family as his own child, and thus become entitled to every privilege which actual sonship could expect. We find one instance of this in the history of Moses; Pharaoh's daughter took him to be her son. (Ex. ii. 10.) Daughters were sometimes adopted in the same manner; an example of which we have in the case of Esther: "When her father and mother were dead, Mordecai took her for his own daughter." (Esth. ii. 7.) It is not clear that this way of receiving children was very common among the Jews; but they could not but be familiar with its practice, as it existed in other countries, especially in latter times, when they were brought, by their national calamities, to mingle so much with people among whom the custom was general. The Scriptures, accordingly, make several allusions to it. God is said to *adopt* persons into his family, when, by his grace, he converts them from the power of sin, and gives them, through Jesus Christ, a title to the rich inheritance of his people. To as many as receive Christ, is given power to become the sons of God. (John i. 12.) They are then no more foreigners and strangers, but fellow-citizens with the saints, and *of the household* of God. (Eph. ii. 19.) The spirit of adoption is sent forth into their hearts, whereby they cry, Abba, *Father;* and they become assured of an eternal inheritance, being made heirs of God, and joint-heirs with Jesus Christ. (Rom. viii. 14—17.)

SECTION III.

OF SLAVES.

SLAVERY seems to have existed before the flood. Noah speaks of it as a thing well known. Among the ancient patriarchs it was very common. The *servants* of whom we hear in the history of their times, were properly *slaves*, who might be bought and sold without any regard to their own will. Some of the richer shepherds, like Abraham and Job, appear to have had thousands of them belonging to their households. The government of the master, however, was probably, in these cases, of the mildest kind; so that it would be considered a privilege, by such as were not able to establish a great, independent family for themselves, to be admitted as servants into the prince-like household of another, beneath the protection of whose power they might dwell in safety and comfort. By the law of Moses, no Jew could be held, by one of his own countrymen, as a bond-servant or slave for life. Unless he himself insisted on staying with his master, he became free after a service of six years; and whenever the year of Jubilee came, all Hebrew servants, whatever had been their time of past service, were to be dismissed with liberty, as a matter of course. (Ex. xxi. 2—6, Lev. xxv. 39—55.) Strangers might be kept in continual bondage. They were acquired, either by being made captive in war, or by purchase: the children of servants were, by their birth, placed in the same state; these were distinguished by the name of *home-born*, or *born in the house*. A man might also become a servant, on account of a debt which he could not pay. (2 Kings iv. 1, Matt. xviii. 25.) Sometimes, a man oppressed with poverty sold *himself* to a master. The law denounced sentence of death against the person who should steal a fellow-being, to sell him for a slave. (Ex. xxi. 16.)

By their law, the Jews were required to treat their servants with humanity; and particular commandments were given, to secure for them several important privileges, both of a civil and of a religious kind. (Ex. xxi. 20, 26, 27, xx. 10; Deut. xii. 18, xvi. 11.) In a large household, the servant who was considered most faithful and discreet, was placed over the rest, as superintendent, in the general management of the house. He was called the *Steward*. Such was Eliezer, in the house of Abraham. (Gen. xv. 2, xxiv. 2.) Ministers of the gospel are styled, in the New Testament, "*Stewards* of the mysteries and of the manifold grace of God;" because they are principal servants in the household of Christ, appointed to watch over its affairs, and intrusted, in a peculiar manner, with the distribution of its spiritual provisions. (1 Cor. iv. 1, 2, 1 Pet. iv. 10.) This is a trust that calls for the greatest diligence and the most vigilant care; unfaithfulness in the discharge of its duties, will be visited with dreadful punishments. (Matt. xxiv 45—51.)

The condition of slaves among the Gentile nations, especially the Greeks and the Romans, was far less tolerable than among the Jews. They were not supported by those to whom they belonged, and yet were allowed to have only the smallest private possessions; these, moreover, were entirely subjected to the will of their masters. To them, the rest of the Sabbath never came, and no sacred festival interrupted the course of their labour, with its regular and joyful return. Among the Romans, slaves were considered no better than cattle, without any civil or religious right: the law protected them with no care; the master ruled them with unrestrained authority. For the smallest offences, they were cruelly scourged; and when the wrath of the owner was greatly kindled, he might cause them to suffer a painful death. The common way of inflicting capital punishment upon slaves, was by the *cross*. It was not unusual to *brand* them; sometimes, by way of punishment, and often, merely for the sake of marking them with their master's *sign*, so that they could not escape, if they ever wished to run away. The brand was burned, generally, upon the forehead, and sometimes on the hand. Soldiers were frequently branded on the hand, in a similar manner. This was a custom of very ancient times. From it, probably, arose another custom, not uncommon in idolatrous countries, of receiving a brand or mark in the body, as a sign of obedience and consecration to some particular false god. The Jews were forbidden to *print any marks* upon themselves, perhaps with reference to some heathen custom of this kind. (Lev. xix. 28.) There is allusion to the practice, in the book of Revelation: "He caused all, both small and great, rich and poor, free and bond, *to receive a mark in their right hand or in their foreheads.*" (Rev. xiii. 16.) The apostle alludes to the custom of branding slaves, in his epistle to the Galatians: "I bear in my body the marks (or brands) of the Lord Jesus." (Gal. vi. 17.) These marks were the scars of wounds, received for the sake of Christ, which, wherever he went, showed him to be the property of that glorious Master

CHAPTER VII.

DISEASES AND FUNERAL CUSTOMS.

SECTION I.

OF DISEASES.

Sickness and death are the melancholy fruit of sin. Were there no sin in the universe, there would be in it neither pain nor sorrow. The innumerable forms of suffering that crowd upon human experience, in this world, are but innumerable signs of guilt in the sight of a holy God. Death entered into the world by sin, and furnishes the sad evidence of that most awful evil, wherever it is found. (Rom. v. 12—14.) It was, therefore, no vain imagination, which led the ancient Israelites to refer their diseases to the displeasure of God; for although they come, for the most part, according to the laws of nature, without any miraculous interference of the Almighty, we are to remember that those laws have no necessity except in His appointment, and that His appointment, in this case, has, from the beginning, flowed, according to his own word, from holy indignation against sin. Hence, Moses, the man of God, in the beautiful Psalm which he composed on the subject of human frailty and mortality, ascribes all to this lamentable source: "Thou turnest man to destruction, and sayest, Return, ye children of men. Thou carriest them away as with a flood; they are as a sleep! In the morning, they are like grass which groweth up: in the *morning* it flourisheth and groweth up; in the *evening*, it is cut down, and withereth! *For we are consumed by thine anger, and by thy wrath are we troubled. Thou hast set our iniquities before thee, our secret sins in the light of thy countenance. For all our days are passed away in thy wrath*" (Ps. xc. 3—12.) In like manner, David piously acknowledges the hand of God: "I was dumb, and opened not my mouth, because Thou didst it! Remove *thy stroke* away from me: I am consumed by *the blow of thine hand!* When Thou with rebukes dost correct man for iniquity, Thou makest his beauty to consume away like a moth!" (Ps. xxxix. 9—11.)

But, besides the ordinary diseases which, in the righteous providence of God, were appointed to be the *natural* and *gene-*

the scourges of human depravity among the Jews, as among all other people, there were others of a more *extraordinary* and *peculiar* kind, which they were taught to ascribe to no natural source whatever, but to the *direct* power of some unseen and unearthly agency. Sometimes, the finger of the Almighty was put forth, to blast, as it were, by its *immediate* touch, the vigour of health and life. More commonly, however, an inferior ministry was employed to execute his will. Either an angel, rejoicing to do his commandments, rushed from his presence on the errand of judgment and wrath; or some foul spirit of hell, permitted in his holy counsels to pass over the common boundaries of its restraint, went forth with malicious satisfaction, and inflicted the heavy stroke. In Egypt, at the dead hour of midnight, Jehovah went through the land, and smote all the first-born, "from the first-born of Pharaoh that sat on his throne, unto the first-born of the captive that was in the dungeon; and all the first-born of cattle." (Ex. xii. 23, 29.) So in the days of David, we are informed that the Lord sent a pestilence upon Israel, which destroyed seventy thousand men as it passed over the land. This was no natural plague; the angel of the Almighty was sent forth to accomplish its destruction, and was discovered to the guilty monarch himself, standing between earth and heaven, with a drawn sword in his hand, stretched out over Jerusalem. (1 Chron. xxi 12—16.) Thus also in the camp of the impious Sennacherib an angel smote, in one night, an hundred and eighty-five thousand men, so that "in the morning they were all dead corpses." (2 Kings xix. 35.) In much later times, Herod, because he gave not glory to God, was smitten by an angel's hand, and in consequence, was eaten of worms, so as to give up the ghost. (Acts xii. 23.) We have an example of the agency of evil spirits, in the case of Job, whom Satan, by permission of God, afflicted with sorest disease. Saul, the first king of Israel, was troubled greatly by *an evil spirit from the Lord*. But in the time of our Saviour, an unusual liberty seems to have been given to the devil and his angels. They were suffered, in a great number of cases, to take complete possession of the bodies of men, to govern them according to their own will, and distress them with various forms of painful and unhappy disease.

The unfortunate person with whom one or more of these unclean spirits thus took up a residence, was deprived, to a greater or less extent, of the free use of his natural powers. Sometimes, particular organs of his body were entirely restrained from doing their office: thus he became deaf, or dumb or blind, or afflicted with other similar calamities. At other times, the spirit itself acted through the organs of the sufferer, so that *he* only *seemed* to act, and in reality, had no control whatever over the movements of his own body. Thus, when a person possessed with a devil appeared to speak, it was often the case that he himself had not the smallest agency in producing the words or the sound; his organs of speech were moved altogether by the demon within, so as to utter what it pleased. So, in like manner, the wretched demoniac was frequently driven, by a force which he had no disposition or power of himself to exert, into the most extravagant and unruly actions. We read of such being compelled to go forth into wild and lonely places, and take up their abode in the tombs, without house and without clothing; and from these desolate hiding places they rushed forth with amazing strength, on all that passed by that way, handling them with the greatest violence: neither could they be kept with chains and fetters; but, with prodigious power, they would break them, and rush forth again to the wilderness, hurried away by the unholy spirit. Of another, we read that the spirit often caused him to fall into the fire and into the water, or threw him down and tare him with exceeding cruelty. We are not to suppose, however, that the evil was confined, in *all* cases of possession, merely to the *body;* or that, while this was actuated like a machine, in some instances, by the unclean spirit, the *mind* of the sufferer was always free from disorder. *This*, also, not unfrequently, perhaps always in some degree, seems to have fallen under the satanic influence. Sometimes, it was brought under the power of a deep and wretched melancholy, which destroyed its energy and spoiled its social sympathies, and stamped upon the outward visage the expression of sullen and settled gloom. At other times, a more wild insanity seized upon the soul; malignant and hateful passions burst forth without control; and, occasionally, a fierce ungovernable phrensy carried its derangement through the whole inward man, and drove him to the utmost extreme of extravagance and madness. Hence, one person who was under the power of an unclean spirit, is called, in the New Testament, a *lunatic*. (Matt. xvii. 15, compared with Luke ix. 38—40.) And of another it is said, that he was found, after the demons had been cast out by the command of Christ, sitting "clothed and in *his right mind*." (Mark v. 15.) From the fact that persons possessed with devils were generally more or less disordered in mind, in the different ways we have mentioned above, it became common to ascribe to the same source, by way of reproach and scoff, *any* language or conduct

142   BIBLICAL ANTIQUITIES.

in another which seemed unreasonable or absurd. Thus th
phrase *to have a devil*, was often used to signify that the person of whom it was said acted in a strange, offensive manner,
or talked with extravagance and nonsense; as we say of a man
in such cases, *he dreams; he raves; he has lost his senses; he
is crazy*, &c. When John the Baptist came, with his austere
manner, refusing to taste the common enjoyments of social
life, and rigorously confining himself to the simplest and most
frugal diet, many of the Jews said: "He hath a devil." His
conduct appeared to them unreasonable and unlovely, savouring
of the unsociable melancholy which often hung over the demoniac's mind, and led him to delight in wild, uncomfortable
solitude, more than in the society of men. (Matt. xi. 18.)
So, also, on one occasion, they said to our Saviour, "Thou hast
a devil:" meaning to charge him with falsehood and nonsense.
On another, some of them exclaimed, "He hath a devil, and
is mad; why hear ye him?" (John vii. 20, x. 20.)

Many of our Saviour's miracles, while on earth, were
wrought for the deliverance of persons who were suffering under the dominion of evil spirits. He cast them out by a word.
The same power he gave likewise to his disciples; and for some
considerable time after his departure from the world, devils
were compelled, by the authority of his name, to come out of
multitudes into whom they had entered. There were, at the
same time, a class of persons among the Jews, who pretended
to cast out devils by various kinds of incantations and drugs.
These were called *Exorcists*. Such were the seven sons of
Sceva, a principal priest, and certain other vagabond Jews of
Ephesus, who took upon them to use the name of Jesus, as a
mere charm, for this purpose. (Acts xix. 13—16.) It was to
this class of men among the Jews, that our Lord referred, in
that question to the Pharisees: "If I by Beelzebub cast out
devils, by whom do your children cast them out?" (Matt.
xii. 27.)

On the subject of those extraordinary visitations of sickness
and death, which, as we learn from the Bible, God has at times
sent upon men, by an instrumentality more than natural, it
may be remarked, that the calamity did not, in all such cases,
approach under some strange and unheard-of form, or without
any appearance of natural disorder, so that the touch of an invisible hand might be clearly manifest. In many instances,
no doubt, the secret agency was exerted simply to produce
some violent and desperate disease, which, on other occasions,
sprang from a purely natural cause, and which would effectually
accomplish the intended purpose. To the eyes of men, there-

fore, an individual might sometimes seem to be sinking under fatal sickness, without any thing miraculous, while, in reality, the supernatural stroke of Heaven was crushing him to the grave. Thus when the angel smote Herod, it is probable that his friends and attendants ascribed the calamity to a mere natural disease which was not very uncommon in the east: it was enough that the persecuted followers of Christ could discover the operation of a higher hand, and perceive the glory of Zion's God, in the awful but righteous judgment. And is it unreasonable to suppose that the hand of the Almighty may still move, at times, in the same mysterious way, to accomplish his holy purpose? May not the angel of destruction, as in ancient years, still go forth occasionally from before the Eternal Throne, on his errand of vengeance and death? Who will undertake to say that the profane and licentious sinner, cut off so generally in the midst of his days, is *in no case* taken away by the unseen stroke of such a messenger? It matters not that the sword of wrath is not openly revealed, glittering over its victim or sinking into his bosom, and that the thoughtless crowd will not perceive the judgment of a righteous God; there may be, still, a sufficient manifestation of His presence, to leave the ungodly without excuse, in refusing to notice the operation of his hands, while the righteous and the truly wise are led to consider and understand. There may be, too, a reason for such an extraordinary interposition in the holy character of Jehovah himself, which, without respect to the display of his justice in the eyes of men, may require unusual, and, as it were, untimely dispensations of wrath, in cases of uncommon transgression; thus, also, the guilt of the offender may receive its more appropriate recompense in the appalling dismay which must seize upon his soul, on finding himself thus dragged, as it were, by the grasp of his Maker, before his insulted throne.

From the representation which has just been given, it appears that no absolute and marked distinction, as to appearance and character, existed universally, between maladies of a merely natural kind, sent in the general providence of God, and those which proceeded from the direct and extraordinary stroke of his power. Any fatal disease might become the channel of the Divine displeasure, as it flowed thus, in its unwonted stream, from the Fountain of holiness and truth. Still, there were certain forms of disorder more generally employed for this purpose than others. On this account, *these* came to be associated, in a peculiar manner, with the idea of anger and judgment from Heaven, and were commonly considered to proceed from the presence of God, if not altogether with miraculous visitation, yet at least with more direct and special appointment than the other ordinary calamities of life. Such, in a particular manner, were the *Pestilence* and the *Leprosy*.

The Pestilence, or *Plague*, is a terrible distemper, known in the east from the earliest ages down to the present time. It arises from a poisoned condition of the air, and, while it lasts, scatters desolation and death over the whole region of its influence. The symptoms of the disorder are painful and violent, commencing generally with cold shivering of the frame. Soon a burning fever succeeds, with distressing pain about the heart, and swelling in the flesh. All is quickly terminated, in most cases, with miserable death, which comes often in a few hours, and, at the farthest, after two or three days. The plague has sometimes raged, at one time, over different countries, for several thousand miles in extent; thus the whole of Asia, the greater part of Europe, and a large portion of Africa, (making up the principal part of the inhabited world,) have been wasted at once, with the awful scourge. Nor has it, in every case, endured but for a season or a single year; for fifteen years together its ravages have been felt; and on one occasion, as history relates, the whole period of half a century was distinguished by the long havoc of a wide-spread pestilence. The pestilence was frequently employed by God, in the execution of his extraordinary judgments. (Num. xi. 33, xvi. 45—50, xxv. 9.) The destruction of the Israelites, in the time of David, by the hand of the angel, was accomplished, as we are told, in the way of a pestilence. (2 Sam. xxiv. 13, 15.) It was probably by the same method of destruction, that the Assyrian camp was so dreadfully spoiled, in the days of Hezekiah. We are not to imagine, however, that the *plague*, in Scripture, always means this particular disease, called the pestilence. It is frequently used to signify any great calamity whatever. Such are the plagues mentioned in the book of Revelation. Any rapid, desolating destruction might well be called a plague.

The Leprosy.—It should be matter of thankfulness with us, that this loathsome and afflicting disease is not known to us, except by report from other times or from other regions of the world. It has always been peculiar to warm climates, and in such, especially in Egypt and other regions of the East, it is still found, agreeing, in all its general symptoms, with the description of its ancient character, as left in the Bible by Moses. The disease seems to commence deep in the system of the body, and generally acquires a thorough settlement in the person of its victim, before it discovers itself on the outward skin. It may lie thus concealed, even for a number of years; especially when it is seated in the constitution by birth, as it often is, when it does not commonly unfold its outward symptoms, until the child is grown up to years of maturity. After its appearance too, it does not proceed with any rapid ruin. Not until a number of years, does it reach its full perfection of disorder; and not until a number more have passed away, does this disorder terminate in death. A leprous person may live twenty or thirty, or if he receives the disease with his birth, forty or even fifty years; but years of such dreadful misery must they be, that early death might seem to be better. The horrible malady advances with slow but certain steps, from one stage of evil to another, diffusing its poison through the whole frame, while the principle of life is still suffered to linger in the midst of the desolation; and one after another the pillars of strength are secretly undermined and carried away, till the spirit finds, ere yet she can escape from its imprisonment, the house of her earthly tabernacle literally crumbling, on every side, into dissolution and dust. The bones and the marrow are pervaded with the disease, so that the joints of the hands and feet gradually lose their powers, and the limbs of the body fall together in such a manner as to give a most deformed and dreadful appearance to the whole person. There is a form of the disorder, known in some places, in which the joints, beginning with the furthest of the fingers and toes, one after another separate and fall off, and the miserable sufferer slowly falls in pieces to the grave. Outwardly, the leprosy discovers itself in a number of small spots, which generally appear first on the face, about the nose and eyes, but after some time on other parts of the body, till it is all covered over. At first these spots have the appearance of small reddish pimples, but they gradually spread in size, till after some years they become as large as a pea or bean, in the surface which they cover. When scratched, as their itchy character constantly solicits, a thin moisture oozes out of them, which soon dries and hardens into a scaly crust; so that, when the disease reaches its perfect state, the whole body becomes covered with a foul, whitish scurf. Particular directions were given in the law of Moses, to distinguish the spot of the real leprosy from others, that might resemble it in appearance. These are contained in the thirteenth chapter of Leviticus.

There are various kinds of leprosy, some more malignant and loathsome than others. According to the appearance of its spots, it is called by different names. There is a *white*, a *black*, and a *red* leprosy. It has been generally supposed, that one of its most dreadful and disgusting forms was selected by Satan, when he smote righteous Job "with sore boils, from the sole of his foot unto his crown;" so that "he took him a potsherd to scrape himself withal, and sat down among the ashes," in deep distress. How horrible and dismal must have been the ruin, wrought in his person by that deforming distemper, when his friends were unable to recognise his appearance; "they lifted up their eyes afar off, and knew him not!" They were overwhelmed with the picture of misery; "they lifted up their voice and wept; and they rent every one his mantle, and sprinkled dust on their heads, toward heaven. So they sat down with him upon the ground, seven days and seven nights, and none spake a word unto him; for they saw that his grief was very great!" Who can read, without emotion, the strong and affecting language, in which the sufferer himself describes his calamity, and pours forth the complaints which it wrung from his bosom! "O that my grief were thoroughly weighed, and my calamity laid in the balances together! For now it would be heavier than the sand of the sea: therefore my words are swallowed up. For the arrows of the Almighty are within me, the poison whereof drinketh up my spirit; the terrors of God do set themselves in array against me!—I am made to possess months of vanity, and wearisome nights are appointed to me. When I lie down, I say, When shall I arise, and the night be gone? and I am full of tossings to and fro, unto the dawning of the day. My flesh is clothed with worms and clods of the dust; my skin is broken and become loathsome.—My kinsfolk have failed, and my familiar friends have forgotten me. They that dwell in my house, and my maids, count me for a stranger; I am an alien in their sight! I called my servant, and he gave me no answer; I entreated him with my mouth. My breath is strange to my wife, though I entreated for the children's sake of mine own body! Have pity upon me, have pity upon me, O ye my friends, for the hand of God hath touched me?"

This shocking disease is contagious; so that it is dangerous to have much intercourse with leprous persons. On this account, it was wisely ordered among the Jews, that such should dwell alone, "all the days wherein the plague should be in them," and should be held *unclean*, so that no one might touch them without defilement.—Hence too, it was so strictly enjoined, that the earliest appearance of any thing like the spot of leprosy should be immediately and thoroughly examined The leper, in whom the plague was ascertained really to exist, was required also to distinguish himself, by having his clothes rent, his head bare, and his lip covered, (all of which were common signs of deep sorrow;) and to warn others from coming near him, by crying out, *Unclean! unclean!* (Lev. xiii. 45, 46.) The leprosy is still more fearful, as it may be handed down from one generation to another by birth. The leprosy of a father descends to his son and even to his grand-children of the third and fourth generations, assuming indeed a milder form, as it passes down, but still showing some of its disagreeable effects, in each successive case.

The leprosy was regarded, among the Jews, as a disease sent, in a peculiar manner, from the hand of God, and designed to mark his displeasure against some great sin, found in the person who suffered its affliction. Nor was this idea without some support, in the dispensations of judgment which their history recorded, and in the especial solemnity with which that disease is noticed in the Levitical law. When Miriam was punished for reproaching Moses, she was miraculously smitten with this malady in its full state. So when Gehazi sinned, the hateful scurf settled like snow upon his body, at the word of the prophet, and its plague descended to his seed after him. Thus also, when Uzziah the king profanely undertook to burn incense in the house of God, the leprosy burst out on his forehead, in the very act. (Numb. xii. 10, 2 Kings v. 27, 2 Chron. xxvi. 16, 23.) No medicines appear to have been employed for its cure; the sufferer looked for relief, to the compassion of God, without hope from the remedies of human skill. When it pleased the Almighty to heal a leper, the law appointed very peculiar ceremonies to be observed, for his cleansing; as may be seen by reading the fourteenth chapter of Leviticus. Our Saviour was careful to remind such, when he restored them to health, of their duty in this respect, bidding them to show themselves to the priest, and offer the commanded gift. (Matt. viii. 4, Mark i. 44, Luke xvii. 14.)

The leprosy, in the peculiar character which it held under the ceremonial system of the Jews, as well as in its natural features of horror, was a striking emblem of the evil of sin. This great moral disease fixed itself, with like strong hold, in the constitution of the soul, and spread its awful poison through its whole nature. The grace of spiritual life and health withers before its defiling contagion; loathsome and abominable ulcers break forth in every part, leaving no vestige of soundness or beauty; and the universal system sinks into disorder and melancholy wreck, proceeding from one woful stage of ruin still onward to another and a worse. This is the true *unclean* plague, which separates the soul from the presence of God, and shuts it out from the glorious *camp* of Heaven; which calls for deepest lamentation, and sorrow, and forbids every feeling of solid contentment or peace. The uncleanness, the separation from the earthly congregation of Israel, and the sorrow and shame which the law appointed in cases of natural leprosy, were but typical shadows of these far more momentous things. So were the ceremonies of purification, which it prescribed, but emblematic images of that great mysterious method of mercy, whereby the blood of Jesus Christ purges the conscience from dead works, so that the sinner may draw near to the living God with acceptance. (Heb. ix. 13, 14.) This disorder will not yield to the medicines of human art; it cannot be cured by any other than a Divine power. The blood of Christ alone can cleanse from its deep pollution; his Spirit only can destroy its malignant force. To him the soul must come, like the leper of old, casting itself down at his feet and crying, " Lord, if thou wilt, *Thou* canst make me clean!" He is still ready to answer, with that transporting word, " I will; be thou clean."

Of the other diseases which were common at different times among the Jews, it is not necessary to say any thing. They were less remarkable in their character, and generally such as are not uncommon in other parts of the world at the present day, if not exactly under the same form, yet with no material difference.

In the time of Christ, it was the custom, in many cases, to anoint the sick with oil. This was counted a remedy in some particular diseases, and was originally applied merely on account of its natural healing power. It came, however, to be abused by the Jews, as a magical charm. That people, in later ages, gave themselves up very much to the folly of enchantments and superstitious rites of various kinds; some such form of sorcery seems to have grown into use, in making applications of oil to the sick, whereby it was thought the remedy would be rendered powerful and certain. When the disciples of our Lord were sent forth, they thought proper not to neglect this common sign of healing, although the cures which they performed were altogether miraculous; " they anointed with oil many that were sick and healed them." (Mark vi. 13.) So the apostle James directs the elders, to pray over the sick, " anointing him with oil in the name of the Lord;" by which he means, that *while* they observe the customary usage, in this matter, they should do it in the name of Christ, and with prayer to him for healing power, when his blessing

Mourning Women.

might be expected to raise the sick to life and health. (James v. 14.) There might be, perhaps, in the exhortation, a reference to the superstitious manner in which the Jews sought to render the application effectual; as if he had said, "Be ye not like unto them."—"I show unto you a more excellent way."

SECTION II.
CUSTOMS WHICH ATTENDED DEATH AND BURIALS.

WHEN a person died, some one of his nearest friends immediately closed his eyes. The relations rent their garments, from the neck downward in front to the girdle, and a cry of lamentation and sorrow filled the room. This continued, bursting forth at intervals, until the corpse was carried away from the house. In many cases, the ceremonies of grief lasted eight days; for kings or other persons of distinguished rank, the time was extended commonly to a whole month, or thirty days. (Numb. xx. 29, Deut. xxxiv. 8.) It was usual, at the death of individuals of any importance, to employ some women to act as mourners on the occasion. These were not friends of the deceased, but persons whose professed business it was to conduct the ceremonies of wailing and lamentation, whenever they were wanted, and who received always some compensation for their services. They chanted, in doleful strains, the virtues of the dead, thus raising, to a higher pitch, the sorrowful feelings of the relations, and causing them to find relief in floods of gushing tears. Such were the *mourning women* of whom the prophet speaks, in his pathetic lamentation over the miseries that were coming on his country. (Jer. ix. 17—20, Amos v. 16.) These wailings were often accompanied with some melancholy music of instruments. (Matt. ix. 23.) The company of mourners did not confine their songs of lamentation to the house; when the funeral procession moved to the grave, they accompanied it, all the way, filling the air with sadness, and compelling others to weep with their mournful sounds. The children in the streets sometimes imitated these ceremonies in their playful sports; as we learn from that comparison employed by our Saviour, in which children are represented as complaining to their fellows, in the markets or public places, that they would not bear their part in any play which was proposed to them: "We have piped unto you, and ye have not danced; we have mourned unto you, (that is, sang mournful funeral songs,) and ye have not lamented," according to the custom of such occasions. (Matt. xi. 16, 17.)

Besides rending the garment, sorrow was expressed, at times, by beating the breast; tearing the hair; uncovering the head; walking barefoot; covering the lip, or more properly the chin; scattering ashes or dust into the air; putting on sack-cloth, and spreading ashes over the head, or sitting down in the midst of them. Sometimes they tore their faces with their nails, and wounded their flesh with painful cuttings; though this was a heathenish practice, expressly forbidden in the Jewish law. (Lev. xix. 28, Deut. xiv. 1, 2.) It was common also, to take off the ornaments of dress, and neglect all attention to personal appearance; they refused to anoint their heads, to wash themselves, to dress their hair, to trim their beards, or to indulge themselves with any of the common comforts of life. (2 Sam. i. 2, 11, xiii. 19, xiv. 2, xv. 30, xix. 4, 24.) These forms were not, of course, all, or even most of them, employed on common occasions of grief, or confined by any means to funeral seasons; they were the general signs of affliction, on any account, and were displayed to a greater or less extent, according to the measure of sorrow, real or pretended, which it was designed to express.

After death, the body was washed. (Acts ix. 37.) From a natural, though foolish, desire to preserve the remains of beloved friends, as long as possible, from corruption, it became common to use various methods of *embalming*. We read of this practice in the history of the most ancient times. Jacob and Joseph were embalmed, with great care, in the land of Egypt. No people ever equalled the ancient Egyptians in this art. Their physicians, who were at the same time priests, had three methods of embalming; one far more expensive and effectual than the other two, which was not therefore used, except when persons of great rank, or at least considerable wealth, died. In this case, the entrails were taken out of the body, by an opening in the left side, and the brain drawn from the head, with a crooked piece of iron, through the nostrils: then the inside of the body was washed with wine of the palm tree and filled with aromatic substances: spices of the strongest kind were crowded into the skull: the whole body was anointed with a composition of myrrh and other powerful preservatives, and afterwards kept for a number of days in a solution of the salt of nitre: lastly, it was wrapped round with numerous folds of linen, dipped in oil of myrrh, and besmeared with gum. This process occupied forty, or more days. The other methods were less complete, but were more commonly used on account of their cheapness. When the body was embalmed, it was returned to the relations, who put it into a box of syca-

more wood, so fashioned as to resemble the human form, and
set it up in some part of the house, leaning against the wall.
In this way bodies were often kept, for ages. Sometimes the
box or coffin was placed in a tomb, or family vault. Bodies
embalmed in the first way have been preserved for some
thousands of years; some of them are still found in Egypt,
preserved, without doubt, from most ancient times, and are now called *mummies*.
We have no account of any sort of embalming used by the more ancient Jews.
It is probable, however, that they were
not without some practice of the kind,
as we find it common in later ages.
Their method was far more simple than
that of Egypt. It seems to have been
generally little more than wrapping the
body round with several folds of linen,
well supplied with aromatic substances,
such as aloes and myrrh. Thus, as we

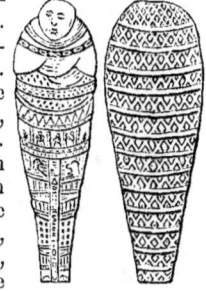

are told, Nicodemus showed his care for the body of our Saviour, in company with Joseph of Arimathea, who took it down
from the cross. He " brought a mixture of myrrh and aloes,
about an hundred pound weight: then took they the body of
Jesus, and *wound it in linen clothes with the spices, as the manner of the Jews is to bury.*" (John xix. 38, 40.) Mary, with
some other pious women, prepared still more spices and ointments, and carried them early on the first day of the week, to
the sepulchre, to be used in showing respect of a similar kind
to their Lord. (Luke xxiv. 1.) The use of a large quantity
of spices, on such occasions, was expressive of great regard for
the deceased, and was considered an honour to his person.

The Jews used no box or coffin for the dead. The corpse,
wrapped in folds of linen and bound about the face with a napkin, was placed upon a bier, and so carried by *bearers* to the
tomb. The bier was a kind of narrow bed, consisting, in common cases, we may suppose, of only a plain and simple frame,
but sometimes prepared with considerable ornament and cost.
The bier or *bed* in which king Asa was laid after his death,
was " filled with sweet odours, and divers kinds of spices, prepared by the apothecaries' art." (2 Chron. xvi. 14.) On one
of these funeral frames lay the widow's son, when our Saviour
met the mournful procession, without the city-gate. At his
almighty word, the dead man immediately *sat up.* (Luke vii.
15.) It was common, at least in the later times of the nation,
to bury soon after death. It was always inconvenient to keep

a corpse long, because, by the law, every person who touched it, or who merely came into the apartment where it lay, was rendered unclean from the time, a whole week; and so was cut off not only from sacred privileges, but also from all intercourse with friends and neighbours. To be deprived of burial, was counted, among the Jews, as among ancient nations universally, a great misfortune and disgrace. (Eccles. vi. 3.) Hence it was considered not only an act of humanity, but of religious duty also, to bury the dead; and the war was deemed uncommonly cruel, in which the conquerors would not permit the dead bodies of their enemies to receive this kind attention. (1 Sam. xxxi. 8—13, 2 Sam. xxi. 9, 14, 1 Kings xi. 11—15, Ps. lxxix. 2, 3.) So, the prophets, in their representations of the awful calamities of war threatened by God, often make use of this dreadful image,—the carcasses of the unburied slain given up to be meat for the fowls of heaven and the wild beasts of the forest. (Jer. xvi. 3—7, xxxiv. 20, Ezek. xxxix 17—20, Rev. xix. 17, 18.)

The Jewish sepulchres were situated without their towns and cities.—Jerusalem seems to have been the only city in which it was ever allowed to bury, and there the privilege was granted only to the royal family of David, and one or two other individuals, as a mark of peculiar respect. (2 Chron. xxiv. 16.) Sepulchres were often private property; one family or several families united, having their own separate burial place. There were, also, however, common and public burial places, generally some distance out from the city or village, in a lonely and unfrequented spot. In these, as is not uncommon in our own country, particular families appear to have had their separate little lots, often surrounded with a wall like a garden, where their ancestors for many generations quietly slumbered together. The private sepulchres were frequently situated in gardens, and, in early ages especially, beneath the shadow of some large and venerable trees It was considered a most desirable privilege, to be buried in the sepulchre of one's ancestors. (Gen. xlix. 29—32, 2 Sam. xix. 37.) Hence, by way of disgrace and punishment, wicked kings were sometimes not permitted to be buried in the tombs of their fathers. (2 Chron. xxi. 20, xxviii. 27.)

Sepulchres were, in common cases, dug merely in the ground. Those of the more wealthy and noble were prepared with greater labour. They were often cut out from rocks, so as to form quite a considerable room, surrounded on every side, and roofed above with the solid stone. Sometimes caverns, formed by nature, were fitted up for the purpose. In these dark

Interior of a Rock Sepulchre

chambers, the dead were placed around the sides, each resting in a separate niche or open cell formed in the wall. Not unfrequently, sepulchres were very large and divided into several distinct apartments. They were generally entered by descending a few steps, and where there were more rooms than one, those which were farthest back from the entrance were often dug somewhat deeper than such as were nearer, so as to have another little flight of steps leading down to their deep solitude. The entrance was closed with stone doors, or by a simple large flat stone placed against the mouth. The sepulchre in which Lazarus was buried, was a cave, with a stone laid upon it: at the call of Jesus, he *came forth* from his resting-place, folded in his grave-clothes, and bound about the face with a napkin. (John xi. 38, 44.) The sepulchre of Joseph was hewn out in the rock; and, when the body of Christ was laid within it, he rolled a great stone to the door for its security. (Matt. xxvii. 60.) Several of these ancient sepulchres are still found in the land of Palestine. They sometimes furnish, as they did also in ancient times, a hiding-place for thieves and robbers. We read in the New Testament, of miserable persons, possessed with devils, taking up their abode in such solitary places. Over sepulchres, were sometimes erected monuments of more or less elegance, by way of honour to the buried dead; as we may infer from that which is spoken concerning the Pharisees: "Ye build the tombs of the prophets, and garnish the sepulchres of the righteous." (Matt. xxiii. 29.) They made a great pretence to piety, in constantly repairing and decorating the places where holy men slept in death, while they imitated all the wickedness of their fathers in killing them, by their persecution of Him, concerning whom Moses and all the prophets spake. In the same chapter, they are compared to "whited sepulchres, which indeed appear beautiful outward, but within are full of dead men's bones, and of all uncleanness." Hence we learn that it was common to white-wash tombs. This might perhaps have been considered, in some measure, an ornament; but there appears to have been another reason for the practice. By the law of Moses, whoever touched the bone of a man or a grave, was rendered unclean for seven days. (Numb. xix. 16.) As such defilement unfitted a man for the privileges of the sanctuary, it was highly important that the possibility of contracting it by accident or through ignorance should be prevented; especially at those seasons when the people came from every quarter of the country to celebrate the great sacred festivals, at Jerusalem. On this account, it became customary to paint the sepulchres with white, that they might be easily noticed, and so warn those who were passing near them, to keep off. This, it is said, was required to be done a short time before the Passover, each spring, just after the long rains were over; and as there were no rains through the summer to wash it off, it lasted till the next fall. It was only three or four days before the passover, when our Lord compared the Pharisees to such sepulchres, which, we may suppose, were then to be seen with their fresh covering of white on every side of Jerusalem.

A grave or sepulchre is sometimes called in Scripture a *pit* Hence the phrase *to go down to the pit* is several times used to signify descending into the tomb by death. Thus the Psalmist complains: "My life draweth near to the grave. I am counted with them *that go down into the pit:* I am as a man that hath no strength; free among the dead, like the slain that lie in the grave, whom thou rememberest no more; and they are cut off from thy hand. Thou hast laid me *in the lowest pit,*—in darkness—in the deeps." (Ps. lxxxviii. 3—6, 10—12, xxviii. 1, xxx. 3, 9.) The prophet Ezekiel represents the ruin of several nations, threatened by the Almighty, in the same style. By the sword of destruction, they were speedily to be brought down to *the nether parts of the earth, with them that go down to the pit*—to lie in their *graves, set in the sides of the pit,* that is, in the funeral niches ranged along the walls of the sepulchre. (Chap. xxxii.)

HADES.—It became common, especially in the language of poetry, to employ the imagery of a sepulchre in representation of the *general* condition of the dead. A vast cavern was conceived, stretching abroad with immense extent, in the deepest parts of the earth. Continual gloom hung over all its scenery, and the most profound silence reigned on every side. No step of living man had ever descended to its unknown depth; nor had the eye of such ever discovered one of its secrets. It was all wrapt in awful mystery; it was *the land of silence;* it was the region and *shadow of death.* Round its sides, the forms of departed men rested, every one in his separate place; and when its powerful gates unfolded, it was but to admit some new inhabitant to its dreary mansion, as he came from his state among the living on earth, to mingle with the countless multitudes below. This unseen unknown condition of the dead, was called, in the ancient language of the Jews, *Sheol;* and in the Greek language, which was used in writing the New Testament, *Hades.* In the English Bible, it is sometimes styled simply *the Grave;* at other times, it is designated by the word *Hell.* In the 32d chapter of Ezekiel, lately referred to, something of this image of the general state of those who have left the world is presented to our view. The prophet is commanded to cast down Egypt with her multitude, and all the daughters of the famous nations, unto the nether parts of the earth, with them that go down to the pit; that is, according to the style of prophecy, to pronounce the decree of utter ruin which God had determined against these people. Then, the kingdoms are severally represented, as if they were themselves human persons, taking their places in the deep region of silence; while around each, the multitude of her mighty ones, once terrible in the land of the living, but now slain and fallen by the sword, lie without strength, and without glory, round the sides of the pit—in the vast abyss of Sheol, Hades, or *Hell*. In the 14th chapter of Isaiah, the image is brought forward with full and clear repre sentation, in one of the most magnificent pictures which the inspired poetry of the Bible has described. The powerful and oppressive monarch of Babylon is suddenly cut off from power and life. The earth, for gladness, breaks forth into singing; the fir trees and the cedars rejoice. But not only the world which he has left is made to exult in his fall; *Sheol* from beneath is moved to meet him at his coming: it stirreth up the dead for him, even all the chief ones of the earth, and raiseth up all the kings of the nations from their thrones. "Art thou," they cry, "also become weak as we? art thou become like unto us? Thy pomp is brought down to the *Grave!*"

This Sheol, or Hades, is the *Hell* intended in that expression of the Psalmist: "Thou wilt not leave my soul in hell, or suffer thy Holy One to see corruption." (Ps. xvi. 10.) The apostle Peter teaches us that David, in this declaration, spake of the resurrection of Christ, foretelling that *his* soul should not be left in hell, or *his* flesh see corruption; that is, that he should not continue in the condition of the dead, like other mortals, but, by the power of God, would soon forsake their dark and silent world, in all the fulness of recovered life. (Acts ii. 25—32.)—This also is the *Hell* of which John speaks in that passage; "I looked, and behold a pale horse: and his name that sat on him was Death, and hell followed with him." (Rev. vi. 8.) So, likewise, in his awful description of the last judgment; "The sea gave up the dead which were in it; and death and hell delivered up the dead which were in them.—And death and hell were cast into the lake of fire." (Rev. xx. 12, 13.) *Death* and *Hell*, or *Hades*, are represented as real persons: the last receives all its power directly through the triumphs of the former, and when the one is compelled to release its captives, the dominion of the other is also over. So it shall be in the end: the whole mysterious state of separation between the body and spirit shall come to an everlasting conclusion; Death and Hell shall be for ever stripped of their ancient power—swallowed up, as it were, in that infinitely more tremendous ruin which is to follow. *That* will be the *second death*—the lake that burneth with fire and brimstone, where the ungodly shall be tormented day and night for ever and ever—the true *Hell* where the lost soul, having, between death and judgment, tasted the awful punishment of sin only in its single state, shall ever after, in union with its risen body, drink the wine of the wrath of God poured out, without mixture, into the cup of his indignation. Blessed is he who shall have part in the resurrection of the just unto eternal life, on whom this second death shall have no power!

This mysterious, unknown mansion of the dead, was conceived to lie in the deepest region of the earth, toward its lowest foundations—as far *beneath* its upward surface as the starry heavens are lifted *above*. Hence, its image was frequently employed to denote any amazing depth, as the heavens were sometimes used to express, on the other hand, the idea of any exceeding height. Thus Job; "Canst thou by searching find out God? Canst thou find out the Almighty to perfection? It is *high as heaven*, what canst thou do? *deeper than hell*, what canst thou know? The measure thereof is *longer than the earth*, and *broader than the sea!*" (Job xi. 7—9.) That is, without figure, "It is impossible to find out God to perfection; such knowledge transcends the boundaries of created intellect infinitely, *in every way*." In similar style, we find the Psalmist making use of the same images; "If I ascend up into *heaven*, Thou art there! If I make my bed in *hell*, behold Thou art there! If I take the wings of the morning, and dwell in the uttermost parts of the *sea*, even there shall thy hand lead me, and thy right hand shall hold me!" (Ps. cxxxix. 8—10.) By which he means, that no height, nor depth, nor distance—no change of place, *in any way*, however great—could separate him from the presence of God. In a like figurative way we must understand the language of God, in that threatening of old; "Though they dig into *hell*, thence shall my hand take them; though they climb up to *heaven*, thence will I bring them down." (Amos ix. 2.) The apostle employs the same style; "Say not in thy heart, Who shall ascend into heaven?—or, Who shall descend into *the deep?*" That is, the gospel requires no hard or impossible thing—it demands only what may be accomplished with the greatest ease, if the heart be willing. (Rom. x. 6—9.) The sentence pronounced against Capernaum, introduces the contrast with awful meaning; "Thou, Capernaum, which art exalted to *heaven*, shall be brought down to hell!" In other words; thou shalt sink from the most exalted condition of privilege and blessing, to the lowest state of wretchedness under the fearful displeasure of God. (Matt. xi. 23, Luke x. 15.)

Hades signifies an *unseen* or *hidden* place, and well expresses the idea which the Jews represented under their ancient word *Sheol*. Something of its signification is found in the language of perhaps every people. When it is wanted to speak of the general condition into which men are brought by death, merely as it stands contrasted with this present state of life, and without any respect to its happiness or its misery, some indefinite term or phrase is employed; which, while it may distinguish it from all that belongs to the life we now live, leaves its precise character utterly out of view, and expresses only its most vague and universal notion. This notion is naturally formed, either by clothing that unknown state of being, which it contemplates, with some general imagery borrowed from the gloomy circumstances which attend the *body* after death—or by denying to it all the principal features of this present scene of existence, and opposing it in the way of contrast to all of life and condition that is felt or known this side the grave. Thus in our own tongue, we employ the phrases, *invisible world*, *world of spirits*, *the other world*, &c. They are used to distinguish the state of the dead in general, without reference to character or destiny, from the state of the living on earth; and so have only a negative significance, waking in the mind a conception only of what is *wanting*, rather than of what *belongs* in any way, to the thing spoken of. The Jews, however, as well as most other ancient people, clothed the idea with somewhat more of definiteness and form. Locality and figure were assigned to the world of departed spirits; and, though all its imagery was vague and shadowy and dark, there was still something of positive reality in the scenery of it, which the imagination laboured not altogether in vain to discern and rest upon. At the same time, the Jewish idea of this mysterious place seems not to have been altogether uniform in its particulars; it is presented with occasional variety of representation, and appears to have undergone in the course of time some considerable alteration. Thus, at one time, it borrows its drapery, as we have said, from the lonely sleep of the tomb; it is silent, and dark, and sad, and its inmates are lodged in awful stillness around its sides. But again, we find it represented with more of life and activity among its inhabitants, and without any such conformity to the arrangement of a sepulchre.

The word *Hades* is found in the Greek original of the New Testament *eleven* times. Once it is rendered, in the English translation, *Grave*, (1 Cor. xv. 55;) in the other ten cases, it is called *Hell*. Only three of these have not been already mentioned, viz. Matt. xvi. 18, Luke xvi. 23, and Rev. i. 18. When the word "Hell" occurs in other passages, it is the translation of a different word, which always means *the place of endless torment*, where fallen angels and ungodly men suffer the heavy wrath of the Almighty without hope.

CHAPTER VIII.

MISCELLANEOUS MATTER.

SECTION I.

OF WRITING.

The art of writing is most ancient. The account of its origin is lost in the distance of time. It is clear, however, from all history, that it had its commencement at a very early period, in some region of the East, and from thence was carried into every other part of the world, in which it has been ever found. Many have supposed that the knowledge of letters was given to men, like the knowledge of speech, by direct revelation from God himself; and, indeed, when we consider the mysterious and marvellous nature of the invention, it is hard to conceive how it could ever have been contrived by the unassisted wisdom of man. The Bible gives us the earliest notice on the subject that is anywhere to be found. Moses, we are told, received the two tables of the covenant on Mount Sinai, *written* with the finger of God; and before that, Moses himself was not ignorant of the use of letters. (Ex. xxiv. 4, xvii. 14.) There is, therefore, much reason to believe that the art of writing was understood among the Jews while other nations were yet without it, and that from them it has passed into all other countries, and been handed down to our own times. Hence, the alphabets of all languages that have ever been written, present a striking conformity with the ancient alphabet of that people, whether we consider the number of their letters, their names, their sounds, their order, or the original forms to which they may be traced backward. Some refer the origin of writing to the time of Moses; others, to that of Abraham; while a still different opinion throws it back to the age of Adam himself.

It was long, however, before the art came to be used with any thing like that convenience and ease which are now known. The materials and instruments with which it was performed, were, in comparison with our pen, ink and paper, extremely rude and unwieldy. One of the earliest methods was to cut out the letters on a tablet of stone. Another, was to trace them on unbaked tiles, or bricks, which were afterwards thoroughly burned with fire. Tablets (that is, small, level surfaces or plates) of lead or brass were sometimes employed. When the writing was wanted to be most durable, the last was chosen. Tablets of wood were more convenient. Such was the *writing table* which Zacharias used. (Luke i. 63.) In some countries, it was common to cover these with wax, on which the letters could be easily written, and, if necessary, blotted out again.

The instrument employed for making the letters on these tablets, was a small, pointed piece of iron, or some other hard substance, called by the Romans, a *Style:* hence, a man's manner of composition was figuratively termed his *style* of writing; 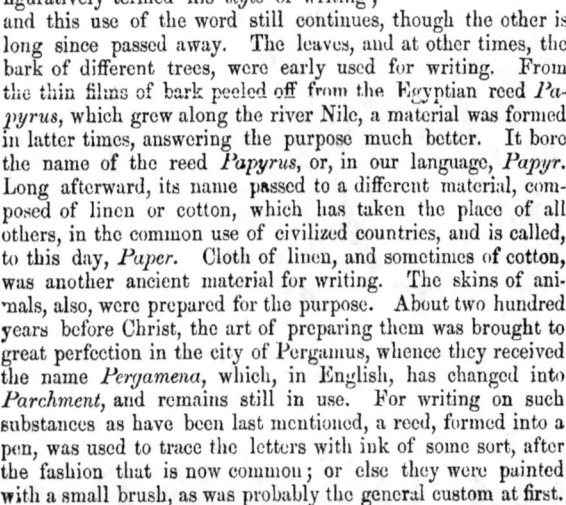 and this use of the word still continues, though the other is long since passed away. The leaves, and at other times, the bark of different trees, were early used for writing. From the thin films of bark peeled off from the Egyptian reed *Papyrus*, which grew along the river Nile, a material was formed in latter times, answering the purpose much better. It bore the name of the reed *Papyrus*, or, in our language, *Papyr.* Long afterward, its name passed to a different material, composed of linen or cotton, which has taken the place of all others, in the common use of civilized countries, and is called, to this day, *Paper.* Cloth of linen, and sometimes of cotton, was another ancient material for writing. The skins of animals, also, were prepared for the purpose. About two hundred years before Christ, the art of preparing them was brought to great perfection in the city of Pergamus, whence they received the name *Pergamena*, which, in English, has changed into *Parchment*, and remains still in use. For writing on such substances as have been last mentioned, a reed, formed into a pen, was used to trace the letters with ink of some sort, after the fashion that is now common; or else they were painted with a small brush, as was probably the general custom at first.

Books were written generally upon skins, linen, cotton cloth, or papyrus; parchment, in later times, was most esteemed. The several pieces, or leaves, were joined one to another, so as to make a single long sheet from the beginning to the end. This

was then rolled round a stick; or, if it was very long, round two sticks, beginning at each end, and rolling till they met in the middle. When any person wanted to read, he unrolled it to the place he wished, and when he was done, rolled it up again. Hence, books of every size were called *rolls:* our word *volume* means just the same thing in its original signification. (Jer. xxxvi. 2, Ps. xl. 7, Isa. xxxiv. 4.) The roll was commonly written only on one side; that which was given to Ezekiel, in vision, was written on both, *within* and *without* (Ezek. ii. 10.)

From this account of the ancient books, it is easy to understand how they might be sealed, either once or a number of times, so that a new seal might have to be opened, after unrolling and reading a part, before the reader could proceed to the remainder. (Isa. xxix. 11, Rev. v. 1, 2, vi.)

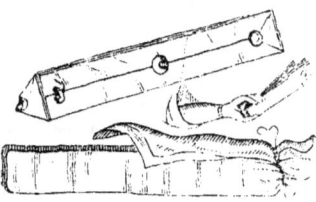

Letters were generally in the form of rolls, too. They were, probably, as is the eastern custom at present, sent in most cases without being sealed; while those addressed to persons of distinction were placed in a valuable purse or bag, which was tied, closed over with clay or wax, and so stamped with the writer's signet.

BIBLICAL ANTIQUITIES.

[The Roman Scrinium, or book-case, shows how these rolls were preserved.—The labels at the top contain the titles.]

Those persons among the Jews who were skilful in the use of the pen, were, as we have already seen, of considerable importance in society. They were distinguished from other men, by having an ink-horn fastened to their girdle. (Ezek. ix. 2, 3, 11.)

SECTION II.

OF MUSIC AND DANCING.

Music had its origin in Heaven. (Job xxxviii. 7.) It was designed to celebrate the praises of God, and to give to the devotion of cherubim and seraphim its most lofty expression, as it sounded long since, and is sounding still, through the courts of his Temple on high. So, no doubt, in the garden of Eden, our first parents worshipped the great Creator with songs of sacred melody. The *fall*, which spoiled every thing, has caused this heavenly art to be too often, ever since, perverted from its high and proper character. How often has the power of music, in every age, been employed on earth to turn away the soul from all that is holy, and to promote the darkest interests of hell! Musical instruments were first invented by Jubal, the son of Lamech. (Gen. iv. 21.) Among the Jews, music was always cultivated with much care, and was employed not only about the tabernacle and the temple, but also in the common scenes of domestic and social life. Marriages, birth-days, and other festival seasons, were enlivened with its sound; it was heard from the shepherd, as he reclined at ease near the steps of his flock, and from the fields of the farmer, as his harvest or his vintage was gathered with joy; it rose from the chamber of piety, in gratitude and adoration to God; it poured its more melancholy strain on the wind, from the funeral march, as it moved with the dead to the house appointed for all.

MUSICAL INSTRUMENTS were of three general kinds; such as had strings, such as were played upon by blowing, and such

as were sounded by being struck. Of the first class were the Harp and the Psaltery; of the second, the Organ, the Pipe of different sorts, the Horn, and the Trumpet; of the last, the most common were the Cymbal and the Tabret or Timbrel.

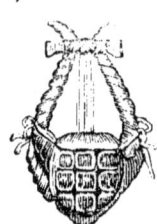

The *Harp* is mentioned with the organ, as the earliest of musical instruments. (Gen. iv. 21.) It was formed after different fashions, with a smaller or greater number of strings. Sometimes it had only three; sometimes, eight, when it was called *Sheminith*, as we find in the titles of some of the Psalms; at other times, it had ten. In the time of David, the strings seem to have been swept by the hand in playing;

afterward, a small bow was used for the purpose. The *Psaltery* had ten and sometimes twelve strings, which were played upon with the fingers. It was formed in the shape of a triangle; the body was hollow, with a piece of leather tightly drawn over it, and on the outside of the leather, the strings were stretched across. It is sometimes called a *Viol*, in the English Bible. (Isa. v. 12, Amos vi. 5.) On each of these ancient instruments, the royal Psalmist of Israel loved these games, which lasted some days, were witnessed trials of strength and skill, in the exercises of *Leaping, Wrestling, Boxing*, and throwing the *Discus*, or Quoit; also *Races* on foot, on horseback, and with chariots. An almost innumerable multitude of spectators from all Greece, and from other countries far and near, assembled to witness the contests. It is hard for *us* to conceive the greatness of the interest which was excited by one of these occasions, or the extreme anxiety to obtain the victory, which was felt by those who contended in the games. It was, in fact, considered one of the most distinguished honours on earth, to win such a victory, especially in the Olympic games; and, accordingly, it was coveted by persons of the greatest rank, nor were any pains reckoned too great, which might conduct a man to such a height of glory. Many, therefore, were the candidates for distinction and fame, by this road, though only a few happy individuals could secure the prize, while all the rest must necessarily come off with disappointment and shame. None but freemen, and such as were clear from infamous stains upon their character, were allowed to contend. For any of these, at the same time, to have entered into such contests without the most careful preparation beforehand, would have been the height of presumption and folly. For months, the candidates submitted themselves to strict rules of diet and exercise, and rigidly refrained from every indulgence which might, in any measure, hinder the full strength and activity of their bodies. At the appointed time, they made their appearance before the crowd of spectators. A *Herald* proclaimed their names, and recited aloud the rules they were required to observe in the games; for unless a man strove lawfully, he could not, though he came out conqueror, receive the crown. The combatants were entirely naked, that they might not be hindered in any degree by the weight of their clothes, or by their becoming entangled around their limbs. When the signal was given to commence the contest, every muscle was instantly in motion, while the eyes of the surrounding multitude hung, fixed with the deepest attention, on the struggling parties.

To inspire them with zeal and courage, the prize was placed in full view before their eyes. Judges were appointed to overlook every exercise, to see that the rules were strictly observed, to decide who came off conqueror,

to play, bidding its sounding numbers rise on high, with the touch of his skilful hand, while his voice poured forth in unison its hallowed song to Jehovah, his God.—The *Organ* seems to have consisted of several pipes made out of reeds, and having different sounds, which were passed back and forward under the mouth, and thus blown into so as to make music. It had, in its most perfect form, about seven of these pipes. The *Pipe* had some general resemblance to the flute, and was made in different forms. The *Horn*, made out of the horns of oxen or rams, was chiefly used in war: it is sometimes called a trumpet. There was, however, another *Trumpet*, formed of metal. The *Cymbal* consisted of two flat pieces of brass: the musician held one in each hand, and struck them together occasionally, with a ringing sound, as an accompaniment to other instruments. It is often seen in bands of military music in our own country. The *Tabret* was a round hoop of wood or brass, over which was tightly drawn a piece of skin, while a number of little bells were hung around to increase its noise. It was held in the left hand and beaten with the right. It is sometimes called a *Timbrel*. With such instruments in their hands, Miriam and others of the Israelitish women went forth, dancing and singing their song of triumph, after the awful miracle of the Red Sea. The women in the east, it is said, are accustomed to dance, in like manner, to the sound of tabrets, to this day.

The sacred music of the tabernacle and temple was conducted by the Levites. It consisted of psalms sung with the voice and various accompaniments of instrumental sound. It will come more properly under consideration, when we are brought to speak of the Sanctuary with its solemn service. The Jews had also their sacred *dances*, which were practised, as expressions of joy and thankfulness to God, in the celebration of their religious festivals, and on other occasions when his special goodness called for triumphant praise. The notes of the timbrel appear to have been generally employed to direct and regulate the dance. The company went forth, following one who acted as their leader, keeping time with the simple sounds of the music, in regular movements of the feet, and answering one another in songs framed to magnify the glory of Jehovah, Israel's God, by declaring his majesty, goodness, and power, and exciting the soul to love and joyful confidence in his name. This mode of showing religious joy was particularly practised by women. (Exodus xv. 20, Judges xxi. 21—23.) Men, however, not unfrequently danced before the Lord, in like manner. Thus King David leaped and danced, in company with others, before the ark; and so all the saints of God are called upon, with the voice of inspiration itself, to praise the Lord, according to the usage of the times, in the movements of the dance, with the music of timbrels, and harps, and organs, and cymbals sounding high. (Ps. cxlix. 3, cl. 4, 5.) Even when there was no regular dance, it was common to express joy by acts of leaping and skipping. (Luke vi. 23, Acts iii. 8.)

Dancing was employed, also, at times, to express gladness, on occasions of mere social and worldly rejoicing. As far back as the days of Job, rich and ungodly families had their music and dancing, without any respect to the worship of the Most High. (Job xxi. 11—15.) On occasions of national triumph, dances were sometimes led forth in honour of those whose bravery had been successful in war. (Judg. xi. 34, 1 Sam. xviii. 6, 7.) So, at seasons of mirth and joy on any account, they seem to have been not uncommon. (Jer. xxxi. 4, 13.) In the time of our Saviour, we learn from the parable of the prodigal son, that dancing was customary, in the celebration of domestic joy. (Luke xv. 25.) On Herod's birth-day, the daughter of Herodias danced before the company; no doubt, in conformity with what was often done on such occasions. We have no evidence that both sexes ever mingled together in the Jewish dance, unless it should be sought in the idolatrous confusion which reigned around the image of Egypt's deified calf, at the foot of Sinai. (Ex. xxxii. 6, 19.) In religious dances, they appear sometimes to have united in the same procession, but in *separate companies*. (Ps. lxviii. 25.)

SECTION III.

OF GAMES AND THEATRES.

In the time of our Saviour, the Greeks and Romans had various kinds of public exhibitions or shows, for the entertainment of all classes of people. The restless desire of interest and excitement which ever attends the lost condition of human nature on earth, in its ignorance of the TRUE GOOD, combined with its perverted and trifling taste, has led to the invention of such time-killing and sin-promoting amusements in every age, and, more or less, among every people. Barbarous or civilized, the disposition is the same, however much, in one case, the outward semblance of refinement may seem to surpass the rude, uncultivated style which is found in another. Cock-fights, Bull-baitings, Bear-hunts, Horse-races, shows of Jugglery and Legerdemain, and Theatric representations, are all indeed *different* modes of diversion, fashionable with *different* classes of society; but the taste which makes them acceptable is the same in all cases, confined only by circumstances to such particular forms as it may select, in any instance, for its gratification. The Jews, we may suppose, were not altogether without some such methods of finding diversion for their idle hours; but they seem to have prevailed to little extent among them, in comparison, with their customariness in other nations. The Greeks took the lead in multiplying public shows and giving them refinement and splendour. Long before the birth of Christ, they had their *Games* and their *Theatres*, brought to their highest state of perfection. Their Games especially were celebrated through the whole world; and, when their regular seasons came round, spectators came from distant countries, in every direction, to witness their exhibition. From them other nations borrowed much, in the plan of their similar entertainments. The Jews became acquainted with these exhibitions, after the success of the Grecian arms had carried their customs into Asia. In the time of Antiochus Epiphanes, the more licentious of the nation, who were inclined to adopt the manners of the heathen, endeavoured to introduce their games into Judea. Herod, something more than a hundred years after, with the same disposition to bring foreign usages into the country, builded at Jerusalem a Theatre and an Amphitheatre, and caused shows to be exhibited and games to be celebrated, after the manner of the Romans and in honour of the Emperor Augustus. The generality of the Jews, however, greatly disliked these steps, as being contrary to their religion, by reason of the idolatrous character which belonged to such amusements among the heathen.

There are, in the New Testament, several allusions to games which were so common in that age. These were and striking to all who read them, while the continu such sports, in different countries, rendered their min liar with the things to which they referred; but canno fully apprehended, without some explanation fro history.

GAMES.—There were, in ancient Greece, four pri brations of games, which returned at regular season held always in their fixed places, time after time. pic, which were the most important, and the P were celebrated every fifth year; the *Nemean* once in three years. The last were held near and to reward his victory with a crown of honour. On the race-ground, they had their seat raised near the goal or farthest extremity of the course, where they might impartially determine who reached the mark first. They were persons venerable for age, and respected for integrity of character. The contests were not carried on without considerable danger of wounds and bruises, and even death itself. The *boxers* were not satisfied with the mere weight of their fists, but had, besides, a piece of iron or lead, rolled up in a leather strap that was fastened round their right hands, which they employed to give destructive force to their blows. It was common, therefore, to spill much blood, to break bones, and to put limbs out of joint; and the man would have been deemed a pitiful fellow, who should have consented to resign the hope of victory without submitting first to such honourable injuries. The conqueror had his name proclaimed, by a public herald, amid resounding shouts from the vast assembly of spectators, and was immediately presented with his hard-earned *crown*. A branch of palm also was given him, to carry in his right hand as a sign of triumph. The crown was a thing of no value in itself, being composed merely of sprigs of palm, pine, laurel, or wild-olive, or stalks of common parsley; but, as the token of victory and honour, it was worn with the greatest pride; for the fortunate individual whose brow it encircled, became an object of admiration

to the whole assembly, and heard his name sounded with the most extravagant applause, upon every side. His native city or district of country exulted in the honour of its citizen, and took no small share of glory to itself, for having given birth to a personage so exceedingly worthy of universal esteem. To testify their proud satisfaction, he was lifted into a triumphal chariot, and conducted home with the greatest pomp. Instead of throwing open the gates of the town to bring him in, they chose to throw down a portion of the wall; as much as to say— " A city which contains within it such extraordinary excellence and courage as ours, may well do without walls altogether." If the parents of the hero were alive, they blessed the day which brought such a weight of honour to their house, and everybody was ready to congratulate their happy fortune in having the treasure of so prodigious a son. Peculiar privileges, different in different places, were granted him, to enjoy till the day of his death. Thus honourable was it, to obtain only one victory in these games : the man who came off conqueror in several of the contests, or in all, as was sometimes the case, was almost literally adored.

We have said that these exhibitions were provided to entertain the public taste. We must not, however, imagine that they had their origin, like our puppet-shows, in no other reason. In early times, strength and swiftness were the most important qualifications for a soldier. Gunpowder has, by its discovery, entirely changed this state of things. Exercises of the several kinds that have been mentioned, grew into fashion for the sake of cultivating these bodily perfections; and their great importance naturally caused them to be greatly honoured wherever they were found. Hence gradually arose the Grecian games. Religion, too, had a name in their institution; for they were all celebrated in honour of some false god or deified hero. Still, in their actual character, they derived their interest and encouragement from the mere gratification which their spectacle furnished, and the direct nourishment which they yielded to ambition and pride.

From the representation which has been given, it appears that the care and diligence which were required to secure a victory in these games, were of the highest kind. On this account, the apostle more than once compares the Christian life to such a contest, and so most impressively exhorts those who are engaged in its trial, to give all diligence to make their success sure, while he places before their eyes, for their encouragement, the crown of glory which the righteous Judge will give them, if they continue faithful to the end. " Know ye not," he exclaims, " that they who *run in a race*, run all, but one receiveth the prize ? So run, that ye may obtain. And every man that *striveth for mastery*, is *temperate in all things*. Now, they do it to obtain a *corruptible crown;* but we, an *incorruptible*. I therefore so run, not as uncertainly ; so fight I, not as one that beateth the air : but I keep under my body, and bring it into subjection, lest that, by any means, when I have preached to others, (or proclaimed like a *herald,*) I myself should be a castaway," (or, rejected person;) that is, should fail in securing the approbation of the *Judge,* and so, of course, come short of all reward. (1 Cor. ix. 24—27.) The Corinthians, who had the Isthmian games celebrated but a little distance from their city, could not but feel the impressive force of such an exhortation. In similar style he addresses the Hebrews: "Wherefore, seeing we are compassed about with *so great a cloud of witnesses, let us lay aside every weight, and the sin which doth so easily beset us*, and let us run with patience *the race that is set before us*, looking unto Jesus, the Author and Finisher of our faith, who *for the joy that was set before him*, endured the cross, despising the shame, and is set down at the right hand of God. For consider him that endured such contradiction of sinners against himself, lest ye be *weary* and *faint in your minds.*" (Heb. xii. 1—3.) In this passage, all the saints who have gone before, are represented as looking down upon Christians, as they struggle through their earthly trials, with the interest of friendly spectators. Their presence and example should quicken their zeal; but above all should the pattern of Jesus, who himself has led the way to the reward of glory, through conflicts far surpassing all that his followers can know, animate and encourage their hearts. Timothy is admonished to be faithful, by an allusion drawn from the same quarter: "If a man strive for masteries, yet is he not *crowned*, except he strive *lawfully.*" (2 Tim. ii. 5.) The apostle likens himself to a racer straining every nerve to win the prize. He did not consider his work to be over, on this side of eternity, but continually strove to get forward, with all his might: "Brethren, I count not myself to have apprehended: but this one thing I do; forgetting those things which are behind, and *reaching forth* unto those things which are before, *I press toward the mark for the prize* of the high calling of God in Christ Jesus." (Phil. iii. 12—14.) It was not till near the close of his life, when he considered the time of his departure to be just at hand, that he allowed himself to say: "I have *fought a good fight;* I have *finished my course;* I have kept the faith. Henceforth there is laid up for me a *crown* of righteousness, which the Lord, the *righteous Judge*, shall give me at that day." (2 Tim. iv. 6—8.) This crown, unlike the frail chaplets which were given in the games, *fadeth not away.*" (1 Pet. v. 4, i. 4.)

From the circumstance that a branch of palm carried in tne right hand was a token of victory, in the celebration of these contests, we may understand that image in the vision of the apostle John: "I beheld, and lo, a great multitude, which no man could number, of all nations, and kindreds, and people, and tongues, stood before the throne and before the Lamb, clothed in white robes, and *palms in their hands.*" (Rev. vii. 9.) So thoroughly, indeed, has the emblematic meaning thus attached to the palm, established itself in human ..., ... to this day, in our own as in many other languages, ... is used to signify *victory*, without any thought of its figurative application; and the phrase, *to bear the palm*, or ... ... *palm*, is everywhere common.

THEATRES.—The theatre of ancient times was built in the form of a half-circle, with seats rising one above another round the inside of the wall. Sometimes the building was made, as it were, double, with an oval shape; then it was called an *Amphitheatre*. They were left open at the top, or only covered with cloth of some close kind, to keep off the sun or lighter showers of rain. Various exhibitions were displayed in the centre. Plays were acted here, for the entertainment of the fashionable multitude. Among the Romans, sports of various kinds were also exhibited. One amusement in which that refined people greatly delighted, was the deadly sword-fight between gladiators. These were persons trained to the use of the sword for the express purpose of gratifying the public taste, or their own pride, by such bloody spectacles. Captives, and slaves, and condemned malefactors, were the only gladiators at first; but, in time, free-born citizens, induced by hire, or by the vain imagination of glory to be acquired in such an exhibition, presented themselves in the disgraceful scene of battle. Another show, common in the Roman amphitheatres, was the *Fight with wild beasts*, which condemned persons were often compelled to endure, by way of capital punishment. Amid the mockery of unfeeling spectators crowded around, the wretch on whom the sentence of the law had fallen, was brought into the open space in the middle. Then a lion, or tiger, or bear, or some equally terrible animal, was let loose upon him, and excited to attack him with the greatest fury. To such cruel exposures in the theatres, the apostle seems to allude, when he speaks of Christians being made a *gazing stock*, or *theatrical show*, in their fight of affliction, from the enemies of the truth. (Heb. x. 32, 33.) In another place, we hear him saying: "After the manner of men, I have fought with beasts at Ephesus," (1 Cor. xv. 32;) where he means, either that he had literally been condemned to this punishment, in the Ephesian theatre, or that he had been called to struggle in that city with angry, violent, and powerful enemies, who assaulted him like wild beasts; as David calls such *dogs* and *lions*, in the book of Psalms. Some who fought with beasts were allowed to have armour of some sort, to defend themselves, and to give them some chance of killing the animal; while others were exposed quite naked, and without any weapon. These last were devoted to destruction, without any possibility of escape; for if they came off with life in one conflict, it was only to be slaughtered in another. In the exhibition, those of the former class were brought out first, in the early part of the day; those from whom all favour was cut off, were reserved till afterward, and produced upon the stage last. To this circumstance Paul appears to refer, in describing the great trials of himself and his fellow apostles: "I think that God hath set forth us the apostles *last*, as it were, *appointed unto death;* for we are made a *spectacle* to the world, and to angels, and to men." (1 Cor. iv. 9.) The theatre was also a place in which it was common for assemblies of the people to be held, when they met to deliberate on public business. (Acts xix. 29.)

SECTION IV.

MODES OF DIVIDING AND RECKONING TIME.

DAYS.—The Jews reckoned their *Days* from evening to evening, according to the order which is mentioned in the first chapter of Genesis, in the account of the work of creation: "The evening and the morning were *the first day.*" Their Sabbath, therefore, or seventh day, began at sunset on the day we call Friday, and lasted till the same time on the day following. When our Saviour was in Capernaum, it was thought wrong to bring the sick to him to be healed, while the Sabbath lasted; but "*at even, when the sun did set,* they brought unto him all that were diseased, and them that were possessed with devils: and all the city was gathered together at the door." (Mark i. 21—35.) This manner of giving the night the first place in the reckoning of days, has been found among several other nations. The custom in such cases, was, no doubt, handed down from the practice of the most early times, founded upon the original order, in which evening was made to exist before any morning had been; and thus the account of the Bible is confirmed, in this case, as in many others, by the voice of heathen tradition.

HOURS.—The time between the rising and the setting of the sun was divided into twelve equal parts, which were called *hours.* (John xi. 9.) As this period of time, however, is longer at one season of the year than at another, it is plain that the hours also would be of different length, at different times. In winter, they were, of course, shorter than in summer. They were numbered from the rising of the sun, and not from the middle of the day, as is common with us. Thus the hour of noon, which we call the *twelfth*, the Jews reckoned the *sixth* hour; while the twelfth hour with them was just at sunset. When the days and nights were just equal, their hours would be exactly equal to those we use now, and would begin to be counted precisely from our six o'clock in the morning: then their *first* hour would be our *seven* o'clock; their *third*, our *nine* o'clock; their *ninth*, our *three* o'clock in the afternoon; and so of the other numbers in their order. But in the middle of summer, when the days are longest, and the sun in that country rises about five and sets about seven of our time, it is evident that each Jewish hour would be longer than one of ours, and that no one of them could answer exactly to any one of ours, except the sixth, or twelve o'clock: their third hour would come a short time *before* our nine, and their ninth, a short time *after* our three. So in the middle of winter, when the sun rises there about seven and sets about five of our time, the Jewish hour would be as much shorter; and then their third hour would come a short time *after* our nine, and their ninth, a short time *before* our three. (Matt. xx. 1—12.) The dreadful darkness that covered the whole land when Christ was crucified, began precisely in the middle of the day. (Matt. xxvii. 45.)

Hours are not mentioned till after the captivity; it is reasonable, therefore, to suppose that the Jews borrowed this mode of dividing time from the Chaldeans, from whom also it passed to the Greeks and Romans. In more ancient times, the day seems to have been divided merely into four general parts, according to the position of the sun in the heavens. Hence, the notices of its earlier or later periods are expressed only in general terms; such as the *morning*, the *heat of the day*, *mid-day* or *noon*, the *cool of the day*, and the *evening*. It appears, however, that some advancement toward a more regular and artificial division was made before the captivity, as we read of a *sun-dial* which belonged to king Ahaz. (2 Kings xx. 11.) Perhaps it was brought from Babylon, (where such instruments appear to have been first used,) as a curious ornament and convenience for royal use, and so was carefully preserved for many years. The word *hour* sometimes signifies, in Scripture, any determinate and fixed season or opportunity; as in those expressions: "My *hour* is not yet come;" "This is your *hour* and the power of darkness," "The *hour* is coming, and now is;" and in others of like kind.

The evening consisted of two parts. The first commenced some time before sun-set, perhaps as early as the ninth hour the second, about the going down of the sun. The lamb of the passover, and the lamb of the daily evening sacrifice were required to be killed *between* these two evenings.

WATCHES.—Before the captivity, the night was divided into three parts, called *watches*, because they were severally the periods of time which watchmen were required to spend in their nightly service, before they could retire from their posts. They were named the *first*, the *middle*, and the *morning* watch. In the time of Christ, the Roman and Greek method of dividing the night into *four* watches was in use among the Jews. It was also, like the day, measured into twelve equal hours, from sunset to sunrise. The first watch, or *evening*, lasted till about nine o'clock of our time; the second, or *midnight*, from nine to twelve; the third, or *cock-crowing*, from twelve to three; the fourth, or *morning*, from three till it was day. All of them are mentioned in our Saviour's exhortation: "Watch! for ye know not when the master of the house cometh; at *even*, or at *midnight*, or at the *cock-crowing*, or in the *morning*." (Mark. xiii. 35.) The Jews were accustomed to distinguish the last-mentioned period into the *first*, the *second*, and the *third* crowing. Thus it is foretold of Peter: "Before the cock crow *twice*, thou shalt deny me thrice," (Mark xiv. 30;) even as it accordingly happened: the cock crew directly after his first denial, and then crew a second time after the third. The other evangelists write: "*before* the cock crow," or, "the cock shall *not* crow, till thou hast denied me thrice." They referred to the whole time of cock-crowing; meaning that this should not be over before this melancholy fall would all take place, as it did in fact before it was half over. Or, it may have been so said, because the second crowing was the one principally regarded in the course of that watch, and so was readily understood to be meant, when one only, by way of distinction, was mentioned.

THE WEEK.—The *week* had its origin with the commencement of time; when, after six days employed in the work of creation, God rested on the seventh, and blessed it, and set it apart to be continually observed as a day of holy rest, and a sacred memorial of that great event. We find, in the account of the flood, that it had continued in use down to that age, and so was a measure of time familiar to Noah. (Gen. vii. 4—10, viii. 10, 12.) After the flood, it was handed down by the sons of Noah to their descendants. In this way it has happened, that some traces of the ancient *week* are to be found in every quarter of the world. Nations the most distant from each other, and of every character, have united in giving testimony to the truth of the Bible account; either by retaining, in their common reckoning of time, the regular division of seven days, or at least, by showing such regard to that definite period, as can in no way be accounted for, if it was not received by tradition from the earliest ages. Not only has this been the case, in all the countries of the East, such as Egypt, Arabia, Assyria, India, China, and others; but among the most ancient people of Europe also, the Greeks, the Romans, the Gauls, the Germans, the Britons, and the several nations of the north,—and this, long before they had any knowledge of Christianity, as is evident from the *names* of the days found in use among them, which were all of idolatrous origin. Even among the uncultivated tribes of Africa, travellers have met with the same division of time. It is not only, however, by retaining the number of days which compose a week, that the tradition of the world so evidently confirms the account of Moses; the testimony is rendered still more striking, by the very general idea of some peculiar *sacredness* belonging to the seventh day, which has existed in every age. The week, it must be remembered, is not a *natural* period of time, like a *day*, a *month*, or a *year*, which are all suggested by the revolutions of the heavenly bodies, and so naturally come into use among every people; there is no reason in the nature of things, why days should be counted by *sevens*, rather than by *eights*, *tens*, or any other number. The division, therefore, wherever found, must have had its origin in arbitrary appointment. To imagine, that all the nations of the world united in forming the *same* arbitrary appointment, by mere chance, would be ridiculous. Nothing but the authority of the original appointment made by God himself, can be admitted as a sufficient cause for such a fact.

The Jews had not particular names for the first six days of the week, but distinguished them merely by their order; thus, what we now call *Sunday* was termed the *first day* of the week, *Monday* was the *second*, *Tuesday* the third, and so of the rest. The seventh day, which we name *Saturday*, was styled among them the *Sabbath*, that is, the day of *rest*. And because this was the most important day of all in the week, the whole week came to be called, from its name, a *Sabbath;* whence the other days were called also the first day of the Sabbath, the second day of the Sabbath, and so on in their order. The day before the Sabbath, (our Friday,) because part of it was employed in making ready for the sacred *rest* of the Sabbath, was called, in later times, the *preparation*. (Mark xv. 42.) In addition to the week of *days*, the law appointed a week of *years*, making every seventh year *Sabbatical*, or a season of rest from cultivation, to the whole land. After counting again, *seven* of these weeks of years, the fiftieth year was set apart as the great *Jubilee.*

MONTHS.—The Jewish *months,* like those of all other ancient nations, were *lunar,* measured from one new moon to another. In the age of Noah, each month consisted of thirty days, as may be determined from the several notices of time in the history of the flood. The Jews, however, after their settlement in Canaan, seem to have reckoned each month from the first *appearance* of each new moon, without regard to any fixed number of days; only, if the new moon was not seen at the end of *thirty days,* they would not continue the old month any longer by waiting for it, but the next morning began a new one, because they were certain, in that case, that clouds or some other cause had hindered the moon's appearance after the actual time of her change. While, therefore, the longest months consisted of thirty days only, others would have no more than twenty-nine, and sometimes but twenty-eight, according as the moon was discovered sooner or later at different times. That the moon might be seen as early as possible, it is said that persons were appointed to watch, about the time it was expected, on the tops of the mountains; who, as soon as they saw its light, gave notice, when it was proclaimed to the people by the sounding of trumpets, and by lighting fires on high, which rapidly carried the news through the land. Each new moon was, in some measure, a holy day; for although any kind of business might be attended to, it was honoured with peculiar offerings, and ceremonies at the sanctuary. (Num. xxviii. 11—15.) It was observed also with particular respect, throughout the country, as a season of religious joy. (1 Sam. xx. 5, 6, 24—29, 2 Kings iv. 23, Isa. i. 13, 14, Amos viii. 5, Coloss. ii. 16.) Hence arose the necessity of carefully marking the first day of every month, and causing it to be published among the people. Originally, months had no particular names, but, like the days of the week, were distinguished merely by their numerical order; thus they were called the *first* month, the *second,* the *third,* and so on to the last. In the time of Moses, the first month was called *Abib,* that is, "the month of *new fruits,* or *young ears of corn."* The others continued still without names. In the age of Solomon, we find three other names in use, viz. *Zif, Bul,* and *Ethanim.* Whence these names came, cannot be certainly known; they were probably borrowed from some foreign calendar. We hear nothing of them afterward. From the time of the captivity, *all* the months were called by the names which the Chaldeans and Persians were accustomed to use.

The Year.—The common *Year* was made up of twelve of these months. Lunar months, however, it is well known, will not exactly measure a true year according to the sun. Twelve such months are nearly eleven days less time than such a year. Of course, if the year of any people was always counted by that number, and no more, it would begin every time nearly eleven days sooner than before; and thus, it would run backward till, in no great while, its first month would be found where it started, after having gone round all the seasons and so got a whole twelve-month out of its place. In this way, most of the Mohammedans are accustomed to reckon their years. But such a method is extremely inconvenient. To regulate their year therefore, and keep it near its right place, the Jews added, when it seemed to be necessary, a whole month to its common length. This must have been done, once in three years at most, and sometimes once in two. Attention to this important matter was continually secured, by the manner in which the yearly times of the sacred *festivals* were appointed. While these were fixed, each to its certain month in the year, they were also closely connected with particular *seasons;* so that the festivals would have come altogether out of place, if their months had been allowed to move like those of the Mohammedans, to any extent. The feast of the *passover*, for instance, was to be kept from the fifteenth to the twenty-first day of the first month; at the same time, it was required that a sheaf of barley should be offered before the Lord, on the second day of its celebration, as the *first-fruits* of the new harvest and a sign of *its* commencement. Thus there was a necessity, that the middle of the first month should always come as near as possible to the time when the grain began to be ripe. If, therefore, at the end of twelve months, it appeared that the middle of the next month would come *before* that time, so that a sheaf of ripe barley could not by any means be gathered for the passover, the priests would be reminded, and, in a measure, compelled to add that month also to the old year, and to put off the beginning of the new one till another new moon. In this way, the year, though measured by the changes of the moon, was kept in tolerable conformity with the true natural year, which depends upon the sun. It *might* begin, some one spring almost a month from the time it began some other spring; in such cases, however, it would never, if properly managed. vary more than two weeks from the true year, being in the one instance, only that much too *fast*, and in the other, only that much too *slow*. Generally, the variation from the correct time would be considerably less.

The year was divided into six seasons, each consisting of two months. Some account of these has already been given, in speaking of the *climate* of Palestine. There were, among the Jews, two points from which the months of the year were counted. Their *sacred* year was reckoned from the month *Nisan*, or the ancient Abib, because on the fifteenth day of that month they had departed out of Egypt; God himself, on that occasion, appointed it to be the beginning of the Israelitish year. (Ex. xii. 2.) The sacred feasts were determined by this reckoning, and the prophets made use of it, in dating their visions. The *civil* year, which was the most ancient, was reckoned from the month *Tisri*, just six months after the beginning of the other. It was an old tradition, that the creation of the world took place at that time. By the reckoning of this year, contracts, births, reigns of kings, and other such matters, were dated. The month *Nisan*, with which the sacred year began, commenced with the new moon that appeared immediately before harvest. This would take place generally in April of our time; but when the new moon of April would not occur till late in the month, the preceding one, which appeared toward the end of March, was made, we may conclude, the commencing point of the sacred year. Thus, it was so managed that the passover fell always not far from the middle of April, which was about the time that the grain became ready for harvest. The month *Tisri* began of course with the sixth new moon after that of Nisan, which would cause it to fall principally, sometimes more and sometimes less, in the time of our October. The names and order of the Jewish months, after the captivity, were as follows, commencing with Nisan, the first of the sacred year. 1. NISAN. 2. ZIF. 3. SIVAN. 4. TAMMUZ. 5. AB. 6. ELUL. 7. TISRI, or ETHANIM. 8. BUL. 9. CHISLEU. 10. TEBETH. 11. SHEBAT. 12. ADAR. When it was necessary to add a thirteenth month, it was called VEADAR, which means the second Adar.

In counting time, the Jews were accustomed to reckon any *part* of a certain period for the whole. Thus in Scripture we sometimes find a *part of a year* counted as if it were a whole one, and so also *a part of a day*. Thus a child was said to be circumcised when it was *eight* days old, though according to the law this was to take place *upon the eighth* day. (Lev. xii. 3, Luke ii. 21.) If a child was born in the last hour of the day, that hour was counted as a whole day, and his circumcision might take place any time upon the eighth day from that. It is in this way we are to reckon the time, when we are told that our Lord rose *three days after* his death, and that he was *three days and three nights* in the heart of the earth (Mark viii. 31, Matt. xii. 40.) He was crucified on the afternoon of Friday, which was therefore reckoned the *first day* of his death; Saturday, during all of which he lay in the sepulchre, was the *second:* when the first day of the week commenced, on the evening of Saturday, he was still under the power of death, and did not break its bands till about sunrise on Sunday morning; so that it was the *third* day when he rose. Thus, according to the Jewish way of counting, he was in the sepulchre *three days*.

CHAPTER IX.

POLITICAL INSTITUTIONS.

SECTION I.

PATRIARCHAL GOVERNMENT.

The first form of government was what has been called the *Patriarchal*. This arose naturally from the authority of parents over their children. The father was considered the proper ruler of his own family, as long as he lived. His authority rested upon his children, even after they were grown up and had formed new families of their own. His descendants around him were taught to look up to him as their supreme *head*, both religious and civil. When the father died, each one became the proper independent ruler of that branch of the general family which was descended from himself. But it was not natural for kindred families to break off all social connection; especially in early times, when the feeling of relationship was greatly cherished, and carried its powerful sympathy far out with the most distant flowings of kindred blood. They did not therefore generally choose to separate into entirely distinct societies. While the father of each house continued to be the head of all his own descendants, it was agreed to have all the families still united under the authority of another *common* head. The first-born seems originally to have been always the person who was honoured with this dignity. From various causes, however, the union of families in this way would not long continue to hold all together Men, on some account, would be led to move off from the society of their relations, and form new similar patriarchal establishments in other places. As societies became very large too, the bond of connection could not but become less secure. Jealousies and difficulties between the several branches would naturally arise. At length they would fall asunder into separate independent communities.

The union of kindred families under one head arose at first out of natural affection, rather than from any policy. They considered themselves one people, because they were of one blood. Any *general* government which was wanted to bind them together was very small. The head of each separate house directed all its concerns, and in this way it was not hard for a simple people, while not yet very numerous, to live connected together as one general society, with but little other control. The control of the common head, therefore, was not exercised with much actual command over the general body He was honoured merely as the central point, around which the connection clustered. He was the natural representative of its kindred whole. Such was held to be the relation which the eldest born sustained by his birth to the rest of the family. He enjoyed on this account peculiar respect and veneration

His counsel was sought. His advice carried decisive weight. But a prince-like sovereignty, as the general interests did not need it, he was not expected to exercise.

Before long, however, as separate communities gained strength, and bad men became heads of independent families, injustice, violence and war made their appearance. Then there arose a new motive for union. Related families were led by policy, as well as by friendship, to keep together; that by united strength they might defend themselves from plundering enemies, or that they might be the better able, where such a disposition was felt, to do violence on the rights of others. Hence also the central head of their connection naturally came to exercise a more active authority. A society that needed little general government in times of peace, could not get along without a good degree of it, when called to take any thing of a warlike character, in the way either of violence or of mere defence. When war and oppression became common, new ways also of enlarging societies grew into fashion. The weak were sometimes compelled by force to submit to the strong, and to add yet more to their strength by serving them. And sometimes, to avoid this fate, they of their own accord put themselves under the authority of some neighbour more powerful than themselves, and became his willing servants in order to enjoy his protection. The custom of buying servants also came into use, in consequence of the violence which began to prevail in the world. Those who were taken captive in war were considered the property of their conquerors, and were often sold for money.

In some such way as this, things seem to have proceeded after the flood; and though we know exceeding little of the history of earlier times after the fall, the general manner of society then was no doubt in this respect after the same fashion. Men lived so long then, that the patriarchal government might have been continued without any trouble. It might have been expected that the whole family of man would have been held together in one friendly society while its generations were so near to the original common head. But *sin* hindered the natural union. Cain went off very early from the rest of his father's family, under the curse of Heaven, and established a new community. Afterwards, as the ungodly part of the world increased far above the pious, they seem to have been split asunder into various petty societies. Great violence grew common among them. (Gen. vi. 11.) Many men distinguished themselves by daring boldness and terrible valour, in committing outrage upon others. They filled the earth, as far as it was then peopled, with war, bloodshed and oppression. Thus they got to themselves a great name in those times, as many by the mere greatness of their violence and butchery of human life have done since. They were celebrated and feared for their wonderful strength, and spoken of as *giants, mighty men, men of renown.* (Gen. vi. 4.) Slavery was one of the evils which sprung out of these wars and fightings, as we may learn from the fact that it was a thing well known to Noah. (Gen. ix. 25—27.)

The descendants of Noah, after the confusion of tongues at Babel, separated into different parts of the world, and formed different patriarchal societies. In a short time, some of them began to take a more regular and settled form of government. The authority of the common head glided into the formal sovereignty of a *king*. Some kingdoms arose in an orderly way; others were established by violence. People that followed agriculture to some considerable extent were brought into the form of regular kingdoms sooner than those who made it their chief business to keep herds and flocks. Among these last, the more simple patriarchal government was naturally cherished, as being suited to their manner of life, and sufficient for all its wants. Even when their societies took the name of kingdoms, and their heads were called kings, they were often in fact only patriarchal establishments still. They consisted generally of several separate tribes or families, descended from a common ancestor, connected together as one people, while yet each had its own particular head who ruled it with a kind of sovereign authority. These heads, under the general head or *king*, were the *princes* of the nation. Sometimes, there was no general head at all, but the prince of each tribe was in every respect an independent monarch, while yet all were classed together as one people, and had a general name in common.

When compared with the kingdoms that have since been in the world, most of those which received the name in these early times were very small. Sometimes a single city, with the neighbouring country a little distance round it, formed such a kingdom. Hence, though the whole land of Canaan embraced not near as much country as some of our single states, we find it contained a large number of independent governments of this sort. The Israelites under Joshua, we are told, smote no less than thirty and one kings, all of that country, when they took possession of the land. (Josh. xii. 7—24.) Abraham did not hesitate, with three hundred and eighteen servants, to pursue after Chedorlaomer and the kings that were with him, after they had subdued several kingdoms. (Gen. xiv.) He was himself, in every respect, an independent sovereign in the country, and his vast family of servants formed a little kingdom around him. He was even considered a *mighty prince* among the inhabitants of the land. (Gen. xxiii. 6.) Such, also, Isaac was held to be. The king of Gerar said unto him, "Go from us, for thou art much mightier than we!" (Gen. xxvi. 16.) Soon, however, some nations began to show a much larger appearance. They grew to be great and strong. This tended gradually to put an end to such very small kingdoms. They could not stand alone, when powerful empires were rising in the earth. Yet there were always in the East, some who never could be brought to forsake the simple manner of government which prevailed among their ancestors. They remained independent tribes, each ruled by its own head with sovereign power, and forming, in reality, a little government by itself, though many of them might be classed together as one general people, and might consider themselves such by reason of their common origin. These were such as dwelt in the wilderness, moving through it with unsettled habitation, and bidding defiance to the mightiest monarchs of the earth in the midst of its safe and broad retreat. They are found there in the same independent condition to this day.

SECTION II.

GENERAL MANNER OF THE ANCIENT ISRAELITISH GOVERNMENT.

Amid the nations of the earth in ancient times, the Jews were a peculiar people. Not only their religion, but their government also, was established by divine authority. The principles according to which it was to proceed, were solemnly settled by God himself, after their deliverance from the bondage of Egypt.

Before that time, the simple, original patriarchal manner of government had prevailed among them. They were separated into tribes, and these again into various branches or families, according to their generations. Each great family had its *head*, and each tribe its *prince*, chosen out of the several heads of the families it contained. These were called the *elders of Israel*. This general plan of having the nation divided into tribes and families, with particular heads appointed over them, was not given up when the government of the nation was regulated with new authority afterwards. On the contrary, it was sanctioned by the Most High, and secured by the system of laws which he published through his servant Moses. There was, as we shall soon see, a wise reason in the general design of God for keeping the whole people thus separated into its several branches, from age to age.

The common natural object of government is to promote the happiness and comfort of men in society, by securing to them life, liberty, property and peace, and assisting their improvement in knowledge and every useful art. Considered in this light, it is a most merciful appointment of God, though often abused by the wickedness of men, like other good gifts of Heaven, and turned into an instrument of oppression and evil. But the Jewish government was formed peculiarly with a view to answer another great end. While it was so arranged as to be suited well to the proper design of other governments, its particular frame was organized and adjusted by the Almighty with special reference to the interests of his *church*. God chose the Jewish people out of the nations of the earth, to be his visible church, to maintain his worship, and to preserve the true religion in the midst of an idolatrous world, till the fulness of time appointed for the coming of Christ. This was the great design of their separation, and their civil, as well as their religious state, was ordered with a peculiar regard to the securing of it. The one was made to agree with and assist the other in promoting the same high purpose. The *kingdom*, therefore, was intimately connected with the *church*. They were made up of the same society; to belong to the one, was to belong to the other, and to be cast out of the one, was to lose at the same time the privileges of the other. God was, in a special and direct way, concerned with the institution and order of each. The two were blended closely together, so as to make one complex system. The laws which were made for the government of the nation were associated with those which regarded directly the interests of religion, in such a manner as to form together a single plan, wisely arranged for that most excellent end which has been mentioned. The Israelitish commonwealth was organized and established by divine care, merely that it might be a sort of outward frame for the preservation of the Israelitish church. Although, therefore, the laws and institutions given by the Lord to the Jewish people are properly distinguished into two general classes, such as relate to religion, and such as relate to civil society, a religious design, nevertheless, may be discovered in some measure running through all; and the reason of most of the peculiar features which civil society was made to bear, is to be sought in their relation to religion, rather than in any mere political purpose.

The whole system of government aimed to secure the worship of the only true God, and to preserve his truth from corruption. It was formed therefore in such a way as to be a strong barrier against all idolatry, and in such a way as was likely to render it *lasting* as well as *effectual*. Its laws, while they were adapted to secure the temporal peace and prosperity of the people, and to perpetuate the kingdom for many ages, were framed in the most wise manner for shutting out every form of false religion and maintaining the worship of the one God that created heaven and earth.

As a first grand measure for securing the end which he had in view, God offered himself to be the *king* of the nation. While he was the supreme ruler of all the earth, he proposed to take that favoured people, to be *a peculiar treasure* unto him *above all people*, and to govern them himself with a special care as their Lawgiver and Sovereign. By a most solemn covenant at Mount Sinai, they agreed to receive him as such, and to be governed entirely by him, not only as a *church*, but also as a *holy nation*. (Ex. xix. 3—8.) In this character he afterwards gave laws. decided important questions of duty, threatened punishment and caused them to be executed, and provided ways in which he might be at any time consulted in cases of difficulty or doubt. He interposed continually with his authority in the affairs of the nation, making known his will and reproving what was wrong in the measures of the kingdom, by his appointed messengers; and oftentimes putting forth his sovereign power, to control or correct those measures, by means of his almighty *providence*, in such a way as was not used with other people. The form of government under him was allowed to vary, but his special sovereignty was still maintained. Moses was his servant, who published his laws, and under his continual direction led the nation from Egypt to the borders of Canaan. Joshua, under the same direction, was made its commander in chief, to conduct the people into the promised land, and to lead them in their battles till they got possession of it. Afterwards, at various times, extraordinary *Judges* were raised up to govern. They were intrusted with great power, and regarded with much honour; but they were only officers acting for God, as he called them one after another, from time to time, into service. At length, in the latter part of Samuel's life, the people demanded a king, such as other nations had, to judge them. God commanded the prophets to reprove them, as having sinned against him by this demand. "They have rejected me," he declared, "that I should not reign over them." Yet he suffered them to have their desire. (1 Sam. viii. 5—22, xii. 12.) Still, however, he did not withdraw himself from the supreme direction of the kingdom. (1 Sam. xii. 16—22.) He pointed out the king who should be chosen, and required him to rule the nation with continual regard to divine direction. Because Saul refused to obey, the kingdom was taken from him and given to David. By his prophets the Lord continued to direct and reprove the proceedings of government, and from time to time he punished obstinate resistance to his will, by calamities sent in his righteous providence for that express end. Thus king and people were made to remember and feel that God was the proper sovereign of the nation. At last, by way of severe punishment, he sent them into captivity; yet he soon brought them back again, and established them under his care, once more, in their own land. There, though his immediate direction by means of his prophets was in a short time withheld, he still watched over their affairs with a peculiar and continual providence, afflicting sorely for sin, and yet preserving the nation from ruin with great deliverances, till the great end of their separation from the rest of the world was answered fully, with the introduction of a new and better covenant by the Lord Jesus Christ. (Heb. viii. 6—13.) Then he cast them off; and for their dreadful guilt, scattered them "among all people, from the one end of the earth even unto the other," as they are found to this day. (Deut. xxviii. 64.)

God being properly the king of the nation, the people were placed under a two-fold obligation to honour him, and to observe that religion which he appointed. As the Lord of heaven and of earth, their Maker, they were bound to obey him in all things, and to delight in his service; but besides this, they were bound to yield obedience and homage to him as their national monarch. All such general duties as subjects in all kingdoms owe to their king, were, among the Israelites, due to God. Thus, the claims of religion at once became also claims of government, and the good order of the state was, in its nature, essentially blended with the good order of the church. Regard to the principles and institutions of the true religion could not be dispensed with, without unfaithfulness and insult to the sovereign of the kingdom, as well as to the infinite and eternal Ruler of the universe. Such neglect, therefore, called for punishment as a *civil* offence, as well as exposed to the anger of Heaven, in its character of a *religious* one. Idolatry was not only *impiety*, as a departure from the true God, but *treason* also, as it set itself directly in opposition to the authority and honour of the king. The whole law of the kingdom, therefore, exerted its utmost force to prevent it, and to punish it, when it did appear under any form, with the most extreme severity. In corrupt times, indeed, it prevailed, notwithstanding, in the land; but it was because there was no faithfulness among those whose duty it was to maintain the principles of the government; they were all, in such cases, trampled under foot.

The evil of idolatry was guarded against in two general ways; by regulations *directly* opposing its errors and *directly* enforcing the principles of the true religion, and also by regulations that tended *indirectly* to the same end, by hindering, as far as possible, all free and general intercourse with idolatrous nations. Idolatry reigned through the world, and the Jews discovered themselves ever ready to be carried away by its temptations. There was need, therefore, of a bulwark doubly secured, to keep that single people, for hundreds of years, safe from its total desolation.

How strongly every thing opposed to the worship of the one only living and true God was directly and positively forbidden, and what severe punishments were decreed against all such offences; and how solemnly the several duties of obedience to that God, and regard to his appointed worship were required to be observed, it is needless to say. The law was full of ex press precepts of this sort. It set itself not only against every actual idolatrous practice, but also against the use of customs in any way that were connected with idolatry among the heathen; lest by any means such customs might prove an enticement to lead men into the evil with which they were commonly joined. Thus it was forbidden to plant a grove of any trees near the altar of the Lord; to round the corners of the head, or to mar the corners of the beard; to make baldness between the eyes for the dead, &c. These were customs connected with idolatry. Thus, there is reason to believe, a number of particular laws had a special reference to superstitious and idolatrous usages that were common among other people at that time. Some that now seem strange and difficult to explain, probably had much of their meaning and design in a regard to usages of this sort, which they were made to prevent.

It was altogether necessary, however, in order to secure the end in view, that, in addition to all the care of direct and positive laws, the people should be kept as much as possible separate from all other nations. Evil communications always tend to corrupt good manners; and the Israelites for a long time showed themselves very prone to be spoiled by the smallest intercourse with their idolatrous neighbours. It was, therefore, a wise and merciful arrangement in the general plan of their government, to cut them off, by every means, from such familiar intercourse, and to make them a people *dwelling alone*, and "not reckoned among the nations." (Num. xxiii. 9.)

For this end, they were settled in the land of Canaan; a country not large enough to invite or to allow other people from abroad to come and dwell among them; yet sufficient in all respects for their support, and abounding with the most excellent natural advantages. (Lev. xx. 24, 26.) They were required to drive out or destroy all the idolatrous Canaanites, that they might not be a snare to lead them into sin. The destruction of that race was called down upon them by their sins. The measure of their iniquity was full, and the Israelites were commanded to destroy them without mercy. Without a command from God, they would have had no right to attack them in this way; because it is not for men to decide when and how the anger of God, in such cases, calls for the execution of punishment. But when the command is given, it would be sin not to obey. The will of God is the best reason in the world for whatever measure it demands. He may use whatever means to himself seem best, to accomplish his righteous purposes. He had as much right to send the Israelites to destroy cities, men, women, and children, as to send upon them the same destruction by means of a famine, a pestilence, or an earthquake. There was not, therefore, any thing to be blamed, in the severe treatment of the Canaanites. It was the work of God, the Judge of the whole earth, performed by such instrumentality as he saw fit solemnly to employ.

While care was taken to root out these wicked nations, the Jews were forbidden, also, to make marriages with idolaters. "Thy daughter," says the law, "thou shalt not give unto his son, nor his daughter shalt thou take unto thy son; for they will turn away thy son from following me, that he may serve other gods." (Deut. vii. 3, 4.) Again; no encouragement was given to commerce. The manner in which the state was arranged, tended to hinder it. The law which forbade the taking of interest for money lent, which under any form is called *usury* in the Old Testament, implied that commerce was not to be pursued, and served to prevent it. Where there is no interest lawful on money, merchants cannot thrive. Thus, while the Tyrians, just above them, were the most commercial people in the world, and carried on a traffic with almost every nation, the Israelites, though their country was bordered all along on one side by the sea, for a long time had nothing to do with this business at all, and never were brought, for any considerable period, to engage in it, except to a small extent. In this way they were greatly preserved from intercourse with strangers, and the introduction of strange fashions and notions. They were a nation of farmers. There was made a *necessity* that they should be such, in the way the land was divided.

By the direction of God, the whole land was regularly divided, when it was first settled by the Israelites, so as to secure to every family its proper, particular share. (Num. xxxiii. 53, 54, xxxiv. 13—18.) First, each *tribe* was to receive its district of country, distinct from the rest. Then each great *family* was to have allotted to it, its right proportion out of the district that fell to its tribe. Lastly this proportion of each such family was to be again measured off into as many parcels as it contained men who were to inherit. Thus every Israelite had his own inheritance assigned to him in the beginning, to be handed down to his posterity after him. He lived, too, in the midst of his kindred. Every neighbourhood was made up of relations, nearly connected by blood in proportion as their ands lay nigh to each other. Care was taken, too, that this state of things should not alter. Land was forbidden ever to be sold from one to another, so as to pass entirely away from the family to which it had been given. "The land," God said, "shall not be sold for ever; for the land is MINE; for ye are strangers and sojourners with me." (Lev. xxv. 23.) Land might be parted with, but only for a time. In the year of jubilee, it was required to come back to the original owner or his children. When sold, therefore, and bought, the price was always determined according to the time that was yet to come before the next jubilee. It was just what the use of it for that time, longer or shorter, was considered to be worth. Nor was the person obliged to wait till the jubilee, if he became able himself, or if his near friend was willing for him, to buy it back again sooner. Whenever a price, answering to the time that was still to come according to the rate at which it had been sold, was offered to the purchaser, he was obliged at once to give it up. (Lev. xxv. 13—28.) In this way, no family was allowed ever to be left without its proper inheritance. Every Israelite was born an heir to some land, and forced, in some measure, to be a farmer. There could be no great estates owned by single men; nor, on the other hand, was there room for such a thing as perfect, hopeless beggary. A pretty general equality was secured. Every jubilee made every Israelite an independent man. There were times, indeed, when this advantage was not enjoyed. We read of wicked men joining house to house, and laying field to field, till there was no place, that they might be placed alone in the midst of the earth, (Isa. v. 8;) but it was done in defiance of law. Those were times of dreadful corruption, in which the rights of men were torn from them by violence, and justice had no place in the government. We have seen before, that only *sons* inherited, if there were any; the distinction of families was kept up in the male line. But if there were no sons, daughters were to receive the inheritance; they were, however, in such case, to marry within the "family of the tribe of their father," and their children were to be counted as belonging to the family of their father, and representatives of his name, instead of passing into the lines of the houses to which their husbands belonged. (Num. xxvii. 1—11, xxxvi. 1—12.) In other cases, daughters might marry into any tribe; and when married, they passed altogether away from the inheritance of their fathers.

While this plan of securing to every family its estate, tended greatly to promote the happiness and strength of the nation, and to bring the whole country into a state of the most perfect cultivation, it could not but have a powerful influence, too, to keep the Israelites in their own land, and to hinder strangers from settling much among them. It is easy to see how it must have hindered foreign commerce. Besides, however, it formed a strong hold upon every Israelite, to keep him from withdrawing to other nations. He had property in his own country, which, at the same time, he could not sell, if he wished to leave it. To go abroad to live, was to lose his estate. A strong attachment, too, was naturally formed to the place where his fathers had always lived, which would not endure the thought of forsaking it.

While God himself was the supreme ruler of the nation, ordering its civil as well as religious affairs with a special direction, there was still, at all times, some regular form of human government under him, by which the business of the kingdom was carried on, and its laws put in execution. This, as we have seen, was in some respects different at different periods.

In the original form of this government, each tribe had its own rulers, and formed, in many respects, a distinct and independent government within itself. The manner of government, in its general plan, was according to the ancient patriarchal fashion, from which it had been received. Every tribe had its *prince*, and each of the greater and also of the lesser families into which it was divided, had its *head*. The law required *judges* to be appointed in every city, whose business it was to judge the people not only of the city itself, but also of the country, with its villages, for some distance round; so that in this way the whole land was furnished with judges. (Deut. xvi. 18.) There was another class of persons, clothed with some authority and much respect, who were scattered in like manner throughout the land. They are called, in the English Bible, *officers*. Mention is made of these in the account of the oppression which the people suffered in Egypt. (Ex. v. 6, 14.) The same law, afterward, which required judges to be appointed in every city, commanded that these *officers* should be so appointed also. The judges and officers had both their particular business to attend to; their particular departments of duty, which, by their office, they were called to have in charge; but besides this, they bore a part also in the business of public government. Each city was governed by a *council* or *senate*, that seems to have been made up of all the *heads of families*, or *elders*, *judges*, and *officers*, who belonged to it or to the neighbourhood around it. When measures of a more general sort, such as concerned several cities or the whole tribe, were to be considered, a general *assembly* was called of all the *heads*, *judges*, and *officers* in the tribe, together with its *prince*. This assembly, in each tribe, managed its government, in all cases that did not touch directly the interests of other tribes or of the nation in general, as if it had been an independent state. Thus we read of particular tribes even undertaking and carrying on wars on their own account, with which the rest appear not to have meddled. (Josh. xvii. 15—18, Judg. iv. 10.) In the time of Saul, the two tribes and the half one which lived on the east side of Jordan, carried on in this way, by themselves, a very great war. (1 Chron. v. 18—23.) So, also, the tribe of Simeon had its own wars, as late as the reign of Hezekiah. (1 Chron. iv. 39—43.) Hence we find the Israelites, as their ancient history his set before us, continually proceeding, in all their political movements, by *tribes* or *families*.

The government which each tribe had within itself, answered a large part of the purposes for which government is wanted in any country; but still there was need of something more to bind all into one nation. There was, therefore, a national *assembly* or *senate*, made up of the princes, heads, judges, and officers of all the tribes, which met at times, to deliberate upon questions which concerned the general interest, and to decide upon measures that regarded the order or welfare of the whole people. (Josh. xxiii. 2, xxiv. 1.)

It is not altogether clear, what was the particular business of the *officers* mentioned above, who were to be appointed in every city. They are supposed to have been persons chosen to keep the *genealogical tables* of the Israelites. In these tables were carefully recorded all the births, marriages, and deaths of every family. Among the Jews, it was a matter of great importance to have accurately preserved, from generation to generation, every line of descent along the male side of houses. The custom had its beginning with the commencement of society. The whole manner of the Israelitish commonwealth tended to cherish and confirm its power. The way in which inheritances passed downward in families, rendered it necessary to keep regular records of genealogies, such as never could be disputed. It was, therefore, a public care. The office of those who were appointed to take charge of it was regarded as one of great importance, and persons of more than common abilities were sought to fill it. By reason of this care, every Israelite could, without any difficulty, trace the line of his pedigree back to Abraham, the father of the nation, and so back to Adam, the father of the human race. Thus, Matthew and Luke were able, without any trouble, to give the genealogy of our Saviour. (Matt. i. 1—16, Luke iii. 23—38.) There was a wise counsel of God, for the manifestation of his truth, in so ordering it by his providence, that there should be such a careful distinction of families among the Jews, and such a careful record kept of their genealogies. By this means, a most satisfactory fulfilment of several great prophecies concerning the Messiah was made to appear, when he came. It had been foretold that he was to be the seed of Abraham, of the tribe of Judah, and the son of David. (Gen. xxii. 18, xlix. 10, 2 Sam. vii. 12—16, Ps. lxxxix. 4, cxxxii. 11, Acts ii. 30.) When Jesus appeared, he answered to all these prophecies; and there was such evidence of it in the public records of the families of the tribe of Judah, that nobody could dream of contradicting it. Matthew, therefore, from these records published his genealogy, tracing the line of Joseph's house down from Abraham and David. Luke has given us the pedigree of Mary's family, starting with her father Heli and carrying it back to the same sources. Soon after, all this business of recording genealogies was thrown into confusion. The nation was scattered and its families disordered. They are still a separate people, but no one among them can declare his ancient pedigree. By this, they ought to know that the Messiah has come; for how could it now be certainly known, if he were yet to come, that he was of the tribe of Judah and of the house of David? Since God has long ago made it impossible to prove such a descent in any case, they ought to believe that the Messiah has already long ago made his appearance. But they blindly expect him still, and refuse the only Saviour, Jesus of Nazareth.

We do not hear of *Judges* among the Israelites, till after their departure out of Egypt. For a while, at first, Moses himself was the only judge, and all causes, great and small, were carried before him. By the advice of Jethro, however, which God sanctioned, he made a great number of higher and lower judges for the nation. "He chose able men out of all Israel, and made them heads over the people, rulers of thousands, rulers of hundreds, rulers of fifties, and rulers of tens. And they judged the people at all seasons: the hard causes they brought unto Moses; but every small matter they judged themselves." Cases which judges of a lower kind could not decide, or in which their decision was not considered just, were carried before those of a higher order; and if the matter was too hard for the highest of all, the judges of thousands, it came before Moses himself. After their settlement in Canaan, the people, as we have seen, were always to have judges in every city. Weighty causes were to be carried to the place chosen of God, and there laid before the priests and the person who should be, at the time, clothed with the authority of supreme judge. (Deut. xvii. 8—10.) When the nation came to be ruled by kings, the king himself was the supreme judge It was com

mon for him, however, to consult with the high priest, and to
seek judgment from his lips.

The tribe of Levi held a most important place in the nation
The influence which it possessed, extended itself throughout
the whole frame of government. It was consecrated especially
to the service of God; withdrawn from the common pursuits
of life, not allowed to possess a particular territory like the
other tribes, and scattered into every district of the land. To
it, was committed the care of religion, and naturally along
with this, came the care of education. The nature of their
profession led them to cultivate knowledge more than others,
and afforded them, also, opportunity, such as no others had,
for acquiring it. The learning of the nation, therefore, was
found principally in this tribe. Hence, places of trust and
authority came, very naturally, to be filled in general by
Levites. As they were skilful to handle the pen, they were
made, wherever they could be found, scribes and keepers of the
genealogies. As they were called to be familiar with the law
and with learning in genera., they were, in like manner, selected, in preference to others, to be judges. In the time of
David, we are told, six thousand of them were *officers* and
judges through the land. (1 Chron. xxiii. 4.) The law made
it the business of the priests to explain its meaning, and to pronounce judgment in all difficult cases. The priest's lips were
to keep knowledge, and the law was to be sought at his mouth.
It was not *required*, however, that the common judges should
be taken out of any particular tribe. It was only the general
superiority of the tribe of Levi over the rest, in point of learning, which caused the judges, in the time of the kings, to be
commonly taken out of it.

Kings in the East, at the present day, exercise a most unlimited power over their subjects, being restrained by no law,
and having respect to no other regular authority. We know
that it was in this way, also, they ruled, in most of those countries, in ancient times. In the Israelitish government, however, their power was in many respects restrained. The whole
nature of the government tended to forbid absolute or tyrannical
authority in the monarch. God was the supreme Sovereign of
the nation, and its affairs were at all times so ordered, that its
kings were made to feel themselves under his control. The
system of religious *law* which he had established, was a strong
barrier in the way of proud presumption. The *priests* were the
ministers of the Most High, appointed to maintain the authority of that law, and to withstand all departure from its principles: if faithful, their influence was sufficient to check ever

royal power, when it transgressed its proper line. The *prophets* were messengers of the Almighty, which kings were constrained to hear, and compelled to respect—even such of them as hated their message and desired to cast off their allegiance to God. The peculiar *providence* with which the nation was governed, conspired with all this influence, to confound the ambition of princes, and make them mindful of their subjection to the Holy One of Israel. The general manner of the kingdom, too, which we have just been considering, tended to prevent arbitrary power in kings. There was too much of the old patriarchal style in its confederacy of tribes and families, to allow any thing at all like despotism in the throne. The law of Moses, because God foresaw that the nation would have kings, prescribed certain rules, to be observed when they should be chosen. (Deut. xvii. 14—20.) It appears, moreover, that a formal contract, or covenant, was made between the elders of the people and their kings, in which the royal duties and powers were solemnly stated. The covenant was committed to writing and carefully preserved. Thus, we are informed, when Saul was made king, "Samuel told the people the manner of the kingdom, and wrote it in a book, and laid it up before the Lord." (1 Sam. x. 25.) So, when David was anointed in Hebron, it is said that he *made a league* with the elders of Israel, before the Lord. (2 Sam. v. 3.) Rehoboam foolishly refused to agree to the reasonable terms which were proposed to him by the people, and in consequence of it, ten tribes immediately rejected his claim to the kingdom, and sought for themselves another monarch.

It was the business of the king to secure obedience to the laws, and to punish such as broke them. He had power to declare war and to make peace, and to administer justice with supreme authority. He could grant pardon to offenders, and he could sentence them to immediate death. He was considered the military head of the army. He was not, however, expected to go always himself to war; he might employ generals to conduct his forces in his stead. It is hardly necessary to say, that in some instances his power was greatly abused, and that not unfrequently the boundaries of right were daringly overleaped, and the privileges of the people disregarded, in spite of all the security with which they were defended. The wickedness of man has produced such instances of evil in every government.

SECTION III.

JEWISH GOVERNMENT AFTER THE CAPTIVITY.

The *Captivity* put a complete end to the *kingdom of Israel*, made up of the ten tribes who revolted from Rehoboam. The *kingdom of Judah* was still preserved. It embraced the tribe and family from which the Messiah was to come; and all the privileges and promises which had been granted to the seed of Abraham, the church of God, were confined to it as the only proper stock of the Jewish nation. During their captivity, they were still allowed to retain something of the plan of government which had been in use before. We read of their *elders*, and of the *chief of the fathers of Israel*. It appears, also, that they had a prince or governor of their own, who ruled them under the supreme authority of the king of the country. After their return to their native land, while they continued in subjection to the Persians and afterwards to the Greeks, they had, we know, a chief magistrate as well as other officers of their own, by whom the government was managed. When there was no other regularly appointed chief magistrate, it seems that it was common for the high priest to exercise the duties of that office. In the time of Antiochus Epiphanes, the nation recovered its freedom, after a long war, carried on with great bravery under the conduct of Judas, surnamed Maccabeus, and his brothers Jonathan and Simon. These held, one after another, the office of high priest, and became, at the same time, *princes* ruling the kingdom with independent and sovereign power. For something more than a hundred years, the affairs of the nation were managed by persons of this illustrious family, who sustained at once the dignity of high priests and the authority of kings. Then it fell under the dominion of the Romans, about sixty years before the birth of our Saviour.

For a time, the Romans made but little change in the manner of the government. They exercised, however, the right of appointing its highest ruler. Instead of leaving the chief civil authority with the high priest, as it had been before, they bestowed it upon Antipater, the father of Herod. Afterwards, Herod himself was intrusted with the government, and had conferred upon him the title of *king of Judea*. By his will, which the Roman Emperor Augustus allowed to stand, he divided his dominions among his three sons, Archelaus, Herod Antipas, and Herod Philip. Archelaus had Judea, Samaria, and Idumea, and bore the title of *Ethnarch*, which means, *Ruler*, or *chief of the nation*, with a promise from Augustus that he should, after some time, receive the name and all the dignity of a king, if he conducted himself in a manner worthy of such distinction. Herod Antipas and Philip bore the title of *Tetrarchs*. (Luke iii. 1.) The word *Tetrarch* signifies, in its original meaning, *Ruler of the fourth part* of a country. The office is said to have been borrowed from the Gauls Three tribes of these barbarous people, at a certain time, came into Asia Minor, and by force took from the king of Bithynia a part of his country, where they settled themselves, and called the district from their own name, *Galatia*. The Galatians to whom Paul wrote, were their descendants. Each of these tribes was divided into four parts, and each fourth part had a chief magistrate of its own, under the general authority of the king. These chief magistrates were Tetrarchs. Afterwards, the name was given to governors who ruled some district of country under an emperor or king, though it was not the *fourth part*, precisely, of any kingdom. Herod and Philip ruled each over less than a fourth part of Judea. A tetrarch, though dependent on the Roman Emperor, was yet allowed to govern the people who were under him, altogether according to his own pleasure. An ethnarch, however, was superior in point of rank; he was honoured and addressed by his subjects as a king. (Matt. ii. 22.) A tetrarch was sometimes distinguished with the same title. (Matt. xiv. 9.)

In the tenth year of his reign, Archelaus, for his exceedingly bad government, was deprived of his authority and banished out of the land. His territories were then annexed to the province of Syria, and so came under such government as was common in other provinces of the great Roman empire. This took place when Quirinus, or *Cyrenius*, was President of Syria. A governor was placed over Judea, who had the title of Procurator, and was dependent upon the President of Syria. Such were Pilate, Felix and Festus. These procurators, or governors, though they were officers under authority in the great empire, had, nevertheless, very great authority in the provinces which they ruled, and held in their hands the power of life and death. Herod Agrippa reigned over the country a while, with the title of king, after our Saviour's death; but only a short time. (Acts xii. 1—4, 19—23.)

The procurators of Judea resided generally at Cesarea; but on the great festivals, or when any tumult was feared, they went to Jerusalem, that by their presence they might hinder disorder, or suppress it if it made its appearance. They were allowed to keep in the country, for the purpose of maintaining their authority, six companies or bands of Roman soldiers, each consisting of several hundred men. Five of these bands were stationed at Cesarea and one at Jerusalem, in a tower close by the temple. (Matt. xxvii. 27, 28, Acts x. 1, xxi. 31, xxvii. 1.) The *Centurions* who are mentioned in the New Testament, were officers under the chief captain of a band. (Matt. viii. 8, 9.) The name signifies one who has the command of precisely a hundred men; but each centurion had not always so many. We must not confound the chief captain of the Roman band, with another officer, called the *captain of the temple*. This last was a Jewish officer, a priest of high standing, who had command of the bands of Levites that were appointed to guard the temple. (John xviii. 3, 12, Acts iv. 1, v. 24, 26.) When more than one such captain is spoken of, we are to understand the captains of single bands under the command of the chief officer. (Luke xxii. 4, 52.)

As a Roman province, the nation was required, under the government of the procurators, to pay regular tribute. It was a privilege granted to the Jews, which was not commonly allowed, that persons from among themselves were generally appointed to manage and collect the taxes. The office of chief tax-collector, was one of some distinction and of much profit. Each had a particular district appropriated to his management, having paid to the government a certain price for the right of collecting all its taxes. To secure the collection, he employed a number of inferior tax-gatherers, who took their several stations in places where tribute was to be received, and took in all the particular tolls. These were usually taken from the lowest rank of society, and were often very worthless in their character. Greedy of gain, they were frequently guilty of fraud and extortion. Accordingly, they were in all the provinces heartily hated and despised; but especially were they detested among the Jews, who always felt the whole matter of paying tribute to a foreign power to be an exceeding grievance and disgrace, and could not endure such as bore any part in collecting it. Hence, the tax-gatherers, or *publicans*, were reckoned in the same class with the vilest sinners, such as thieves, harlots, &c. It was considered a great scandal, that our Saviour consented to sit at meat with persons held to be so infamous. But he came to seek and save that which was lost; and among this low class of unprincipled men, the grace of his gospel was made far more effectual than among the self-righteous Pharisees. Zaccheus was one of those chief collectors that have been mentioned, who employed the common tax-gatherers under them. Matthew, the apostle, was a publican of the latter sort; a common tax-gatherer, who seems to have been caring only for filthy lucre, till the voice of Jesus fell upon his ear, as he sat at the *receipt of custom*, with the solemn call FOLLOW ME. That call was attended with a divine power; for at once, "he left all, rose up, and followed him!"

Judges, as well as other magistrates, were regularly appointed in sufficient number among the people, on their return from the captivity. (Ezra vii. 25.) Cases that were more than commonly difficult, were brought for some time either before the chief magistrate of the state, such as Zerubbabel was, and Ezra, and Nehemiah, or before the high priest. At length, however, a supreme court of justice was established, called the *Sanhedrim*. No mention is made in history of this council being in existence before the time of the Maccabees. Some indeed have thought, that its origin is to be found as far back as the time of Moses. On a certain occasion in the wilderness, when Moses was greatly distressed with the weight of the burden that rested upon him, God commanded him to choose seventy men of the elders of Israel, whom he promised to qualify by his Spirit that they might assist him in the heavy charge. (Num. xi. 16—17, 24—30.) This council, according to the opinion just mentioned, was intended to be a lasting supreme court in the kingdom, and was actually continued age after age till the latest times of the nation; so that the Sanhedrim, of which we hear after the captivity, was in reality but the same institution. But we find no notice of such a council being in existence, during the whole period from the death of Moses to the captivity, and the history of the Bible naturally leaves upon the mind the idea, that no tribunal of the sort was known. The council of seventy appointed in the wilderness seems to have been formed merely for the time which then was, that it might take a share with Moses in the burden of government, and contribute by its influence to support his administration in the midst of so rebellious a people. As its members one after another died, their places were not filled up, and so it came to an end with that generation. The Sanhedrim after the captivity was entirely a new council; though, no doubt, it was meant to be an imitation in some respects of that ancient institution.

The Sanhedrim was composed of seventy or seventy-two members selected from the *chief priests*, the *elders*, or heads of families, and the *scribes*. The high priest was its *president*. When they met, it is said that the members took their seats in such a way as to form a semicircle, with the president in the

centre so as to face them all. On his right side sat the *vice-president*, next in authority to himself, and on his left, the *second vice president*.

The *council room* in which they commonly assembled was not far from the temple, some think *in* the temple; when they pretended to try our Saviour, however, they met in the palace of the high priest.

The authority of the Sanhedrim was very great, reaching to the affairs both of the church and of the state. In the time of Christ, however, its power was considerably limited by the Romans. It had still liberty to try and pass sentence, but the power of executing the sentence, if it called for capital punishment, was taken from it and placed altogether in the hands of the Roman Governor. Thus, when our Saviour was taken to be destroyed, he was brought first before the Sanhedrim, hastily assembled in the high priest's house, and there, after the empty show of a trial, declared to be worthy of death. Then, when they had bound him, they led him away in the morning to the Judgment Hall of the Governor, and urged him to pass sentence for his crucifixion. Pilate had full power, as he said himself, to release him, (John xix. 10;) but, though he was convinced of his innocence, he had not virtue enough to let him go, while there seemed a danger that his own interest might suffer by a refusal to gratify the Jews. To get clear of the difficulty, he told them to take him themselves, and judge him according to their own law. But they replied, "It is not lawful for *us* to put any man to death;" they were determined to be satisfied with nothing less than his death, and this could not be without sentence from Pilate. (John xviii. 31.) At length, after an ineffectual attempt to reason them out of their purpose, the unfaithful man yielded, and delivered up the Lord of glory to be nailed upon the cross. When Stephen was stoned, it was not done by the authority of the Sanhedrim, but in an unlawful riot

It was the council of the Sanhedrim that met after Lazarus were raised from the dead, to consider what measures were to be taken to stop the growing credit of Jesus, when Caiaphas, the president, at once declared that nothing ought to be thought of but his death; uttering at the same time a striking prophecy, of which he was not himself aware. (John xi. 47—53.) Peter and John were brought before it, at a later period, for preaching "through Jesus the resurrection from the dead." (Acts iv. 5—21.) Afterward, all the apostles together were brought before it, and beaten. (Acts v. 21—41.) We read of it also in the history of Paul. (Acts xxii. 30, xxiii. 1, 15, 20, 28.)

In the time of our Saviour, there was, according to Josephus an inferior tribunal or court of justice in every city, consisting of seven judges, which decided causes and punished crimes that were not so important or difficult as to require their being carried before the Sanhedrim. Before the Romans took away the power of capital punishment from the nation, this court could sentence a criminal to death by the sword, which was considered the least severe sort of execution. Stoning was held to be a heavier punishment, and could be inflicted only by the great council, or Sanhedrim. Our Saviour referred to these different tribunals, when he set forth the true spirit of the sixth commandment in his sermon on the mount. He taught, that wrath and malice, which the Jews hardly felt to be sins at all, would certainly be called into account and punished, and represented anger without cause to be worthy of a punishment as great as that which was commonly inflicted for killing a man,—which they looked upon as the only crime that broke the commandment. "Whosoever is angry with his brother without a cause, shall be in danger of the *judgment*, (or inferior court;) and whosoever shall say to his brother, Raca, (a word of scorn and contempt,) shall be in danger of the council, (or Sanhedrim;) but whosoever shall say, Thou fool, (a word of spite and malicious reproach,) shall be in danger of hell fire." (Matt. v. 22.) Josephus says, this court of seven in every city, was the same which the law of Moses established from the first, when it required judges and officers to be appointed, as we have seen already. There was a still smaller court of *three* judges, which became common under the Roman government. It was not, however, a standing tribunal like the others, but chosen merely for the occasion, when a particular case of law was to be decided, and the parties were willing to have it settled in this way. Each party chose one man, and the two thus chosen selected a third, which made up the temporary court. The same plan of settling disputes *by arbitration*, is common among ourselves. This privilege the Roman laws allowed to the Jews, even when they were settled in other countries; and as the Christians were at first regarded as only a sect of the Jews, they likewise enjoyed the same advantage Hence, the apostle censures the Corinthian Christians for carrying their causes before heathen magistrates, when they had full liberty to settle them among themselves in the way now mentioned. (1 Cor. vi. 1—7.)

The Jewish nation enjoyed many privileges under the dominion of the Romans. They were allowed to practice their sacred rites and to continue their whole manner of religion without restraint; to hold fast their ancient customs; and to live in a considerable degree according to their own laws. Yet after all, as appears from the view which has just been taken, their condition was one of complete dependence and subjection. With the coming of SHILOH, we beheld the sceptre departing from Judah and the lawgiver from between his feet, to be restored no more. (Gen. xlix. 10.) The governors who ruled the country were very unjust and cruel, and the affairs of the nation were miserably managed. For want of energy in the government, the land was overrun with robbers. The spirit of the people too continually tended to make the matter grow worse and worse. They bore the yoke with extreme reluctance. The idea of being in bondage and paying tribute to a Gentile nation was not to be supported quietly by Jewish feelings. "We be Abraham's seed, and were never in bondage to any man!" was the language which these feelings prompted, in the very midst of their national subjection. (John viii. 33.) Such feeling, excited as it was by continual provocation, could not fail to give rise to frequent tumults and insurrections; and these still served to produce new evils, only causing the chain of bondage to be drawn with more galling tightness, till at length, after desperate confusion, violence, and war, they drew down complete and tremendous destruction upon the whole nation. History informs us of various insurrections made under different leaders, who persuaded a multitude to follow them with the wild hope of breaking the Roman yoke. There was always a large class of men in the country who maintained that it was unlawful to pay tribute to a foreign power; the law of Moses forbade setting up a stranger to be king over the nation, and this, according to their interpretation, made it wrong to acknowledge submission to any Gentile king or emperor. (Deut. xvii. 15.) The Pharisees in general, held this sentiment, though they did not carry it out in open rebellion. The *Galileans*, however, who sprung chiefly out of the sect of the Pharisees, pushed the doctrine even to this extremity. They rose about the twelfth year of Christ, when Judea was first joined to the province of Syria, and taxed under the government of Cyrenius. One Judas of Galilee was their leader. He publicly taught that such taxing was contrary to the law of Moses, and "drew away much people after him." (Acts v. 37.) He perished, and his followers were dispersed; but they still continued to form a sect in the land, and to propagate their doctrines afterward. It is supposed by some, that the Galileans slain by Pilate in the court of the temple were of this sect. (Luke xiii. 1, 2.) The *Herodians* were a political party, who leaned altogether to excess the other way. They had their name from Herod, and seem to have been a sort of court-pleasing tribe, who cared very little for law or religion, when they did not appear to agree with worldly interest. They were in favour, therefore, of entire submission to the Romans, and were not unwilling to have introduced into the country many of their heathen practices. How malicious was the policy which the Pharisees employed on a certain occasion to "entangle the Redeemer in his talk." (Matt. xxii. 15—22.) Though violently opposed to the Herodians in general, they got some of them to unite with them in this plan to injure Christ, and sent them together with some of their own disciples to propose to him the much disputed question, "Is it lawful to give tribute unto Cæsar or not?" If he had said, *It is not lawful*, the Herodians were ready to accuse him to the Roman government as a person opposed to its authority; if he had said, *It is lawful*, the Pharisees would have charged him with being unfriendly to the liberties of the people, so as to bring upon him their displeasure. His answer, however, by its excellent wisdom, defeated their malevolence.

In this state of bondage and uneasiness which the nation endured, its expectation was strongly turned toward the Messiah that was to come. According to the Scriptures, they believed that the time appointed for his appearance was that particular age, and all looked for it as a thing just at hand. But, alas, they had a false notion entirely of his character. They expected one who would come with great splendour and power, to deliver them from *earthly* bondage, and to restore their kingdom to all the glory of *earthly* freedom, prosperity, and victorious strength. They thought, that the throne of David which he was to establish, would be the same throne of worldly dominion that had been set up of old in the midst of Israel after the flesh; and hence they imagined, that the promises of God concerning the continuance of this throne, made it impossible that the nation should be given up to complete ruin.

When Jesus of Nazareth, therefore, a man of poor and obscure birth, presented himself as the Messiah, they turned from him in unbelief. To the glory of that spiritual kingdom which he proposed to establish, they were blind. False christs, vain pretenders to be the Messiah, who took upon them the character of worldly importance and promised to deliver them from the power of the Romans, were more favourably received. Several such rose, and became leaders in insurrection, drawing multitudes after them. (Matt. xxiv. 23—27, John v. 43.) On one occasion, after a great miracle, the multitude were filled with a persuasion that Jesus was the Messiah, the Great Prophet that was to come, and then immediately they wanted to take him by force and make him a king. (John vi. 14, 15.)

As the spirit of opposition to government prevailed so much in those times, being greatly stirred up by injustice and oppression, and as among the Jews it was attempted to be justified and even proved a duty on principles of religion; we find the apostles, in their epistles, strongly urging upon Christians the necessity of quiet obedience, not only for fear of punishment, but also for conscience' sake. (Rom. xiii. 1—7, 1 Pet. ii. 13—17.)

SECTION IV.

OF KINGS.

ANOINTING with oil was a principal ceremony among the Jews, in introducing kings to their office. It appears, however, that it was not thought necessary to anoint in every new succession to the throne. If the first in a royal line had been thus set apart, it was, perhaps, considered sufficient for those that followed, unless the right to the crown was disputed. We do not, at least, read of the ceremony being used in other cases. Hence the king was called, *The anointed one.* This is just the meaning of the word *Messiah*, and also of the word *Christ*. These names, which are only the same in different languages, were given to the Redeemer, because he was spiritually anointed by the Holy Ghost to be a PROPHET, a PRIEST, and a KING; for the same ceremony was used for setting apart prophets also, and priests to their office. (Isa. lxi. 1, Luke iv. 17—21, Ps. cx. 1—4, ii. 2, 6, Acts iv. 25—27, x. 38.)

The *Robe* which kings wore was very costly. It was common, in the East, to have it of purple colour.—The *Diadem* glittered with pearls and gems. It was a fillet, about two inches broad, bound round the head so as to pass the forehead and temples, and tied behind. Its whole workmanship was exceedingly rich and valuable. The colour of it was different in different countries. This ornament, as well as the neck-chain, and bracelets for the arms, was worn at all times. In the English Bible, it is called a *crown*. Other *crowns*, however, were also in use, which covered the whole head; but of their form, nothing certain is known.—The *Throne* was a magnificent seat with a back and arms, of such height as to need a *footstool* for the feet to rest upon. That of Solomon, was all of gold, ornamented with ivory, and was so high as to have six steps leading up to it. The "*throne*" became a natural emblem of government and power. Hence God is represented as sitting upon one; and the image is clothed with exceeding grandeur, by making heaven itself his throne, and the earth his footstool. (Isa. lxvi. 1, Matt. v. 34.) The *Sceptre* had its origin perhaps from the Shepherd's staff, as kings were styled shepherds frequently in early times, and their office seems to have been derived from the authority of the ancient patriarchal chiefs, who were so often, like Abraham and Job, but great master-shepherds, at the head of their extensive families. Generally, it was a wooden rod or staff, nearly as long as the height of a man, overlaid with gold or adorned with golden studs and rings, and having an ornamental ball on the upper end. (Ezek. xix. 11.) A sceptre figuratively denotes dignity and dominion; *a sceptre of righteousness* is used to signify just government.)

In eastern countries, anciently as well as in modern times, the courts of kings were distinguished with much pomp and princely state. Their attendants were very numerous. Their palaces were constructed in magnificent and expensive style, and richly furnished with ornaments. Large gardens were connected with them, in which walks, groves, and fountains were made to unite in the most agreeable variety. Great profusion marked the royal table; and large wealth of costly garments filled the royal wardrobe. The Jewish kings do not seem to have generally indulged the same degree of luxury and extravagance that was common in some other countries, such as Babylon and Persia; yet we find notices of much that was according to the general eastern style now mentioned. Solomon was not surpassed by the monarchs of any country in the splendour of his royal state. He made full experiment of all that wealth, labour, and taste could procure of worldly magnificence: but according to his own account, he found it to be all vanity and vexation of spirit. (Eccl. ii. 4—11.)

Eastern kings of the present day very rarely make their appearance in public, and it is a matter of great difficulty to get access to them in any way. We find that the same seclusion was customary in ancient times. Among the Persians, it was death for any person to come into the presence of the monarch, without being invited. (Esther iv. 11.) Among the Jews, however, no fashion of this sort ever had place; their kings allowed themselves to be seen in public, and approach to them was not forbidden. Those who came into the presence of the king, even if they were the highest officers in the government, appeared before him with respectful obedience, and stood, like servants, before their master. Hence the phrase to *stand before the king* means to be occupied in his service. So the priests and Levites are said to have been set apart, to *stand before the Lord* to minister unto him. (Deut. x. 8.) Gabriel is spoken of as *standing in the presence* of the Lord, to signify his readiness to perform his commands, as well as his high dignity in being so admitted to appear before the King of kings. (Luke i. 19.) To behold the king's face was considered an honour and happiness; much more to see it habitually, that is, to be employed in his immediate service and enjoy his favour. Thus, also, the expression *to see God* signifies to experience his friendship, and to be admitted to the greatest happiness in his presence; whereas, *not to see him* is to be shut out from his favour, and to be under his awful displeasure. Christ says of his humblest followers, that in heaven their angels do *always behold the face* of his heavenly Father; referring to the usage of earthly courts, where such as always beheld the monarch's face were highest in office and regard. By this, he signified that these "little ones" had a powerful interest in heaven, and were peculiarly dear to God himself; so that it became men to take heed how they despised them. (Matt. xviii. 10.) To *sit* next the king, especially on his right hand, was a mark of the highest honour and dignity. (1 Kings ii. 19, Matt. xx. 20—23, Heb. i. 3.)

As we have already seen, it was expected in early times that those who approached kings should come with some sort of a present. The most profound reverence was required to do him honour, according to the ceremonious manner of the East. Among the Persians, the homage thus presented to the sovereign was little less than idolatry outright. A similar homage was required also to be paid to his chief courtiers and favourites, and to refuse it was considered a grievous offence. Thus, when Haman was promoted, "all the king's servants that wer in the gate *bowed and reverenced* him," and great wrath was excited against Mordecai because he would not do him this honour. (Esth. iii. 1—6.)

When eastern sovereigns go abroad, they are always attended with a great and splendid retinue. The same custom prevailed of old. The Hebrew kings rode on asses or mules, or in cha riots, accompanied by their guards; these were called, in the days of David, *Cherethites* and *Pelethites*.—When a monarch in those regions took a journey into distant provinces, because broad and convenient roads, such as we have, were not known it was common to send a messenger before him, to give notice of his coming, that the way in which he was to travel might be made ready, and every thing else necessary prepared for his approach. When they were to pass through strange and untravelled regions, they had a way opened before them, some times with vast labour; precipices were digged down, and hol low places were filled up, and every hinderance cleared away To this practice, there is beautiful allusion in that prophecy of Isaiah: "The voice of him that crieth in the wilderness Prepare ye the way of the Lord; make straight in the desert a highway for our God! Every valley shall be exalted, and every mountain and hill shall be made low: and the crooked shall be made straight, and the rough places, plain: and the glory of the Lord shall be revealed, and all flesh shall see it together." (Isa. xl. 3—5.) While the prophet thus signified that happy return from the Babylonish captivity which should take place in the time of Cyrus, when God should conduct the Jews, as it were, in all the majesty and splendour of a royal march back over the wilderness and hills to their native land; his words, full of divine animation, looked forward at the same time to a far more glorious accomplishment, which that first fulfilment itself, in the wise ordering of God's providence, was made to shadow forth beforehand as its feeble type. We are taught in the gospel, that John the Baptist was the messenger sent to cry in the wilderness, and that the Lord whose way was to be prepared, was the Redeemer, Jesus Christ, God mani fest in the flesh. (Luke i. 76, iii. 3—6. See also Mal. iii. 1

In many nations, there was a sort of general royal name that was applied to their monarchs one after another as matter of course when they came to sit upon the throne Thus, among the Romans, the emperors were for a long time successively styled by the name of *Cæsar*. So the kings of the ancient Amalekites seem to have carried in common the name of *Agag;* while that of *Hadad* was appropriated to the king of Syria. *Abimelech* was used in the same way among the Philistines for some time. The ancient monarchs of Egypt were called in succession *Pharaoh,* and those of Persia, in many cases, *Darius;* each of these two names were originally only common words, in the languages of those countries, which signified simply *king* or *monarch.* In later times, the kings of Egypt bore the general name of *Ptolemy.*

Among the officers that were commonly connected with the royal court among the Jews, we find mention made of *Counsellors.* Such were "the old men that stood before Solomon while he lived." (1 Kings xii. 6—12.) *Prophets* also were a sort of royal officers. Pious kings always consulted them; while those of ungodly character, after the example of heathen monarchs, applied to soothsayers and false prophets. Then we read of the *Recorder,* or *writer of the state-chronicles,* who kept in writing a regular account of all the transactions of the king's reign; also of the *Scribe,* or royal secretary, who registered the acts and decrees of government. The *High Priest,* as the chief minister of God the sovereign of the nation, held an important place also in the king's court, as was to be expected in such a government. These that have been mentioned were employed to give counsel or to act, officially, in *state* business. Then there were others, whose business connected them more particularly with the king's *domestic* establishment. Such were the officers who provided supplies for the king's table. Such was the *Governor of the palace,* or royal steward, who had charge of all the servants, and of the whole household management. He wore, it seems, a particular kind of robe, bound with a precious girdle, and carried a key upon his shoulder, as a mark of his office. (Isa. xxii. 15—22.) The *king's friend* or *companion* was a person whom he admitted to his most familiar confidence, and who was trusted, when occasion required, with the most important charges. As we have already noticed, the king had also his *Lifeguard,* who in the time of David were called Cherethites and Pelethites These were soldiers, employed particularly to guard the palace and the king's person. When sentence of death was pronounced on any person by the king, they carried it into execution. They were sometimes also called *Runners,* because they were required to carry tidings of the royal laws and edicts into distant parts of the kingdom, and at times to run before his chariot.

In the Roman empire, it was not unusual for those who

wanted to be clothed with the dignity of kings in the tributary kingdoms, to go to Rome for the purpose of soliciting such favour in their own persons. It was thus Archelaus went there, some time after his father's death, to have his will confirmed by the emperor, and to receive the government of Judea. The Jews, by reason of their great hatred to him, sent an embassy of fifty men at the same time, with a petition to Augustus that they might be allowed to live according to their laws, under a Roman governor. Archelaus, however, received the kingdom, and when he came back inflicted severe punishment on those who wanted to hinder him from reigning. In one of his parables, our Lord beautifully alludes to this custom of the times, and seems to have had the well-known case of Archelaus particularly in his eye: "A certain noblemen went into a far country, to receive for himself a kingdom, and to return. But his citizens hated him, and sent a message after him, saying, We will not have this man to reign over us," &c. (Luke xix. 12—27.) The application of the parable to Christ himself is clear and striking. He was going to heaven to receive all power from his Father, and would afterward return to take vengeance on those who rejected him.

SECTION V.

OF PUNISHMENTS.

TRIALS in early times were simple and short. The places where they were held, as we have seen already, were the gates of cities. Here the judges were accustomed to sit, as the place of greatest public resort. The accuser and the accused appeared before them, *standing*. The witnesses were sworn, and examined separately: two besides the accuser himself were necessary to establish a charge. The sentence was then pronounced, according to the wisdom and honesty of the judges, and without any delay carried into execution.

The common time for trying causes seems to have been in the morning. (Jer. xxi. 12.) By the later Jews, it was held unlawful to try any cause of a capital nature in the night; and also, to try, pass sentence, and put it in execution on the same day. This last particular was entirely disregarded, in the zeal with which our Saviour's life was taken away. He was seized and brought to the high priest's palace in the night; *as soon as it was day*, he was tried with the unholy mockery of justice; early in the morning he was led away to the go vernor to be sentenced to death; and before the sixth hour, or noon, he was lifted up upon the cross.

The design of punishments in human governments, is to hinder new crimes, or, as Moses expresses it, *that all the people may hear, and fear, and do no more presumptuously.* Of the different sorts of punishments mentioned in the Scriptures, some were peculiarly Jewish in their use, and others were employed by people of other countries. They are naturally divided into two general classes;—such as were capital, or took away life, and such as were not thus fatal. We shall notice those of the last kind first.

PUNISHMENTS NOT CAPITAL.

I. SIN AND TRESPASS OFFERINGS.—If a man wilfully and presumptuously transgressed the ceremonial law, he was cut off from the people; but if he transgressed without such deliberate purpose, through error, ignorance, or forgetfulness, the law could be satisfied by the offering of an appointed sacrifice. Sacrifices of this sort had in them the nature of punishment. If they were withheld, in the cases which called for them, the punishment which belonged to wilful transgression was incurred. Some offences, also, that were not of a ceremonial nature, and even in certain cases such as had been committed with knowledge and design, might be atoned for in the same way. Cases of the latter class were all, however, such as the law had no power to discover, except by the voluntary confession of the offender, and of that character that the general good of society was likely to be promoted by the encouragement which was thus offered to his guilty conscience to make acknowledgment of its sin. Together with the Trespass offering to be made in these instances, the property that had been dishonestly acquired was to be restored, together with a fifth part of its amount added to it. The offerings of which we speak could not, of course, do away the evil which any action had in the sight of God most Holy; they satisfied merely the civil and the ceremonial law, while they shadowed forth in type, the Great Atonement that was to come. For an account of these Sin and Trespass Offerings, and of the cases in which they were to be employed, see the fourth, fifth, and sixth chapters of Leviticus.

II. FINES.—These were sometimes determined by the person himself who had been injured, in certain cases where the law appointed a severer punishment, but allowed *him* to accept, ·f he chose, a satisfaction of this sort in its stead. (Ex. xxi. 30, Num. xxxv. 31, 32.) In other instances, fines were fixed by the decision of the judges, or expressly determined by the law. In cases of theft, the general law was, that double the amount stolen should be restored; but if a *sheep* or an *ox* that had been stolen was already slain or sold, the restoration for the first was to be *four-fold;* for the second, *five-fold.* When the thief was unable to make restoration, he was sold, with his wife and children, into bondage. (Ex. xxii. 1—4.) All fines were paid to the injured person; the government received nothing in this way.

III. SCOURGING.—This was a very common punishment among the Jews, in all ages of the nation. The law directed that the person to be beaten should lie down, and that the blows, which were never to be more than forty, though they might be any number less, according to the crime, should be applied to his back in the presence of the judge. (Deut. xxv. 1—3.) In later times, he was tied by the hands to a low pillar, and stripped down to the waist. For fear of going, by mistake, beyond the precise number of lashes allowed, it became customary not to give over thirty-nine; and that the reckoning might be more sure, the scourge employed had three lashes or thongs, so as to give three stripes at once. In this way, thirteen blows made out the thirty-nine stripes. In the time of our Saviour, the punishment of scourging was not confined to the regular courts of justice, but was often inflicted also in the synagogues, which, as we shall see hereafter, were of the same nature with our churches. (Matt. x. 17, Acts xxii. 19.) Paul was scourged with *forty stripes, save one,* no less than five times. (2 Cor. xi. 24.) The instrument of scourging used in early times, was commonly a *rod;* hence, in the Old Testament, the rod is used oftentimes to signify any punishment. Cruelty invented, for its own gratification, a horrible whip, by fixing sharp iron points, or nails, or pieces of lead, to the end of thongs. This seems to have been called a *Scorpion.* (1 Kings. xii. 11.) Among the Romans, scourging was very severe, and was not limited to any number of blows, as with the Jews. Thus the blessed Redeemer was cruelly beaten, till he became so weak that he was not able to carry his cross to Calvary. (Luke xxiii. 26.) There was a law, however, by which it was forbidden to punish one who was a *Roman citizen,* in this way. (Acts xvi. 22, 23, 37, xxii. 25.) Paul had this advantage, some think, because he was born at *Tarsus,* which, for its services, had been made a free city by Augustus Cæsar. Others, however, suppose that the freedom of Tarsus was not the same thing as having the rights of Roman citizenship, because, though the chief captain knew that Paul was of that city, he yet ordered him to be scourged, (Acts xxi. 39, xxii. 24;) they maintain, therefore, that the apostle's family had obtained the privilege in some other way. However it was, he enjoyed by *birth*, what Lysias had secured only by paying a great *price* (Acts xxii. 28.)

IV. CONFINEMENT.—As sentence of punishment was in general carried into execution very soon after it was pronounced. there was not the same need of *Prisons* as among us. Criminals were sometimes put under the care of a guard; and not unfrequently, in early times, they were shut up in empty cisterns. At a later period, prisons of different sorts became more common, and were used not only to keep criminals safe for trial, or till the proper time for executing upon them some other punishment, but also for mere confinement itself as a punishment. Prisoners were often, in addition to their confinement, bound with *chains*. After the captivity, it became customary to shut up in prison persons who failed to pay their *debts*, after the example of other nations. Such were also liable to be beaten with stripes, and to be put to different kinds of torture. (Matt. v. 25, 26, xviii. 28—34.) There was a singular way of binding persons, so as to deprive them of liberty, in use among the Romans. It was, to fasten the prisoner to a soldier, by a chain passing from the arm of one to that of the other. In this way, he was continually attended with a guard, who could not for a moment forsake his charge, even if he had himself been so disposed. The apostle Paul was confined in this manner. Thus coupled to a soldier that kept him, he "dwelt two whole years in his own hired house," at Rome. (Acts xxviii. 16, 30.) He was not, therefore, hindered from seeing any that chose to visit him, and might, if he pleased, go abroad out into the city. But to be, in this way, compelled to wear a chain at all times, was to be constantly under the greatest disgrace in the eyes of the world. Hence, many who before showed some friendship to him, became ashamed to acknowledge acquaintance with him, and treated him with cold neglect. Thus acted not all, however. "The Lord give mercy to the house of Onesiphorus," he writes, "for he oft refreshed me, and was *not ashamed of my chain;* but, when he was in Rome, he sought me out very diligently, and found me!" (2 Tim. i. 16, 17.) Sometimes the prisoner was bound, by a chain from each arm to *two* soldiers. Thus Peter was sleeping in prison, on that memorable night when the angel of the Lord delivered him by miracle. (Acts xii. 6.) Persons who were trusted with the care of prisoners were liable, not unfrequently, to be punished with death if they let them escape. (Acts xii. 19, xvi. 27.)

V. RETALIATION.—The nature of this punishment may be learned from Ex. xxi. 23—25, and Lev. xxiv. 19—22. See also Deut. xix. 16—21, where the punishment for false witness is determined on the same general principle. The injured person might agree with the offender, in common cases where retaliation was appointed by the law, to receive a sum of money as a satisfaction in its room, and this either before or after the decision of the judge. The law which authorized retaliation was merely a *civil* one, appointing punishment in this way on the same principle that was regarded in the appointment of any other punishment, and did no more give countenance to feelings of private revenge, than the law which commanded the use of the scourge gave liberty to indulge a malicious or cruel disposition. The Jews, however, in the time of our Saviour, did not make this distinction, but interpreted the law as if it was a *moral* one, and furnished a right rule for the regulation of the heart and life. Our Lord taught that a very different rule ought to be followed when this was in view. (Matt. v. 38—42.)

VI. EXCOMMUNICATION. As religion and government were blended inseparably together among the Jews, to be cast out of the church was a *civil* punishment as well as an *ecclesiastical* one. We have no account of it being employed till after the captivity. The later Jews made three degrees of it. The *first* was, when a person was cast out of the synagogue and forbidden to have any intercourse with society, even with his own family, for the space of thirty days; and if he did not repent at the end of that time, the excommunication was repeated. The *second* was more solemn and severe, being pronounced with a curse: it was not lawful for anybody to sell to such as were under it, even the necessaries of life. The *third* was even more severe, cutting off the guilty person absolutely and entirely from all connection with his countrymen, and solemnly committing him to the hands of God, whose awful judgment was near at hand.

CAPITAL PUNISHMENTS.

We come now to the consideration of CAPITAL punishments. The first mention of such punishment is found in Gen. ix. 6. *Whoso sheddeth man's blood, by man shall his blood be shed.* Such was the commandment of God. The *way* in which the criminal was to be put to death, was left to be determined by men

The Blood-avenger.—In the earliest times, it was left altogether to the nearest relation of the person that had been killed, to execute punishment upon the murderer. In the common sentiment of society, this was not only his *right*, but his *duty*, also; so that disgrace and reproach fell upon him, if he failed to perform it. Hence, it became with such an one, a great point of honour not to leave the blood of his kinsman unrevenged, and this, added to the keen feeling of anger which naturally raged in his bosom, urged him to make the greatest exertions to overtake and destroy the person by whose hand it had been shed. This plan of punishment was the most natural one in that simple state of society which was first common. Hence, it prevailed among all people; and because the manners of many nations in the East have been handed down with very little alteration from the most ancient days, it still prevails to a considerable extent in that part of the world. It is in use also among the Indians of our own country, and in various countries of Africa. It is easy to see, however, that such a plan must be attended with most serious evil. It is adapted to cherish feelings of bitterness and revenge, and to make them seem honourable; it is not likely to distinguish between wilful murder, and such as happens without design; and more than this, it tends to produce lasting feuds between families, one revenge still calling for another, and blood continually demanding new blood, so that, in the end, instead of one life, many are cruelly destroyed, in consequence of a single murder. Thus it is remarkably among the Arabs: families, and sometimes whole tribes, are set against each other in deadly hatred and war, by the retaliation which a crime of this sort produces; and the enmity is handed down from fathers to sons as a sacred inheritance, until either one party is completely destroyed, or satisfaction made, such as the side to whom the injury was first done may agree to accept. The true interest of society, therefore, requires that a different plan of punishment should be secured; that its execution should be taken out of the hands of the nearest relation, and put into those of the civil magistrate

This most ancient plan of punishment, in case of murder, was the one in use among the Jews before the time of Moses; for the *Avenger of blood* is spoken of, in the law which he gave, as a character well known. Under the direction of God, he did not do away the old custom altogether; for although in its whole nature it was an evil, the feelings of the people were, nevertheless, so thoroughly wedded to its usage, that, without a miraculous control upon their minds it was not to be ex pected they would consent to relinquish entirely the right of private vengeance which it allowed. Some indulgence, therefore, was granted in this case, it seems, like that which was permitted in the case of divorce, "on account of the hardness of their hearts." (Matt. xix. 8.) At the same time, a most beautiful and wise arrangement was made, to *correct* the most serious disadvantages with which it had been before accompanied, which, in fact, while it left some *form* of the ancient

custom, gave it a new *nature* altogether. *Cities of refuge* were appointed, three on each side of Jordan, with straight and good roads leading to them from every direction, to any of which the murderer might fly; and if he got into it before the Avenger overtook him, he was safe from his rage until he had a fair trial. If it was found that he was indeed guilty of wilful murder, he was delivered up to the Avenger to be destroyed, and not even the altar was allowed to protect him; but if it was found that the murder had not been intentional, he was allowed to remain in the city of refuge, where none might come to do him evil; and on the death of the high priest, he might return in security to his own home. (Ex. xxi. 12—14, Num. xxxv. 9—29, Deut. iv. 41—43, xix. 1—13, Josh. xx. 1—9.)

STONING was the punishment which the law of Moses most generally appointed for crimes that called for death. The witnesses were required to throw first, and then all the people that were present, till the miserable criminal was overwhelmed with death. (Deut. xvii. 7, John viii. 7.) This seems to be the punishment we are to understand, in all cases where the way of putting to death is not expressly mentioned. (Lev. xx. 10, compared with John viii. 5. Also Ex. xxxi. 14, with Numb. xv. 35, 36.) Another method of taking away life was by the SWORD. Among the Egyptians, *Beheading* was a common punishment, (Gen. xl. 17—19;) and in the later times of the nation, the rulers of the Jews sometimes made use of it. (Matt. xiv. 8-12, Acts xii. 2.) But among the ancient Israelites, this way of execution was not practised. Punishment by the sword, which has been sometimes confounded with it, was inflicted in whatever way the executioner found it most convenient to use the weapon; he probably thrust it most commonly into the bowels of the criminal. Hence, he was said to *rush* or *fall upon him*. (1 Kings ii. 25, 29, 31, 34, 46.)

These two were the only capital punishments that belonged properly to the Israelites. There were, however, besides them, certain marks of infamy sometimes inflicted on the dead bodies of criminals, to add to the shame and disgrace of their death. Such was—1. *Burning* the body after it had been stoned. (Gen. xxxviii. 24, Lev. xxi. 9, Josh. vii. 15, 25.) 2. *Hanging* it on a tree or gibbet: the person thus suspended was said to be *accursed of God*, an abomination in his sight. (Deut. xxi. 22, 23.) 3. *Heaping stones* over the place where it lay, as a monument of shame. (Josh. vii. 26, viii. 29, 2 Sam. xviii. 17.)

Various other capital punishments are mentioned or referred to in the Bible, that were in use among other nations, some of which also were introduced among the Jews, as they came to have more intercourse than at first with foreign countries. Of this sort were *Beheading*, already noticed, which was practised among the Egyptians, Persians, Greeks and Romans; *Strangling*, (1 Kings xx. 31;) *Burning alive* in a furnace, which was used among the Chaldeans, (Dan. iii. 6, 11, 15—27, Jer. xxix. 22;) *Exposing to wild beasts*, (Dan. vi. 7, 12, 16—24, 1 Cor. xv. 32;) *Beating to death*, which among the Greeks was inflicted on slaves; *Cutting asunder*, and *Sawing asunder*. (Dan. ii 5, Luke xii. 46, Heb. xi. 37.) Isaiah, the Jews say, was sawn asunder by Manasseh; but perhaps the story is only one of their numberless fables. There were various other contrivances, some of them very cruel, to put men to a violent death, which it is not necessary to mention. One more, however, calls for notice; and it is entitled to particular consideration. I mean the *Cross*.

CRUCIFIXION was a common method of punishment among several ancient nations; especially among the Persians, Carthaginians, and Romans. It was according to its use with the latter people, that the Jews became acquainted with it; and it was because he was put to death by Roman authority, that the Lord Jesus Christ was made to suffer its cruel torture. (John xviii. 31, 32, xii. 32—34.) The cross was employed among the Romans as a punishment for robbers, assassins, and rebels. Slaves especially, when they were guilty of great offences, were put to death in this way. Hence, crucifixion was held to be the most shameful and degrading death which a man could suffer. The *cross*, in public opinion, had in it even more of disgrace and reproach than the *gallows* now has with *us*. It was therefore an exceeding humiliation which the ever-blessed Redeemer, who thought it not robbery to be equal with God, consented to endure, when, " being found in fashion as a man, he humbled himself and became obedient unto death—*even the death of the cross.*" (Phil. ii. 6—8, Heb. xii. 2.) So great was the degradation of such a death esteemed to be universally, that a most powerful prejudice against the gospel was everywhere excited, on account of its author having suffered the shame of dying in this way. The Gentiles were ready to treat the apostles with the greatest contempt, for preaching a religion, that offered salvation by the death of a man that had been *crucified;* and it continued to be long after a taunting reproach cast upon Christians, that their leader, whom they worshipped as a God, had expired as a malefactor on the *cross.* The scandal of such a death was no less in the estimation of the Jews; and besides, they considered the person who suffered it to be *accursed of God*, according to the law in Deut. xxi. 23, which declares every one that is hanged upon a tree to be thus made a curse. (Gal. iii. 13.) To trust in such an one as the great Messiah and Saviour, was therefore in their view the greatest madness and folly. (1 Cor. i. 23, 24.) The apostles, on the other hand, and all such as were led by the Spirit of God to lay hold of eternal life by faith, gloried in their Master's cross What to others seemed shameful and vile, they esteemed most precious and worthy of all admiration. In the face of the world, they counted all things but loss for the sake of *Christ* and HIM CRUCIFIED. (Rom. i. 16, 1 Cor. ii. 1, 2.)

When the sentence, *thou shalt go to the cross*, was passed by the magistrate upon any one, the unhappy man was in the first place stripped of all his clothes, with only a single covering left around the loins, and severely scourged with rods or whips. So cruel was the scourging, that death sometimes took place under it. After this treatment, which in a great measure took away all his strength, he was compelled to carry the cross on which he was to be hung, (and it was by no means a light burden,) to the place of execution. This was commonly a hill near the public road, not far out of the city or town. As he passed along the way to this place, smarting with pain, and ready to faint by reason of the dreadful stripes he had already received, and groaning under the weight of his own cross, the unfeeling rabble loaded him with insult, mockery and wanton cruelty. Having reached the appointed spot, the *infamous tree*, as it was sometimes called, was taken from his shoulder and firmly fixed in the ground. It consisted of a piece of timber standing upright like a post, not generally more than ten feet high, and crossed by another considerably smaller, either altogether at the top, so as to resemble in its whole form the letter T, or only a little distance below it. The person to be crucified, having first been presented with some kind of stupifying drink, to deaden the sense of pain, was then lifted up, and nailed to the fatal wood by four large spikes, driven one through each hand and foot. The hands were fastened to the cross piece, with the arms stretched out and raised somewhat

above the head; the feet, to the upright beam, down toward the ground. To prevent the hands from being torn away from the nails by the weight of the body, there was a short piece of wood made to stick out from the middle of the beam just mentioned, for the sufferer to sit upon. Hence, he was sometimes said to *ride upon the cross*, or, *to rest upon the sharp cross*. On the cross piece, directly over his head, as he hung thus exposed to the gazing multitude, an inscription or *title* was fixed, declaring, in large letters, the crime for which he was thus punished. In some cases, the condemned person was nailed to the cross before it was set up, and so lifted up together with it, when it was raised and fixed in its proper standing position. The first method, however, seems to have been the most common. The execution was performed by four soldiers, each of them driving one of the spikes, who, it appears, had a right, on account of this service, to the garments of the man that was put to death. (John xix. 23, 24.) In this awful situation the victim of the cross was left to suffer, till death came to relieve him from its power. This, however, did not take place commonly till the third, and frequently till the fourth or fifth day. (Mark xv. 44.) While any signs of life appeared, the cross was watched by a guard.

After death, the body was often left hanging till it wasted away with corruption, or was devoured by birds of prey and ravenous beasts; (for it was generally so low, that these last could reach at least the lower part of it.) In the province of Judea, however, it was allowed to depart from the general practice, by way of indulgence to the Jews, with whom it was not lawful to leave a malefactor's body all night upon a tree or any sort of gibbet. (Deut. xxi. 23.) Among them, therefore, crucified persons were buried on the day of their crucifixion; and their death, on that account, was hastened by other means, such as kindling a fire under the cross, letting wild beasts loose upon them, or breaking their bones with a mallet. In the case of our Saviour, no such means were necessary: he died in a few hours; but to be sure that he was really dead, one of the soldiers pierced his side with a spear. (John xix. 31—35.)

Such was the manner of death which the Lord of glory humbled himself to endure, when he laid down his life for a sinful and ruined world. His crucifixion was attended, while it lasted, with all the circumstances of indignity and horror that usually accompanied the punishment. But it was marked, besides, with peculiar and extraordinary inhumanity, such as common custom was not acquainted with. It was a scene of the most unfeeling insult and cruelty, from its commencement to its close. Jews and Gentiles joined to accomplish the work of shame and awful guilt. In the high priest's palace it began. There, we are told, the Son of God was treated with the most bitter and malicious scorn. They insulted him by spitting in his face; they buffeted him; they covered his eyes and then struck him with the palms of their hands, saying, in mockery of his claim to be the Messiah from heaven, Prophecy unto us, thou Christ, who is he that smote thee? (Matt. xxvi. 67, 68.) The very servants were encouraged to abuse him in this way. (Mark xiv. 65.) When sent to Herod, the proud prince with his men of war sat him at nought, and mocked him, and arrayed him in a gorgeous robe. Before Pilate's bar, the chief priests and elders accused him, in language of bitterness and reproach, of the worst crimes; charging him with sedition and blasphemy, and representing him to be a malefactor whose guilt cried loudly for the heaviest vengeance of the law. The multitude without, excited by their religious rulers, insisted with tumultuous and violent cry, that he should be sentenced to the cross. The governor, though he had no doubt of his innocence, at length gave way to their importunity, and ordered him to be scourged, as a preparatory step to his execution The Roman soldiers then caused the work of wanton mockery to be renewed. In derision of him, as one that aspired to be a king, they stripped him, and put on him an old robe of royal colour; and when they had platted a crown of thorns, they put it upon his head, and a reed in his right hand, for a sceptre; and they bowed the knee before him, and mocked him, saying, Hail, king of the Jews! Then they spit upon him, and took the reed, and smote him on the head, cruelly forcing the thorns to pierce it on every side. Thus arrayed, exhausted, and torn with the stripes of the scourge, and disfigured with blood trickling from his temples and over his face, the governor brought him out before the people, hoping that they might yet be moved to pity by such a sight, and consent to his release. But the cry of priests and people was renewed with unrelenting rage, Crucify, crucify him! Away, away with him! And when he seemed determined to let him go, on account of some new conversation which he had with him, a loud threat was sounded in his ears: "If thou let this man go, thou art not Cæsar's friend." (John xix. 1—12.) This overcame his resolution: he knew that the emperor, Tiberius Cæsar, was a most suspicious and jealous prince, and ever ready to listen to charges of treason and opposition to his authority, that were brought against inferior rulers in the empire; and that it was not at all unlikely that an accusation against himself, such as the Jews threatened, might, if carried to Rome, be enough to ruin him. Accordingly, for the sake of his worldly interest, he resisted all the remonstrances of conscience, and ordered the execution to proceed. So they led him away to be crucified. Bearing his cross, and ready to sink under its weight, he went forth through the city toward the place of death, insulted, derided, and abused, no doubt, by the surrounding multitude, the whole way. His strength, however, was found before long to be so far taken away by his sufferings, that he could not possibly support his burden: as they came out of the gate of the city, therefore, they laid hold upon one Simon, a Cyrenian, that was coming from the country, and on him they laid the cross, that he might bear it after Jesus. When they had reached Calvary, they offered him the stupifying liquor, (which he refused to drink,) and nailed him to the dreadful tree, placing him between two malefactors, as if he was not merely of the same infamous character, but vilest of the three. It was probably as they were driving the spikes through his hands and feet, that he lifted to Heaven that affecting prayer: "Father, forgive them, for they know not what they do!" The four soldiers who fastened the nails, with cold-blooded indifference, took his raiment as their spoil, and parted it among them in his preence. While he hung, tortured with anguish through all his frame, he was assailed on every side, in the most hard-hearted manner, with taunting irony and scornful ridicule. "They that passed by reviled him, wagging their heads, and saying, *Thou that destroyest the temple and buildest it in three days, save thyself! If thou be the Son of God, come down from the cross!* Likewise, also, the chief priests, mocking him, with the scribes and elders, said, *He saved others; himself he cannot save! If he be the king of Israel, let him now come down from the cross, and we will believe him. He trusted in God; let him deliver him now, if he will have him; for he said, I am the Son of God.*" It was surely an awful spectacle, when the Holy and Just One was thus subjected to anguish and loaded with reproach, by sinful mortals.

The pain that was suffered in crucifixion was exceedingly severe. By reason of the scourging, the back was all torn with wounds, and these being exposed to the air, became, by their inflammation, a source of keen distress. Because the hands and feet abound particularly with nerves, which are the instruments of all feeling, nails driven through these parts could not fail to create the most lively anguish. The body was placed, moreover, in an unnatural position, the arms being stretched back, in order to be nailed to the cross piece above, in such a manner as to produce an oppressive feeling of uneasiness and constraint through the whole breast, which became, in a short time, an occasion of indescribable misery. This position, of course, could not be altered in the smallest degree, and the least movement which the sufferer might be led to make, must have served only to provoke new torture from every wound. The cross, therefore, was full of cruelty as well as of shame, and might well be dreaded. But are we to suppose that the Lord Jesus Christ could not endure its horrors with as much ease as many of his followers, through the assistance of his grace, have been able to endure the same or similar anguish of body in their deaths? Whence, then, that extreme anxiety and dismay with which he was filled in view of his last sufferings? Whence that awful distress that overwhelmed him on the cross? What was the *cup*, the thought of which produced such agony in the garden of Gethsemane, when he prayed that, if possible, it might pass from him, and his sweat was as it were great drops of blood falling down to the ground? What was the *cup* which, while he was drinking it, wrung from his bosom that piercing cry of sorrow: "My God! my God! why hast thou forsaken me?" Ah, the terrors of the cross were but a feeble representation

of the horror that compassed his soul from another quarter
There was wrath laid upon him by a righteous God, for the
guilt of sin. It pleased the Lord to bruise him, and to put
him to grief, and to make his soul an offering for sin, because
the great work of redemption which he had undertaken required it. He made him to be sin for us, who knew no sin,
and laid on him the iniquity of us all; therefore, he was
wounded for our transgressions, he was *bruised* for our iniquities, the *chastisement* of our peace was upon him, and with
his *stripes* we are healed. (Isa. liii. 4—11, 2 Cor. v. 21,
Heb. ix. 28, x. 4—13, 1 Pet. ii. 22—24.)

Having considered what it was literally *to bear the cross*,
we may without much difficulty understand what it signifies
figuratively. It can mean nothing less than to be ready to
undergo the severest hardship, to face the most formidable
danger, and to lay down even life itself, if the sacrifice should
be required. Such a *cross-bearer* every follower of Christ is
commanded to be. (Matt. x. 38, xvi. 24.) And he may not
dream that his faithfulness will not *actually* be brought into
trial. The way to heaven is through much self-denial, labour,
and tribulation.

SECTION VI.

OF MILITARY AFFAIRS.

AMONG the Israelites, armies were made up altogether of
what we call the militia of a country. A general enrolment
was made of all that were *able to go forth to war*, from twenty
years old and upward. (Num. i. 2, 3, xxvi. 2.) Out of this
whole number, in case of war, as many were called into actual
service as the occasion appeared to demand. All, however,
held themselves ready to assemble on the shortest notice; and
if the occasion was extraordinary, the whole body might be
summoned to meet in one vast army at once. (Judg. xx. 1—
11, 1 Sam. xi. 7.) In common cases, only a small part was
chosen. (Ex. xvii. 9, 10, Num. xxxi. 4, 5, Josh. vii. 3, 4.)
When we consider the way in which soldiers were raised, we
need not be surprised at the accounts that are contained in
the Bible, of uncommonly large armies being formed in a very
short time. In the time of the kings, especially, such vast
armies were frequently gathered for the field. They sometimes consisted of several hundred thousand men. It was the
more easy for the government to call out hosts of this sort, be-

cause, in ancient times, soldiers did not receive any wages; they were supported at their own expense, or by their parents. (Judg. xx. 10, 1 Sam. xvii. 17—20.) Every man had to find likewise his own arms. This plan of making soldiers provide for themselves tended to make wars in those days generally of short continuance. Long campaigns, such as are now common, in which whole seasons are sometimes passed away in marches and manœuvres, without much actual fighting, could not be sustained, when each soldier had either to carry his provisions along with him for the whole term, or to have them sent all the while from home. Hence, when armies were collected, they commonly came as soon as possible to battle, and so in most cases decided the war with a single stroke. Valour, indeed, was sometimes encouraged with the offer of reward; but only in special instances, and never to any general extent. (Josh. xv. 16, 1 Sam. xvii. 25, 2 Sam. xviii. 11.) In time, however, the practice of making public provision for the wants of soldiers and of allowing them some pay, began to grow gradually into use. In the time of the Maccabees, military service was rewarded with regular wages. Accordingly, we find in the New Testament, which belongs to a later period, mention made of wages of this sort. (Luke iii. 14, 1 Cor. ix. 7.)

When the army was made up, and ready to proceed to battle, a proclamation was made, releasing certain classes of men entirely from the duty of service, and allowing them to return home. (Deut. xx. 5—8.) Moreover, when a man married a wife, he was not required to go forth to war for a whole year afterwards. (Deut. xxiv. 5.) At first, the whole army was always dismissed, as soon as the war was over, and all its soldiers were converted at once into quiet husbandmen. Under the government of the kings, however, it became common to have *always* some soldiers in service. (1 Sam. xiii. 2.) Besides his *Life-guard*, David had, at all times, twenty-four thousand men employed in military duty. His whole army was divided into twelve bodies of so many men each, and every one of them was required to perform this service in course, a month at a time. (1 Chron. xxvii. 1—15.) The practice of having a standing force in this way, led necessarily to the making of some provision for their support at the expense of the government; and also for supplying them with arms. (2 Chron. xi. 12, xxvi. 14.)

The commander-in-chief of the whole army was called *the captain of the host*. His authority and importance were very great. (2 Kings iv. 13.) Both kings and generals had *armour bearers;* they were chosen out of such as were most valiant in the army, and were employed not merely to carry the arms of their masters, but also to give their commands to the inferior captains.

Before the time of Solomon, the Israelitish army was composed altogether of footmen. He multiplied horses in the country, and from his day, horsemen and chariots were not unknown in the wars of the nation. (1 Kings x. 26, xxii. 35.) They were, however, never so important for military use in the land of Israel as in most other countries; its hilly surface hindered them from being of much service. But on account of their benefit to nations in general, and the dependence which it was common to place upon them, we find them used figuratively to signify protection and defence of the most effectual kind. (2 Kings ii. 12, xiii. 14.) The strength of war among the Israelites was, in every age, their infantry. This was made up of two general classes of soldiers,—such as engaged with their enemies in battle hand to hand, and such as fought them at a distance. The first class were armed with spears, swords, and shields; the second, with javelins, slings, and bows.

In the days of our Saviour, as has been noticed already, a considerable number of Roman soldiers were stationed in the country, to support the authority of the governor. The Roman armies were mighty in war, consisting of footmen and horsemen joined in suitable proportion, and distinguished by the most complete discipline. They were divided into great bodies called *legions*, each of which was divided again several times into less bands and companies. The proper number for a legion was six thousand men, though it was not always the same. In common language, the word was used to signify any great number, as the words *thousand* and *million* are with us. (Matt. xxvi. 53, Mark v. 9.)

The *war-chariot* was in use at a very early period. (Ex. xiv. 6, 7.) The Canaanites employed it much in their battles, and among the Eastern nations generally it was in no small reputation. We read that Judah could not drive out the inhabitants of the valley, in the territory assigned to that tribe, because they had chariots of iron; that is, we may suppose, chariots which had much iron-work in their structure, so as to be very strong. (Judg. i. 19.) They could act with advantage only where the country was somewhat level. The war-chariot, like all others in ancient times, had only two wheels, and was drawn generally by two horses, though sometimes by three or four, abreast. It carried two persons, a *driver*, who directed its course over the battle ground, and a *warrior*, who, standing upon his feet, fought from it with spear or bow, as it wheeled through the tumult of death. Cyrus, the great king of Persia, introduced chariots of such size that twenty men, it is said, could fight from each of them. But what made them still more terrible was the way in which they were themselves armed. On both sides of them were fixed great iron  scythes, strong and sharp, with which they rushed at full speed upon the ranks of the enemy, bearing terror and destruction wherever they came. Some have thought that the iron chariots of the Canaanites just noticed, were so called on account of some such deadly contrivance that belonged to them.—*Elephants* were used in war, especially in later times, among some Eastern nations. Great machines, like towers, were fixed upon their backs, from which sometimes as many as thirty-two soldiers fought. Mention is made of such elephants, and also of *chariots armed with hooks*, or scythes, in the books of the Maccabees.

Let us now attend to the arms with which the ancient soldier was equipped for the battle. We may divide them all into two general classes, as they were designed either to protect the warrior himself or to injure his enemy; that is, as they were either *defensive* or *offensive*. We will notice such as were of the defensive sort first.

224   BIBLICAL ANTIQUITIES.

The head was guarded with a *Helmet*. It was a strong cap, made of thick ox-hide, and often covered with brass; sometimes it was made of brass altogether. The practice of having it crowned with some ornament on top, such as a horse-tail crest, or some kind of plume, was in use among different people at an early period.—The *Breastplate* consisted of two parts, one of which covered the fore part of the body, and the other the back; both being joined together at the sides by clasps or buttons. It was made sometimes of flax or cotton woven very thick and close; at other times, of some sort of metal, especially brass. Some of this last sort were composed of scales, either brazen or iron, laid one over another like the scales of a fish Such was the *coat of mail* which Goliath of Gath wore. In the English Bible, this piece of armour is called gene rally *a coat of mail*, sometimes a *habergeon* and *brigandine*.— The feet and legs were sometimes protected with *Greaves* or boots; those of Goliath were of brass.—The *Girdle* was an important article, as we have already seen, in common dress; but to the soldier it was especially needful. In marching and in fighting, he wanted to have his loins well girded, so as to move without the smallest hinderance. Military girdles were often very beautiful and valuable. Fastened to his left arm, the warrior's *Shield*, when skilfully managed, afforded better protection to his whole body, than all the rest of his armour together. There were different kinds of them, some large, and others comparatively small. Some were large enough to guard the entire body at once; others of less size were passed with dexterous movement from one point to another, as the eye gave warning where the enemy's weapon was likely to strike. Shields were manufactured sometimes of light wood, or oziers woven together, with a covering of tough bull's hide, or, in some instances, of brass; sometimes of a bull's hide alone, two or three times folded over. They were so formed as to present on their front side, toward the enemy, a surface more or less rounding from the centre to the border, so as to turn aside whatever struck them. To make them smooth and slippery for the same purpose, as well as to keep them from being injured by the wet, it was common to anoint them with oil. (Isa. xxi. 5.) Among all ancient nations, it was held to be a great disgrace, and so a great misfortune, to lose the shield in battle. God is called a *Shield* and a *Buckler*, because he affords the most secure protection to all who put their trust in him; *with favour he compasses the righteous as with a shield.* (Ps. v. 12, xviii. 2, lxvii. 9.)

Offensive weapons were of two sorts; such as were used in fighting hand to hand, and such as were used in fighting at a distance. Of the first kind were the sword and the heavier kind of spear. The *Sword* was short, in comparison with ours. There appear, however, to have been two kinds of the weapon, one larger than the other; the first had only a single edge, the second had an edge on each

226   BIBLICAL ANTIQUITIES.

side, like a dagger. The edge of a sword was often called its *mouth*, with which it was said to *devour* flesh and to *drink* blood. The weapon was carried in a sheath fastened to the girdle, so as to hang upon the thigh; whence the expression *to gird on the sword*, or to make ready for war. (Ps. xlv. 3.) The justice of God is represented as being armed with a sword, to destroy the guilty; and sometimes the *means* which he makes use of to accomplish punishment are figuratively styled his sword. (Ps. xvii. 13, Isa. xxxiv. 5—8, Jer. xii. 12, xlvii. 6, 7.) In like manner, the Assyrian is called *the rod of his anger*, sent against a hypocritical nation; and the Medes and Persians, led by the illustrious Cyrus, before

whom Babylon's glory fell, are declared to have been his *battle-axe* and *weapons of war*, employed to break in pieces the nations, and to destroy kingdoms. (Isa. x. 5—15, Jer. li. 20—24.) The *Spear* was a long wooden staff with an iron point.—For fighting at a distance, javelins, bows, and slings, were used. The *Javelin* was a spear of lighter make than the one used in close fight, which was darted with the hand against the enemy. The *Bow* and the *Arrow* are of very ancient origin. Bows were generally made of wood; sometimes, however, of brass. They were so strong, that it required frequently the greatest force to bend them: hence they made use of the foot as well as the hands for this purpose, treading on one end, and pressing on the other with the left hand, under the whole weight of the body, till the string was brought to the right point and fixed there by the other. Bending a bow, accordingly, they used to call *treading it*. *Arrows* were made of reeds, at first; afterwards of light wood pointed with iron. The *Quiver* was hung upon the back; so that the soldier might reach his hand over his shoulder and draw out the arrows as he wanted them. The *Sling* also was one of the earliest weapons of war. Most wonderful was the skill which was sometimes acquired by practice, in the use of it. The Benjamites excelled in such skill; many of them *could sling stones at an hair's breadth and not miss*, and could use their left hand about as well as their right. (Judg. xx. 16, 1 Chr. xii. 2.)

Cities were generally surrounded with a wall, to protect them from enemies; and sometimes with a double one. On the top of walls, towers were raised, which often rose to a great height. From these, stones and arrows were discharged upon besieging armies. Guards also were kept constantly stationed in some of them, to look out for the approach of any danger, and to sound an alarm when it appeared. Great engines were sometimes placed in them to hurl destruction upon the enemy

Besieging Engine.

with more dreadful force. These were either immense bows, which were bent by means of powerful machinery, and shot arrows enormously large; or prodigious slings, which were put in motion in like manner, and hurled great stones and balls of lead. Engines of such sort, *invented by cunning men, to shoot arrows and great stones withal,* king Uzziah caused to be placed upon the towers and bulwarks of Jerusalem. (2 Chron. xxvi. 15.) It was common to erect single high towers also in other places through the land, especially on the borders of the country, in which military guards were kept. When an army besieged a city, they often dug a ditch around it, between themselves and the wall, to keep their own camp in security; and sometimes another on the outside of their own camp, to have it protected behind and before. Then they *cast up a bank*, or *mound* of earth, against such parts of the wall as seemed to be least strong, which ran slanting upward from the ditch so as sometimes to equal the wall itself in height. From

this, they shot with their weapons into the city. The *Battering-ram*, too, was employed at a very early period. It was a long, heavy beam of solid wood, with a head of iron or brass mounted on one end. This was at first borne on the arms of the soldiers and driven with violence against the wall; but afterwards, it was hung by means of long chains, so as to be fairly balanced in the middle, and thus made to swing head foremost against it with much greater force. Where the strength of the walls and the watchful skill of the besieged were such as to baffle all attempts to take the city by storm or by stratagem, the more tedious way of starving it into a surrender was resorted to. Sieges of great cities lasted sometimes in this way a great while; and awful beyond description, in some cases, were the sufferings they occasioned. (Deut xxviii. 52—57, 2 Kings vi 24—30, Jer. xix. 9.)

The onset of a battle was very olent, and was made with a great shout. In the ancient way of fighting, the qualifications of a good warrior were very different from what they are now, since the invention of gunpowder has changed the whole manner of war. Personal activity and strength were then all-important. Soldier was often called to join with soldier, in direct individual combat, in which he must destroy his antagonist or die; and when he escaped with victory from one such desperate trial, it was only to engage in another equally critical. Battles conducted in this way, it is easy to perceive, must have been commonly very full of blood and death. Terrible was the slaughter accomplished by war in ancient times, and sad was the desolation which the monster scattered abroad to mark its fatal path. Even the tender mercies of victory were cruel. In the treatment of its vanquished foes, the successful army owned no restraint but its own pleasure; and it was too often hurried by the wrath excited in battle to glut its vengeance, by using its power with the utmost rigour. Fields and houses and cattle, men, women and children, became, by right of war, the property of the conquerors. They considered the spoils of the conquered the proper reward of their warfare. The soldiers, who, as we have seen, received no wages, felt themselves entitled to these as the only compensation which they could expect for their services. The hope of securing a reward to themselves in this way, was one powerful motive that animated them in their trials and toils; and accordingly the division of the spoils after battle was always an occasion of the most boisterous joy, such as rose from the fields in the time of harvest, or rung through the hills when the season of vintage was come. (Isa. ix. 3, Ezek. xxix. 18 20.) Oftentimes, captives of every age and sex were sold into bondage; and not unfrequently the most brutal outrage and violence were employed in their destruction, without the smallest compassion (2 Kings viii. 12, Isa. xiii. 16—18, Zech. xiv. 2.) When the wrath of the conqueror had been provoked in more than a common measure, he passed like an overflowing flood through the land, reducing it to waste and barrenness the most deplorable. Whole nations were sometimes carried away out of their own countries, and settled in others far remote, that they might be the more effectually subdued into complete obedience. Thus Israel and Judah were carried off into distant regions, and other people were brought from different countries to occupy the desolate cities of Samaria. (2 Kings xvii. 6, 23, 24, xxiv. 14—16.) In some instances, however, more humanity was exercised, and conquered countries were allowed to remain under the government of their own kings, on condition of paying tribute, and thus continuing to acknowledge their subjection from year to year. But if such rebelled, they were punished with dreadful severity if again overcome.

Such was the character of war among ancient nations in general. The Israelites, however, had much more humanity

in their common manner of warfare, than was exercised by
other people: and if much of their conduct, in this respect,
seems after all to be marked with cruel severity, when tried
by the principles of later times, we are to recollect, that in the
matter of war a nation's behaviour must necessarily be regu
lated, to some considerable extent, by the general usage and
spirit of the age to which it belongs. For its own security, it
must employ with its enemies, measures in some degree of the
same nature with those which other governments adopt. We
are to bear in mind too, that in the case of some of their wars,
the Israelites acted under the express direction of God. Thus
they were commanded to destroy the Canaanites without
mercy, because the measure of their iniquity was full. God
had a most perfect right to give such a command, and they, in
the execution of it, discharged a solemn religious duty. To
find fault with them for this, would be as if one should quarrel
with the storm, or charge the lightning with injustice, when
they fulfil in terror the judgments of the Almighty.

When the consequences of being overcome in war were so
dreadful as we have seen, it is no wonder that great consternation and grief were felt by a conquered people. They often
betook themselves to flight, willing to forsake every thing for
preservation from the cruelty of their enemies. Not unfrequently they fled to the tops of the mountains, and lonely
caves and wild rocks became their places of refuge from the
overflowing scourge. Great, on the other hand, was the rejoicing which the news of victory spread through a nation.
Among the Jews, the conquerors were received, as they returned home, with the most unbounded gladness. The people
came out to meet them from different cities, with songs of congratulation and praise. Bands of women especially went forth
in this way, with instruments of music in their hands, and
welcomed their approach with dancing and singing. Thus,
"the women came out of all the cities of Israel, singing and
dancing to meet king Saul, with tabrets, with joy, and with
instruments of music." (1 Sam. xviii. 6, 7, 2 Chron. xx. 27,
28.)

The image of a battle, or continual warfare, is employed in
the Scriptures, to set forth the difficulty of the Christian life
in this present evil world; and the Christian himself is represented to be a soldier, whose safety requires him to be at all
times clad in complete armour, and to abound in watchfulness
and labour to the end. The enemies to be opposed and overcome are terrible in strength. "We wrestle not," says Paul,
"against flesh and blood, but against principalities, against

powers, against the rulers of the darkness of this world, against spiritual wickedness in high places. Wherefore take unto you the whole armour of God, that ye may be able to withstand in the evil day, and having done all, to stand. Stand therefore, having your loins girt about with truth, and having on the breastplate of righteousness; and your feet shod with the preperation of the gospel of peace; above all, taking the shield of faith, wherewith ye shall be able to quench all the fiery darts of the wicked. And take the helmet of salvation, and the sword of the Spirit, which is the word of God: Praying always with all prayer and supplication in the Spirit, and watching thereunto with all perseverance." (Eph. vi. 10—18.) This fight the apostle calls, in another place, "the good fight of faith." (1 Tim. vi. 12.) The man that endureth to the end obtains the *victory*, and for his reward receives *a crown* of life. It is only "to him that overcometh," that the blessedness of heaven is promised. (Rev. ii. 7, 17, 26—28, iii. 5, 12, 21.) What holy joy the aged Paul felt, when he found himself, after all the dangers, and toils, and discouragements, and sufferings of this great fight, able to shout toward its close, "Victory! victory!" (2 Tim. iv. 7, 8.) This victory is won, through the helping grace of God, by means of *faith*, and without this it is not possible. (1 John v. 4, 5.)

We have already seen how the Christian life is represented under the image of a laborious race, such as was common in the ancient Grecian games. The Holy Ghost has made use of the most significant *things*, as well as the most forcible *words*, to teach us the greatness and difficulty of the work to which religion calls us, and to stir us up to earnest concern and untiring continual diligence in its pursuit. (Matt. vii. 13, 14, 22, x. 37, 39, xi. 12, xiii. 44—46, xx. 16, xxiv. 42—44, Luke xiii. 23—30, xiv. 25—33, Acts xiv. 22, 1 Cor. ix. 24 —27, Phil. ii. 12, iii. 7—17, Heb. iii. 12—14, iv. 1, 11— 13, vi. 12, xii. 1—3, 1 Pet. iv. 18.) How strange, that men, with the Bible in their hands, should so generally feel as if religion did not need uncommon interest or uncommon exertion! Multitudes, who call themselves Christians, are passing onward through life hardly conscious of any struggle or trial of a religious sort whatever, and yet they dream that they are on the way to heaven. If you talk to them of spiritual discouragements, anxieties, toils, and conflicts, they know not what you mean, or perhaps regard all such language as the sickly cant of fanaticism or gloomy superstition. They show far more concern about the affairs of this world, than about all the infinitely interesting realities of that which is to come, and seldom allow these last to engage their thoughts or their conversation; yet they pretend to be followers of them who *through faith and patience* have gone to inherit the promises. But let us beware of such delusion. The devil would like to persuade us, that the road to heaven requires no great care or effort to be found and travelled; but Christ has assured us, that it is difficult and narrow, and that few find it. The devil will whisper to the soul, that there is no need to be continually watching and striving in order to secure eternal life; but the Bible warns us to work out our salvation *with fear and trembling*. The redemption of the soul is precious. The ruin out of which it is to be raised is most awful. All Heaven is moved with interest for its salvation. The Son of God has laid down his life a ransom for it. And shall we dream of having lifted such a height from corruption to holiness, with no corresponding interest or exertion on its own part? No: religion claims, and certainly deserves, our highest regard and most serious labour. It sets before us a RACE; and we must run, laying aside every weight and casting off every hinderance, if we would win its prize. It sets before us a BATTLE; and we must fight, arrayed in all the armour of righteousness, and resisting evil within and without, on to the close of life, if we would secure its victory and be crowned with immortal glory. By grace we are saved, it is true, through faith, but this gift of God is not obtained without hearty desire and endeavour on the sinner's part; and then, faith must lead to **earnest** and diligent labour in the work of purifying the heart and overcoming the world—or else it will be but a dead faith, vain and unprofitable.

BIBLICAL ANTIQUITIES.

PART II.

Priests removing the Old and placing the New Bread

PART II.

CHAPTER I.

GENERAL HISTORY OF RELIGION.

Our first parents, before the Fall, were altogether holy The law of God was written upon their hearts, and, while they delighted in it as perfectly good, they obeyed it in all its length and breadth. Their religion was, in its nature, the same with that of Heaven. According to the universal and perpetual order of the Divine Government, they were *entitled*, on account of their own righteousness of character and conduct, to the favour of their Maker, which is happiness and life. They were not, however, placed out of the reach of evil. They had a trial of their faithfulness to stand, before their moral state should be rendered eternally secure. In that trial they failed. The commandment of God, through the temptation of the devil, was wilfully transgressed. Thus, "by one man sin entered into the world, and death by sin; and so death passed upon all men, for that all have sinned." (Rom. v. 12.)

The ruin was awful. The greatest calamity in the wide universe of God, is *sin*. The human race was now brought into that condition which is the most deplorable that any mind can conceive. Struck out from the order and happiness of the general creation, and cut off from all intercourse with God, it presented only a spectacle of horror and terrific desolation, uncheered by the smallest gleam of hope. The state of man was the same with that into which a part of the angels had fallen; a state of rebellion against the Almighty, of exclusion from peace, a state of infinite wrath, of death without hope and without end.

But God had mercy. When no arm but his own could save, he determined to help. He left the angels to perish without relief, but stretched forth his hand to rescue sinking man. (Heb. ii. 16.) A great Salvation was provided. A wonder ful arrangement had been, from the beginning, made in heaven, to recover the lost. The eternal Son of God engaged to become a *sacrifice* for their guilt, and the Father consented to receive once more into favour, and, by his Spirit, to restore to holiness, as many as should be willing to accept the atonement thus wonderfully secured. And because the nature of man's depravity was such, that not one of all the race would ever be naturally willing to embrace the offer of mercy, even after such condescension and love on the part of God, the arrangement of Divine compassion extended yet farther. It was determined that, in consideration of the Saviour's work, the Holy Spirit should be sent forth into the hearts of men, to enlighten and persuade them, to the end that they might become willing to be saved; that thus, as the prophet declares, the Redeemer should "see of the travail of his soul, and be satisfied," (Isa. liii. 11;) and that, out of the multitude of Adam's fallen children, a portion should yet gloriously rise from ruin and find a happy restoration to the great family of God. Here originated the *Church*.

The church is a society made up of the Redeemer's people. In its *visible* character, as a body regularly organized in this world, it comprehends all who, in any age, *profess* to be his people, and externally are placed under that constitution which he has appointed for their government and improvement. In its *invisible* character,—that is, as it appears to the eye of God, who searcheth the heart,—it embraces only those who are *really* and *truly* the people of Christ, redeemed by his blood, and made meet by his grace "to be partakers of the inheritance of the saints in light." Many belong to the church as an outward body on earth, who have no part in its glorious reality, as a body spiritually united to its Great Head. The *institution* of the church had respect, no doubt, only to those who become truly thus united to Christ; its object was, by means of the truth of God, (which it was appointed to preserve from age to age, and to employ instrumentally for the salvation of men,) to bring out from the darkness of the world, as many as might be moved to comply with the Divine invitation in deed and in truth, and so, by salutary preparation and discipline, to gather their whole number, from the beginning to the end of time, into one great family in heaven. But, in its actual outward form and history, in this world, *all* are regarded as being interested in its existence, who participate in its external privileges, whether truly pious or not; because man cannot try the heart, and God unfolds not *his* judgment of its character before the Great Day.

In consequence of the Redeemer's undertaking, our race was, immediately after the Fall, placed in new circumstances. They were fallen still, but a way of recovery was thrown open. The wrath of the Almighty still hung suspended over their heads with tremendous terror; but for a little time its destruction was delayed; the full bursting forth of its fury was restrained; and in that awful pause room was left for complete escape; a REFUGE was provided within reach, strong and secure, to which the criminal might run and be eternally safe. Thus, in the midst of earth's moral desolation, there was to be displayed, down to the end of time, a spectacle of returning life. Heaven was to receive, with universal rapture, millions from the very jaws of hell. The accomplishment of this mercy was to be, however, only through the mediation and suffering of the Son of God. The Holy One of Heaven could deal no longer with men *directly*, save as their judge and destroyer. From the time of the Fall, therefore, no communication of friendship could exist between God and man, except *through* Christ. For his sake, the Infinite Judge forbears for a while the full execution of death, and to him is committed, in a peculiar manner, the care of our fallen world. The Father has withdrawn himself from immediate concern with it, such as he employs in his general government. It has been given over into the hands of the Son, in view of his mediatorial work. He has been constituted *Head over all things to the church*. (Eph. i. 22.) He has undertaken, and it has been left to him, to maintain the full honour of God's law in the case of the human family, while yet redemption from its curse should be made possible for all, and multitudes should actually obtain the deliverance. He governs the world, therefore, with continual regard to the church, which he has determined to gather out of its ruins, and conduct to glory. All the kindness which the world experiences now from God, comes through *him*, and is only in consequence of that new position in which it is placed before God, by his mediatorial undertaking. And because the world is thus given into his hands, with the trust of completely vindicating the holiness of the Divine law, its final judgment will also proceed from his authority. "The Father judgeth no man, but hath committed all judgment unto the Son. He hath given him authority to execute judgment, because he is the SON OF MAN." (John v. 21—29, Acts xvii. 31.) As many as refuse to embrace his mercy, he will himself sentence to the everlasting death, which sin deserves, and God's righteous law demands. Thus he will reduce *all things* to order, by grace or by justice, and wind up, as it were, in unalterable and perfect arrangement, the affairs of this apostate part of creation. "Then cometh the end, when he shall have delivered up the kingdom to God, even the Father; when he shall have put down all rule, and all authority and power: for he must reign till he hath put all enemies under his feet. And when all things shall be subdued unto him, then shall the Son also himself be subject unto him that put all things under him, that God may be all in all." (1 Cor. xv. 24—28.) Thus will be accomplished that *restitution of all things*, foretold by all the prophets. (Acts iii. 21.) Then, having put an end to disorder, and brought all opposition into subjection to God, the Redeemer, God and man in one person, shall reign in the glory of his kingdom, as Head of the church, under the general government of Him who is all in all, without interruption and without end. For it is written, "He shall reign over the house of Jacob for ever, and of his kingdom there shall be no end." And again, "Unto the Son he saith, thy throne, O God, is for ever and ever." (Luke i. 33, Heb. i. 8.)

The church, then, though it has been all along despised by the great body of our race, has ever been infinitely the most interesting and important institution in the world. It is the kingdom of Jesus Christ, proceeding under his own direction and government to that great end of victory and glory, which it is ordained to reach. The world derives all its mercies from heaven, through its relation to this kingdom, established in the midst of its ruin. And because the government of the world is upon the shoulders of Zion's King, all the changes that take place among the nations of the earth, which are directed by his providence, are made to help forward the interests of this same kingdom. The world is ruled for the church. The mighty ones of earth little dream of the designs which God has in view to accomplish, by all the revolutions and schemes, which, from age to age, occupy their thoughts and call forth their labours. Their imaginations are directed to ends of mere temporal advantage to themselves, or their particular countries; but God employs their work to bring about far other ends, such as the prosperity of His own kingdom requires. Thus, ambition, and pride, and every unhallowed passion, which fill the world with war and change, are all made subservient to the will of Christ, and conspire to promote his glorious plan of mercy to the church. (Isa. x. 5—7.) In the vast machinery of this world's action, unnumbered wheels are constantly at work; and though, to human sight, many of them seem to be acting for particular separate purposes, the eye of God, whose wisdom has united the universal frame, beholds all its parts contributing their ultimate influence to the same point, and combining their multiplied movements to accomplish the same grand result. That result is the advancement of the Redeemer's kingdom to its victorious consummation. This will be clearly seen, when the history of the earth shall have come to its close. It may, however, be even now discovered with striking certainty, in looking back upon the history of ages that are past When we read the record of what has been done among the nations, in different ages of the world, this great truth should be kept at all times in view. History is studied correctly and understandingly, only when this relation of God's general providence, in all the changes of earth, to his will concerning the church, is seriously and attentively regarded. Here we find a reason and a meaning, an order and a connection, in the events which it unfolds, such as cannot appear under any other view.

From what has been said already, it is manifest that the church has been, and must be, in every age, the same body. The kingdom of Christ began to be formed just after the fall; and the same kingdom has been going forward ever since, and will go forward till the end of the world. The method by which fallen sinners are restored to the family of God, has always been one and the same. Men were saved before the coming of Christ, as well as since that time, only by his death. "There is none other name under heaven given among men, whereby we must be saved," but the name of Jesus. (Acts iv. 12.) True, the saints who lived before he came into the world, could not have any clear knowledge of the precise way in which atonement was to be made for sin; but they knew and believed that God had devised and was about to execute a plan which should fully answer the purpose, and make it possible for him to be just, while he yet justified the sinner who embraced his offered mercy. They knew, for it was clearly promised, that a Divine Deliverer, able to satisfy God's law and to save men, would in the latter days appear on earth, to take away sin and to bring in an everlasting righteousness for as many as would trust in his name Being assured of this by the testimony of God, they believed it, renounced all hope of being justified with God by their own goodness, and fixed their whole expectation and trust upon the Great Salvation which was to be made known in latter times. Thus Abraham and all other holy men of old were justified by faith. (Rom. iv. 1—8, Gal iii. 6—8.) They "all died in faith, not having received the promises, but having seen them afar off, and were persuaded of them, and embraced them, and confessed that they were strangers and pilgrims on the earth." (Heb. xi. 13.)

But, although the church has been substantially the same in all ages, its measures of spiritual advantage, and its outward constitution, have been greatly altered with the progress of time. It has had, as it were, an infancy, a childhood, and a full grown manhood. (Gal. iii. 23—25, iv. 1—6.) Its light has gradually proceeded from glimmering feebleness to the full splendour of rising day. Compared with the bright revelation of the gospel, the scriptures of the Old Testament shed only a faint light upon the world. (2 Tim. i. 10.) They were a light, which shined in a dark place, until the day should dawn, and the day-star should arise. (2 Pet. i. 19—21.) Still, however, it was a great and glorious light, sufficient to conduct the benighted sons of men to heaven. (Ps. cxix. 105—130.)

The first revelation of mercy through Christ, was made to our original parents just after their fall. In the midst of the curse, which Justice pronounced, it promised that the SEED of the woman should bruise the serpent's head. (Gen. iii. 15.) This Seed, the same with that in which the great promise made long after to Abraham, was to be fulfilled, was Christ. (Gal. iii. 16.) Adam and Eve, we may hope, being filled with godly sorrow for their guilt, believed the gracious word of God, and were saved. Their children were made acquainted with the great truth, and instructed in the fear of the Lord. And so down to the flood, the knowledge of God and of the way of salvation by faith was continued among men; and there were all the while some who loved and obeyed the true religion. These formed the church in those days. There was no written Bible, to make known the will of the Most High. But what God revealed to Adam, and others after him, was carefully remembered and handed down by word of mouth. When men lived so long, it was easy to preserve knowledge in this way. Some holy men of those times had a very great intimacy with God, and received many communications of instruction and favour directly from himself. We have, however, no means of knowing very much about the extent of religious knowledge, or the manner of religious worship, which belonged to that early age. Still, this much we learn from the Bible: —The solemn worship of *sacrifice* was common from the beginning; in which the believer acknowledged his guilt before God, and looked forward, with holy trust, to the satisfaction which God himself had promised to provide. The *sabbath* was observed, and was attended, no doubt, with rich spiritual blessings. There was also a regular church, united in the service of God, which secured most important privileges of religious education and of social worship. There was exhortation too, and preaching, which tended to edify and assist the people of God, while it warned, and left without excuse, the ungodly around. (2 Pet. ii. 5, Jude xiv. 15.)

Abel was a believer, and went to heaven. Cain despised religion, and belonged to the Wicked One. (1 John iii. 12.) He was driven out, for his sin, from the presence of the Lord, and became the father of a worldly and unbelieving race. The church was found in the family of Seth, whom God raised up to take Abel's place. Those who belonged to it were called, it seems, *children of God;* while the unbelieving were styled, *children of men.* The number of the ungodly was soon increased greatly; the children of the pious were, many of them, seduced to join them. "The *sons of God* saw the *daughters of men*, that they were fair; and they took them wives of all which they chose." Corruption thus rapidly became stronger and stronger, till it filled the earth, and Noah's family embraced the *whole* church. The flood came with the wrath of the Almighty, and buried the guilty race in destruction.

This awful event should have been remembered, to keep men from repeating the apostasy which was its occasion. But the posterity of Noah soon began again, with an evil heart of unbelief, to depart from the Lord. Idolatry gradually took the place of true religion. To such extent did it prevail at length, that the very existence of the church in the world seemed to be brought to a termination. But in its low estate, God interposed to recover it to new dignity, and to establish it with better privileges. He selected Abraham, the Chaldean; communicated to him the clear knowledge of religion, with new and more explicit promises of that Great Salvation which was to be made known in the latter days; and set him apart, with his posterity, to preserve the truth amid the corruptions of the world, and to hand it down, without interruption, until the time of Jesus Christ. The line of Abraham's ancestors seems to have been distinguished for piety, from the time of Noah, longer than most other families; but idolatry had at last corrupted it as well as the rest. (Josh. xxiv. 2.) Called by God, however, the patriarch left his country and his friends, and came into Canaan. The Lord promised that he would give that land to his descendants; that they should be his peculiar people—his church; and that in his Seed all the nations of the earth should be blessed. As a seal of the covenant into which he and his posterity were thus graciously allowed to enter, he received the sign of circumcision

Isaac and Jacob were heirs of the same promises, and distinguished with like spiritual blessings. Their religion was committed to their descendants. Among these, its form, and something also of its power, continued to be known in Egypt till the time of Moses. It appears, however, to have fallen, by that time, into very general neglect. Many of the Israelites, there is reason to believe, were carried away with the idolatries of Egypt.

With a mighty hand and an outstretched arm, the Lord recovered his people from oppression. He led them, by the hand of Moses, to the foot of Sinai. There he formed a solemn covenant with the whole nation, and gave them a written law. The church was now made to assume a new and more conspicuous form. It was blessed with a fuller knowledge of the Divine Will; it was admitted to greater privileges; and much more effectual provision was made for protecting its existence, and guarding its truth, in the midst of an apostate world. The principles of true morality and religion were made clear to all, by particular precepts of duty toward man and toward God. The manner in which God was to be worshipped was carefully prescribed. A great system of rites and ceremonies was established; which, while it served like a hedge to secure the proper form and the continuance of the church, was, at the same time, so full of important instruction, and so framed to shadow forth spiritual and heavenly truth, that to every true believer it could not fail to be a source of continual improvement in grace, and a most valuable help to devotion.

After a long discipline in the wilderness, the chosen nation was settled in Canaan, with all the advantages which thus, by its new form, the church was appointed to enjoy. That form was intended to be continued until the time of the gospel. Age after age, however, the measure of religious knowledge, with which it was distinguished, received important increase. The Bible, whose first five books had been written by the hand of Moses, was gradually enlarged, by the addition of others equally inspired. The light, that was shining in a dark world, grew stronger and clearer. Prophecy multiplied its revelations, and by its sure word pointed with more certainty and emphasis to the glory that was to come.

The Jewish state was very peculiar. As we have seen, when considering its manner of government, its civil and religious institutions were closely blended together, so as to form a single system harmoniously conspiring in all its parts toward the same general point. The whole was designed, in the wise plan of God, to preserve the true religion, and prepare the way for the introduction of the full brightness of the gospel in the fulness of time. The Jewish *church* was the special object regarded, in the separation of the Israelites from the rest of the world to be the peculiar people of the Most High; and their whole *government*, accordingly, was constructed with a view to the interests of the church, and in such a manner as to fall in with and assist the particular constitution under which it was placed. Hence, as already remarked, a religious design is to be discovered running, in some measure, through the whole system, and much of the meaning of those laws and institutions which moulded and fixed the shape of the civil government, is to be sought in their relation to religion, rather than in any merely political purpose. Still, it is proper to distinguish the nation as a *church*, from the nation as a *civil community*, and to distribute its institutions and laws into two general classes—such as related more directly to religion, and such as had regard to the government of the state as an earthly kingdom.

But the laws which related entirely to religion were not all of the same nature. As a *church*, the Jews were placed under a twofold system of law. They had the Moral law, which rests upon all men, in every age; and they had a Ceremonial law, peculiar to their dispensation, and designed to pass away with it.

In discoursing of divine laws, it has been common to divide them altogether into two kinds—NATURAL and POSITIVE. *Natural laws*, which are the same that are usually called *Moral*, are such as arise necessarily from the character of God and the nature of his moral creatures, and which every man's conscience, if it be not completely seared by sin, tells him, as soon as they are known to him from the light of nature or revelation, that he is under solemn obligation to obey. *Positive laws* are such as have no necessary and unalterable reason in the nature of things, but derive their authority from the particular appointment of God, made known by revelation; having no force, except where they are thus expressly enjoined, and being designed to continue only *for a time*, determined in the purpose of the Most High; after which, all their obligation is done away. Each of the ten commandments is a natural or moral law: the laws which required the Jews not to eat certain animals, the laws which regulated inheritances among them, and others of a like sort, were positive laws. A positive law, when it is enjoined, is no less binding than a moral one. The obligation to obey rests, in both cases, upon the same reason, namely, the *will of God:* when that will is made known in any way, whatever it may require, the duty of complying with it is at all times the same, and at all times of the highest force; whether the requirement is perpetual and universal, or whether it is limited to times and individuals, is an inquiry that does not touch at all upon the nature or extent of its claim to be regarded and obeyed. Positive laws, again, have been divided into POLITICAL and CEREMONIAL. The laws which God gave for the government of the Jewish republic, in its civil character, were of the first class; such were the statutes that were made concerning magistrates, marriages, inheritances, punishments, &c. : many of them, as already noticed, partook at the same time of a religious character. The laws which among the same people prescribed the peculiar rites and forms of religious worship, private or public, were of the latter class—*ceremonial:* such were those that related to meats and washings and sacrifices, and all the outward service of the tabernacle or temple.

While, therefore, the Moral law, and that which has been styled the Ceremonial, were alike altogether religious in their character; and so may be with propriety classed together, in distinction from the Political or Civil law; they were distinguished nevertheless from each other by a wide and clear difference. The one had its origin with the beginning of creation, flowing necessarily out of its divine plan, and being essential to, and inseparable from, its constitution, as long as that constitution shall endure : the other had its commencement only when the sovereign wisdom of God revealed its appointment, and had no necessary existence in the original order of being, but was made to answer some particular end in the general system of God's grace; and having accomplished this design, had no longer any authority whatever. A moral law, accordingly, includes its reason in itself; and finds its end answered *directly* and *immediately* in the obedience which it receives; a ceremonial one, on the contrary, had its reason entirely *out* of itself, and always contemplated some other end than what it directly required to be done, as its original and principal design.

The MORAL LAW, summarily comprehended in the ten commandments uttered from Mount Sinai, requires in all its precepts a spiritual obedience. It contemplates the heart. It carries its authority into all duties; even such as were ceremonial in their nature were enforced by its power; because when the will of God is understood, whatever it may prescribe, the obligation to regard it flows from the first principle of natural and unchangeable reason; namely that the creature should in every thing render a willing obedience to its infinitely perfect Creator. Thus, for an ancient Jew to eat swine's flesh, while it brought him under the penalty of the Ceremonial law, was an offence, also, if wilfully done, against the Moral law, not less truly than it would have been for him to take his Maker's name in vain, or to steal his neighbour's property. Our Saviour teaches us, that the sum of all the Moral law is expressed in two great precepts. (Matt. xxii. 37—40.) Love to God will secure natural obedience to all his will, and "love worketh no ill to his neighbour; therefore love is the fulfilling of the law." (John xiv. 23, Rom. xiii. 8—10.) This law is that which Paul speaks of as being written in the hearts of men. (Rom. ii. 15.) Man was originally made so as to have a *natural* sense of its obligation, and a natural knowledge of its precepts. And although, by the fall, the clearness of this knowledge has been much obscured, it has not still been utterly taken away; but some vestiges of it are to be found, in every age, among all people. (Rom. i. 19—21.) It is still only by reason of sin, that men do not all learn the glory of God from his works, and are not all moved by their inward sense to understand the Moral law and to make it the rule of their conduct.

This law, we have said, never loses its force. Every human soul is at all times under its authority. Nor will it in any case give up the smallest part of its claim. It requires *full* obedience, or tremendous punishment, such as falling upon a creature, like man, must doom him to everlasting misery. The law is holy, just and good—and whosoever offendeth in one point is guilty of all—for it is written, "Cursed is every one that continueth not in all things written in the book of the law to do them"—and again, "Till heaven and earth pass, one jot or one tittle shall in no wise pass from the law, till all be fulfilled." (Rom. vii. 12, James ii. 10, Gal. iii. 10, Matt. v. 18.) According to this law, we are to be judged in the Great Day. Reader! have *you* not broken it times without number? How then will you appear before the judgment-seat of God? How will you stand in that awful trial, where a single offence is enough to condemn you for ever? Can it be that you have not yet begun to look out for some way of escape from so fearful a prospect?

The CEREMONIAL LAW of the Jews comprehended a vast number of precepts. It stood in meats and drinks, and divers washings, and carnal ordinances, imposed on them till the time of reformation. Some of its institutions were appointed long before the time of Moses. Such was the institution of *sacrifices*, with the regulations which governed the pious in offering them, appointed in the very commencement of the church, immediately after the fall. Animals were divided into *clean* and *unclean* before the flood. (Gen. vii. 2.) As early as the time of Noah, the commandment was given, *not to eat blood*. Abraham received the appointment of *circumcision*. From his time, we find in the brief history of the Bible, traces of several other important regulations afterwards embraced in the Mosaic ceremonial law. So that some have imagined, we should find, if we had a complete account of the religious usages of that early age, that almost all the principal rites, which their law required the Jews to observe, existed to some extent before, among their pious ancestors; or at least, that observances *similar* to them, and evidently having the same principle and intention, were not unknown. Moses, by the command of God, formed for the nation a full and regular system of ceremonial laws. Such rites as had been before appointed and in use, he sanctioned with new authority, and prescribed, with particular care, the manner and various circumstances which were to be connected with their observance. What was partial and imperfect before, he set forth with new, more formal and systematic, more extensive, and more expressive arrangment. Various precepts, altogether unknown till that time, were added to complete the divine plan. The whole, thus framed together, made one harmonious scheme, conspiring in all its parts to secure the great purpose of its appointment.

One use of the ceremonial law was to keep the Israelitish nation separate and distinct from the rest of the world, and to guard them from idolatry. To preserve the true religion, and to prepare the way for the coming of the gospel, God, in his wisdom, designed the Jewish people to be *a people dwelling alone*, amid the other nations of the earth. (Num. xxiii. 9.) The whole system of laws, civil and religious, under which they were placed, was such as was adapted to secure this end. Their Ceremonial law, especially, could not fail, if regarded in any measure, to keep them separate. It embraced many very peculiar precepts, and many that stood in direct opposition to the usages and manners of other people. It could not be completely observed except in the land of Israel; and its operation tended continually to shut out all foreign customs, and to draw a broad line of distinction between the seed of Abraham and every stranger. There was need of such a security, to keep the people from becoming utterly confounded with the nations around them, whose idolatry they were, for a long time, so ready to imitate. The safety of the church required that it should be burdened and shut up with restraint, in this way

Hence, the apostle calls the Jewish law, a *Schoolmaster*, which, by salutary but severe care and discipline, secured the church under proper training, as it were, until the time when the gospel was introduced. Its obligation imposed a sort of bondage, such as children, not yet of age, were made to feel under tutors and governors: which ceased only when the fulness of the Father's appointed time was come, giving way to the liberty of a far more glorious dispensation. (Gal. iii. 19—24, iv. 1—11.)

But there was another, which we are to regard as the principal design of the Ceremonial law. It was framed to shadow forth, with figurative representation, the most important spiritual truths; so that by its serious observance, believers who lived before the time of Christ might continually grow in knowledge and grace; and so that it should be afterwards, to the end of time, a most striking evidence of the truth of the gospel; by the wonderful prophetic image of gospel realities which men might discover in its whole system. It was adapted continually to remind the ancient Jews of the great evil of sin, and of the absolute need of complete atonement for its guilt, before it could be pardoned. It represented strikingly the infinite holiness of God, and the necessity of his favour. It pointed to the great Provision, which God intended to reveal in its proper time, for the taking away of sin, and directed the eye of faith and hope to the perfect salvation that was to come. By signs, it foretold the sufferings and death of Christ, and the whole work of redemption which he was to accomplish; and emblematically represented the great spiritual benefits that were to be secured in consequence. Altogether, it was a grand TYPE of the system of grace unfolded by the gospel, and its several parts were, in general, figurative of particular most interesting realities, comprehended in that system. Thus we are told, the law had a shadow of good things to come. (Heb. x. 1, Col. ii. 17.) In the Epistle to the Hebrews, the apostle teaches its meaning in this way, in many important particulars. Christ fulfilled this law by bringing actually to pass all that it typically signified, as he fulfilled the moral law by his life of obedience, and death of atonement for sinful men. (Matt. v. 17.)

We ought, therefore, always to inquire after their spiritual and typical meaning, when we read of the various institutions of this ancient law. We ought to consider what reference they had to Christ and the wonders of the gospel. In this way, that part of Scripture which treats of these things is to be rendered most profitable for instruction in righteousness. If it be not read thus, it is not read aright. We are now able to see more clearly, a great deal, than the ancient Jew could, the full signification of the ceremonial ordinances he was commanded to observe. Their meaning has been interpreted by events. Time, by unfolding the accomplishment of the things they represented, enables us to understand *types* which were once dark, just as it explains *prophecies* that were formerly as much obscure. Types are, in fact, of the same general nature with prophecies, only foretelling things to come in a different way. It becomes us, therefore, to study them with the same sort of attention, and to seek like instruction and spiritual benefit from both. The Holy Ghost designed one as well as the other to be so improved.

The history of the Jews, recorded briefly in the Bible, shows them to have been a rebellious and stiff-necked people in religion. They were ever ready to forsake the Lord, and fall in with the idolatrous practices of the heathen around them. Yet by the force of their law, and the oft-repeated judgments of the Almighty, they were kept a distinct people. For their sins, they were at length carried away, however, into distant captivity. The kingdom of Israel, which had broken itself off from the house of David, and offended God with most dreadful apostasy, was then allowed to become lost among the nations. The kingdom of Judah alone was regarded as the visible church, with which the truth and promises of God were to remain deposited till the time of Christ. It embraced the tribe and family from which the Redeemer was to rise. (Gen. xlix 10, Ps. cxxxii. 11.) It was enough, therefore, to answer the original design of God in separating the Jewish nation, that this portion of it, with whom were the promises, the written law, and the sacred service of religion, should be thenceforward preserved a separate people. Accordingly, they were so preserved in the land of their captivity, and, after seventy years, brought back again to their ancient country. The temple was once more builded, and the worship which the law prescribed solemnly renewed. Thus the nation and the church were continued till the great Messiah appeared.

After the captivity, the Jews never again showed any inclination to fall into idolatry Other sins of the worst kind prevailed greatly, but this they held in continual detestation. Their religion became, in the end, without *life* and without *power* almost entirely; but the *letter* and *form* of it they cherished with the most scrupulous care. No doubt, the affliction which the nation was made to suffer by its captivity, had much to do in producing this change. This was felt and remembered as an awful warning not to repeat the idolatry of former times, which had occasioned it. Its whole history, too, from the beginning to the end, by clearly fulfilling many prophecies, and unfolding many signal displays of divine power, afforded a demonstration most convincing, that Jehovah was the true God, and that besides HIM there was no other. Moreover, after the *return* from that captivity, new means were employed to secure the advantage of general religious instruction This served to keep alive the memory of what was past, and so impressed the great truths of revelation upon the minds of all, that the evil and folly and danger of idolatry could never be forgotten. Religious instruction was secured, principally by the establishment of *Synagogues* and *Schools*. Synagogues were a sort of churches, where the people met by congregations through the land on every Sabbath, to hear a portion of the Scriptures read and explained, and to join in social prayer before God. Regular schools for the instruction of the young, under the care of distinguished men, came also into use; and as this instruction was concerned chiefly with the knowledge of the sacred law, it tended much to preserve it among the people.

The ancient dispensation, together with all the movements of Providence, in the revolutions of kingdoms and nations in the world, looked forward to the introduction of the gospel, and operated to prepare the way for its coming. Since that event, all things have been conspiring toward another point—the establishment of the Redeemer's kingdom over the earth, and the great winding up of the work of redemption which the Son of God has undertaken, since the fall, to accomplish in this miserable world. The gospel sheds light upon the whole ancient testament of the Jews, and lifts the veil away from their wonderful institutions. (2 Cor. iii. 14—18.) It ought to be remembered, that the sum and substance of the entire Bible is JESUS CHRIST CRUCIFIED TO SAVE A LOST WORLD; and that without this object in view as its grand end, the whole Jewish system of religion can have no meaning.

As *we* look *backward* many hundred years, and find the hope of the church in a redemption long since wrought out, so the *Jew* was taught to stretch his expectation *forward* and to found all hope toward God upon that same redemption to be revealed at a future time. What *we* learn from inspired *history*, was set before him by inspired *prophecy* and *types*: in his case indeed, compared with ours, the representation was shadowy and dark, yet altogether sufficient to lead the soul of the pious believer to confidence and peace.

Prophecy, though from its nature it could not but be wrapped to some extent in obscurity, was nevertheless very explicit in declaring the general truth, that a Great Salvation was to be disclosed in coming time, and an age of happy and glorious privilege unfolded, far surpassing all the previous state of the church. This testimony was strikingly confirmed by the great system of types, which God ordered for the help of faith. What was predicted in one case with *words*, was prefigured in the other by shadowy *signs*. A general belief, accordingly, was cherished by the whole nation, that a far more excellent and happy state than the one under which they lived was to be revealed at a future period. It was universally agreed, too, that this happy state was to be introduced by a powerful and glorious Deliverer, called emphatically by the prophet Daniel, the MESSIAH, or Anointed One, and spoken of repeatedly in other places under different names—such as the SEED of the woman, the SEED of Abraham, SHILOH, the BRANCH out of Jesse's stem, IMMANUEL, &c. Hence they were accustomed to speak of the whole period of the world, as being divided into two great ages—the first reaching from the beginning to the time when the Messiah should appear, and then yielding place to the second, which was to abound with righteousness and peace. The first, in which they lived themselves, they styled *This age*, or *The present age;* the other was distinguished as *The age to come*.

Great error, however, came to mingle itself with this expectation which the nation cherished. The Scripture representations were understood in a low and narrow sense. The descriptions of that coming age, the latter time, when the reign of the Messiah was to be established in glorious and happy triumph, had been set forth by the prophets under striking imagery of an earthly kind. The Great Deliverer was represented under the character of a *Prince*, clothed with highest majesty and power, coming to occupy the throne of David, completely overthrowing all the enemies of his people, reducing the world to subjection, and reigning with most wise, righteous, and beneficent authority, so as to make his dominion full of all blessedness and peace. His people, too, were spoken of as the Jewish kingdom, and called by the names of *Israel*, *Jacob*, &c. All this had a meaning far more lofty and excellent than was signified by the terms employed when taken in an earthly sense. The kingdom to be set up was spiritual; the deliverance was redemption from sin; the triumphant glory was victory over death and hell; the blessings of the government were holiness and eternal life; the people crowned with such benefits was the church gathered out of all nations—the true Israel comprehending all in every place that embrace the promises of God by faith. A serious consideration of the *whole* revelation of prophecy on this point, should have led to such a spiritual interpretation of the worldly imagery used in many cases in relation to it. But a worldly temper perverted it into an occasion of error. The notion of an earthly and temporal kingdom dazzled the imagination. The Messiah, it came to be expected, would appear with irresistible power to restore the Jewish nation to glory—to raise it far above even its most triumphant state in the days of Solomon—to introduce and establish a long reign of liberty, virtue and happiness. As the nation sunk under the pressure of foreign power, the expectation and hope of such a deliverer was indulged with more and more fondness.

There were always, however, some who entertained more correct ideas on this subject. Taught by the Holy Spirit, they directed their faith toward a higher end. They looked for spiritual blessings, as the most desirable in the promises of God concerning the Messiah. Such were old Simeon, who waited for the consolation of Israel, and pious Anna, and others in Jerusalem *that looked for redemption*, to whom she spake of Christ when he was yet an infant. (Luke ii. 25—38.) Yet even such appear, for the most part, to have entertained the notion that the benefits of the Messiah's kingdom were to be enjoyed especially by the Jews, and that the Gentiles, in order to have part in them, would be required to unite themselves, as proselytes, with the Israelitish church. The imagination of a worldly dominion too, so generally indulged by others, was ever apt to creep in and mingle itself to some extent with their best conceptions. How this imagination cleaved to the minds of Christ's disciples for a long time, may be learned from Matt. xvi. 22, xviii. 1, xx. 20—28, Mark x. 35—37, Luke xix. 11, xxii. 24. Our Saviour repeatedly corrected the error, declaring that he was shortly to die a violent death, and that all who became his true followers must expect no earthly victories and distinctions, but persecution and tribulation; that the blessings of his kingdom were to be secured only by giving up all the expectations of worldly happiness which men naturally cherish, and that they far excelled all that the Jews imagined concerning the reign of the Messiah, being spiritual altogether and heavenly in their nature. Still, so strong was the general notion in their minds of a kingdom to be set up on earth, that as long as he lived it was not relinquished. Accordingly, after his death, we hear them sorrowfully saying, "we trusted that it had been he which should have redeemed Israel;" and with his resurrection, we find the expectation revived in all its strength—"Lord," they said, "wilt thou at this time restore again the kingdom to Israel?" (Luke xxiv. 21, Acts i. 6.) The Holy Ghost, however, in a short time, guided them into a knowledge of the truth. They learned to conceive with wider and loftier views of Christ's kingdom. Their former impressions were swallowed up in the discovery of its moral glory—its divine grandeur—its eternal blessedness.

Not only was the expectation of the Messiah universal among the Jews, but there was, likewise, a general agreement about the *period* when he might be looked for. Ancient prophecy had pointed to the *time*, as well as the *place*, of his appearance. (Gen. xlix. 10, Dan. ix. 24—27.) It came to pass, accordingly, that in that very age in which our Saviour appeared on earth, the people were expecting the promised Deliverer as just at hand. The opinion prevailed, that the time was then come for all to look for the speedy accomplishment of the sure word of prophecy on this subject. Thus Simeon and Anna, and many more in Jerusalem, we are told, were waiting. The Samaritans united with the Jews in this hope, and seem on the whole to have formed juster notions than *they* had of the character of the Messiah. (John iv. 25, 29, 42.) Nor was the expectation confined to the land of Palestine. The Jews, being scattered at that time into many foreign countries, caused it to take root in other regions; so that there came to be a general idea through the East, that a great prince was about to rise out of Judea in its low estate, who should obtain supreme dominion in the world. This fact is mentioned by two of the most respectable heathen historians of those times. (Matt. ii. 1—12.)

It was foretold also by the Spirit, that the Messiah should have a *forerunner*, to come immediately before him, and prepare, as it were, the way for his manifestation. Great and powerful kings in the East were accustomed, when making a journey, to send such before them to have the road made ready all along for their approach: so it was represented, a voice should be heard in the wilderness of this world, when the heavenly King was about to appear, giving notice of his coming, and calling upon men to make the way ready for his presence. (Isa. xl. 3—5.) What sort of *office* was signified by this figurative account of the forerunner, going before the Messiah, we learn from the history of the gospel. (Luke i. 76, 77, iii. 2—18.) In the close of the Old Testament, the name of *Elijah the prophet*, was applied to this forerunner. (Mal. iv. 5, 6.) Hence an opinion came to prevail, that Elijah himself would actually return from the other world, and make his appearance in this important character. It was a doctrine of the scribes, the great interpreters of Scripture, that Elias in his own person should come immediately before the Messiah. (Matt. xvii. 10 —13.) The Jews accordingly put the question to John the Baptist when he appeared, after he had told them that he was not the Christ, *Art thou Elias?* They meaned by Elias no other than the ancient prophet of Israel himself: John therefore assured them, he was not that holy man. (John i. 21.) Yet he *was* the very person to whom that name had been applied in prophecy—the great forerunner of the Messiah : Jesus declared of him, "This is Elias, which was for to come." (Matt. xi. 14.) But when he was called by that name, it was intimated only that he should resemble Elijah in holiness, self-denial and faithful boldness—or, as an angel once explained it, that he should come to perform his ministry "in the spirit and power of Elias." (Luke i. 17.) There were some who imagined Jesus himself to be Elias returned to the world. (Luke ix. 8, 19.)

In the fulness of time, the long-expected Christ, the Son of the living God, came. But the nation knew him not; "he came to his own, and his own received him not." With the Jews the promise had been deposited, and they had given the world to understand their expectation of its glorious accomplishment; but the accomplishment itself they were not able to see, while others saw and believed, and rejoiced in the unspeakable grace of God.

By this event, a new and far more glorious dispensation was introduced. The old one, having answered all its purpose, was commanded to pass away for ever. The ceremonial law lost all its obligation, having been imposed only till this "time of reformation." (Heb. ix. 10.) The *middle wall of partition*, between the Jews and other nations of the world, was broken down : " the enmity, even the law of commandments contained in ordinances" was abolished. (Eph. ii. 14, 15.) All distinction between Jew and Gentile as to any peculiar favour of heaven, was over. One was invited as freely as the other to join the family of God, and take part in the rich blessings of his grace. Peace was commanded to be preached *to all*—those that were *far off* as well as those that were *nigh*.

To those who had been trained up with the notions and feelings of Jews, this could not but seem a most wonderful doctrine. They had grown up with a strong impression, which all their education tended to fix deeply in the mind, that God had shut out all other people entirely from his regard, and that the blessings of the true religion were, by his unalterable purpose, to be confined to their own nation; so that no Gentile could ever be admitted to the friendship of God, except by numbering himself with the Jews as a proselyte to their church When the gospel, therefore, declared that all difference was taken away, and invited all alike to embrace its benefits, many needed no other objection to lead them to reject it at once (Acts xxii. 21, 22.) Even those who were truly converted to receive its truth, were slow in coming to a clear understanding of this point. It was hard for them to feel that the door of grace stood as widely and as freely open to the Gentile, without any respect to the law of Moses, as it did to the circumcised Jew. (Acts x. 10—16, 28, 45, xi. 1—18.) Hence we find it declared so often in the New Testament, with a sort of peculiar emphasis, as a thing new, wonderful, and contrary to former prejudice, that the gospel offered its blessings to the *Gentiles* —to *all*—to the *world*—to the *whole world*, without distinction of nation or place. (Matt. xxviii. 19, Luke xxiv. 47, 48, Acts xiii. 46, 47, xvii. 30, 31, xxvi. 17, 18, xxviii. 28, Rom. i. 16, iii. 29, 30, 1 Tim. ii. 4—6, Tit. ii. 11, 1 John ii. 2.) Paul speaks of it as a glorious mystery. (Eph. iii. 3 -6.) The word *mystery* in this case, as generally in his epistles, means simply something that was utterly *unknown* before God revealed it by the gospel—a thing that was for a long time *hidden;* not implying that there was any thing in its nature which could not be explained or understood, as the term commonly means with us.

Neither was it easy for the converted Jew, even when he had learned *that the gospel unfolded its privileges equally to all,* either to cast off all regard himself to the system of religion which he had so long been accustomed to reverence as appointed of Heaven, or to be satisfied that the Gentile converts should be entirely free from its observances. We are not able fully to enter into the difficulty which *he* naturally felt on this point. It is not therefore strange, that we find such persons still clinging to some of their ancient rites in the Christian church, making it a matter of conscience to observe them. (Acts xxi. 20, 21, Rom. chap. xv.) With feelings of this sort, it is not strange likewise that they should sometimes have insisted upon it as a duty for others also, even those who had never been Jews, not to neglect them. False teachers, from various motives of pride or worldly policy, were very ready to take advantage of this prejudice, and to spread it with all their might in different churches; endeavouring to persuade those who had been Jews, that they should hold fast part of their old religious usages, and those who were Gentiles, that they ought to be circumcised and pay some regard to the Ceremonial law. (Acts xv. 1, 24, Gal. ii. 3—5, vi. 12, 13.) Hence arose, generally, the first errors in the churches. The Galatian church was turned away almost altogether from the truth of the gospel by this means, as we learn from the severe letter which Paul wrote to them on account of it. In his other epistles, we find notices of a similar evil at work in other places also. It took, however, different forms. A vain philosophy endeavoured to connect its new and wild opinions with a portion of the Jewish law, and then under this mixed character crept into the Christian church, showing various features of error in different congregations. "Men of corrupt minds and destitute of the truth," "proud and knowing nothing, but doting about questions and strifes of words," "unruly and vain talkers," "deceived" themselves, and worse "deceiving" others, introduced these corruptions, spoiling the tranquillity of churches, and turning men aside from true godliness. (Col. ii. 8—23, 1 Tim. i. 3—7, iv. 1—8, vi. 3—5, 2 Tim. ii. 14—18, 23, iii. 6—9, Tit. i. 10—16, iii. 9.)

The apostle Paul did not in every case forbid, as sin, all compliances with Jewish observances. When they were such as not to interfere with the spirit of the gospel, or were not used as entering into the *substance* of true religion, he suffered the conscientious scruples of weak Christians in regard to them to be indulged. He exhorted others also, who felt no such scruples themselves, to give way in their practice to such prejudices of their brethren around them, so far as the things which they respected were in their nature indifferent. (Rom. xiv. 14—23.) He himself acted on this principle, forbearing to use his Christian liberty in all lawful cases, whenever it was likely to give offence. (Acts xvi. 3, xviii. 18, xxi. 21—26, Rom. xv. 1, 1 Cor. ix. 20.) But when a disposition was discovered to rely upon these observances as a ground of confidence toward God, and as entering essentially into his plan of salvation, the apostle condemned them in the strongest terms, and would not countenance such as clung to them, with the smallest ndulgence. To such he said, "If ye be circumcised, Christ shall profit you nothing; for I testify to every man that is circumcised, that he is a debtor to keep the whole law. Christ is become of no effect unto you, whosoever of you are justified by the law; ye are fallen from grace." Thus he expostulated with the Galatians, who had been drawn aside from the simple truth of the gospel, by false teachers, into this ruinous error. Especially, he thought it necessary, steadfastly to resist all compliance on the part of *Gentile* Christians with the Ceremonial law. The considerations which made it proper to allow some indulgence to the Jewish converts, had no place with such as had not been educated from childhood in the Jews' religion. a converted Jew might be supposed to cleave to some of his ancient usages, under the force of conscientious prejudice, without falling from or abandoning the doctrine of free grace through faith, while the observance of the same usages on the part of a Gentile convert, who had no such natural prejudice to entangle his conscience, would argue a deliberate confidence in the Jewish law as a method of obtaining favour with God, and so give reason to fear a fatal departure from the great fundamental truth of the gospel, *that a man is justified by the faith of Jesus Christ alone, and not by the works of the law.*—The apostle, therefore, would not give place to such as wanted to draw the Gentiles into the observance of Jewish rites, no, not for an hour: and he anxiously guarded against every thing, in example as well as precept, among Christians of this class, which might have the smallest influence to make them think that any thing of this sort belonged to true religion. He thought it necessary, accordingly, on one occasion at Antioch, to withstand Peter to the face, and publicly to reprove him for his unfaithfulness on this point, in the most solemn manner. (Gal. ii. 11—14.)

CHAPTER II.

THE TABERNACLE.

THE TABERNACLE was made in the wilderness according to the commandment of God. By a solemn covenant, the Israelites had engaged to be his obedient people, and he had taken them, as a nation, out of all the nations of the earth, to be a holy kingdom for himself. They were to be under his special and extraordinary care, and to be governed in their whole civil and religious state by his peculiar and extraordinary direction. They were to be his *church*, and the whole frame of their commonwealth was to be constructed with reference to the great interest for which the church was established. Accordingly, the Most High gave them a law, and agreed to dwell among them with his continual and special presence, in a sanctuary which he directed to be prepared for this high and solemn use Thus the Tabernacle had its origin

It was required to be made, together with all its furniture, from the offerings which the people might be willing to present for the purpose. All were invited to contribute something for an end so important; but it was left to each individual to act in the matter with perfectly free choice. The offering of every man was to be given willingly with his heart. By reason of the great readiness of the people to offer, materials more than enough were soon collected. Men and women united in showing their zeal, by contributions of every various sort that could be useful, till an order had to be publicly given for them to bring no more. (Ex. xxv. 1—8, xxxv. 4—29, xxxvi. 3—7.)

As the work to be accomplished needed various materials of the most costly sort, so it called for peculiar skill to execute it in the way which its magnificent design required. Accordingly, God raised up Bezaleel the son of Uri, and Aholiab the son of Ahisamach, filling them with wisdom and understanding in all manner of workmanship, to have the entire charge of the whole business. They were qualified, with more than ordinary or merely natural ability, to perform themselves the most difficult and curious sorts of work, such as belonged to arts entirely different, and also to teach others, who might be employed, under their direction, to help forward, in various ways, the general labour. (Ex. xxxi. 1—6, xxv. 30—35.)

It was not left, however, to these workmen, or even to Moses, to contrive the form or manner of the sacred building in any respect. No pattern of earth was to be regarded—no device of man was to be followed, in its whole construction and arrangement. It was to be the dwelling-place of God, symbolical, in all its visible and material order, of realities infinitely more grand and glorious; God himself therefore devised its entire plan, and unfolded it with most particular direction, in all its parts, to his servant on Mount Sinai. Careful and minute instruction was given relative to the materials to be used, the manner of workmanship to be employed, the form and size of the building, and every article of sacred furniture that was to belong to it. And more than this, there was presented to the eyes of Moses a pattern, or model, of the whole, as the Lord intended it to be made and arranged, with a solemn injunction to have all finished exactly according to it. "According to all that I show thee," was the charge of the Almighty, "the pattern of the tabernacle and the pattern of all the instruments thereof, even so shall ye make it:" and again, "Look that thou make them after their pattern, which was showed thee in the mount." (Ex. xxv. 9—40, Heb viii. 5.) There was no wisdom wanted in the workmen, therefore, to *contrive* any part of the work to be done, but merely to *execute* it according to the divine plan which Moses was appointed to explain.

The very great care which God showed about the manner in which this holy tabernacle was to be made, teaches us that it was designed to have a meaning in all its parts vastly more important than any mere visible and outward use. Something far more exalted than what struck the eye of sense, was intended in its construction. Under its earthly and material show, there was designed to be a representation of things heavenly and spiritual, such as should be full of instruction to the church till the end of time. In this consideration we have unfolded a satisfactory reason for that extraordinary care with which the original plan was divinely determined, and also for the care of the Holy Spirit, in causing so full and particular an account of it to be preserved in the Scriptures for the use of piety in all ages. And should not this reflection excite us to seek an intimate and familiar acquaintance with the ancient sanctuary? Surely it becomes us to consider all the parts of its plan with serious and careful attention, remembering at every step the heavenly origin of all, and humbly endeavouring to penetrate through the shadow of its earthly service into the sublime and glorious realities, which, according to the wisdom of the Spirit, it proposes for our solemn contemplation.

To have a right conception of the sacred dwelling-place which the Most High caused to be made for Himself among the Israelites in the wilderness, we must consider the Tabernacle itself, its furniture, and its Court. Let us attend first to the Court.

THE COURT OF THE TABERNACLE was a lot of enclosed ground which surrounded the Tabernacle, and all that was connected with it, comprehending room enough for the accommodation of all that were to be at any time directly concerned with its religious services. It was required

to be a hundred cubits long from east to west, and fifty broad from north to south. It was enclosed to the height of five cubits on every side, with curtains of fine twined linen These were hung from brazen pillars, ranged at equal distances one from another in a row on each side, either by being fastened to them merely by hooks of silver, or else by means of silver rods reaching all along from one to another. The pillars had sockets of brass to stand upon. There were twenty of them on the north, and on the south side, and ten in each of the end ranges, east and west. The entrance into this court was on the east end, and exactly in the middle of it. It was twenty cubits wide. It was closed by a hanging different from the other cur tains, "of blue, and purple, and scarlet and fine twined linen, wrought with needlework." This was hung from four pillars, and could be drawn up by means of cords, so as to leave the entrance open when there was occasion to go in or out. (Ex. xxvii. 9—18.)

The TABERNACLE stood well toward the west end of the court just described, and in the middle of its breadth from north to south, so as to face exactly the entrance upon the east side. It was made of boards of shittim wood overlaid with gold, and four coverings of different materials thrown over its whole frame, to shield it from the weather, and to shut out completely the light of day. When set up it was thirty cubits long, ten broad, and ten high. Like what has been noticed of the court, it was required always to be placed  with its length from east to west, and its entrance was at its east end. This end, accordingly, was not boarded. The boards were all ten cubits long, and a cubit and a half broad, and had each two tenons fashioned on one end. In the building, they stood upright, joined edge to edge, and every one resting by its two tenons on two silver sockets. Thus on each of the sides, north and south, were twenty boards, which standing in the way now mentioned made a wall just thirty cubits long The west end had six boards, and there was one besides at each of the corners of that end, which, while they served to connect it with the sides, seem also to have added somewhat to its extent, so as to make the breadth of the tabernacle ten cubits, that would with only the six boards have made no more than nine. Altogether then there were forty-eight boards standing upon ninety-six sockets of silver. Every socket weighed a talent The boards, however, needed something to hold them together Bars, therefore, or poles, of shittim wood overlaid with gold, were made to pass across them through rings fixed on each one for the purpose, by which means all the boards of each side, or of the end, were firmly bound one to another. Five bars were employed in this way on each side, and also on the end : the middle one reached from end to end, across all the boards : the other four were, according to one opinion, each only half as long, two of them together making a whole length across at the top, and the other two a whole length across in like manner at the bottom. Another opinion is, that all the bars were of full length, and that what is said about the middle one, means only that it was fixed in its place in a different way from the others, being either sunk *into* the boards in a sort of groove, all the way along, or else thrust *through* them, by means of a bar passing clear across from one to another. (Ex. xxvi. 15—30.)

Such was the frame of the tabernacle, presenting, when erected, on each of its sides and its western end, a heavy wall of shittim planks gorgeously covered over with gold, and supported beneath on ninety-six massy sockets of silver. It left the top, as well as the end toward the east, entirely open. But to make the sacred tent complete, over this frame were to be spread four great coverings, one above another. The first was very beautiful and costly. It was composed of ten curtains of fine twined linen, and blue, and purple, and " scarlet, made with cherubim of cunning work ;" that is, of fine twined linen into which pictures of cherubim were curiously wrought with various colours, blue, purple and scarlet. Each of these curtains was twenty-eight cubits long and four broad. Five of them were coupled together, side to side, so as to make one large piece, twenty-eight cubits long and twenty broad, and so in like manner were the other five united into another piece. Along the edge of the outermost curtain on one side of each of these great pieces, or *couplings*, were made fifty loops of blue, so placed, that those which belonged to one piece answered exactly to those which were on the other. Then fifty hooks or clasps of gold were provided, by which these loops might be

A SIDE VIEW OF THE TABERNACLE WITH ITS COVERINGS.

P, the five pillars at the entrance; L, the under covering of fine linen curtains; G, curtains of goat's hair; R, covering of ram's skins; D, coverings of badger's skins.

THE TABERNACLE UNCOVERED.

A, the Holy Place; B, the Most Holy of Ho

al, along linked one to another, and the two pieces thus knit together into one rich and magnificent covering. They were thrown across the frame of the tabernacle from north to south, and hung down on each side within a cubit of the bottom; for, since the frame was ten cubits high and ten wide, the measure *over* it from the base of the wall on one side to its base on the other, was just thirty cubits, that is, two cubits more than the length of the curtains.

One of the pieces seems to have been laid across, so as to reach from the front of the tabernacle, covering the top and sides, as far as twenty cubits back: then the other, linked upon it by the loops and clasps, was spread over the hinder part, covering the top and sides in like manner from where the first stopped, and falling down in loose folds over the western end. Over this fine inner covering was spread another more substantial. It was composed of eleven curtains of goats' hair, each thirty cubits long and four broad. These also were united into two large pieces, one being made up of five, and the other of six; and provision was made, as in the case of the inner covering, for linking the pieces together by loops and clasps. The clasps used in this case, however, were made of brass, and not, as they were in the other, of gold.

These pieces, being thrown across the tabernacle like the others, reached down on each side to the row of silver sockets on which the boards stood; because they were thirty cubits long, which, as we have just seen, was equal to the distance from one base over to the other. The piece that was composed of six single curtains, lay toward the fore-part of the tabernacle, and the sixth curtain was doubled in the fore-front of it, so as to hang somewhat perhaps over the entrance. It is not easy, however, to determine precisely how this covering was disposed, in front and on the western end behind, so as to have its cloth which it had more than the other, completely occupied. But in whatever way arranged, it spread entirely over the top, and sides, and back part of the frame, so as to hide the inner covering altogether out of sight, and shield it on every part from injury.—But still more effectually to shut out harm, there was added a third covering of rams' skins dyed red, and over that again a fourth one, made of the skins of some sea-animal. Thus the whole was most perfectly defended from the weather. (Ex. xxvi. 1—14.)

Across the east end, or *entrance*, of the tabernacle, were ranged five pillars of shittim wood, overlaid with gold, standing upon sockets of brass; and from these was suspended a curtain or hanging of blue and purple, and scarlet, and fine twined linen, wrought with needlework, large enough to cover the whole front. This was the *door of the tent*. There was probably another curtain of coarser materials hung over this fine one on the outside, to keep it from being spoiled; at least we may suppose it was so when the weather was bad. (Ex xxvi. 36, 37.)

The inside of the tabernacle was divided into two apartments, by another curtain hung entirely across it from the top to the bottom. This curtain was richly wrought with figures of cherubim, like the fine inner covering spread above, and was suspended upon four shittim pillars overlaid with gold, that stood on so many weighty sockets of silver. It was called *the veil*, and sometimes *the second veil*, as the one which hung over the entrance had to be passed through before coming to it. (Heb. ix. 3.) The front apartment formed by this hanging partition, which reached from it to the door of the tent, was twenty cubits in length: it was called *the Holy Place*, and also *the First Tabernacle*. The other apartment, reaching from the dividing veil to the western end of the tabernacle, was of course completely square every way, its length, its breadth, and its height, being each exactly ten cubits: it was called *the Most Holy Place, the Holy of holies*, or the *Holiest of all*, and sometimes also *the second* or *inner tabernacle*. (Ex. xxvi. 31—33, Heb. ix. 2—8, 12, 24.)

The FURNITURE of the sanctuary and its court next claims our consideration. Here we are to notice the altar of burnt-offering and the brazen laver that stood in the court; the altar of incense, the candlestick, and the table of shew-bread which belonged to the holy place; and the ark of the covenant, with its mercy-seat overshadowed by the cherubim of glory, which abode in awful retirement within the holiest of all.

1. *The Altar of burnt-offering*, or the Brazen Altar, stood directly in front of the door of the tabernacle, off from it toward the centre of the courts, so as to be in a line between the tabernacle and the entrance of the court on the east end. Its frame was square, and hollow within, in length and in breadth five cubits, and in height three. The sides were made of boards of shittim wood completely overspread with brass: some think, however, that they were boarded in this way only from the middle upward, while below they were composed of some sort of brazen net-work. It is not altogether clear either, in what way the inside was occupied. We are told in the Bible, that *a grate of net-work of brass* was put *under the compass of the altar beneath*, so as to *be even unto the midst of it*. This some suppose to have been hung within the hollow frame, (which

they conceive was cased with boards all the way down,) just in the middle between the bottom and the top of it, and that it was the sacred fire-place where the sacrifices were to be burned: it was made full of holes, they say, round about and below, to let the ashes fall through to the bottom of the altar, where there was a little door on one side by which they might be taken out to be carried away. Another opinion is, that across the middle of the frame there was fixed some kind of flooring, and that the whole upper half above this was filled with earth, on which the sacrifice-fires were kindled; while the lower part, it is imagined, was altogether unoccupied, being enclosed only with grated sides, according to the idea already mentioned, through which in certain cases the blood of the victim was poured under the altar. (Lev. iv. 7, 18, 25.) This opinion, therefore, supposes the *grate of brazen net-work put under the compass of the altar beneath*, to be nothing else than the lower half of the frame itself made with grated sides, on which the upper half, closely boarded and filled with earth, was made to rest. There is certainly the best reason to believe, that the sacrifices were burned upon a surface of earth, and not upon a metal grate, from the direction in Ex. xx. 24. We are to suppose, therefore, that such a surface, on its top, the altar of burnt-offering did present, and that its brazen frame was formed only to support and hold together the earthy pile in which it especially consisted. It had four horns, one rising from each of its corners. These seem to have been clothed with a peculiar sacredness, as in particular cases of solemn sacrifice the priest was required to put on every one of them some of the blood. (Lev. iv. 25, 30, xvi. 18.) Hence it was usual for those who fled to the altar for protection and safety, (according to an ancient custom which caused it to be regarded as a sanctuary or sacred asylum,) to lay hold upon its horns. (1 Kings i. 50—53, ii. 28—34, Ex. xxi. 14.) At the same time, the horns added to the goodly appearance of the whole structure, and they were made so strong, that animals, when about to be sacrificed, might be secured to them with cords, as it seems they sometimes were. (Ps. cxviii. 27.) A sloping walk of earth heaped up, was made to rise gradually on one side to the top of the altar, by which persons might go upon it. (Ex. xx. 26.) Connected with the altar were several different sorts of instruments; such as *pans* to carry away the ashes, *shovels* for taking them up, *basins* for receiving the blood of the victims, and *flesh-hooks* for turning pieces of flesh in the fire: all of them were made of brass. (Ex. xxvii. 1—8.)

On this altar the fire was required to be kept ever burning

A short time after it was set up, there came fire in a miraculous manner, from the Lord, and kindled upon the offering that was laid in order on its top. This sacred flame was cherished with the greatest care from year to year, and none was allowed to be brought ever afterwards from any other quarter, to be employed in the service of the tabernacle in any way. For presumptuously making use of fire not taken from the altar, immediately after their consecration to the priestly office, Nadab and Abihu were destroyed by an awful judgment from the Almighty. (Lev. vi. 12, 13, ix. 24, x. 1—10.)

The altar was fed with the unceasing sacrifice of life. The place where it stood was a place of daily slaughter. The stain of blood was at all times fresh upon its sides. From its summit, rose, almost without interruption, the smoke of burning flesh; and dark oftentimes and exceedingly heavy was the cloud with which it mounted toward heaven. Thus it was a continual remembrancer of SIN, displaying in lively representation its awful guilt, and the consuming wrath of Heaven which it deserves. It stood in front of the sacred dwelling-place of God, to signify that his holy nature could not endure sin, or allow it to pass unpunished; and that he never would therefore admit the sinner to come before him in peace, without the law being completely satisfied, and guilt atoned for by suffering equal to its desert. At the same time, the altar was a sign of peace and good will to men; because while it taught that justice must be satisfied before God could be reconciled to the sinner, it declared also, that the satisfaction was provided without expense to man—that the necessary atonement was secured—that the wrath of Heaven, which, left to light upon his own head, must crush him downward in eternal death, had found for itself another victim; and thus God could be just, while he threw open a way for the guilty to draw near to his throne and be restored to his favour. In this way, the obstacle that shut up the way of life, and the removal of that obstacle by infinite grace, were at once presented to view. The blood-stained altar, with its dark column of smoke soaring on high, was a standing monument of God's unyielding justice, and yet a standing memorial of his victorious mercy; clothed with severity and terror, yet the significant pledge of goodness, friendship and peace.

"This Brazen Altar," to use the words of a learned and holy man, "was a type of Christ dying to make atonement for our sins. The *wood* had been consumed by the fire from heaven, if it had not been secured by the *brass;* nor could the *human nature* of Christ have borne the wrath of God, if it had not been supported by a *divine power.* Christ sanctified himself for his church, as their altar, (John xvii. 19,) and by his mediation sanctifies the daily services of his people who also have 'a right to eat of this altar,' (Heb. xiii. 10,) for they serve at it as spiritual priests. To the horns of this altar poor sinners fly for refuge, when justice pursues them, and there they are safe in the virtue of the sacrifice there offered."

2. *The Brazen Laver* stood between the altar of burnt-offering and the door of the tabernacle. The name which it has in the original language of the Bible, implies that it was round in its shape, and it is reasonable to suppose that its pattern was followed in the general form of the much larger one which was made for the temple afterwards, and called a *molten sea;* this, we are told, was round all about. The laver, therefore, was a circular vessel, rounded toward the bottom, it seems, after the manner of an urn or a tea-cup, so as to rest upon a single foot at its base below. It must have been of considerable size, but we are not informed what were its dimensions. It was for holding water, which was required to be kept constantly in it, for the priests to wash their hands and feet with, when they went into the tabernacle, or when they came near the altar to minister before the Lord. This they were solemnly charged never to neglect; *they shall wash their hands and feet,* was the injunction of God, *that they die not.* There were spouts or cocks by which the water might be let out through the lower part of the vessel, as it was wanted for use. The Jews say, that the laver stood near the entrance of the tabernacle, so, however, as not to be directly between it and the altar, but a little off toward the south side. They tell us, too, that fresh water was put into it every morning. (Ex. xxx. 18—21, xxxviii. 8.)

The washing of the body, in the outward service of the ancient sanctuary was intended to teach the necessity of inward purity in all who would draw near to Him in spirit and in truth. (Ps. xxvi. 6, lxvi. 18.) Thus the apostle exhorts believers to draw near to God with a true heart, in full assurance of faith, having "their hearts sprinkled from an evil conscience, and their bodies washed with pure water." (Heb. x. 22.) So we need to be washed every day, and are required every day to come with repentance and faith to Christ, that we may be cleansed from guilt, and so fitted to come before the Lord with an acceptable service. (James iv. 8, 1 John i. 7—10.) More especially, the laver was, moreover, a continual sign that the nature of man had become polluted, and that until the pollution was entirely taken away, it could find no entrance into heaven. As on the altar the eye of faith might behold, as it were, this inscription, *without shedding of blood there is no remission;* so, also, it might read upon the laver, *without holiness no man shall see the Lord.* It is not enough that sacrifice and atonement are made for sin, so as to satisfy the law; the soul needs at the same time to be delivered from its deep-rooted power, to be washed from its dark-coloured stain—to be sanctified as well as justified, and so made meet for the inheritance of the saints in light. A laver, therefore, as well as an altar, was planted out before the tabernacle; and it stood *between* the altar and the sanctuary, showing that pardon through the Great Sacrifice is the first benefit which the believer receives, and that this is followed by the complete sanctification of his nature, before he passes into the House not made with hands on high. Thus the laver also was a symbol of rich mercy. While it forcibly called to mind the deep depravity of the soul, and presented before it the alarming truth, that in its native character, or while one spot of its pollution remained, it could never see God; it gave assurance at the same time, that this great purification was not an object of despair, as it must have been if left for man to accomplish by his own power, but that the grace of God had made provision for it altogether sufficient and sure—that a *fountain for the uncleanness of sin* was wonderfully secured, by the same love that procured *redemption from its guilt*, in which the soul might be made as white as if it had never been defiled with the smallest stain. (Eph. v. 26, 27, Rev. i. 5, vii. 14.)

We are now ready to move the curtain aside, and enter within the holy place, the first apartment of the sanctuary. No window, or opening of any sort was provided in the tabernacle, to let in the light of day; but this room was never dark. Night and day it was brightly lighted with burning lamps. All its furniture, therefore, was clearly exposed to view, as soon as it was entered. This consisted of only three principal articles; the altar of incense, the table of shew-bread, and the candlestick from which the light proceeded. It was not allowed, however, for a common Israelite to enter into this sacred tent, and behold its furniture: no one but a priest might pass the outer veil and go in even so far as the first apartment.

3. *The Golden Candlestick* was placed on the south side of the holy place, so as to be to the left of any person when he came into the room by the middle of the entrance. It was made entirely of pure gold. It consisted of a *shaft* or principal stem rising upright from a suitable base, and six branches. These branches started out at three different points from the

Supposed form of the Golden Candlestick. p. 267.

main stem, and turned upward with a regular bend, so as to reach the same height with it. From each point went out two, one directly opposite to the other, and those above went out exactly in the same direction with those below; thus all were in the same range, three on one side, and three just over against them on another—the lower ones bending round in a larger curve, and the upper ones in a less, so as to bring all their tops to the same height, and in the same line, at equal distances one from another. The stem and each of the branches were adorned with artificial bowls, knops and flowers. The size of the candlestick is not mentioned in the Bible, but the Jewish tradition is, that it was as much as five feet high, and three and a half along the top, from the outmost branch on one side to the outmost branch on the other. Each of these seven tops, of the branches and their common stem, was made to terminate in a lamp. Connected with the candlestick were *tongs* and *snuff-dishes*, all made of gold; also *oil-vessels* for use in filling the lamps. The tongs were made probably after the fashion of scissors, to clip off the snuff, when it was immediately dropped into the snuff-dishes. (Ex. xxv. 31—39.)

The lamps were supplied with the purest olive oil; such as was procured, not by the common way of pressing it out, but by bruising or beating the olives while yet somewhat green, in a mortar. The priests were required to take care that the candlestick was never without light. Every day its lamps were to be examined, and dressed, and supplied with oil, as they might need. The Jews say, that only *three* of the lamps were kept burning through the day, but that all of them were lighted in the evening, to burn during the night.

The light of this candlestick was symbolical of the spiritual knowledge which God communicates to his people through his word, the Bible, and by the enlightening grace of the Holy Spirit. The law of the Lord is a glorious light set up in the church. (Ps. xix. 8, cxix. 105, 130, Prov. vi. 23.) *In it life and immortality are brought to light*, and truth revealed that guides the soul to heaven: it unfolds the knowledge of God, and of Jesus Christ, the True Light of a world made dark and desolate by sin. (John i. 4—9, viii. 12.) But all this light shines without being *comprehended* or perceived by the natural mind of man. A divine influence is needed to open a way for it through the midst of the thick darkness that is in him by reason of sin, and to introduce it fairly and effectually to his view. Such an influence of mercy is exerted by the Holy Spirit. "He shines into the hearts" of all who are saved, "to give them the light of the knowledge of the glory of God in the face of Jesus Christ." (1 Cor. ii. 10—12, 2 Cor. iv 4—6.) This enlightening agency, the source of all true wisdom to man, was that which was particularly signified by the candlestick with its seven lamps shining before the Most Holy place. Thus we are taught by divine revelation itself, in the Vision of John, the apostle, "There were seven lamps of fire burning before the throne, *which are the seven spirits of God.*" (Rev. iv. 5, i. 4.) The number seven denotes *perfection*—complete sufficiency in every way, and fulness in all respects, according to the nature of the thing spoken of.

4. *The Table of Shew-bread* was placed over against the candlestick, on the north side of the apartment, so as to be to the right of the priest when he walked up toward the second veil. It was made of shittim wood, and was two cubits long, a cubit broad, and a cubit and a half high. It was overlaid with gold, and had round the edge of its top, or leaf, an ornamental rim of gold, called its crown; and just under this, as it seems, the frame was compassed about with a border, a handbreadth broad, which was crowned with a similar rim. It was provided with vessels for different kinds of service, which are called in the English translation, *dishes, spoons, covers and bowls, to cover withal*. The *dishes*, there is reason to believe, were broad plates on which the shew-bread was placed: what are called *spoons*, seem rather to have been vessels in which incense was kept, (Num. vii. 14, 20, 86;) incense we know was used on the table, (Lev. xxiv. 7;) what are named *covers* and *bowls*, appear to have been two different sorts of vessels for holding wine; the first large, in which a continual supply of it was kept, and the second smaller in size, which were filled from the others, for the purpose of presenting drink-offerings before the Lord—so their use, instead of being to cover withal, was, it is most probable, *to pour out withal*, according to the more common signification of the word. (Ex. xxv. 23—30.)

Twelve loaves of unleavened bread were continually kept upon the table. They were placed in two piles, one loaf upon another, and on the top of each pile there was put a small quantity of pure frankincense. They were called *shew-bread*, or *the bread of the face*, because they were set solemnly before the Presence of the Lord as it dwelt in glory behind the second veil. Every Sabbath day, the loaves were changed by the priests—the old ones taken away and the new ones put in their place. The bread that was taken away was given to the priests to eat, and no person else was allowed to taste it; neither were they suffered to eat it anywhere else except within the court of the sanctuary: because it was most holy, it was to be eaten only by sacred persons, and only upon holy ground. The incense that was on the piles was still burnt; when the bread was changed, as an offering by fire unto the Lord, *for a memorial instead of the bread*, or an acknowledgment that all belonged to him, while the greater part was, by his permission, consigned to the use of his servants. (Lev. xxiv. 5—9.) David, on a certain occasion, when he was an hungered together with those that were with him, and no other bread could be procured, did not hesitate to eat the shew-bread that had been removed from the sanctuary. (1 Sam. xxi. 1—6, Matt. xii. 3, 4.)

"As the Ark," says one, "signified the presence of God in his church, so this table with the twelve cakes signified the multitude of the faithful presented unto God in his church, as upon a pure table, continually serving him : made by faith and holiness as fine cakes, and by the mediation of Christ, as by incense, made a sweet odour unto God." Thus each loaf represented a tribe. There is reason to believe, however, that while it may be considered to have been a continual thankful acknowledgment of God's goodness in providing for his people their daily food, this *perpetual bread* was more especially designed to be a symbol of the never-failing provision which he has made in the church for the spiritual nourishment and refreshment of all the truly pious. In the words of the writer quoted a short time since, it was "a type of the spiritual provision which is made in the church, by the gospel of Christ, for all that are made priests to our God. *In our Father's house there is bread enough, and to spare;* a loaf for every tribe. All that attend in God's house shall be abundantly satisfied with the goodness of it. (Ps. xxxvi. 8.) Divine consolations are the continual feast of holy souls ; however, there are those, to whom *the table of the Lord*, and the *meat thereof*, because it is plain bread, is contemptible. (Mal. i. 12.) Christ hath a *table in his kingdom*, at which all his saints shall for ever eat and drink with him." (Luke xxii. 29, 30.)

5. *The Altar of Incense*, or the Golden Altar, was situate between the Table and the Candlestick, so as to stand very near to the second veil, equally distant from both sides of the tabernacle. "Thou shalt put it," was the direction of the Lord, "before the veil that is by the ark of the testimony before the mercy-seat that is over the testimony, where I will meet with thee." It was a cubit long, a cubit broad, and two cubits high; made of shittim wood, and overlaid with gold, not only upon every side, but also over the top; furnished with four horns all overlaid in like manner, and compassed

round about its upper surface with an ornamental crown, or border, of the same precious metal. No flesh ever burned upon this altar; nor was it ever touched with blood, except on the most solemn occasions; and then its horns alone were marked with the crimson stain. The smoke that rose from its top was never any other than the smoke of burning incense. This went up every morning and every evening, filling the sanctuary with its fragrant cloud, and sending a refreshing odour out through all the court and far over the country on every side for miles beyond. Because it was thus renewed every day, it was called *a perpetual incense before the Lord.* It was not simple frankincense that was burnt, but a compound of this with other sweet spices, made according to the particular direction of God for this special purpose, and so considered holy, such as no man was allowed to make any like unto for common use. (Ex. xxx. 34—38.) The priest was charged never to offer *strange incense,* that is, any other than the sacred composition, upon the golden altar.

The pious writer, from whom some remarks on the meaning of the other altar have been lately borrowed, observes:—"This incense-altar typified, 1. *The mediation of Christ.* The brazen altar in the court was a type of Christ dying on earth; the golden altar in the sanctuary was a type of Christ interceding in heaven, in the virtue of his satisfaction. This altar was before the mercy-seat; for Christ always appears in the presence of God for us—he is our advocate with the Father, (1 John ii. 1;) and his intercession is unto God of a sweet smelling savour. 2. *The devotions of the saints,* whose prayers are said to be set forth before God as 'incense.' (Ps. cxli. 2.) As the smoke of the incense ascended, so must our desires toward God rise in prayer, being kindled with the fire of holy love and other pious affections. When the priest was burning incense, the people were praying, (Luke i. 10,) to signify that prayer is the true incense. This incense was offered daily; it was *a perpetual incense;* for we must *pray always,* that is, we must keep up stated times for prayer *every day,* morning and evening, at least, and never omit it, but thus pray without ceasing. The lamps were dressed or lighted at the same time that the incense was burnt, to teach us, that the reading of the Scriptures, (which are our light and lamp,) is a part of our daily work, and should ordinarily accompany our prayers and praises When we speak to God, we must hear what God saith to us; and thus the communion is complete. The devotions of sanctified souls are well-pleasing to God, of a sweet-smelling savour; the prayers of the saints are compared to 'sweet

Probable form of the Altar of Incense. p. 270.

odours.' (Rev v. 8,) but it is the *incense* which Christ *adds* to them that makes them 'acceptable,' (Rev. viii. 3,) and his blood that *atones* for the guilt which cleaves to our best services. And if the heart and life be not holy, even the *incense is an abomination*, and he that offers it is 'as if he blessed an idol.' " (Is. i. 13, lxvi. 3.)

"This altar was to be placed *before the veil*, on the outside of that partition, but *before the mercy-seat*, which was within the veil. For though he that ministered at the altar could not see the mercy-seat, the veil interposing, yet he must look towards it, and direct his incense that way : to teach us, that though we cannot with our bodily eyes see the throne of grace, that blessed mercy-seat, for it is such a throne of glory, that God, in compassion to us, *holdeth back the face* of it, and *spreadeth a cloud upon it;* yet we must in prayer by faith set ourselves *before it, direct our prayer* and *look up.*"

While the incense was burning, it was customary for all the people, as many as were standing without before the sanctuary, to put up prayers to God, every one silently by himself. It was understood that the holy offering was significant of that spiritual service of adoration and holy desire which God should receive from every heart. It was understood too, by the serious believer, that there was something more signified by it : the incense, presented by the priest, and rising pure and acceptable to God most Holy, from off the golden altar, represented to his faith prayer made efficacious and well-pleasing by something *added* to it to bear it upward and recommend it before the throne; he felt that his prayers in themselves were too feeble and impure to come up with acceptance before the Lord, and saw with gratitude, in the symbol of the sanctuary, a divine assurance that provision was made to remedy the defect : the nature and manner of the provision he could not indeed comprehend, but still he reposed confidence in its certainty, and by grace was enabled, through the sign, to lay hold of its consolation and benefit. It was natural, therefore, and certainly proper, to feel that the time of the going up of the morning and the evening incense was peculiarly suitable t be employed in prayer, and that there was an advantage in di recting the desires of the heart toward heaven at the very moment that the fragrant cloud was rising from the altar; not because the incense in itself could give value to any prayer, much less sanctify a hypocritical one, but because it was a divinely appointed ordinance admirably adapted to encourage and assist faith and devotion by its typical meaning. Many pious persons accordingly, who lived in Jerusalem, used often to go up to the temple, (which took, we know, the place of the tabernacle,) at these particular seasons, to put up prayers before God's holy house while the priest was ministering at the golden altar. Hence there was commonly a great multitude standing in the different courts of the temple at such times. When the priest went into the holy place to perform the service, notice was given by striking a great instrument that sounded like a bell, and might be heard all over Jerusalem; and then immediately the priests that were without, the Levites, and the whole multitude, addressed themselves in deep and solemn silence to the business of devotion. Thus it was on that memorable occasion when Zacharias ministered in the sanctuary, and suddenly beheld the angel Gabriel standing close beside him on the right side of the altar. (Luke i. 8—22.)

We are now prepared to look into the second apartment of the tabernacle—the Most Holy place. Beyond the second veil no mortal might ever pass but the high priest; and only on one great occasion in each year was it lawful even for him to do so; and then, only with the most solemn preparation and the most reverential care. The holiest of all was clothed with the solemnity of another world, and filled with unearthly grandeur. The whole tabernacle was the sanctuary of God, but here was the awful residence of his PRESENCE—the special dwelling-place of his visible glory. Well might sinful man tremble to move aside the veil, and present himself within so holy a place.

6. At the extreme of the apartment, the western end of the whole tabernacle, rested the *Ark of the Covenant*. It was in form a box, a cubit and a half broad and high, and two cubits and a half long, made of shittim wood, and covered within and without with the purest gold. Like the table of shew-bread and the golden altar, it was crowned with an ornamental border or rim, round about its top. Above upon it was the *mercy-seat*. This was made of solid gold of the best sort, exactly answering in length and breadth to the ark, on which it rested as a flat cover or lid, so as completely to close it over. On each end of it was fixed a *cherub*, wrought in like manner, of pure solid gold, rising above it, and overshadowing it with wings stretched forth on high. The faces of these sacred figures were turned toward each other, bending somewhat downwards towards the mercy-seat, on which they stood. Between these cherubim dwelt the uncreated glory of God. "There," He said to Moses, " I will meet with thee, and I will commune with thee from above the mercy-seat, from between the two cherubim which are upon the ark of the testimony."

The Most Holy Place.

In this ark Moses was required to put the two tables of
stone on which the ten commandments were written with the
finger of God. These were called the *testimony*, because they
were the testimony, or evidence and witness, of the *covenant*
between God and the Israelites; whence the ark was styled
sometimes the *ark of the testimony*, and sometimes the *ark of
the covenant*. We are expressly told, that the ark contained
nothing besides these tables. (1 Kings viii. 9.) By the side
of it, however, that is, at one end, in a coffer it seems, made
for the purpose, there was deposited a copy of the five books
of Moses, while a golden pot full of manna, and Aaron's rod
that budded, were laid up as memorials *before* it. (Ex. xvi.
32—34, Numb. xvii. 10, Deut. xxxi. 26. The apostle Paul
nevertheless seems to say, that the golden pot and the rod
were in the *inside* of the ark itself, with the tables of the covenant. (Heb. ix. 4.) Either we must understand him to mean
simply, that these things belonged to it, and were laid up for
security beside it; or else we must suppose, that they were
really placed within the ark at first, but afterwards were
taken out by some presumptuous hand, and so lost, during its
captivity and unsettled condition, before it was carried into
Solomon's temple:—at which time, we are told in the passage
referred to above, "there was nothing in it save the two tables
of stone which Moses put there at Horeb."

What was the particular form and appearance of the cherubim over the ark, we are not told. In the first chapter of
Ezekiel a description is given of four *living creatures*, as they
appeared to the prophet in vision, which supported the throne
of God, and bore it in majesty from place to place. Each of
them had four faces, the face of an ox, the face of a lion, the
face of an eagle, and the face of a man; all attached to a body
resembling that of a man, which was furnished with four wings,
together with hands such as men have, under them, and stood
upon feet like those of a calf. These are called cherubim.
(Ez. x. 15, 20.) Some have imagined, that the appearance
which they are represented to have had, was the common and
proper appearance that belonged to *all* figures of cherubim;
and so, of course, that we are to consider those which stood
over the mercy-seat to have been made after the same fashion.
But it seems more natural, from the account that is given of
these last, to suppose that they had each only a single face;
for it is said that their faces were made to look one toward another, which could not well be if they had more than one a
piece. No intimation is given, either, that these had more
than two wings, though it is not asserted that they had only

the one pair, and may be imagined, that, while they stretched these before them, so as to meet over the sacred covering of the ark, they were furnished with others to cover the lower parts of their bodies, in token of reverence and humility. (Isa. vi. 2, Rev. iv. 8.)

It appears most probable, therefore, that the cherubim mentioned in Scripture were not, in every case, of the same form. We are not to imagine, that in any case their figure and appearance were such as actually belong to any kind of existing creatures. They were mere emblems, intended to represent something else by symbolical signs, whether seen in vision, as they appeared to Ezekiel and to the apostle John, or formed by art, as they were for the tabernacle and the temple. They appear evidently to have been designed to represent the holy angels, who attend continually before the throne of God, and delight to perform his will. Their wings signified the readiness and swiftness with which they execute the Divine commands. Their faces, which seem always to have been one or more of those four that have been mentioned, denoted wisdom and power, activity and irresistible strength. Those which Ezekiel and John saw, were full of eyes, to express the great knowledge that belongs to the ministering spirits of heaven, the quickness of understanding with which they receive every intimation of God's most holy pleasure, and the clear, unerring certainty with which they instantly move to carry it into accomplishment. (Ezek. x. 12, Rev. iv. 6—8.) To present still more significantly their characters as *ministering servants*, and to emblem, at the same time, the unutterable grandeur of the Divine Majesty, they were represented as bearing the Almighty with immeasurable speed wherever it was his will to go. In the vision of the prophet, he saw, stretched forth over the heads of the cherubim above, the likeness of a firmament as the colour of the terrible crystal; and above upon the firmament, was *the appearance of the likeness of the glory of Jehovah*, throned in magnificent splendour. The cherubim lifted up their wings, when directed, and bore the whole whithersoever the Spirit was to go, with movement of awful sublimity; when they went, the noise of their wings was like the noise of great waters, as the voice of the Almighty, the voice of speech, as the noise of a host! In another magnificent description of the majesty and power of the Most High, it is said; "He rode upon a cherub, and did fly; yea, he did fly upon the wings of the wind!" (Ps. xviii. 10.)

The *Glory of the Lord* visibly displayed above the mercy seat was in the appearance of a cloud. "The Lord said unto

Moses, speak unto Aaron, thy brother, that he come not at all times into the holy place within the veil, before the mercy-seat which is upon the ark; that he die not: for *I will appear in the cloud upon the mercy-seat.*" (Lev. xvi. 2.) This manifestation of the Divine Presence was called, among the Jews, the *Shechinah.* Its appearance was attended, no doubt, with an *excellent glory,* of which we can form no proper conception, and such as it was exceedingly awful for dying, sinful man to look upon. Out of this cloud, the voice of God was uttered with deep solemnity, when he was consulted in behalf of the people, so as to be heard through the veil in the Holy Place. (Num. vii. 89.) This was the appointed way of holding direct intercourse with the Holy One of Israel; "There I will meet with thee," was his declaration, "and I will commune with thee from above the mercy-seat." There is some reason to think, that it was on this account the tabernacle was called, at times, the *Tabernacle of meeting,* (translated, also, Tabernacle of the congregation:) this name, however, may have been given to it, because it was the great centre of worship round which the congregation was wont to be assembled. From the situation of the glorious Shechinah, God is spoken of as "dwelling between the cherubim." (Ps. lxxx. 1, xcix. 1.) Hence, also, the ark is represented as his footstool, above which he sits, enthroned as it were, upon the wings of the cherubim. (1 Chron. xxviii. 2, Ps. xcix. 5.)

The Holiest of all was a figure of heaven, where God dwells in infinite and eternal glory; where his throne is established in righteousness and in judgment; where thousand thousands and ten thousand times ten thousand, all pure and happy spirits, minister before him, and contemplate, with adoring wonder, the perfections of his character, as they unfold upon their vision, with ever new discovery, age after age, without end. Thus we are taught by the apostle Paul, in his epistle to the Hebrews.

As God was, in a peculiar sense, the king of the Israelitish nation, it may not be improper, perhaps, to look upon the tabernacle as being, in some sort, the *royal palace* in which he was pleased to dwell among the people; from which he issued his laws, and to which his subjects were required to come to do him honour, presenting themselves before him with their homage and tribute. In this view, the priests also were *royal servants* attending upon the monarch, and composing his court; and all the furniture of the sacred tent had relation to the idea of a princely house, in which it is common to find full and rich provision made for comfort and convenience in every way

Thus it was *lighted* in brilliant and expensive style, as befitted a palace, and furnished with a *table* supplied with its various utensils, and continually spread with provision. This idea, however, if it be not utterly without reason or truth, enters only secondarily, and as it were, accidentally, into the original design of the tabernacle. The analogy imagined between its arrangement and service, and the manner of an earthly royal court, is slight in every case, and in most particulars fails altogether; so that it is evident its whole constitution and order had regard, in the Divine plan, to something entirely different. Its great purpose was to present, symbolically, the glorious reality which the gospel unfolds—the mystery of mercy into which angels desire to look, whereby God can be just, while he justifies the sinner, renews his intercourse of friendship and love with a fallen rebel race, and out of the deep pollution of guilt and the abyss of infinite ruin, raises a multitude which no man can number, to mingle in spotless purity with the great family of Heaven, where in his presence there is fulness of joy and pleasure for evermore.

It signified, that a fearful separation had taken place between God and the human race. It represented God as seated upon a throne of holiness, and jealous of the honour of his perfect laws; a being in whose sight iniquity can never stand, and whose righteousness *will by no means clear the guilty*. It represented man to be under the condemnation of sin—polluted, ignorant, helpless and lost. It was intimated, accordingly, that communion, direct, free and happy, with his Maker, such as is granted to pure and unfallen spirits, was, in his case, forfeited completely; that sin had created a hinderance in the way of it, which no power of his was sufficient ever to remove; that he was shut out from the favour of God; that his prayer could have no regard in heaven; that the presence of the Almighty, if he were brought into it, could be to him only a consuming fire, full of terror and death. The way into the Holiest of all was barred against approach with awful solemnity.

At the same time, it was signified, that God had, with amazing goodness, provided a remedy for the dreadful evil, and devised means to remove entirely the hinderance, so terrific, that rose to shut the sinner for ever from his favour. Indeed, the nature and extent of the evil were displayed only in the representation of the remedy; the picture itself was, in all respects, a picture of mercy; of mercy triumphant over sin and death: and it was in the exhibition of the victory alone, that the terribleness of the difficulty which it had to overcome was brought into view. God was represented as seated upon the throne of grace as well as of holiness and justice: the ark, while it guarded the tables of the eternal law, was covered with the mercy-seat. Righteousness and mercy, it was intimated, were met together in mysterious union, such as infinite wisdom alone could contrive, and only infinite power could accomplish; such as fills all heaven with adoration and wonder, and causes angels to bend forward, as it were, with the most earnest interest, to contemplate its unspeakable glory. (1 Pet. i. 12, Rev. v. 11—13.) Communication was represented to be restored between the Holy One and the ruined sinner. God could regard the prayer of man, pardon his guilt, remove his impurity, extend to him the richest blessings of his grace, and in the end receive him into his own presence in glory, as if he had never offended. But all this is secured only through a most extraordinary array of means, and with expense beyond all parallel. The way to the throne is open, but not for the guilty to rush before it in his own person: his desires may be presented there and answered, but only as they come recommended by the mediation of another: that mediation is all-prevailing, but only as it is founded in full and complete atonement, equal to the utmost demand of a broken law. Thus, in the service of the tabernacle, there was provided a priesthood, to stand between the Most High and the tribes of his chosen people; and so before the Most Holy Place there was erected an altar of perpetual intercession; and without, in front of the entrance of the sanctuary, an altar of continual atonement. By *blood*, and by *water*, and by *incense*, God was to be approached. In the church of Jesus Christ, we find the great realities themselves which were thus represented in shadowy type. The Son of God is the glorious Mediator, who makes reconciliation for iniquity, by whom sinners may draw near to Jehovah, and by whom the grace of Heaven finds its way in overflowing streams to their dark and polluted souls. He is able to save to the uttermost all that come unto God by him, because he ever lives to make intercession for them; and his intercession cannot fail to be prevalent, because it is founded upon an atonement of infinite value—he has appeared on earth to take away sin by one amazing and sufficient sacrifice, THE SACRIFICE OF HIMSELF. (Heb. vii. 25, ix. 26.) In the church, there is thus secured every thing that is needful for man, in order to restore him to fellowship with his Maker here on earth, to create him anew in knowledge, righteousness, and true holiness, after the image in which he was originally made, and to introduce him at last without moral spot or blemish into the full happiness of heaven.

We have now surveyed the whole of the ancient tabernacle. Every person must be struck with the exceedingly expensive style in which it was made. What an amount of labour, what an expense of the most skilful and curious workmanship, what an astonishing worth of the most rare and precious materials, were joined in the erection of a single tent! Hereby it was signified, as it was also in every part of the worship connected with the sanctuary, that God is to be honoured with the most perfect service which men have it in their power to render; and that we can never do too much for the honour of God, or become extravagant in the measure of our zeal and activity for his glory. This costliness and magnificence, however, had also its typical meaning in correspondence with the great design of the whole building. As the whole was an emblematic representation of the great mystery of redeeming grace displayed in the church, it was fit that it should be clothed in every part with the greatest degree of worldly splendour and value, to signify the transcendent glory and preciousness of this mystery, and the moral magnificence of that church in which it is found.

After the work was all finished, it was set apart for the service of God by a solemn ceremony of consecration.—Moses was commanded to set all up in proper order, and to anoint the whole with *holy anointing oil*. This oil was compounded with particular care, according to the direction of God himself, and, like the sacred incense already noticed, might never be employed for any other purpose than that for which it was ordered to be made, nor imitated at all by any composition for common use: thus it became *holy*, and *sanctified* the things and persons that were anointed with it; that is, separated them from common worldly service and dedicated them with solemn appropriation to God. (Ex. xxx. 23—33, xl. 9—11, Lev. viii. 10, 11.) We are informed, moreover, that both the tabernacle and all the vessels of its ministry were sprinkled with *blood*. (Heb. ix. 21.) Thus they were *purified* and prepared for their holy use.

In the wilderness the tabernacle always stood, wherever the Israelites stopped, in the midst of the camp. Immediately around its court were pitched the tents of the priests and Levites; the priests having their place to the east before the entrance, the family of Gershom to the west, that of Kohath to the south, and that of Merari to the north. Outside of these, at some distance, the other tribes encamped in four great divisions, each consisting of three tribes. Each of these divisions had its separate standard and *principal* tribe by whose name it was distinguished. On the east was the camp of Judah, including the tribes of Judah, Issachar and Zebulon: on the south side, the camp of Reuben, including the tribes of Reuben, Simeon and Gad; on the west, the camp of Ephraim, including the tribes of Ephraim, Manasseh and Benjamin; on the north, the camp of Dan, including the tribes of Dan, Asher and Naphtali. When the signal was given to march, the tabernacle was taken down, and all its parts committed to the care of the Levites, to be carried to the next place of encampment. Each of the three families of the Levites had its particular charge in this service assigned to it by the Lord. The care of the most holy things—the sacred furniture of the tabernacle and its court, were intrusted to the sons of Kohath; and they were required to carry the whole upon their shoulders. For convenient carriage, the ark, the table, and both the altars were furnished with rings, through which staves or poles, prepared for the purpose, were made to pass, by means of which they might be lifted and borne. The staves which belonged to the *ark* were never taken out of their rings, but remained there when the tabernacle was set up; those which belonged to the table and the altars were put into their rings only when they were to be used. In marching, the camp of Judah moved forward first; then followed the camp of Reuben; next came the Levites with the several parts of the tabernacle; immediately after them the camp of Ephraim set forward; the camp of Dan brought up the rear. (Num. ii. 1—34, iii. 17—38, iv. 1—33.) Bearing in mind the order both of encampment and march, in which the camp of the children of Joseph had its place always directly *behind* the tabernacle, we may understand that introduction of the Psalmist's prayer,—" Give ear, O Shepherd of Israel, Thou that leadest Joseph like a flock; Thou that dwellest between the cherubim, shine forth! Before Ephraim and Benjamin and Manasseh stir up thy strength, and come and save us." (Ps. lxxx. 1, 2.)

Every encampment and removal was determined by Divine direction. On the day the tabernacle was reared up, in testimony of God's presence and approbation, a CLOUD—the marvellous manifestation of the Divine Presence which had before led them out of Egypt—overshadowed it, and it was filled with the glory of the Lord. By this cloud they were afterwards, continually, in all their journeyings, admonished when to rest, and when and whither to proceed. While it rested over the tent, the Israelites journeyed not, whether it was for a shorter or longer time. But when it was taken up, by day or by night, at once the whole camp was in motion: the ta bernacle was taken down; every necessary preparation was instantly made for marching; and onward, in whatever course the cloud conducted, the tribes, in their appointed order, began to move. Again, when the cloud stood still, and not before, they stopped, erected the tabernacle where it hovered on high, waiting to descend upon its sacred resting-place, and pitched their tents in regular encampment round about. By night this mysterious cloud had the appearance of fire. (Ex. xl. 34—38, Num. ix. 15—23.) To this glorious manifestation of the Divine presence, overshadowing, protecting, and guiding the tabernacle and the chosen people in the wilderness, the prophet Isaiah beautifully alludes, in describing the happy and secure condition of the gospel church. (Isa. iv. 5, 6, Zech. ii. 5.) Through the wilderness of this world, the church, and every individual believer, is guarded and guided by the presence of Christ and the powerful grace of the Holy Spirit, onward to the land of promise—the rest that remaineth for the people of God.

After the Israelites had entered into the land of Canaan, under the command of Joshua, the tabernacle was first set up at *Gilgal*. There it continued till the land was conquered. The ark, however, was separated from it, and carried before the army in the wars of the time. As soon as the affairs of the country were settled in peace, it was removed from Gilgal and set up at *Shiloh*, a town in the tribe of Ephraim. Here it stood till after the death of Eli, considerably more than three hundred, perhaps four hundred years. (Josh. xviii. 1, 1 Sam. i. 3, 7, 9.) Hence Shiloh became a peculiarly sacred place, such as Jerusalem afterwards was, on account of the temples. (Jer. vii. 12—15, xxvi. 6—9.) Here the ark abode in its place, and hither the tribes of the Lord came up to worship. At last, however, being carried out to the field of war, (when Israel had been smitten before the Philistines, and vainly dreamed that its presence would save them, while yet they dishonoured the Lord himself by their sins, and repented not of their idolatries, to give glory to his name,) it was taken captive by the uncircumcised heathen. (1 Sam. iv. 1—22.) The Philistines were soon compelled to send it into its own country again, but it was never after restored, it seems, to its place in the tabernacle. In the days of Saul, the tabernacle was removed from Shiloh to Nob, for what reason we are not informed. (1 Sam. xxi. 1—9.) In the reign of David we find it again removed, and stationed at Gibeon. (1 Chron. xxi. 29.) The ark, meanwhile, having tarried about seventy years at Kirjath-jearim, (to which place it had been brought after its return from the land of the Philistines,) was brought soon after David's settlement upon the throne, to Jerusalem. The first attempt to bring it up was interrupted by the unhappy death of Uzzah, in consequence of which it was carried aside into the house of Obed-edom. After three months, however, the king solemnly assembled the priests, Levites, and elders of the people, and again went to fetch it unto the royal city, with more order and reverence than had been observed on the former occasion. It was now carried, not on a new cart, but on the shoulders of the Levites, as Moses commanded, according to the word of the Lord, and so was happily brought up the rest of the way with the high sounding noise of music and joy. In Jerusalem, it was lodged in a tent which David caused to be prepared there for its reception. (1 Chron. xiii. 1—14, xv. 1—29.) There it continued till it was carried into the temple.—The tabernacle, we are informed, was, in the commencement of Solomon's reign, found still at Gibeon. (2 Chron. i. 2—13.) Finally, its sacred fabric, and all its holy vessels, were removed likewise to the temple, and so all its glory and its use were transferred to this larger and still more magnificent house.

CHAPTER III.

THE TEMPLE.

THE Jewish temple next claims our consideration.—Its general plan was the same with that of the tabernacle; only it was larger, and more splendid, and had the *fixed* structure of a *house*, while the other was a *movable tent*. The meaning of each was the same; the one was but a continuation of the holy sanctuary which had its origin with the other, and took the place of that other, accordingly, as the centre of the same great system of ceremonial worship that was instituted at first in the wilderness. The temple itself did not continue the same building. Its first form perished with the great captivity; afterwards a new house rose in its stead. Thus there was a *first* and a *second temple*. Each of these is entitled to notice. Before we take notice of either, however, it will be proper to take a hasty survey of the city of Jerusalem in which they stood. The holiness of the temple extended itself in some measure over all the city. Jerusalem was not like other cities, ever of the sacred land. It was "the place which the Lord had chosen out of all the tribes, to put his name there." (Deut. xii. 5.) It was the *city of God*—the "city of the Great King, whose gates he loved more than all the dwellings of Jacob." (Ps. xlviii. 1—14, lxxxvii. 1—7.) Hence it was styled emphatically the *Holy City;* and by this name it is distinguished in the east to this day.

SECTION I.

THE HOLY CITY.

JERUSALEM is supposed by many to have been originally called *Salem;* and so it is imagined that the ancient city thus named, of which Melchisedek was king, was no other than this, that became at a later period the capital of the Jewish kingdom. By the Canaanites it was called *Jebus.* When the land was taken by Joshua, the inhabitants of this city, though their king was subdued, could not be utterly driven out by the Israelites; but having fortified themselves in the strongest part of it, they continued to dwell there for several hundred years. (Josh. xv. 63.) At length, however, their strong hold was taken by David, and the Jebusites were for ever cut off from Jerusalem.— The strong hold in which they had so long defied the strength of Israel, was on Mount Zion, which from the time of its capture was distinguished with the name of the "City of David." (2 Sam. v. 6—9.)

Jerusalem was situated on the boundary between the tribes of Judah and Benjamin. It was built over three neighbouring hills, *Zion, Moriah,* and one of less elevation than the others, named in later time, *Acra.* On three sides, it was bounded by valleys, separating it from mountainous heights that girded it round about with perpetual protection. (Ps. cxxv. 1, 2.) On the north it was not provided with the same natural security; its border on that side was distinguished indeed, as on the others, by a considerable declivity, but the country beyond was more open. Hence the city was commonly attacked by its enemies on the north side, as an army could not approach it from any other quarter, without great difficulty. The whole was surrounded with great and strong walls, and each of the hills just mentioned had, besides, a wall of its own. In the time of our Saviour, there was a considerable suburb formed to the north of the town, called the *New*

City; this at length was enclosed also with walls by king Agrippa. All these walls were fortified with numerous towers. The compass of the whole city round about, was between four and five miles.

The most lofty of the three hills that have been mentioned was Zion, called also, as we have seen, the city of David. It appears to have occupied the southern quarter of the city. Close over against it, on the east of its northern part, rose the hill of Moriah. Acra was situated more directly north of it. The part of the town which was built on Mount Zion received also the name of the *Upper City*, while that which extended itself over Acra was called the *Lower City*. Zion was distinguished by noble and costly buildings; among others the citadel of David, and the royal palace, could not fail to attract a stranger's attention. Acra showed the greatest number of streets and houses; the most considerable portion of the whole city spread its population over this hill. Moriah, however, had more honour than either of these hills; on its summit was erected the temple. It was very steep, and so small at the top originally, as not to afford sufficient room for the sacred building and the courts that were to be connected with it. But by means of walls, built up from the valleys at its bottom to the same height with it, the surface above was extended, so as at last to be about half a mile in compass.

The city was separated on the east side from the Mount of Olives, by the deep, narrow valley of *Cedron*, through which flowed the brook of the same name, mentioned in Scripture. This brook, or torrent, commences not far northward of Jerusalem, and having passed along the side of it, through the valley just mentioned, takes afterwards an easterly direction, and finds its way into the Dead Sea. It is completely dry, except during the rainy season, when it gathers a dark and muddy stream from the neighbouring hills. The valley or chasm down which it flows by the city, has been thought to be the same that is called by the prophet Joel, the *Valley of Jehoshaphat*.

The *Mount of Olives* spreads its dry and sandy height immediately east of this inconstant torrent. It rises with considerable steepness right over against the city, and is altogether more lofty than the highest parts of it; so that from the summit of Olivet, the eye overlooks Jerusalem's whole scenery of buildings and streets with perfect ease. This mount was often honoured with the presence of the Saviour. In his visits to Jerusalem, he was not accustomed, it seems, to lodge in the city, but used to go out to the village of *Bethany*, which was about two miles off, over on the Mount of Olives, where he was entertained by a pious and happy family, for which he had a particular regard. (Matt. xxi. 17, Mark xi. 11, 19, John xii. 1—3.) *Bethphage* was on the same hill, not far from Bethany, near the road that led from Jerusalem to Jericho. There the disciples were sent for the colt, on that memorable occasion when our Lord made his last visit to the guilty metropolis of Judea. When it was brought to him, he sat upon it, and rode forward in triumph to the city. As he drew near, it spread before his sight in all its magnificence and pride. But to the kind Redeemer it presented only a melancholy spectacle. He saw it polluted with the deepest defilement of guilt—he saw the cloud of Heaven's awful vengeance hung above its splendour, ready to burst and sweep it with unsparing desolation—he remembered, at the same time, its glory of many generations, its sacred privileges, its holy name —"and he wept over it!" (Luke xix. 29—44.) Not long after, from the summit of the same hill, he rose with a far more excellent triumph, attended by rejoicing angels, and sat down on the right hand of the throne of the Majesty in the heavens. (Acts i. 9—12.) Just over from the bottom of the more northern part of Moriah, between the Kidron and the foot of Olivet, there is shown to the traveller an even plat of ground, about 170 feet square, well planted with olive trees. This, he is informed, is that garden to which Jesus oft-times resorted with his disciples, into which he entered the night before his death, where, in agony, *he offered up prayers and supplications, with strong crying and tears,* and where the wretched Judas betrayed him in the dark and silent hour—the *Garden of Gethsemane.* As from the top of the Mount of Olives, the eye, directed toward the west, looks over Jerusalem, so, when turned the other way, it ranges across a far more extensive prospect. Before it, stretches the wilderness of Jericho; and downward, towards the south, the wilderness of Judea; far forward in the view to the right, it descries the sluggish waters of the Dead Sea, gathered over the ruin of Sodom and Gomorrah; and away beyond Jordan, over against Jericho, the mountains from which Moses beheld the promised land.

On the south side of Jerusalem, starting from the valley of Kidron and running westward, was *Gehenna,* or the *valley of the son of Hinnom,* called also, *Tophet.* (Jer. vii. 31, 32.) It was originally a very agreeable retreat, delightfully shaded with trees. But it became a scene of idolatrous abomination —a place consecrated to the dreadful worship of Moloch. To the image of this idol-god, were offered children in cruel sacrifice. Their own parents brought them forward, and caused them to be placed on the arms of the brazen statue, from which they dropped into a furnace of fire, that was kept burning before it, and perished without pity. To drown the cries of the miserable victims, drums of some sort, it is said, were beaten during the sacrifices; and as the Hebrew name for such an instrument is *Toph*, it has been supposed by many, that the part of the valley where this idol was worshipped got its name of Tophet from this circumstance. Good king Josiah, who vigorously attempted to take away idolatry from the land, defiled this place, we are told, "that no man might make his son or his daughter to pass through the fire to Moloch." (2 Kings xxiii. 10.) He caused it, it seems, to become a place for carcasses of animals to be removed to, and where the dead bodies of malefactors were frequently thrown. (Jer. xix. 2, 6, 11—14.) After the captivity, the Jews regarded it with the greatest abhorrence, and continued to defile it still more than before in the same way, so that it became a great and foul receptacle for all manner of filth and dead animal matter. To prevent the pestilence, which the putrefaction of such a mass was likely to breed, fires were kept constantly burning to consume it. Thus loathsome, dismal, and full of burning destruction, the place came to be considered an image of hell, and the word Gehenna grew at last to be the common name for that awful dwelling-place of the damned, where the worm dieth not, and the fire is never quenched.

From the foot of Mount Zion, where Mount Moriah stands, directly over against it, flowed the fountain of *Siloam* or *Shiloah*. Its waters were conducted into two large pools, the *Upper* and the *Lower*, from which they might be conveniently used; what were not required for use, glided with quiet and gentle stream into the channel of the Kidron. (Isa. vii. 3, viii. 6, xxii. 9, 11, John ix. 7.) At present, according to the account of our late missionaries to Palestine, "the fountain issues from a rock, twenty or thirty feet below the surface of the ground," to which there are steps for persons to go down. "Here it flows out without a single murmur, and appears clear as crystal. From this place, it winds its way several rods *under* the mountain: then it makes its appearance with gentle gurgling, and, forming a beautiful rill, takes its way down into the valley towards the south-east." On the borders of this humble streamlet, were the *Gardens of the Kings*, abounding, no doubt, with shady trees and walks of pleasant beauty. It has been imagined, that the upper pool was designed princi pally for supplying these gardens with water, and so was called also the *king's pool*. (Neh. ii. 14, iii. 15.) Somewhere near this fountain, we may suppose, stood that tower, called by its name, which fell in the days of our Saviour, and killed eighteen persons. (Luke xiii. 4.) There was quite a deep valley in this quarter, between the hills of Zion and Moriah. Over it was erected a beautiful bridge, or causeway, planted on each side with a row of stately trees, which, while they secured the borders of the walk, overhung it also with pleasant and refreshing shade. This was raised originally by king Solomon, among his other magnificent works, and led directly from the royal palace to one of the gates of the temple-court. It was designed to be a convenient and agreeable passage for the king to visit the house of God, and was, accordingly, the common way by which the monarchs of Israel went to, and returned from, its sacred courts. (2 Chron. ix. 4.)

The city was bordered on the west by the valley of *Gihon*. It does not appear to have been very deep, and had nothing about it, so far as we know, worthy of particular remark. Behind it there was all along a height rising considerably above the town, so that when a person was coming from the west, he could see nothing of Jerusalem, till he got on the summit of this elevation; when, all at once, directly before him, its walls and towers and palaces and solemn temple, burst upon his sight

A little distance out of the city, to the north-west, was the hill called *Golgotha* or *Calvary*. It was the place appointed for the execution of malefactors. There our Lord was crucified, though he had done no sin, neither was guile found in his mouth; and thus that spot became the theatre of the most astonishing and interesting transaction that ever took place on earth.

It was a beautiful sight, to look upon Jerusalem in the days of her ancient glory. That glory however has long since passed away. It perished first under the desolating power of the Chaldeans, 588 years before Christ came into the world. Then it was that the eye of the prophet Jeremiah *ran down with rivers of water, for the destruction of the daughter of his people.* "The kings of the earth, and all the inhabitants of the world, would not have believed that the adversary and the enemy should have entered into the gates of Jerusalem:" but a righteous God, for the multitude of her transgressions, gave her into the hands of the heathen. "The Lord covered the daughter of Zion with a cloud in his anger, and cast down from heaven unto the earth the beauty of Israel, and remem bered not his footstool in the day of his anger!" The *beauty of Israel* was the temple, and the *footstool* of Jehovah was the sacred ark of the covenant over which the Shechinah abode in glory between the cherubim. (Lam. ii. 1—8, iv. 12.) Yet afterwards, the city was seen rising again upon its ruins. The Jews endeavoured, with the greatest zeal, to restore it to its former splendour. From age to age it received improvement, and went on recovering beauty and magnificence. Herod the Great, at last, just before the time of our Saviour, brought the glory of its second state to its highest point of perfection. He was fond of great and splendid buildings, and wished to procure respect and honour for himself by the noble works of art which he caused to be finished. Vast, therefore, were the sums of money which he expended in different ways for the embellishment of Jerusalem. Thus the city came to rival, and in some respects to excel, its former self. Again it was a beautiful sight to stand upon Olivet, and look over its irregular extent. But the horror of its first desolation was now to be renewed and surpassed in a second overthrow. The measure of iniquity was at length filled to overflowing, by the crucifixion of the Lord of life and glory. The cry of guilt went up to heaven with exceeding loudness. The vengeance of the Holy One displayed itself in overwhelming terror. Jerusalem, after a siege in which sufferings altogether indescribable were endured, fell once more, utterly crushed beneath the weight of the Roman arm. The abomination of desolation, spoken of by Daniel the prophet, was seen standing in the holy place. The sacred city was trodden under foot of the Gentiles. The name and place of the Jewish nation, in the midst of streaming blood and desolating flames, was taken entirely away.

Jerusalem became a city again; but not to compare in any sort with her former state. Oppression hindered her growth, and war, from age to age, sported with her feeble strength. Her own children were scattered into every corner of the earth, and strangers crowded her streets. For a long time now, it has been pressed under the miserable government of the Turks. So much has it suffered from the ravages of war, and so much have different spots within and around it been altered by other means, that it is no longer easy to trace even the most striking features of its ancient situation. Its hills have been in some cases lowered and its valleys raised; so that to the spectator some distance off, it appears to be all situated upon one general declivity, gently sloping from west to east. But on a nearer view, it is perceived to be still resting on several hills, among which the forms of Zion and Moriah are discovered rising with principal importance. The south wall passes over Zion, near its summit, so that a great part of the mountain is without the city. The north wall, on the contrary, has been made to take in, on that side, more than was anciently enclosed, so as to brin into the north-west part of the town what is supposed to be th hill Calvary. The whole city, it is thought, contains not mor than twenty thousand inhabitants. Half of these are *Mohammedans*, rather more than a fourth part *Jews*, and the remainder nominal *Christians* of different sects, who have lost almost entirely the truth as it is in Jesus Christ. The streets are narrow, and most of them irregular; the houses generally low, with flat roofs and small grated windows. The summit of Moriah, where once the temple of Jehovah rose in sacred magnificence and grandeur, is now crowned with the mosque of Omar, a distinguished place of Mohammedan worship; and none but a Mussulman may pass the wall that surrounds it, on pain of instant death. "After all our research," the missionaries write, "we compare Jerusalem to a beautiful person whom we have not seen for many years, and who has passed through a great variety of changes and misfortunes, which have caused the rose on her cheeks to fade, her flesh to consume away, and her skin to become dry and withered, and have covered her face with the wrinkles of age; but who still retains some general features by which we recognise her as the person who used to be the delight of the circle in which she moved. Such is the present appearance of this Holy City, which was once *the perfection of beauty, the joy of the whole earth.*"

SECTION II.

THE FIRST TEMPLE.

THE idea of building a *Temple* for the Lord was first excited in the mind of David. God would not allow him, however, to execute the design, because he had been a man of war and had shed blood. It was declared to him, nevertheless, that his son who should succeed him on the throne would be permitted to erect the sacred building. (1 Chron. xvii. 1—15.)

Still, the good king was not forbidden to bear his part in the great work, so far as he could help forward its future accomplishment by making preparation for it beforehand. His piety, accordingly, displayed itself in this way in a very interesting manner. All his life, it appears, he had been in the habit of consecrating a very large portion of his worldly pro perty to the Lord, to be employed in his service. (2 Sam. viii. 11.) But in his latter days his zeal and activity for God grew still more conspicuous. The temple, though he was never to see it with his own eyes, became the object of his unceasing and most lively interest. No care or expense which might contribute to its perfection seemed to him too great to be incurred. Great, therefore, exceedingly, was the preparation which he caused to be made for this end. In his trouble he prepared for the house of the Lord an hundred thousand talents of gold, and a thousand thousand talents of silver; and of brass and iron without weight, by reason of abundance; timber also and stone, hewed for use, in great quantity; and all manner of precious stones besides. And over and above all this preparation, because he had set his affection on the house of his God, he left, of his own proper wealth, three thousand talents of gold of Ophir, and seven thousand of refined silver, to overlay the walls of the sacred edifice withal. In addition to the whole, the chief of the fathers and princes of the tribes of Israel, stirred to pious liberality by the generosity of their king, offered willingly a large sum for the same good design. Altogether, therefore, the value of the materials collected for the temple, before David's death, was such as mocks calculation. (1 Chron. xxviii. 2—5, 14—18, xxix. 1—9.)

Not only did the aged monarch make such a vast preparation for the work, for the assistance of his son, but he gave him also the exact plan according to which the whole was to be made. In all this, he was himself instructed by the same God that revealed to Moses the pattern of the tabernacle on mount Sinai. The sacred *House*, as well as the sacred *Tent*, in which the Most High humbled himself to dwell, was not left to be contrived in any sort by human wisdom. The Lord pointed out the hill on which it should be erected, and the very spot upon that hill where the great altar of burnt-offering, that was to be in front of the sanctuary, should stand. (1 Chron. xxi. 18, 26, 28, xxii. 1.) Afterwards, he caused his servant, whose heart was so much set upon the work, to understand clearly the manner after which the several parts were to be constructed. (1 Chron. xxviii. 11—19.) David carefully delivered the entire plan to Solomon, committed the collected materials to his direction, solemnly charged him to be faithful in his great and honourable trust, exhorted the princes of Israel to help him with all their might, and then departed, full of days and honour, to a better world.

Provided with such an amount of materials, Solomon under

took to execute the important work. He added yet more to the preparations of his father, made arrangements with Hiram king of Tyre for aid, set many thousand labourers to work, and in the commencement of the fourth year of his reign began to build. On mount Moriah, where the Lord appeared unto David his father, in the place that David had prepared in the threshing-floor of Ornan the Jebusite, the temple silently ascended. "The house when it was in building, was built of stone made ready before it was brought thither; so that there was neither hammer, nor axe, nor any tool of iron heard in the house while it was in building." At the end of seven years, it stood complete in all its splendour—the glory of Jerusalem—the most magnificent edifice in the world. (1 Kings v. 1—18, vi. 7, 37, 38.)

As has been already intimated, the top of Moriah was enlarged by art, to make room enough for the courts of the sacred house. Solomon caused a strong wall of square stones to be raised from the bottom of it, and then filled up the space between the wall and the side of the hill with earth. Thus the summit was sufficiently extended.

The temple stood, like the tabernacle, with its front toward the east. It consisted of the Sanctuary, or sacred house itself, and a most splendid Porch rising before it. The *Sanctuary* was sixty cubits long, twenty broad, and thirty high, and was divided into two apartments—the Holy and the Most Holy Place. It was built of square stones; but they were not to be seen in any part; for over them, within and without, was a covering of cedar boards overspread with pure gold. The *Porch*, extending along the whole front of the house from north to south, and reaching forward towards the east ten cubits, ascended far above the rest of the building to no less a height than one hundred and twenty cubits. By the entrance of it, were set up two great pillars of brass, one on the right hand and the other on the left, distinguished by the names of *Jachin* and *Boaz*. The passage into this Porch, as it seems, was not closed by any door, but was left continually open.

Passing across the porch, the priest entered, through beautiful folding doors of fir, ornamented with carved figures and covered with gold, into the first apartment of the Sanctuary, the Holy Place. It was a stately room, taking in the whole breadth and height of the house, and extended forty cubits backward in length, floored and ceiled and walled around with fir and cedar, all overlaid with shining gold. Carved figures of various sorts adorned the sides and ceiling, and for beauty they were garnished besides with all manner of rare and precious stones. The apartment was not without windows, though we are not informed of their number or manner. Its furniture was an altar of incense, overlaid with gold—standing before the Most Holy Place, as in the tabernacle—ten tables overlaid with gold and ten golden candlesticks. The tables and candlesticks were ranged on the two sides, five of each on the north and five on the south. All the instruments and vessels connected with them, which were many in number, were made of pure gold. One of the tables, we may suppose, was particularly designed for receiving the shew-bread.

Through another door, that closed with folds of olive-wood, covered with gold, and ornamented as those of the front one were, the high priest, once in the year, entered into the awful Holy of holies. It was twenty cubits in length, in breadth, and in height, having the same measure every way, and all overlaid with fine gold. There, as in the tabernacle, the sacred ark that was made in the wilderness had its secluded place, holding within it the two tables of the law, and overshadowed above by its golden cherubim. At each end of it, between it and the side-wall, Solomon caused another cherub to stand, much larger than those on the mercy-seat. These two cherubim were each ten cubits high, made of olive-wood, and covered with gold. The wings of each were stretched out on either side, reaching on one side to the wall, and on the other extending over the ark, so as to meet in the middle clear above the other cherubim. Over the door and the whole partition-wall before this *Oracle*, or most holy place, where God was consulted, there was hung a great veil, like that costly one that was made for the tabernacle.

As the whole house was thirty cubits high, and the Holy of holies was only twenty, it is plain there was considerable room above it—no less than twenty cubits of length and breadth, and ten of height. How this was occupied, or whether occupied at all, we are not told. It has been conjectured, that the materials of the tabernacle, and its sacred vessels and utensils that were not used in the temple, were laid up there to be carefully preserved.

Close against the wall of the house, in the north and south sides and at the west end round about, there was erected an additional structure. It consisted of three stories, each five cubits high, which seem to have been occupied with *chambers*, having a walk or gallery running round before them, into which they opened. On the south side, there were winding stairs to go up from the first story to the second, and from that to go up to the third. This structure was close up against the walls of the sanctuary, but its beams were not allowed to be fastened into them in any way. From the bottom of the house, along the side of these walls, was started an additional wall, three cubits broad. After this rose up as high as five cubits, one-third of it stopped, and became a resting-place round about for the ends of the beams that supported the floor of the second story of chambers. The remainder of the wall, two cubits in breadth, went up five cubits more, and then there was another cubit left, like the first, for a resting place, on which the ends of the beams of the next floor might be placed. From there, the wall, with only the breadth of one cubit, was carried up yet five cubits more, and then stopped altogether, furnishing a third resting-place, on which were supported the ends of the beams of the roof of the whole structure. Thus, while the lower story of chambers was only five cubits broad across the floor, the second was six, and the third, seven.

The first temple was surrounded with two courts or enclosures,—a smaller one, called the *Inner Court*, or the *Court of the Priests*, and a larger one round this embracing all the rest of the ground that there was to be used, which was styled the *Outer Court*, and also the *Great Court*. There were several gates by which the outer court was entered,—one on the east side, one on the north side, one on the south side, and four, it seems, on the west side The most important of these last, was the one to which the causeway from the royal palace led. There were several gates, also, between the outer and inner courts, to pass through from one to another. Around the courts, there were various buildings, for the use of the sanctuary: some of them furnished places of lodging for those who were employed in the sacred duties of the place, and others were used as depositories for different sorts of vessels and implements, and for various articles, such as flour, salt, wine and oil, that were needed for the temple service.

The inner court corresponded, in general, with the court of the tabernacle. Toward the middle of it, in front of the sanctuary, stood a great Altar of burnt-offering, twenty cubits square, and ten high. (Ezek. viii. 16, Joel ii. 17, Matt. xxiii. 35.) It was furnished, also, with a huge brazen Laver, called a *molten sea*, five cubits high, and ten from brim to brim: this great vessel rested on the back of twelve oxen made of the same metal. In addition to this, Solomon caused ten other lavers, of much smaller size, to be set up in the court, five on the north side and five on the south. They were placed every one upon a base, curiously wrought and fixed upon four wheels: the whole was molten-work of brass. Water was kept in these smaller lavers for washing the flesh of the victims that were sacrificed. Each of them, according to the common calculation of Jewish measures, held between nine and ten barrels, while the great brazen sea could contain about seven hundred. This last was appropriated altogether to *typical* use,—it was the Fountain for uncleanness, where the priests were required to wash, day after day, that they might not die when they drew near to minister before the Lord.

The description that is given of this temple in the Bible is short, and it is not easy to understand it completely in all its parts, by reason of our ignorance of some of the terms employed. We must rest satisfied, therefore, with a general notion of its manner. We are told enough, however, to convince us that its beauty and magnificence were such as to surpass all representation. (1 Kings, chap. vi. vii. 2 Chron. chap. iii. iv.)

It was a most interesting and solemn occasion, when, after its completion, the temple was dedicated to the Most High God. The elders of the nation, and a vast congregation of the people, were assembled. The ark was borne in sacred order from Mount Zion. Sacrifices more than could be numbered were offered before it. The priests conveyed it then into the oracle, and set it in its place, beneath the wings of the two stately cherubim that stood upon the floor. When they came out, an exceeding loud burst of music was sounded from the sacred choir, swelling with the harmony of voices and instruments in vast concert, and rolling its note of grand and thrilling praise all over Jerusalem. In the midst of this solemnity, the *cloud* of Jehovah's glory took possession of the house, as it had long before filled the tabernacle, when it was first erected. Before its majesty the priests were not able to stand, to perform their ministry. On a brazen scaffold, before the altar, king Solomon stood and blessed the people, and, falling upon his knees, with his face toward the people, and his hands extended, poured forth a solemn and affecting prayer to God. When he had ended, a miraculous fire descended from heaven and consumed the sacrifices that were on the altar. Thus the Lord testified his approbation. The whole congregation bowed with their faces to the ground, and worshipped. Then the king and all the people offered sacrifices before the Lord Many thousand were the victims slain. (2 Chron. chap. v. vi. vii.)

After being completely spoiled of its treasures, this beauti ful temple was reduced to ashes by the Babylonians. The ruin took place about four hundred and twenty years from the time of its building, when the nation was crushed and carried *into captivity* for their many sins.

SECTION III.

THE SECOND TEMPLE.

AFTER the return of the Jews from their captivity, according to a decree of Cyrus the Persian king, to which he was moved by a divine influence, the foundation of a new Temple was laid, under the direction of Zerubbabel. Soon after its commencement, the work was stopped for fifteen years. In the second year of the reign of Darius, God sent his word by the prophets Haggai and Zechariah, to reprove the people for delaying to go on with the building, and to encourage them to carry it forward to completion. Then it was renewed, and in a few years finished. We have an account of this in the book of Ezra. Thus rose, on the ruins of the first, the *Second Temple*, about 515 years before the birth of Christ.

When the foundations of this house were laid, the old men, who had seen the temple of Solomon, wept, because they thought it would fall so far short of that in glory. (Ezra iii. 12, Hag. ii. 3.) And, truly, there seemed to be much reason for such an opinion. The other had been erected in the most prosperous age of the nation, with every advantage that wealth the most unbounded, and art the most perfect, could unite: this was to be raised by a broken remnant of the kingdom, just restored from distant captivity to a wasted and almost deserted country. When it was completed, it seemed to labour under a still more melancholy imperfection. It wanted those miraculous manifestations of divine regard, which had been displayed toward the tabernacle and the first temple, and some other most sacred advantages which they had enjoyed. No CLOUD of glorious majesty was seen taking possession of its newly erected sanctuary: no fire descended from heaven to kindle the sacrifice upon its altar: no Shechinah abode between the cherubim in the Most Holy Place. Alas, there was neither ark, mercy-seat, nor cherubim, found there! They had perished, with the two tables of the law, in the ruin of the other temple. Thus, the oracle was without its glory. No voice sounded from behind the veil, as in ancient times, to acquaint the inquiring high priest with the will of Heaven. Silence and darkness reigned together there year after year. Five important things the Jews say, were wanting, in the second state of the temple, that belonged to the first: these were the *Ark*—the *Urim* and *Thummim*—the *Fire from Heaven*—the *Shechinah*—and the *Spirit of Prophecy*.

Yet this was the word of God by his prophet: "I will fill this house with glory—the glory of this latter house shall be greater than of the former, saith the Lord of Hosts." (Hag. ii. 6—9.) The outward glory of the latter house became in the end very great; the silver and gold of the earth belong to the Lord, and he caused them to meet in vast quantity for the decoration of his temple : but the prophecy had in view a different and far more excellent glory. The second temple never equalled the first in the costly magnificence of its work, and wanted much that gave moral dignity and sacredness to the other: but it obtained the pre-eminence, at last, by such a manifestation of Divine Presence within its courts as the first was never permitted to enjoy. It was not honoured with the *Cloud* of Jehovah's glory, but it was distinguished by the presence of JESUS CHRIST, in whom dwelt all the fulness of the Godhead bodily—who was God himself "manifest in the flesh !" (Mal. iii. 1, Col. ii. 9, 1 Tim. iii. 16.)

The second temple was completely rebuilt by Herod the Great. To gratify his pride, and to recommend himself to the favour of the nation, which he was conscious of having justly forfeited by his unheard-of cruelties, he took it into his head to pull down the house which Zerubbabel had erected, and to raise in its room a new one, vastly more beautiful and magnificent. The Jews were afraid, at first, that he was not sincere in his proposal, and might, after taking down the old building, leave them without any; for he was a deceitful and malicious man. It was not, therefore, until they saw the materials made ready for a new one, with prodigious labour and expense, that they were willing to let the other be removed. This was done only seventeen years before our Saviour appeared in the world, and in nine years and a half from that time, the main part of the new building was completed, so as to be fit for its regular service. Still, however, the work of beautifying and adding to the general structure continued to be carried on many years after, even till after the Redeemer's death. Wherefore, the Jews were not wrong, when they said to him, about the thirtieth year of his life, "Forty and six years was this temple in building. (John ii. 20.) So long, at that time, was the period which had elapsed from the laying of its foundations, and all the while it had been receiving new improvement.

Let us now take a rapid view of the several parts of this second temple, as it stood in the days of our Saviour, in all its beautiful grandeur. It was, indeed, as we have just seen, the *third building* erected on Moriah's sacred summit for the worship of God: but, because the temple put up after the captivity, had never been destroyed by enemies, like the first, and had been taken down by the Jews themselves, merely that it might immediately rise again, with a more excellent form, both these buildings were very properly spoken of as together forming, one after the other, the same *Second Temple;* which, accordingly, had its period from the time of Zerubbabel to the destruction of the city by the Romans.

THE COURT OF THE GENTILES.

THE top of Moriah, the *Mountain of the Lord's House*, (which, as already noticed, was so extended by art, as to measure about half a mile in compass, or a furlong square,) was enclosed by a wall, five and twenty cubits high, built around upon each side. This was the *outer wall:* in some parts, perhaps pretty generally all the way round, it took its start, properly, from the base of the mountain, being nothing else than the wall that was built, as we have seen, from the valleys below, in order to increase the surface above, carried upward twenty-five cubits higher than the summit of the hill. Prodigious, then, we may well conceive, was the distance directly downward, in many places, from the top of this wall on the outside, to its deep bottom in the valley beneath.

This outer wall, which was built of stone, beautiful and strong, was furnished with several gates. They were all large, and costly in their workmanship; having each two great folds, covered over with precious metal, and so heavy that they could not be opened or shut without considerable effort. The most stately and costly one of all, was on the east side—if that was, indeed, as some suppose, the magnificent *Eastern Gate*, noticed by the Jewish historian, Josephus. It was covered with Corinthian brass, exceedingly splendid, and more precious than silver and gold. A flight of many steps rose to its entrance, from the deep valley of Kidron, below. A causeway, also, lifted high upon arches, stretched in front of it, across the valley, making a straight and level way over to the Mount of Olives, on the other side. This gate was not situated in the middle of the eastern wall, but considerably farther along towards the north end, in order that it might directly face the porch of the sanctuary, or sacred house of the temple, which was fixed, by divine direction, to the northern part of the enclosed square. It was called the *King's Gate*, because all the eastern side of the hill to which it belonged, had been formed, originally, by king Solomon, with great labour and expense, by means of a wall raised in the way that has been already noticed, from the bottom of the valley beneath. It was called, also, it seems, the *Gate of Shushan*, and had pictured upon it a representation of the city of Shushan, the royal capital of Persia; in memory, according to some, of the great captivity, and so for a warning against idolatry, which was the cause of it; or, as others say, to keep up the recollection of the wonderful deliverance from the malice of Haman, which the nation had experienced in the days of Esther, and to bring to mind, year after year, the feast of Purim, or of Lots, which was then established in that city, to be a memorial from generation to generation of the happy event. (Est. iii. viii. ix.) On the south side of the square, there were two gates, which were called the *Gates of Huldah*. On the west side there were as many as four: one situated well toward the north, directly opposite to the gate Shushan on the east side, which had the name of *Coponius*, and answered to the gate called, in the time of the first temple, *Shallecheth*, to which that royal causeway already noticed led from the dwelling-place of the kings on Mount Zion; another not far south of this, toward the middle, called *Parbar*: and the two gates of *Asuppim*, still farther toward the south. These last three had the names just mentioned, in the first state of the temple. The outer wall, on the north side, also, was provided, it is said, with a gate, situated exactly in the middle of it.

All these gates had towers erected above them. An open space, of several cubits in extent, was left around each, where the people were accustomed to assemble. On either side of them, within, there were buildings or houses, standing close against the wall, two stories high, for the porters and others to lodge in, and for depositories or stores in which were kept various treasures, utensils, and articles for service, that belonged to the temple.

All around, along the inward side of this outer wall, stretching from gate to gate, there were *piazzas*, or covered walks, most beautiful and stately to behold. These were called *Porches*. Along the eastern, northern, and western sides, they were merely *double*, that is, they consisted of two broad covered walks, one adjoining the wall, and the other running by the side of this one, separated from it simply by a row of pillars; but on the southern side, the porch was *triple*, consisting of three such piazzas, or walks. The flooring of these walks was all along, a smooth and solid pavement of marble of different colours: the roof was flat, made of costly cedar, and covered with cement to keep it from being injured by the rain; it rested on rows of pillars, hewn out of white marble, and so large that three men could scarcely stretch their arms so as to meet around them. Where the porches were only double, they were furnished with three such rows of pillars: first, one close up against the wall; then, fifteen cubits over from that, another; and, farther out still from the wall, fifteen cubits more, a third. Thus the two walks formed together a breadth of thirty cubits, divided merely by the middle row of pillars, and overshadowed by a lofty roof. The pillars were about twenty-five cubits high; so that the roof, borne up on the three rows, was lifted to a height equal with the top of the outer wall. Along the south side, as there were three walks, so there were four rows of pillars. The walk that was next to the wall, and the one that was farthest out from it, were just equal in breadth and height with the walks that stretched along the other sides; but the middle one of the three was twice as high and nearly three times as broad as any of the rest, so that its roof was raised as much as twenty-five cubits above the roofs of the common walks that lay along with it on either side, and spread itself out on high at a distance of fifty cubits from the broad and beautiful pavement beneath. It was a most noble piazza, and could not fail to fill the spectator with the highest admiration, when he walked between its gigantic pillars, and lifted up his eyes to its ceiling of rich cedar, extended in lofty grandeur over his head. When a person stood above, on the roof of this middle walk, he could hardly look down into the valley on the outside of the wall, without becoming dizzy, the distance to the bottom of it was so fearfully great. It is said to have been no less than five hundred cubits, or 750 feet. This roof seems to have been that *pinnacle of the temple*, to which our Saviour was brought by the devil, and from which the foul tempter urged him to cast himself down over the outer wall, into the tremendous deep below. (Matt. iv. 5—7.)

These covered walks furnished a pleasant retreat for the people, in warm weather, or when it was raining. They were furnished with convenient seats along the wall, for persons to sit upon. All the day, people might be seen moving backwards and forwards along between the rows of stately pillars, or resting themselves on the beautiful benches, underneath the broad and friendly shelter that was here provided. The porch that lay along the east side, was called *Solomon's Porch*, because, as was stated a short time ago, all this side of the hill had been raised with special labour from the bottom of the valley, by that ancient monarch. (John x. 23, Acts iii. 11, v. 12.)

When a stranger entered the sacred ground, through any of the gates of the outer wall which surrounded the whole, he beheld the House of the temple rising with lofty magnificence, from the north-western part of the hill. But the space was not clear all the way up to it. Going forward a small distance he came to another wall, enclosing a considerable portion of ground that was deemed more holy than the rest of the hill left on the outside of it. The space between this second wall and the outer wall, already noticed, was not by any means of the same breadth on every side. On the west and north sides it was quite narrow, and it was not much wider on the east side; but to the south it took up about half of the whole hill: thus the second wall did not enclose a square with equal sides, but a piece of ground somewhat more than twice as long as it was broad, reaching across from west to east within the northern half of the great square enclosed by the outer one. The space between these two walls round about, was the COURT OF THE GENTILES.

Into this court all persons had liberty to come, whether they belonged to the Jewish nation or not. It was called the court of the Gentiles, not because it was given up particularly to the Gentiles, for their use, but because it was the *only* one to which they were admitted: farther than this first court no uncircumcised person was allowed to pass. It was in this court of the Gentiles that markets were kept for the sale of incense, oil, wine, doves, lambs, oxen, and of every thing, in short, that was wanted for the sacrifices of the temple. These markets appear to have had their particular place on the east side of the court, and toward the southern quarter. Here, persons coming from a distance bought whatever they wished for the purpose of making offerings to the Lord. In the same court the *money changers* sat, to receive Greek and Roman money, such as was in common use, in exchange for Jewish half-shekels, with one of which every man was required to pay his yearly tribute to the sanctuary. They took their stations, a short time before the Passover, in the Porches, with tables full of coin before them, ready to accommodate all who wanted to exchange. In doing this, they required a small fee to be allowed to themselves in every instance, which, because there was so much of it to be done, made their business quite profitable. It was very convenient to have markets at hand, and to have these money-changers to apply to, when persons attended at the temple; but then it was a great abuse to admit this sort of business into the temple-court, for it was mere worldly business after all, and oftentimes was carried on with unjust and avaricious fraud. Yet the unfaithful priests not only suffered this abuse, but encouraged it with their authority. Jesus Christ, however, would not let it pass without chastisement. On two several occasions, at least, as we are informed, he turned the whole company of profane dealers out of the temple, driving their animals out with them, and overthrowing the tables of the money-changers. (John ii. 14—17, Matt. xxi. 12, 13.) When we consider, that quite a number were engaged in this traffic, and that it was carried on according to established usage, and still more, that it was carried on under the approbation and authority of the priests, the rulers of the temple—we must feel, that it was a wonderful miracle which our Saviour wrought in these cases, and that it could only be by a divine power over the hearts of men, to turn them at his pleasure, that a single, poor, and hated individual could accomplish such a measure without assistance.

THE COURT OF THE WOMEN.

WE are now ready to pass onward from the Court of the Gentiles, into the holier ground, that was enclosed by the second wall lately mentioned. By the sides of the gates that were in this wall, pillars were placed, on which were seen inscriptions in Greek and Latin, forbidding, with large letters, all entrance to Gentiles of every nation, and to every person polluted by the dead.

In passing through this wall by any of its gates, persons had to go up several steps till they found themselves on the inside of it, as much as six cubits higher than the level of the Court of the Gentiles, which had just been left. Then there lay before them a level space ten cubits broad, at the other side of which stood another wall, a great deal higher and stronger than the one just passed, which was quite low. Thus all around there was this space, ten cubits in breadth, between these two walls, which persons had to pass over before they got into another court. Wherever there was a gate in the low wall, there was another just over against it in the high one, so that those who were passing out or in might go straight forward from one to the other. The space between the two walls was paved with marble. The high wall just mentioned was considerably higher from the pavement of this space, on the outside of it, than it was from the level of the enclosure which it surrounded, on the other side; because that enclosure was still higher than the space immediately round it between the walls; and as there were several steps to come up to the level of that space through the low wall, so there were more steps to go onward from it, through the high wall, up into the enclosure now mentioned.

This enclosure which, according to a statement already made, was more than twice as long as it was broad, was divided by a wall across it from north to south, into two unequal parts. The part toward the east, which was somewhat smaller than the other, was exactly square: the other part toward the west, while it had the same breadth of course from north to south, was a little longer from west to east. The square one was the COURT OF THE WOMEN. It was so called, not because it was occupied altogether or principally by women, but because women were not allowed to go beyond it toward the Holy House of the temple.

The Court of the Women could be entered from the Court of the Gentiles, by three gates; one on the north, one on the south, and one on the east, each having its situation precisely in the middle of the side to which it belonged. The one on the east side, was directly before the gate Shushan in the outer wall, in a line between it and the sanctuary. This some suppose to have been much more elegant than the rest, and to have been, in fact, that *Eastern Gate*, so richly overlaid with Corinthian brass, of which Jewish history makes mention; and which another opinion, already stated, has imagined rather to have been the same with the gate Shushan. That splendid gate, whichsoever of these two it was, has been thought by many to be the gate that was called *Beautiful*, at which the lame man lay to ask alms of those who were going up to the temple, as related in the first part of the Acts of the Apostles. (Acts iii. 2—11.)

When a person went up by any of these gates, first through the low wall to the level space ten cubits wide, and then, by five more steps, through the high wall, up into the Court of the Women, he found the whole square paved with large slabs of marble, and surrounded with different structures, erected close to the wall round about, as we have seen was the case in the outer court. In the four corners were buildings, or chambers, for different uses; and between these and the gates, on the north, east, and south sides, there were Porches. These Porches were merely *single* along each side, having two rows of pillars: they differed also from those that were in the Court of the Gentiles, by having *galleries* or balconies round about, above the lower walks, and therefore the ceiling of these was not remarkably lofty. On the west side there was no Porch of this sort.

This court was the place where men, as well as women, ordinarily performed their worship, when they appeared at the temple without bringing sacrifices with them. Here Peter and John used to go up with others, to pray toward the temple of the Most High. (Acts iii. 1.) Here it was, that the self-righteous Pharisee and broken-hearted Publican appeared at the same time; the one boldly presenting himself close up to the gate that led forward to the temple, and pleading his own worthiness before a holy God—the other standing afar off, not daring to lift his head toward the dwelling-place of the Lord, but smiting upon his breast and crying, "God be merciful to me a sinner!" (Luke xviii. 9—14.) Paul was in the same court when he was violently seized by his countrymen, and charged, among other things, with having brought Gentiles into that holy place. (Acts xxi. 26—30.)

This court was the place of the *Treasury*, where the people presented their offerings of money for the service of the temple. Several chests or vessels called *Trumpets*, because they were wide at the bottom and small at the top, were placed in some part of it, to receive the gifts: each vessel was appointed to receive some one particular class of them; one, for instance, was for money offered to buy wood for the altar; another, for money to buy frankincense; and so the rest for different uses. Here our Saviour beheld the people casting in their offerings, when the poor widow came forward with her two mites, and cast in all that she had. (Mark xii. 41—44.) In this part of the temple it was, too, that he delivered some of his solemn and impressive discourses, teaching the people, and reproving their unbelief. (John viii. 20.)

THE COURT OF ISRAEL.

In the middle of the high wall that bounded the Court of the Women, on the west side, was the gate called *Nicanor*. Through this, after a rise of fifteen steps, each half a cubit high, a person entered into the COURT OF ISRAEL. These steps were in the half-circle form. On either side of the lowest one, there was a door in the wall, facing the Court of the Women, which opened into a chamber cut out under the level of the Court of Israel above. In these two rooms the Levites deposited their musical instruments. Still, when they had done using them each day in the service of the temple, they came down the fifteen steps, turning to the right or to the left, and laid them away here till they were again wanted.

Besides the gate of Nicanor, there were six other gates, three on the northern and three on the southern side, by which the Court of Israel might be entered. These of course let persons into it directly from the Court of the Gentiles: on the east it was necessary to come into the Court of the Women first, and then from that into this third one, and this was the most common way by which it was entered; but on the north and south, those who went out or came in had nothing to pass through between this court and the outer one but the two walls already noticed, one high and the other low, with the level space of ten cubits' breadth that lay between them round about. Around against the wall, in this third enclosure, there were several houses or chambers standing, as in the courts already noticed, for different sorts of use connected with the service of the temple, and covered walks also along the four sides, from one gate to another, reaching farther out from the wall than the buildings just mentioned, so as to have still room enough, where any of these happened to stand, for persons to pass along in front of them.

This broad covered walk all around appears, indeed, not so truly to have been a walk *along the sides* of what was strictly the Court of Israel, as it was itself the whole extent of that court. The space within, surrounded by this walk, seems to have been *all* comprehended in what was properly another court, about two cubits and a half higher than the pavement of the walk, and separated from it by a low railing. Into this wide walk, or Court of Israel, common Israelites were allowed to come, to attend on particular services of religion, and from it they could look, without difficulty, over the elegant railing just mentioned, toward the holy House of the temple, and see all that was done in the court within.

THE COURT OF THE PRIESTS.

This court within was the Court of the Priests. It had in it the beautiful building of the Sanctuary, with the Altar of burnt-offering, and the Laver standing in front of it. Here the Priests with the Levites performed their daily service Besides these, no other Israelite might even pass the railing that surrounded it, except when he came forward solemnly to lay his hands upon the head of a victim that he offered for sacrifice, or to kill it, or to wave some part of it before the Lord.

Along the eastern end of this court, facing the front of the sanctuary, there was a breadth of eleven cubits, covered with a roof, like the walks already more than once noticed. Thus when a person went up through the gate of Nicanor, towards the House of the temple, he passed first across the covered space of the Court of Israel, lately considered, and then, rising four steps through the low railing that fenced in the Court of the Priests, found himself in this second covered space, of which we now speak, with the broad and lofty front of the temple Porch full before him. Along the back side of this space, just before the railing, a breadth of two cubits and a half was appropriated to the Levites that conducted the music in the solemn service of the Sanctuary. Here, in a row along from the entrance in the middle to the corner of the court on each side, they stood at the appointed times with their various instruments in their hands, playing and singing with a loud voice to the praise of the Most High God. The rest of this covered space, before the narrow range set apart for the use just mentioned, was for the accommodation of the priests, when any of them were not called to be employed in service elsewhere in the court. There were no seats, however, provided for them to sit upon and rest themselves: it was not considered lawful for persons to sit at all, either in the Court of the Priests or in the Court of Israel, around it; reverence towards God and regard for the holiness of these places were required to be continually manifested by standing on the feet.

The Altar of burnt-offering, that stood in this court, was much larger than the one that belonged to the first temple. It had its situation, however, on the same spot—the one that had been anciently pointed out by Divine direction to David. (1 Chron. xxi. 18.) This being the spot where the altar was to be built, it was necessary that the House of the temple should be erected near it; and that was the reason that it was situated so much toward the north-western corner of the hill. Between the altar and the entrance of the sanctuary, somewhat off toward the south side, stood the Laver. The second temple, like the tabernacle, was furnished with only one.

THE SANCTUARY.

The Sanctuary, or Temple, strictly so called, as it stood in the days of our Saviour, was larger in its dimensions than the building erected by Solomon, but constructed after the same general plan. The beauty and costliness of its workmanship were very great. The walls were built with stones of white marble, beautiful and exceedingly large.

In front, toward the east, the *Porch* attracted the admiration of every beholder. It was, it seems, of the same height with that of the first temple, but a great deal broader, and twice as wide; having a breadth of no less than a hundred cubits from north to south, and a width of twenty across through it from east to west. The entrance into it, on the front side, was seventy cubits high and twenty-five broad, and stood always open, without a door of any sort.

The *Sanctuary* itself, behind the Porch, was twenty cubits broad, from wall to wall, sixty in length, and sixty in height. Around it, on the north and south sides, and at the western end, there was a structure of three stories, after the fashion of that which was attached to the temple of Solomon, as it has been described in the account of that edifice. Here were a number of chambers all around in each story, with galleries in front of them, along the outside wall of the structure round about, by which persons, coming out from them, might walk along to the stairs that led down from one story to another, and so go out by some one of the doors below.

The *Holy Place*, in this Sanctuary, which was entered after crossing the Porch, was forty cubits long, twenty broad, and sixty high. It had in it an *Altar of Incense*, one *Candlestick*, and one *Table* for the shew-bread, after the manner of the ancient tabernacle. The Most Holy Place, measuring twenty cubits every way, wanted that which was the perpetual glory of the first temple—the Ark, overshadowed with its cherubim, above which the Divine Presence condescended to dwell. The Jews tell us, that a box, or coffer, resembling it in form, was made to supply its place; but this had nothing of that peculiar and extraordinary sacredness which distinguished the original depository of the Tables of the Law; and therefore the ark has been properly reckoned as one of the five things that were wanting in the second state of the temple. The Holy Place and the Holy of holies, in the last temple, had no wall across between them, but were separated, as in the tabernacle, simply by means of a veil, very costly, and remarkably thick and strong: the Jews say that it was not a *single* curtain that was employed for this purpose, but two of like texture, one being hung before the other, a little distance from it. When our Saviour died, the whole "was rent in twain from the top to the bottom." (Matt. xxvii. 51.) Hereby it was signified, that in the death of Christ the ancient Ceremonial System was brought to an end; that the darkness of the Jewish dispensation was to pass away in the clear revelation of the gospel; and especially that the way into the holiest of all was now made completely open by his blood, for all believers to draw near to the mercy-seat of God, with holy liberty and confidence (Heb. ix. 8, x. 19—22.) The veil that separates man from his Maker is guilt calling for wrath; and nothing can avail to rend the awful curtain but the death of Jesus Christ.

The bottom of the house of the temple was six cubits higher than the level of the court of the priests around it. Thus, as there was a continual rise from one court to another, this holiest, highest spot, on which the Sanctuary stood, was as much as twenty-four cubits and a half above the level of that which was first entered—the court of the Gentiles.

THE TOWER OF ANTONIA.

There was another building on this sacred hill that deserves particular notice. It stood on the outside of the court of the Gentiles, joining the wall on the north, near to its western corner. It was built originally by John Hyrcanus, the Jewish prince, a little more than a hundred years before the birth of Christ, and was used by himself and his successors as a palace, while at the same time it had all the strength and fortification of a castle. It was a square building, measuring two furlongs in compass, that is, as much as three hundred feet along each side. Here the sacred garments of the Highpriests were kept, to be taken out only on the solemn occasions that called for their use. Herod, with his other works of building, caused this also to put on new splendour and strength, and gave it a new name, calling it, in honour of the Roman prince Antony, *Antonia*. It was forty cubits high, and had at each of its corners a tower rising a number of cubits higher, the one at the south-east corner rose in this way as many as thirty, so that from it might easily be seen all that was done in any of the several courts of the temple. In this strong castle the Romans placed a garrison of soldiers, by which they had the whole hill completely under their power, and were enabled to hold the city in awe of their authority. This was considered especially important, as tumults and insurrections were ever likely to be excited, among the vast multitudes that were gathered to the temple at particular times. From the corner tower just mentioned, any disturbance might be at once perceived by the sentinel who was stationed there to keep watch, and immediately soldiers could be sent to quell it. There was a passage from the castle directly into the court of the Gentiles, through the outer wall, by which they could enter the sacred enclosure at a moment's warning.

In this way, that tumult was restrained which was raised

in the temple against the apostle Paul. The Jews dragged him out of the Court of the Women into the Court of the Gentiles, (which was considered less holy, and was spoken of sometimes as being *out of the temple*—the name *temple* being used with a wider or narrower meaning at different times;) and here they purposed to kill him. The chief captain of the Roman band, however, receiving notice of the disorder, very soon appeared on the spot with a number of soldiers, and took him out of their hands, commanding him to be carried into the castle. When he came upon the stairs that led up into it, he was permitted to address the multitude below, till they interrupted him at last with loud and angry cries, when he was taken out of their sight, and lodged within the walls of this magnificent fortress. (Acts xxi. 26—40, xxii. 1—24.)—Some have thought, that the commander of the Roman garrison in this castle is the officer intended by the title *Captain of the temple*, used more than once in the New Testament; but it seems more satisfactory to understand by that title, as hinted in a former part of this work, the chief of the Levites and priests who kept guard around and within the temple. (Acts iv. 1.)

It was a noble sight to look over the summit of Moriah, crowned, as we have now surveyed it, with all the grandeur and beauty of the temple with its different courts. The Jewish historian Josephus speaks of it as exceeding all description. The vast stones of polished marble, the stupendous pillars, the broad and lofty porches, the gates shining with the most precious metals, the towering front of the sanctuary—all united to fill the beholder with the highest admiration. Seen at a distance, by those who were approaching the city, it appeared, it is said, like a mountain covered with snow; for all over, except where broad plates of gold or silver dazzled the eye, it glistened with the whiteness of wrought marble. He that never saw Jerusalem in her glory, say the ancient Jewish doctors, never saw a lovely city; and he that never saw the sanctuary, with its buildings, never saw the most noble fabric under the sun.

It was not without reason, therefore, that the disciples of the Saviour, on a certain occasion, commended with admiration, in his presence, the grand and beautiful appearance of the temple. As he went out of it on the east side, going over to the Mount of Olives, they directed his attention to the rich and splendid style in which it was built and adorned: "Master," said one of them, "see what manner of stones and what buildings are here!" Jesus saw all this; but he looked upon it as

a sight of mere earthly glory that was very soon to pass away
"Seest thou these great buildings?" he replied: "there shall
not be left one stone upon another, that shall not be thrown
down." (Mark xiii. 1, 2.)

And so it came to pass in less than forty years after. The
whole perished in the awful destruction of the city by the Romans. Titus, the Roman general, wished to save it; but the
violence of war was too strong to be restrained in its progress.
It carried its torch to the sacred pile, and wrapped all the
glory of Moriah in wild and terrific flames. This melancholy
ruin of the second temple is said to have been accomplished in
the same month of the year, and on the same day of that
month, which, more than six hundred years before, had witnessed the destruction of the first one by the Babylonians.
After the flames had done their work, the walls were utterly
demolished to the bottom, and the whole ground on which they
stood ploughed up, according to the Roman custom; so that
as Christ had foretold, not a single stone was left in its place
(Micah iii. 12.)

Here ended, for ever, the glory of the Jewish temple. It
was never again to rise on its ruins, as before. Its whole
meaning and use were over. The dispensation to which it belonged was brought to a close. The time was come, when
neither at Jerusalem, nor at any other particular place, the
Father was to be worshipped with such outward service as was
required under the law. (John iv. 21—24.) The purpose of
the Most High, therefore, forbade all restoration of the ancient
sanctuary. An attempt, indeed, was made to restore it, about
three hundred years after its last destruction, which seemed
to have, as far as human calculation could reach, the greatest
prospect of success; but God crushed it at the very start. The
Roman Emperor, Julian, (who had pretended, in early life, to
be a Christian, but afterwards, when he came to the throne,
turned to be a pagan idolater, bitterly opposed to the truth of
the gospel, and so got the name of *Apostate*,) gave the Jews
permission to rebuild their temple, and renew their long neglected worship. They set about the work with alacrity and
high hope. But very soon they were compelled to stop.
While the workmen were clearing away the rubbish, in order
to lay the foundations, great balls of fire, dreadful to behold,
bursting forth from the ground with terrible noise, and repeated earthquakes, full of strangeness and horror, caused every
person to fly from the place, and so put an end to the work.
Thus wonderfully, as we are assured by the most satisfactory
testimony of history, did God blow upon and blast the design
that was formed to counteract his holy will.

CHAPTER IV.

MINISTERS OF THE TABERNACLE AND TEMPLE.

GOD separated the tribe of Levi from all the other tribes, to attend upon the services of the sanctuary. They were taken in room of the first-born. (Num. iii. 5—13, 40—51, viii. 16 —19.) They were not allowed, accordingly, to have any inheritance to themselves as a tribe among the others which composed the nation. The family of Aaron was taken out of this sacred tribe, and consecrated to the *priesthood*, to which the care of the most holy duties, and the privilege of the nearest approaches to the Divine Majesty, were confined. The rest of the Levites were appointed to attend to duties less solemn.

SECTION I.

THE LEVITES.

THE Levites were solemnly set apart to their ministry in the following way.—1. Having washed and shaved the whole body, they presented themselves before the tabernacle with two young bullocks, one for a burnt-offering, the other for a sin-offering. 2. They were sprinkled with water of purifying by Moses. 3. The leading men of the whole nation laid their hands upon them, and by this ceremony offered them to God as substitutes for themselves, and in the room of their first-born. 4. Aaron offered them before the Lord, or, as it is literally expressed in the Hebrew, *waved them for a wave-offering*, before the Lord; perhaps by causing them to fall down before God toward his holy Tabernacle, or, as others have supposed, by requiring them to walk solemnly around the altar, in token of their dedication to the Lord, as *living sacrifices* for his use. 5. They placed their hands upon the heads of the bullocks, which were then offered to make an atonement for them. (Num. viii. 5—22.) By these ceremonial signs was represented the perpetual consecration of the Levites, in place of the first-born of all the Israelites, to the service of the Sanctuary; the purity which God seeks in all who come near to serve him; the necessity there is, that for this end all such as belong to the family of Adam should be cleansed, as it were with *water* and by *blood*, by the sprinkling of the blood of Jesus Christ, and through the sanctifying power of the Holy Ghost.

In the wilderness, the Levites had the charge of carrying the tabernacle, with all its vessels, from place to place. In this business, each of the three great families into which they were divided had its particular department of duty assigned by God himself. In the land of Canaan, they were relieved, of course, from all this service. Only a part of them were needed to attend about the Sanctuary. The rest, scattered in their several cities through the land, seem to have been employed, as we have already seen, in various ways, for the promotion of piety and knowledge in the nation : unless where they forgot their character, and lost the spirit of their office in the spirit of the world. That part of them which attended at the tabernacle or temple were required to see that they were kept clean, and to have continually on hand all supplies, such as wine, oil, incense, &c., that were needed for the sanctuary service. The music of the temple was committed to their care, many of them were employed as porters, and, in later times, it became their business, also, to slay the victims that were brought to the altar. At first, they began to wait upon the service of the tabernacle at the age of twenty-five, and were not admitted to their full ministration before the age of thirty, continuing their service till they reached their fiftieth year. (Num. iv. 3, viii. 24.) Afterward, however, under the temple, they began to attend upon some duties of their ministry as early as the age of twenty. (1 Chron. xxiii. 24—32.)

David divided the Levites into four great classes. The first class, consisting of 24,000, were appointed to assist the priests —to *set forward the work of the house of the Lord*. The second, of 6,000, were made *officers and judges* through the land. The third, amounting to 4,000, were *porters*. The fourth, amounting to 4,000 also, were *musicians*. (1 Chron. xxiii. 3—5.) Those that were appointed to minister at the temple were divided into *courses* or smaller classes, which followed one another in turn, each performing service for a week at a time ; thus only a small part of the whole number were present at once.

The business of the PORTERS was to open in the morning and shut at night the gates of the outer court; to attend them through the day, in order to prevent any thing contrary to the purity or peace of the temple; to have charge of the treasure-chambers near the gates; and to keep watch at different places through the night. The Jews tell us, that there were altogether, about the temple, twenty-four stations occupied every night by guards; three of them, in the Court of Israel, were guarded by priests, and the rest by Levites. Each of these guards, which consisted of several men, had its chief or commander; hence we read of the *captains of the temple*. (Luke xxii. 4, 52.) There was one with still higher authority set over all the guards as their ruler, who is called in a more eminent sense the *Captain of the temple*. (Acts v. 24.) This last, perhaps, was the same with the *Man of the Mountain of the House*, whose business we are told it was to walk round every night and see the guards at every station were not neglecting their duty. If he found any asleep, he immediately struck him, and might set fire to his garments, as at times he did not hesitate to do. Some have thought, that there is allusion to this usage of the temple in Rev. xvi. 15.

The MUSICIANS, by their courses, had an important part to perform in the daily service of the Sanctuary. Each course had its leader placed over it, called the *Chief Musician;* which name we find in the titles of many of the Psalms. Part of them sung with their voices, and the rest played on various instruments, standing all along in a row across the east end of the Court of the Priests, as we have noticed in the last chapter, with their faces toward the broad and lofty front of the temple. The *time* for the performance of this sacred exercise was when the solemn sacrifice was kindled upon the altar. "When the burnt-offering began, the song of the Lord began also with the trumpets, and with the instruments ordained by David king of Israel: and all the congregation worshipped, and the singers sang, and the trumpeters sounded." (2 Chron. xxix. 25—28.) On common days, accordingly, the service of solemn sounding praise was performed twice—namely, when the morning and the evening sacrifice ascended from the altar. On extraordinary days, when other public sacrifices were appointed, the musicians were called of course to additional duty.

According to the Jews, a particular psalm was appointed for each day of the week, to be regularly sung with its ordinary daily service, morning and evening. Thus, the 24th psalm was assigned to the first day, (our Sunday)—because, say they, on the first day of the creation-week God possessed the world as its maker, and so gave it to be for a possession to man: the 48th psalm was assigned to the second day, (our Monday,)—because on that day the Lord divided the waters and reigned over them: the 82d to the third day—because on that day the earth appeared, established by the wisdom of the Most High, and placed under his righteous government: the 94th to the fourth day—because on that day He made the sun moon, and stars, and so will take vengeance on all that worship them: the 81st to the fifth day—because of the variety of creatures made on that day to praise his name: the 93d to the sixth day—because on that day he finished his works, and made man who can understand the glory of the Creator. On the Sabbath, (our Saturday,) they sang the 92d psalm, which is entitled *A Song for the Sabbath day*. On extraordinary occasions, other psalms were sung. With additional sacrifices of the Sabbath, (Num. xxviii. 9, 10,) they sang the two songs of Moses; the one in Deut. xxxii. with the first offering, (or more properly, only a part of it each Sabbath,) and the one in Exod. xv. with the second offering, which was burned in the afternoon before the regular evening sacrifice. Each psalm was divided into three parts; and still, in singing, a considerable pause was made between the first and the second, and between the second and the third. The signal for commencing the song was given by the sound of the trumpets. These were not used in the musical band of the Levites, but only by the priests; certain of whom were stationed on the southwest side of the altar, to sound with them on these occasions. At the proper time, they made the well-known sounding of three successive blasts, (the first and last long and unbroken, while the middle one was brought out in a sort of flourish, with breakings and quaverings,) when instantly the whole band of voices, harps, psalteries and cymbals, raised on high the loud anthem of praise. Having gone through the first part of the psalm, the music was silent. During the pause, the trumpets sounded again, and the people were expected to worship in silent reverence. So it was also during the next pause, when the second part of the psalm was finished; after which, the music started a third time and concluded the service. Such, if we may believe the tradition of the Jews, was the general manner of the temple music.

The Levites were not required to perform themselves the more servile kind of employments about the Sanctuary, such as bringing water, splitting wood, &c. They were allowed servants for these labours. These seem to have been originally such as were devoted to service of this sort by parents, masters, or their own religious choice. (Lev. xxvii. 1—8.) Afterward the number was greatly increased by the subjection of the Gibeonites and others to this business. (Josh. ix. 21—27.) More were added in the age of David and Solomon. (Ezra viii. 20.)—These servants were called NETHINIMS, that is, *given or devoted ones.*

SECTION II.

THE PRIESTS.

THE priestly office had its origin with the earliest times. Sacrifices, as we shall hereafter see, were appointed of God directly after the fall, and so accordingly there were priests, whose business it was to offer them. (Heb. v. 1.) At first, fathers were the priests of their own families. Such were Noah, Abraham, Job, &c. As patriarchal establishments grew to be large communities, their heads seem to have exercised, at least in many cases, a sort of priestly office for the whole, as well as a royal one. We read in the Bible of one ancient priest before the time of Moses, of peculiarly interesting character. He was king of Salem and invested at the same time with the highest dignity of the sacred office; so that even Abraham, though he was priest in his own family, and honoured with the most remarkable favour of God, acknowledged in him a higher and more especially sacred minister of the Most High God. (Gen. xiv. 18—20, Heb. vii. 1—10.) He was constituted a wonderful type of the Lord Jesus Christ, as the apostle fully teaches us in his epistle to the Hebrews. (Ps. cx. 4.)—With the institution of the Jewish Ceremonial Economy, God confined the priesthood to a particular family.

All the male descendants of Aaron were *Priests:* the firstborn of the whole family, in continual succession, according to the regular order of earlier times, sustained the still more important dignity of *High-Priest.* We have an account of the manner in which they were consecrated to their office in Ex. xxix. 1—35, and Lev. viii. 1—36. The ceremonies were solemn and expressive, and for ever separated the family of the priests from all the rest of the nation. 1. They were washed, and then clothed with their holy garments, to signify that they needed to be cleansed from sin, and clad with righteousness for their work.—2. Aaron, the High-priest, was anointed with oil. (Ps. cxxxiii. 2.)—3. A *sin-offering* was offered to make atonement for them. (Lev. viii. 14.)—4. A *burnt-offering* followed, in token of their dedication to God, which could not be acceptable till sin was atoned for.—5. A sacrifice of consecration was next necessary—having, in some sort the nature of a *peace-offering:* by the significant ceremony of putting a little of the blood on their ears, the thumbs of their right hands, and the great toes of their right feet, it was intimated that their whole powers were to be considered as consecrated to God: part of the blood was mingled with holy oil and sprinkled over them, by which they and their garments were hallowed: part of the flesh, together with part of the bread provided for the occasion, was *waved* by the priests themselves, and given to God on the altar; the rest, except the breast, which was given to Moses, became their own share, and was to be eaten on the same day in the holy court of the Sanctuary.—6. They were to abide in the court *seven* days without going from it by day or by night, and every day a new sin-offering was to bleed at the altar, for atonement.

When employed in their sacred duties, the priests were required to wear a particular dress. An account of the holy garments which God directed to be made for their use, we have in the 28th chapter of Exodus. Those which the common priests were required to wear are hardly more than mentioned, toward the end of the chapter; so that we can learn little about them from Scripture, except that they were, on the whole, very beautiful and rich. Reverence, it was supposed, could not allow the use of sandals or shoes in the performance of their holy ministry. Accordingly, they served with naked feet at all times; though the cold marble pavement of the temple rendered such exposure often injurious to health.

The *duties* of the priests at the sanctuary comprehended all the more solemn services of its worship, and such as, by reason of their direct and immediate reference to God, constituted the true life and substance of that worship. They had charge of the altar and its fire, and presented upon it the sacrificial offerings; all the ministry that was done in the *Holy Place* was theirs, &c. To them was intrusted the superintendence of the whole sanctuary, with all its service: all was ordered under their care and direction; it was their business to see that the sacred system of worship which God had appointed was carried forward in all its parts with decent and solemn action from day to day.—The age at which they entered upon their office was the same as in the case of the Levites.

To be qualified for discharging the priestly office, it was necessary, not only that a man could clearly show his descent from Aaron, (Ezra ii. 62,) but that he should also be free from bodily defects. (Lev. xxi. 17—24.) The meaning of this last requirement is plain. In the outward ceremonial arrangement by which the old dispensation shadowed forth things spiritual and heavenly, freedom from *bodily* imperfection represented that *moral* soundness which is needed in such as draw near to the Holy One, and without which no man in the end shall see the Lord. (Heb. xii. 14.) So, in other respects, the priestly character was to be guarded with more than common care from every thing that might seem to detract from its worldly honour, or to stain it with the smallest outward defilement, in signification of the spiritual dignity and purity which should characterize all who come nigh to God. (Lev. xxi. 1— 9, xxii. 1—13.) In later times, it became the business of the Sanhedrim to examine candidates for the holy office, and determine their fitness for it in all respects. If they could not bring sufficient evidence of their descent from Aaron, they were clothed in black, covered with a black veil, and sent home in disgrace. If they had such evidence, they were then examined as to their freedom from blemishes. Such as were found defective in this trial, were excluded from serving in the courts of the priests; but that they might have some service to perform at the temple, they were put to the business of examining the wood that was provided for the altar, in order to detect any pieces that might have worms in them, which were considered unfit for the sacred fire. The wood was deposited for this purpose in the building that occupied the north-east corner of the Court of the Women: here these blemished priests attended from day to day, carefully searching every stick, to be sure that none polluted with a worm was carried to the altar. Thus human authority added its uncommanded ceremonies to the original institution of God, disfiguring it, in this case, as in a thousand others, with vain and foolish superstition.

The priests were forbidden to drink any wine or any strong drink when employed in the service of the sanctuary, lest they should become guilty of irreverence, and so provoke the anger of God. Nadab and Abihu, it seems, owed their crime and their ruin to an undue use of such liquor. (Lev. x. 1—11.)

In the time of David, the whole number of priests, which had then become very considerable, was divided into twenty-four classes, or *courses*, which were required to attend at the sanctuary in succession, each for a week at a time. (1 Chron. xxiv. 1—18.) Thus only a twenty-fourth part were employed, at once, in the service of God's house, and each part was called to engage in this employment only once in about six months The change of one class for another, week after week, always took place on the Sabbath · on that day still, the courses both of the priests and the Levites that had served their week went out, and the next in order came in, to take their turn for the week to come. (2 Chron. xxiii. 4—8, 2 Kings xi. 5—7.) Each course had its own chief, and embraced within itself a particular great family of the general stock. At the return from the Babylonish captivity, as many as twenty of the original courses or families were found to be without representatives: only four, the Jews tell us, were represented among the priests that came back, so far as genealogical inquiry could ascertain. A new distribution, therefore, was necessary, in order to revive the old plan of twenty-four classes. Each of the four families that returned was divided, for this purpose, into six parts, which became so many new courses for the service of the second temple. To these new courses the names of the old ones were assigned by lot, and so they were numbered according to the original order of their first appointment. Thus the twenty-four ancient classes were revived in *form* and in *name*, though so many of them had been lost in *reality*. The ancient course of Abijah, which was the eighth in order, had been so lost with the captivity; but a new one had, in this way, taken its place and name, and this was that *course of Abia* to which Zacharias, the father of John the Baptist, belonged. (Luke i. 5.)

The various daily services to be attended to were distributed among the several priests of each course by lot. Thus it fell upon one *to kill the sacrifice;* upon another *to sprinkle the blood;* upon another *to dress the lamps,* &c. According to this custom of the priests' office, it was the lot of Zacharias, while he ministered before God, in the order of his course, on the occasion mentioned in the gospel, *to burn incense* on the golden altar, in the Holy Place. As the number belonging to each course grew to be large, it seems that when one performed its week of service, *all* its members were not required to minister every day; but a portion of them on one day, another portion on the next, &c., according to their families.

The whole Aaronic priesthood was a ceremonial institution, shadowing, in solemn and expressive type, the mediatorial character of the Lord Jesus Christ. Its meaning was not properly in *itself*, but in this great and glorious reality, of which it was the unsubstantial image. Accordingly, when Christ came, the ancient priesthood was brought to an end, as having accomplished all its purpose: the image yielded to the reality —the shadow to the substance. The priestly office is not wanting in the new dispensation introduced by the gospel. On the contrary, it is found here in its highest dignity, and in its only true worth; not committed to a great family, and handed down from fathers to sons, as under the law, but gathered and consecrated, with unchangeable perfection, in one person. Jesus combines in himself, in the fullest reality, all that the Levitical priesthood represented. It was established in the Ceremonial System, to be a *mediating* ministry between God and the church; it intimated that men, in themselves, are unfit to draw near to their Maker, and that he cannot regard them with any favour, or extend to them any blessing, except *through* some mediatorial agency interposing with sufficient merit on their behalf. All this agency is realized in Christ. He is fully qualified to act for men, in things pertaining to God; and, through him, God is abundantly willing to communicate to the most unworthy of our family the richest blessings of his grace. In every respect the church is blessed, in him, with such a priesthood as her wants demand.

Figuratively, or by way of metaphor, Christians are called priests. In the Old Testament, the whole Jewish nation, because it was so distinguished in religious advantages from the rest of the world, and brought so near to God, in comparison with other people, is thus styled a *kingdom of priests*. (Ex. xix. 6.) So, in the New Testament, believers in Christ are said to be a chosen generation, a *royal priesthood*, a holy nation, &c., (1 Pet. ii. 9,) made kings, and *priests unto God*, by the Lord Jesus Christ. (Rev. i. 6.) Through his redeeming mercy, they are *washed* and *clothed* in robes of righteousness; *consecrated* by *blood*, and by the holy *anointing* of God's Spirit; *separated* from the world that lieth in sin, and permitted to come very near to the Lord in all spiritual services; qualified to offer acceptable *sacrifices* of prayer and praise and sincere obedience, and to *feed* upon the holy provisions of God's house, and to enter within the *Holy Place*, and to approach, with sacred liberty, even to the *mercy-seat*, in the *Holiest of all*. (Heb. x. 19—22, 1 Pet. ii. 5.) Still, however, Christians are in all these respects only *like* priests, not priests in *reality*. Their privileges and services have their whole reason and value only in the priesthood of Christ. There is no other *true priesthood* in the church but this, of the All-sufficient Mediator, now passed into the heavens, and set on the right hand of the throne of the majesty on high.

SECTION III.

THE HIGH-PRIEST.

The office of the High-priest claims a separate consideration It embodied in itself all the attributes and all the meaning of the priesthood, in their highest perfection. The multitude of duties that belonged to the priestly office in the Jewish ceremonial system, made it necessary to have a number of priests; but to show that it was still considered one *single* and *undivided* thing, the whole ministry was united and bound together in subordinate relation to *one* representative head. This head was the high-priest. He was the centre and soul of the entire priesthood, comprehending its most essential agency exclusively in himself, and gathering, as it were, into one simple whole, all the action of its several inferior parts.

We have seen how he was consecrated. His sacred *dress* was still more costly and beautiful than that of the other priests, and is more particularly described in the divine volume. (Ex. xxviii. 2—39.) The *Robe* and *Ephod* have been already noticed, in the first part of this work; chap v. sec. 1. The last was exceedingly splendid, and full of curious ornament. On each shoulder of it was fixed an onyx stone, having graven upon it the names of six of the tribes of Israel; so as to have together all of them thus inscribed, to be borne before the Lord, for a memorial upon the High-priest. The *embroidered coat* was a richly wrought *tunic*, which sort of garment has also been noticed, in the same section, as being the one that was commonly worn by all persons next to the skin. The *Breast-plate* was a square piece, measuring only a span each way, composed of the same sort of highly ornamented stuff as that of the ephod, and made double, in such a way, perhaps, as to form a sort of bag or pouch in the inside. On one side of it was set four rows of precious stones, each row having three, and no two of all being alike, on every one of which was engraved the name of one of the twelve tribes. This was fastened to the front part of the ephod, with the side that was set with stones, outward; and thus the names of the children of Israel were carried by the High-priest upon his breast, as well as upon his shoulders, for a memorial before the Lord, when he went into the Holy Place. In this way it was signified, that he was the mediatorial representative of the whole church; that all its access to God, and acceptance with him, was in and through *his* person, and that he continually acted for its universal body, in all his official ministrations. The *Mitre* was made of fine linen, folded many times round, and finished with peculiar elegance and taste. Upon the front of it was fixed a plate of pure gold, bearing upon it the expressive inscription, HOLINESS TO THE LORD. The robe covered the tunic; and the ephod, as far as it reached down from the shoulders, was girded over the robe, outmost of all. (Ex. xxxix. 1—31.)

Thus splendid was the whole official dress which the Highpriest wore on ordinary occasions. But on the great day of atonement, when he entered into the Holiest of all, he clothed himself with other garments, made altogether of linen, strikingly plain and simple. (Lev. xvi. 4, 23.)

As the High-priest was the most important, by far, of all the priests, and included in himself the highest and most essential dignity of the priestly office, he was required to guard himself with yet more care than the rest of his family, from every thing like degradation or defilement, in the smallest degree. (Lev. xxi. 10—15.) His office was originally held for life, according to the Divine intention. But in later times after the captivity, it came to be oftentimes violently taken away from one, and given to another, without regard to the ancient usage. The right of birth too, which, under the first temple, confined the office to the line of the first-born, was in this latter age trampled under foot. Wicked men sought the distinction in the most corrupt manner. Money and shameful intrigue were employed to get possession of it. More than once, the way to the Aaronic *mitre*, as oftentimes the way to a royal *crown* has been, was through murder itself; while the wearer displayed upon his forehead, engraven in gold, that signature, *Holiness to the Lord*, the guilt of blood polluted his soul with its foulest stain. Thus the office came to be held by the worst of men, following each other in quick succession, and piety had no place where it ought to have been found in its highest perfection. Such unholy men were the high-priests that lived in the time of our Saviour. Such was that *Caiaphas*, who presided in the Sanhedrim when it tried and condemned the Lord of glory. The place had been occupied some years before by *Annas;* on which account he is styled High-priest in the history of Christ's crucifixion, although at that time he did not actually hold the office, having been put out of it to make room for another. Between him and Caiaphas, though both were living at the same time, there had been, in fact, no less than *two* other persons clothed for a little time with the dignity.

The High-priest might, at any time, if he chose, perform the sacred duties which were commonly discharged by the other priests. He was accustomed, the Jewish writers say, to offer a meat-offering of fine flour every day, half of it in the morning, and half of it in the evening, at his own expense; for so the law, in their view, was supposed to require, and not merely that he should present such an offering on the day of his consecration. His most solemn work, however, was performed on the most solemn of all the days of the year—the Great Day of atonement, which will come under consideration hereafter: the duties he had to discharge on that day were such as no common priest could ever attempt to do. It was, moreover, particularly his business to consult God, when the interests of the people made it proper, by *Urim* and *Thummim*.

It has been much inquired, what we are to understand by the URIM and THUMMIM, and how, by means of it, the will of God was discovered when sought in this way. Various conjectures, and some of them very foolish, have been imagined by learned men upon the subject. The account of it is thus given in the sacred volume: "Thou shalt put in the breast-plate of judgment, the Urim and Thummim; and they shall be upon Aaron's heart, when he goeth in before the Lord: and Aaron shall bear the judgment of the children of Israel upon his heart before the Lord, continually." (Ex. xxviii. 30.)

The words Urim and Thummim signify, literally, *Lights* and *Perfections;* but as we are not furnished with any description of the *thing* itself so called, we must necessarily remain in the dark on this point. Whatever it was, it was immediately connected with the solemn consultation of the Divine will; and by its heavenly appointment, it included in it a continual assurance, that when God was inquired of on any suitable occasion in this way, his answer might be confidently expected. Some have thought, therefore, that we are to understand by it, merely a divine *virtue* imparted to the breast-plate of the high-priest, whereby it was, as it were, *consecrated* to its use, and became an effectual means of discovering the will of the Lord; and that thus the breast-plate itself might well be called *Urim*. The language of the Bible, however, seems rather to intimate that some *visible* thing was added to the breast-plate, as the *sign* and *pledge* of this virtue which it was to possess. In either case, these names would denote the *clear* and *perfect* manner in which God made known his will, when consulted by this method. Counsel was asked of God by Urim and Thummim only in difficult and important cases. The high-priest, clad in his sacred robes, with the breast-plate on his breast, presented himself in the Holy Place, and proposed the inquiry. The voice of the Most High sounded in distinct answers, as it seems, from between the cherubim behind the veil. Thus repeatedly, we are informed, counsel was sought and obtained in the time of the tabernacle. Even when the ark was away from its sacred tent, the priest, girded with his wonderful ephod, often stood before it, and had the will of the Lord made known in answer to his inquiries. (Judg. i. 1, 2, xx. 18, 23, 28, 1 Sam. xxii. 10, xxiii. 9—13, xxviii. 6.) We have no account of God being consulted in this way in the time of the temple.

As we have seen already, the High-priest was intrusted with the most important power as a *judge*, not only in sacred matters, but in questions also of a merely civil kind. He sustained, too, a chief rank in the royal court, as a counsellor, to whom the king was expected to have recourse in every great interest of the state.

We read in 2 Kings xxv. 18, and Jer. lii. 24, of a *Second priest* as well as a *chief one*. This seems to have been one appointed to assist the chief or high-priest, in the general oversight of the Sanctuary, and in cases of unexpected necessity, to take his place, even in the most solemn duties. As he might be suddenly unfitted for his peculiar work by sickness or defilement, and yet it was of the most vital importance that on the great day of Atonement, especially, that work should not be omitted, it was certainly altogether expedient to have such a substitute, qualified in such emergencies to take upon himself the whole character of high-priest, in his stead, and so to accomplish the holy services of the season in their proper place. The Jewish writers of later times make frequent mention of such an assistant and substitute (when necessary) of the high-priest. They call him the *Sagan*.

We have seen that the whole priesthood was instituted of God, to represent, in shadowy type, the mediatorial character of our Redeemer, Jesus Christ. To him the priestly office had regard from the beginning. It was only in its relation to him that it had any meaning whatever. Hence, it is plain, the *high-priest*, in the Jewish economy, was, more than any other single priest, a figure of this Great Mediator that was to come. As he was the soul of the entire priesthood, and comprehended in himself, in a certain sense, the universal office, (though necessity required a distribution of its manifold duties among many secondary ministers, and reserved for him exclusively only such as were most vital and essential in their nature,) he of course embodied, in his official person, the largest measure, by far, of that typical significancy that has been mentioned. This will appear with peculiarly striking evidence, when we come hereafter to consider the solemn services which he was required to perform on the day of atonement. The apostle, in his epistle to the Hebrews, dwells at large upon the priestly character of Christ, and shows how infinitely it exceeded, in dignity and glory, all that had belonged, in the earthly pattern of heavenly things, to the Aaronic high-priest. He shows that the Holy Ghost had long before taught, that the Levitical priesthood was not sufficient to secure the great ends to which the priestly office, in its nature, has regard, and that it was, therefore, to be continued but for a season, after which it should give place to one that would possess, in *reality* all the power that this had only represented in *shadow*. A new priesthood, it had been signified, was to be introduced *after the order of Melchisedek;* and the priestly character of that man had been so ordered, in the wise providence of God, as to evince symbolically that this new priesthood, of which it was thus the mystical pattern, should have incomparably more excellence than that which distinguished the Jewish state. The priests under the law were made without an oath; but this one, who was after the order of Melchisedek, with an oath, by which solemnity on the part of God, his office was shown to be far more important than theirs. They were *many*, not being suffered to continue by reason of death; but this man, because he continueth ever, hath an *unchangeable* priesthood. They had *infirmity* and *sin* of their own; he is altogether *holy, harmless* and *undefiled*. (Heb. vii. 1—28.) Yet, though so glorious in his nature, he was not unqualified to *feel* for those on whose behalf he has undertaken to act. To be fit for his work, he clothed himself with the nature of man, so as to become familiar with all its infirmities and miseries, only without sin. Thus he was qualified to represent that nature in his mediatorial agency, and at the same time to sympathize with it in its weaknesses and sorrows. In that he himself hath suffered being tempted, he is able to succour them that are tempted, and can be touched in all points with the feeling of their infirmities. (Heb. ii. 14—18, iv. 14—16, v. 1—9.)

CHAPTER V.

SACRIFICES AND OTHER RELIGIOUS OFFERINGS.

SACRIFICE has been defined to be something that is offered immediately to God in such a way as to be *consumed* or *changed* into some other form. Thus, animals were sacrificed when they were presented to God by being solemnly *killed*, and either altogether, or in part, *burned* upon some sort of altar; and so was wine, when it was offered by being solemnly *poured out*. The Jewish law prescribed many sacrifices, as well as various other religious offerings.

SECTION I.

DIFFERENT KINDS OF SACRED OFFERINGS IN USE AMONG THE JEWS.

SACRED offerings of different kinds were common long before the age of Moses, even from the earliest period of the world Every one that has ever read the Bible knows that sacrifices were in use directly after the fall, and all along down to the time when the Jewish church was separated from the rest of the world. We read of altars and priests. We have notices of *different kinds* of sacrifices. (Gen. iv. 3, 4, viii. 20, xxxi. 54.) We read of *clean* and *unclean* animals. (Gen. vii. 2.) We read also of *firstlings* and *tithes* being consecrated to God (Gen. iv. 4, xiv. 20, xxviii. 22.) In the establishment of the Jewish economy, however, a more regular and extensive *system* of sacrifices and religious offerings was instituted. The number of them was increased; the different kinds of them more carefully distinguished; and the whole manner of them prescribed with particular and solemn direction.

Some of the sacrifices appointed by the Jewish law were *bloody*, requiring the death of animals: others were not so, consisting of cakes, meal, wine, &c.

BLOODY OFFERINGS.

The only animals that might be used in sacrifice were those of the *ox-kind, sheep, goats, turtle-doves,* and young *pigeons.* They were to be in all respects free from blemish or defect, because God ought to be served with the best offerings that man can bring. If we withhold from him our highest regard, and worship him only with a sort of halfway religion, devoting our chief time, care and thought to the world, while with little or no feeling we content ourselves with just so many outward duties of piety as are needed to keep a sleepy conscience quiet, we do but insult the greatest and best of all beings, and provoke his sore displeasure. "Cursed be the deceiver," saith the Lord of Hosts, "which hath in his flock a *male*, and voweth, and sacrificeth unto the Lord a *corrupt thing!*" (Mal. i. 8, 13, 14.) For one particular class of sacrifices *male* victims alone were allowed, except in the case of birds, where the distinction was not regarded. Except in the case of birds also, the victims were required to be not less than eight days, nor more than three years, old. The sheep and goats that were sacrificed were commonly a year old: the bullocks three years. *Wild beasts* were not offered in sacrifice: hence that expression, to intimate that no religious sacredness was to be imagined in the slaying of animals in certain cases; "Even as the roebuck and the hart is eaten, so shalt thou eat them; the unclean and the clean shall eat of them alike." (Deut. xii. 15, 21, 22.)

According to the law of Moses, sacrifices could not be offered upon the altar, except by the priests: nor at any other place than in the Court of God's Sanctuary, the tabernacle first, and afterwards the temple. (Deut. xii. 5—28.)

Animal-sacrifices were of four general kinds: viz. *Burnt-Offerings*, *Sin-Offerings*, *Trespass-Offerings*, and *Peace-Offerings*. We have a particular account of these in the first seven chapters of Leviticus. The three kinds first mentioned had an *expiatory* virtue; that is, they made *atonement* for those that offered them. The Peace-offerings were more particularly sacrifices expressive of *gratitude* and *praise* for mercies received, or of *supplication* for mercies desired. Burnt-offerings, however, were not exclusively expiatory in their character, but had in them also a meaning of thankful and adoring worship presented to the Most High: and in the nature of *every* class, on the other hand, we are to suppose that some regard was had to the guilt of sin, which called for the shedding of blood, before man could be accepted with God in any service. *Blood* poured out in sacrifice of any sort, could have no meaning other than that of *atonement*. It was solemnly consecrated by the Lord to be an expiation for the soul, and accordingly never flowed about the altar without a design of calling to remembrance the existence of sin, and symbolically washing away its evil. (Lev. xvii. 1—14.)

1. BURNT-OFFERINGS. These are sometimes styled *holocausts*, that is, offerings *wholly burned*, because *all* the flesh of the victims employed in them was consumed by the fire upon the altar. The animals used for them might not be, except in the case of birds, any other than males. The sacrifices that were in use before the time of Moses seem to have been most generally of this sort. They appear to have been expressive of religious worship in its widest nature; so as to be employed in it with equal propriety, when it was exercised in the way of praising God for his past mercies, or in the way of imploring his favour and blessing, or of deprecating his displeasure, for time to come. They were offered to God as the Maker, Preserver and Governor of the Universe, worthy of all honour and adoration; and were designed to recommend those that presented them to his holy regard, and to make their services of praise or prayer acceptable in his sight, which, by reason of sin, they could not be, without the *shedding of blood*. Such offerings are said in the law to make atonement for the person that presented them; but no particular cases of sin are mentioned for which they are to be brought to the altar. They seem to have had reference, in this respect, to the *general* sinfulness of heart and life of which a man ought to be conscious in his own bosom, and for which he should continually feel that he needs to have his soul purged by sacrifice. We have an account of the manner of the burnt offering sacrifice in the

first chapter of Leviticus. There we are informed how the offerer was required to bring his victim to the front of the Sanctuary, beside the brazen altar, and solemnly to lay his hand upon its head, and then to kill it before the Lord; how the priests were to take the blood in a proper vessel, and sprinkle it round about upon the altar; how *all* the parts of it, after the skin was taken off, were laid in order upon the wood and fire of the sacred hearth; and how the *whole* was consumed, an offering made by fire, of a sweet savour unto the Lord.

2. SIN-OFFERINGS. These were altogether expiatory, and were to be presented for *particular* cases of transgression. We have an account of the manner of them in the fourth chapter of Leviticus. The victims used for them were different, according to the character of the offerer. A bullock was appointed for the purpose when atonement was to be made for the high-priest, or for the people in general; a male goat, when a civil magistrate was the offender; and a female one, or a lamb, when the guilty person was a common individual of the nation. If the person happened to be so poor that he could not furnish a kid or a lamb, he was required to bring to the altar two turtle-doves, or two young pigeons; one of which was made a burnt-offering, and the other a sin-offering. If he was too poor even for this, he was still not excused; but had to present an offering for his sin, of mere flour, unaccompanied with oil or incense. The victim was presented and slain in the same manner as in the case of burnt-offerings. Its parts, however, were disposed of differently. When it was offered for the high-priest, or for the whole congregation, the ministering priest was required to carry some of the blood into the Holy Place, there to sprinkle it with his finger seven times solemnly, toward the veil of the Holy of holies, and to stain with it the horns of the golden altar of incense; after which, he returned and poured out all the rest of it at the bottom of the other altar without. Then the fat of the animal only was consumed in the sacrificial fire, while all its other parts were borne forth without the camp, to an appointed place, and there burned together. But when the sin-offering was presented by the ruler, or by one of the common people, the ceremonies were not equally solemn. The blood then was not carried into the Holy Place; it was enough to stain the horns of the *brazen altar* with it before pouring it out. The flesh too, after the fat was consumed, was not carried without the camp and burned, but was given to the priests to be eaten in the Court of the Sanctuary. The eating of it was a religious **duty**

that might not be neglected. What it signified, we learn from Lev. x. 16—20.

3. TRESPASS-OFFERINGS. Of these we have an account in the fifth and sixth chapters of Leviticus. Like the sin-offerings, which they resembled in many particulars, they were altogether expiatory, and might not be offered at any time a man chose of his own free will to bring one, as was allowed and encouraged in the case of burnt-offerings and peace-offerings, but were to be presented only for *particular* offences; and when these offences occurred they could not be withheld, without exposing the offender to the punishment of wilful transgression. They were never offered for the whole congregation, as we have seen the sin-offerings sometimes were, but merely for single individuals. The common victim used was a ram. The ceremonies of sacrifice were the same with those that were observed in the common cases of sin-offerings; only the blood was sprinkled round about upon the altar, and no mention is made of its being put on the horns of it. The flesh was to be eaten by the priests.

What was the general distinction between offences that called for sin-offerings and those that called for trespass-offerings, has been much disputed among learned men, and seems to be, on the whole, beyond satisfactory determination. Some have thought, that trespass-offerings were to be made in cases where there was a suspicion, but not a clear certainty, that an offence had been committed; and sin-offerings, in cases where, though at first the offence was unknown, it was afterwards understood. *Sins*, according to some, were offences of a more serious character; *trespasses*, such as were of lighter evil. One of the most learned men the world ever produced has told us, that *trespasses* in this case were offences of commission, such as violated the law by doing what it forbade to be done; and that *sins*, on the other hand, were offences of omission, such as left undone what the law required to be performed. Another, equally learned, has assured us, that it was just the other way; that the *sins* were the faults of *commission*, and the *trespasses* such as consisted in *omission*. Both opinions seem to be without foundation, as well as those that have been mentioned first. Another opinion is, that under the name of *trespasses*, were comprehended cases of two general kinds; viz. such as found a man's conscience in doubt whether he had not committed an offence, which, if certainly known, would have called for a sin-offering; and such as were offences of that nature, that they injured a man's neighbour: while *sins*, or those faults that required sin-offerings, are supposed to have been such transgressions of the law as did not directly affect a fellow-being but had the whole reason of their unlawfulness in their contrariety to the pleasure of God, and which, being done in ignorance, or without thought, were afterwards clearly discovered to conscience. Lastly, it has been supposed by others, that no general distinction between these two classes of offences is to be inquired after; that the distribution of particular offences to one and to the other was made arbitrarily, or in compliance with the common usage of speech, concerning the reason of which it must be idle to seek information; and that, therefore, we are to rest satisfied with the statement, as we find it in the Bible, that certain delinquencies which are mentioned were reckoned as belonging to one class, and certain others to the other, without attempting to discover any specific difference of nature that may satisfactorily account for the arrangement.

4. PEACE-OFFERINGS. The manner of these is told in the third chapter of Leviticus. The animals used for them were bullocks, heifers, rams, ewes, or goats: birds were not sacrificed in this way. Peace-offerings, as we learn from Lev. vii. 11—20, were presented, either in *thankfulness* for some special mercy received, or in the way of *supplication* for some special mercy desired. Sometimes, when a person was in distress, he accompanied his prayers to God for help with a *vow*, that he would afterwards present an offering, if preserved or prospered, and sometimes, of a man's free will he presented his offering beforehand, together with his prayers for Divine help or blessing. Hence arose the distinction of *vow offerings* and *voluntary offerings*, though both of these had in them the nature of supplication-sacrifices, and so differed from the other class of peace-offerings that were designed to express gratitude for favours already enjoyed.—In the case of these offerings, the person that presented the victim, as in the other cases already considered, brought it to the altar, and laid his hand upon its head with solemn ceremony before the Lord. It was not slain, however, to the north of the altar, as the victims offered in the other sacrifices were, but to the south of it. After it was killed, the priests sprinkled the altar round about with its blood, and placed its fat upon the sacred fire, to be a sacrifice of sweet savour unto the Lord; which being done, the flesh was divided between the priest and the offerer—the priest received for his part the breast and the right shoulder, and the offerer had all the rest. The meat was not allowed, however, to be carried away and laid up for common use, but was required to be all eaten on the same day that it was offered, or, at farthest, on the day after; and if any part of it

happened to be left till the third day, it was to be burned. Thus, in these peace-offerings, a communion of friendship was celebrated between God and his people, and he himself, as it were, and his ministers, and those that worship him in this way, partook together of the same sacred feast. At the same time, as already intimated, the *death* of the victim, after the solemn laying of hands upon its head, and the *sprinkling* of its *blood* upon the altar, called to remembrance the guilt of those who aspired to this sacred and precious privilege, and expressively signified, that without atonement God never can hold friendly intercourse in any way with sinful, fallen man.

The number of peace-offerings sacrificed every year was very great. In addition to those that were presented without obligation, as piety or formality led individuals, from time to time, to come before the Lord in this way, a vast multitude were made necessary by the law. From Deut. xii. 17, 18, xv. 19—23, and xiv. 22, 23, it appears, that not only the *tithes* of every farmer's agricultural produce, with a portion of its several *first-fruits*, but the *firstlings* also of his whole flock and herd, were to be consecrated to God as peace-offerings, and solemnly feasted upon year by year; only when the animals happened to have blemishes in them, they were considered unfit for sacrifice, and might be used in the common way, for food, at home; in all other cases, they were either to be taken themselves to the place of God's Sanctuary, or turned into money, which should then be laid out for other victims in their stead, and so entirely consumed according to the manner of thanksgiving sacrifices. In these sacred feasts, not only the families of those to whom the offerings belonged, servants and all, were to participate, but it was enjoined also, that others, who were without portion of their own, should be remembered, and invited to take part in their joyous celebration. The hospitality thus recommended and commanded was powerfully enforced, at the same time, by the consideration, that all the provision made for these entertainments, which was most liberal, was to be consumed on their several occasions, and could not, after the second day, be used at all: thus even those that in other cases were niggardly and inhospitable, could not well refuse to be generous and friendly enough in their peace-offering feasts. How much these feasts of friendship must have tended to promote good feelings among the people, and to secure proper regard to the lower classes of society, and such as were shut out from its more fortunate advantages, the servant, the poor, the orphan, the widow and the stranger, it is needless to suggest.

Under the general class of sacrifices of which we are now speaking, are properly to be reckoned those by means of which it was usual to ratify and confirm *Covenants*. These, indeed, were attended with some ceremonies peculiar to themselves, but had in them, on the whole, the nature of *peace-offerings*. The custom of confirming covenants in this way had its origin very far back in antiquity. The manner of the solemnity, it seems, was for the persons who wished to enter into covenant, to slay and divide the victim, or victims, employed; to place the parts opposite each other; and then to pass through between them, using, at the same time, we may suppose, some form of words suited to the transaction. The *division* of the victim expressed, symbolically, the punishment which ought to fall upon him who should afterwards violate the agreement, while the offering of it in *sacrifice* to God was, in fact, calling upon him to witness what was engaged, and to take vengeance in future on either of the parties that might prove false to it; thus laying conscience under the obligation of a most solemn oath. Part of the flesh, it is to be supposed, was afterwards converted into a feast, of which both parties partook together, in token of friendly agreement and confidence. It was in conformity with human usage in this thing, that God condescended to confirm his covenant with Abraham in the remarkable manner that is recorded in Gen. xv. 8—17, causing a flame and a smoke, as the sign of his own presence, to pass in vision between the parts of the victims prepared for the occasion. We have notice of these *Covenant sacrifices* also in Jer. xxiv. 18, 19; where it is intimated, that the ceremony just mentioned was used in a solemn covenant entered into by Zedekiah and the people of Jerusalem before the Lord. *They cut the calf in twain*, it is said, *and passed between the parts thereof*. From this case, thus incidentally noticed, it would seem that other covenants among the Jews were confirmed in like manner, although it is not expressly mentioned in the Bible, when other cases are spoken of. It is clear, however, that sacrifices were habitually made use of on such occasions. (Gen. xxxi. 53, 54, 1 Sam. xi. 15, Ps. l. 5.) In the great covenant which God made with the Israelites at the foot of Mount Sinai, Moses sprinkled the people with the blood of the sacrifices. (Ex. xxiv. 3—8, Heb. ix. 18—23.)

The sacrifice of the Passover lamb seems to have had in it also much of the nature of a peace-offering. It had, however, a peculiar character belonging to itself. A more particular consideration of it will come in our way hereafter.

As we have already had occasion to notice, some sacrifices

were offered by single individuals for their own advantage, and others were offered in behalf of the nation as a whole. Those of the first sort, if the case in Lev. xvi. 6, be excepted, were not regulated by times and seasons; but were presented, either *freely* at any time a man's heart moved him to render such worship to God, or in conformity with the *requirement* of the law, when persons were brought into certain circumstances, which, according to the Divine will, called for particular offerings, in the way either of atonement for sin, or of thankful acknowledgment of the Lord's mercy. Of such offerings as were presented freely, various notices are found throughout the Bible; of the others that were required from individuals in particular circumstances, besides the cases stated in the 4th, 5th, and 6th chapters of Leviticus, we have instances in Lev. xii. 6, 8, xiv. 10—31, xv. 14, 15, 29, 30, xix. 21, Num. vi. 10—21.—The other general class of offerings, viz. such as were made in behalf of the whole nation, were all, except the particular cases noticed in Lev. iv. 13, 14, Num. xv. 22—26, and xix. 5—10, assigned to certain times, and had their regular periods when they were to be performed. Such were the daily morning and evening sacrifices, (Ex. xxix. 38—41;) the Sabbath-day sacrifices; the new moon sacrifices, and the sacrifices that belonged to those three great festivals. For an account of all these, see the 28th and 29th chapters of Numbers. The paschal lambs, sacrificed in vast multitudes on the first day of the *feast of unleavened bread*, were offered severally in behalf of single families or small companies. The victim required to be slain in cases of uncertain murder, was sacrificed in behalf of a particular city or town. (Deut. xxi. 1—9.) This case, as well as the case of the *red heifer* to which reference has just now been made, was not in all respects a regular *sacrificial offering*, inasmuch as the victim was not brought to the altar and there killed; both heifers, however, had in them the nature of expiatory sacrifices.

The regular stated sacrifices which the law required to be offered for the whole nation, in the course of each year, were as follow: viz. 1. On every day, two lambs; amounting altogether to at least 730. 2. On every Sabbath, two additional lambs; making altogether 104. 3. On the first day of every month, two bullocks, one ram, seven lambs, and one goat; amounting in the year to at least 24 bullocks, 12 rams, 84 lambs, and 12 goats. 4. On each of the seven days of the feast of unleavened bread, the same as in the case of every new moon just stated, (Num. xxviii. 19—25,) and besides, an additional lamb on the second day with the sheaf of first-fruits.

(Lev. xxiii 12;) making altogether 14 bullocks, 7 rams, 50 lambs, and 7 goats. 5. On the day of Pentecost, the same also as for each new moon, (Num. xxviii. 26—31,) and besides, with the two wave loaves, seven lambs, one bullock, two rams, and a goat, together with two other lambs for a sacrifice of peace-offering, (Lev. xxiii. 18, 19;) making altogether 3 bullocks, 3 rams, 16 lambs, and 2 goats. 6. On the Feast of Trumpets, one bullock, one ram, seven lambs, and a goat. 7. On the great day of Atonement, the same, (Num. xxix. 7—11,) and besides a ram and a goat when the high-priest performed his awful duty of entering the Most Holy Place, (Lev. xvi. 5,) making together, 1 bullock, 2 rams, 7 lambs, and 2 goats. On each of the eight days of the Feast of the Tabernacles a number of different victims, equal altogether to 71 bullocks, 15 rams, 105 lambs, and 8 goats. (Num. xxix. 12—38.) --Let us now put the whole together, thus:

	B.	R.	L.	G.
1. Daily Sacrifices for 365 Days,	—	—	730	—
2. Sacrifices for 52 Sabbaths,	—	—	104	—
3. Sacrifices for 12 New Moons,	24	12	84	12
4. Sacrifices for the Passover,	14	7	50	7
5. Sacrifices for Pentecost,	3	3	16	2
6. Sacrifices for the Feast of Trumpets,	1	1	7	1
7. Sacrifices for the Day of Atonement,	1	2	7	2
8. Sacrifices for the Feast of Tabernacles,	71	15	105	8
	114	40	1103	32

Thus many were the victims whose blood was shed each year, in the stated services of the sanctuary, for the whole congregation. The goats, in all these cases, were sin-offerings; and the other animals, except in the one instance noticed in the statement, burnt-offerings. The blood of all these victims, however, formed only a small part of the whole quantity that was poured forth in the sacred court, year after year, from the sacrifices that were there presented before the Lord. The largest stream by far flowed from the various victims that were led to the altar as private offerings.

SACRIFICES THAT WERE NOT BLOODY.

Bloodless sacrifices, it has been already stated, consisted in meal, cakes, wine, &c. Of this class were the MEAT-OFFERINGS, and the DRINK-OFFERINGS that were in many cases required to accompany them. The latter were never presented separately from the first, and in all common cases both were found joined to other sacrifices of the bloody sort. There were, however, some bloodless sacrifices that were offered by themselves without animal victims. We may, for the sake of order, distribute all into three classes, as follow.

1. *Prescribed meat-offerings accompanied with drink-offerings.* When united in this way, they were always attached to particular bloody sacrifices. In Num. xv. 1—12, we have a statement of the different proportions of flour, oil and wine, that were required to be used in such cases for different victims. It seems, that the animal sacrifices which God designed to be accompanied with such offerings as we are speaking of, were all *peace-offerings*, and all *burnt-offerings* of the flock or herd, whether for individuals or for the whole congregation. (Num. xv. 3; and chap. xxviii. 20.) Birds were not so accompanied, except in one case where they were substituted for other animals. (Lev. xiv. 31.) *Sin-offerings* and *trespass-offerings* of every kind were not to be attended even with any thing of the sort; unless it be supposed, that in the single case of the leper's purification sacrifice, mentioned in Lev. xiv. 10—20, such an offering, consisting of a tenth-deal of flour with a proportion of oil and wine, was designed for each of the three victims used on the occasion, out of that general meat-offering which is there noticed: that the case was thus, we are assured by the Jewish writers; but it seems natural and easy enough to consider all that meat-offering as a *single* one of peculiar character, intended particularly to accompany the burnt-offering victim alone.

2. *Meat-offerings voluntarily added to other sacrifices.* The offerings of the first class just considered were made *necessary*, in the cases that have been mentioned, and were accurately determined as to quantity by the law; but these which we are now to notice, were such as individuals were led of their own *free will* to present at the altar, with their bloody offerings, over and above what was absolutely required; or, at least, such as, although they were directed to be presented in certain cases, were nevertheless left to be determined as to their form and their amount by the offerers themselves. Of this sort are to be reckoned all those that are spoken of in the second chapter of Leviticus. From Leviticus vii. 12, 13, we learn that sacrifices of this sort were to be added to all peace-offerings for thanksgiving. No mention is made of wine being joined to them: though no doubt it was often used with victims along with which they were brought to the altar; only, however, as belonging to those other meat-offerings that have been already noticed, which might be presented at the same time, and not as having any thing to do directly with these

that are now in question. Meat-offerings of the first class were all of unbaked flour mingled with oil; but these under consideration might be either thus unbaked or baked in various ways, and sometimes consisted of various fruits of the earth without any preparation. A portion of the first-fruits, together with a tenth part of all the increase of the field, was to be every year employed in this way. (Deut. xiv. 22—29, xxvi. 1—11.)

3. *Independent meat-offerings.* This class comprehends those few bloodless sacrifices that were appointed to be offered, as it were, upon their own account, without being attached to any of the bloody class, or indebted to them for the occasions on which they were to be presented. These were either for the whole congregation, or for particular individuals.—Of the first sort were, 1st. *The twelve loaves of shew-bread*, set forth before the Lord in the Holy Place. 2d. *The sheaf of barley* offered on the second day of the Passover. (Lev. xxiii. 10.) 3d. *The two loaves* of the first-fruits, offered on the day of Pentecost. (Lev. xxiii. 17.) With these last, victims were indeed sacrificed; but they held only a *secondary* place in the solemnities; while the sheaf, in one case, and the loaves, in the other, were of *chief* and *independent* consequence —Of the second sort, such as were offered for individuals were, 1st. *The offering of jealousy*, of which we have an account in Num. v. 15, 18, 25, 26, that was to have with it neither oil nor incense. 2d. *The poor man's sin-offering*, mentioned in Lev. v. 11, that was to be offered in like manner, without oil or incense, when a man was not able to provide for himself even a pair of doves or pigeons. 3d. *The priestly meat-offering*, which Aaron and his sons, it is said, were to present in the day of their anointing. (Lev. vi. 20—23.) Jewish tradition tells us that this last was two-fold; being required of every priest when he first entered upon his sacred office, and being required besides of the high-priest every day during all the time of his ministry; but this does not clearly appear from the Scriptures.

Every meat-offering was required to be seasoned with salt and might not, on any account, have in it a particle of honey, nor yet, in all common cases, a particle of leaven. The two loaves offered on the day of Pentecost were leavened, and we read that leavened bread was brought also with sacrifices of thanksgiving, together with the unleavened cakes and wafers, (Lev. vii. 13;) but no part of such offerings could be presented upon the altar; the universal statute was, that no leaven, nor any honey, was to be burned in any offering of the Lord made by fire. (Lev. ii. 11.) The shew-bread was to companied with incense without oil; the prescribed meat-offering, to which wine was joined, had oil without incense; the poor man's sin-offering, the offering of jealousy, and the sheaf of first-fruits, had neither one nor the other; while all the rest were enriched with both.—The incense, in every case, was all burned upon the altar; in the case of the meat-offering presented by a priest, and as it seems, on the whole, in the case of all those of the first class, such as were prescribed and accompanied with wine, the whole was in like manner given to the fire; but, in other cases, only a part of the flour, or bread and oil, was burned, as a memorial for all, while the remainder was appropriated to the priests, as a gift from the Lord. The wine, when it was used, was solemnly poured out at the bottom of the altar.

In the general class of sacrifices of the bloodless sort, is to be reckoned also, besides those that have been styled meat-offerings, the *sacred incense* that was offered every morning and every evening on the golden altar, and once in the year presented upon a censer filled with coals, within the Holiest of all.

FIRST-FRUITS, FIRST-BORN, TITHES, VOW-GIFTS, ETC.

Besides those to which the name of *sacrifice* has been particularly appropriated, such as we have been hitherto considering, there were other sacred offerings appointed in the Jewish system that claim our attention. The most important of them were of four principal kinds.

1. FIRST-FRUITS. The first sheaf of barley, on the second day of the Passover, and the first loaves of Pentecost, were presented to God as offerings for the *whole nation*. But besides these, offerings of all sorts of first-fruits were required to be made, year after year, by *individuals;* first-fruits of the harvest and the vintage, from the threshing-floor, the wine-press, the oil-press, and the honey-crowded hive, from the first baked bread of the new crop also, and from the fleecy treasures gathered at every time of shearing from the flock. (Ex. xxiii. 19, Num. xv. 19—21.) These were not presented at the altar, but were assigned by God, to whom they were consecrated, for the use of his ministers, the priests. (Num. xviii. 11—13.) How much should be given in these cases, the law left each person to decide for himself. The Jewish doctors of later times, however, gave it as their judgment, that the smallest proportion which a man might conscientiously allow, was a sixtieth part of the whole produce from which it was taken.

In Deut xviii. 3, we find the following statute: "This shall be the priests' due from the people, from them that offer a sacrifice, whether it be ox or sheep: they shall give unto the priest the shoulder, and the two cheeks, and the maw." Th word here translated, *offer a sacrifice*, has at times a more general meaning, and is used to signify the slaying of animals for common use, in cases where nothing of a sacred nature was designed. It was understood accordingly; and, as it would seem, correctly understood, that such an extent of meaning belonged to it in this present case; and so it was the practice throughout the nation, as we are informed, on good authority, still to appropriate the parts that have been mentioned to the priests, whenever, on any occasion, animals were killed at home only for the purpose of ordinary food. This gift may be looked upon as a sort of *first-fruits* of every man's meat, before it might be used for the table. It was not necessary, however, that this should be carried away to the sanctuary; it was enough if it was given to some one of the priests in any place; and, accordingly, every individual used to give it to any one who lived near him, as convenience or personal regard determined his inclination.

2. The FIRST-BORN. Ever after the awful night in which the Lord, for the deliverance of his people, smote all the first-born of Egypt with death, all those of Israel that were males, in commemoration of that event, and in acknowledgment of the mercy that overwhelmed them not at that time with the same desolation, were consecrated to be, in a peculiar manner, the property of God. (Ex. xiii. 2, 12—15.) When the Levites were separated for the service of the sanctuary, they were substituted, as far as their number reached, for the first-born males of the whole people of that generation, and the cattle which they then owned, for all the firstlings of the cattle belonging to the nation; and thus, at the same time, the priestly office, which originally was the right of the first-born, was transferred and confined to this tribe. As on that occasion, however, the number of the first-born was found to be somewhat larger than that of the Levites, it was required that the 273 persons that were thus left without substitutes, should be *redeemed* by the payment of a certain price in money for every one. (Num. iii. 12, 13, 40—51.) So, ever after, all the first-born of man were required to be redeemed in like manner; and the redemption money became a part of the sacred revenue appointed for the support of the priests. (Num. xviii. 15, 16.) A child *could not* be redeemed before it was a month old, and generally *was not*, until the time when its mo-

ther's purification offering was to be presented, which, in the case of sons, was at the end of forty days. Thus, when the infant Jesus was brought for the first time to the temple, *two* duties enjoined by the law were attended to; the mother's sacrifice was offered, and the child was redeemed. (Luke ii. 22—24.) The first-born of such beasts as might be used in sacrifice were to be yielded to the Lord, without the liberty of redemption; and after their blood and fat were given to the altar, their flesh was all appropriated to the priests. (Num. xviii. 17, 18.) The first-born of other animals, such as it was unlawful to sacrifice, might be redeemed; though a man was not *obliged* to redeem them, as in the case of a first-born son. If they were not redeemed, they might be sold or destroyed. (Ex. xiii. 13, Lev. xxvii. 27.)

3. TITHES. A tenth part of all the produce of every Israelitish farmer was to be consecrated, in addition to the tribute already noticed, to the support of the national religion. These tithes were appropriated to the Levites, as their salary, who in their turn were required to give a tenth of all that they thus received, to the priests. (Num. xviii. 21—32.) In the case of the fruits of the earth, the owner might redeem the tithe that was due, by adding a fifth part to what was considered its proper value; whereby, we may suppose, he might save himself the trouble of transporting the articles to the place where they were to be received. In the case of cattle, the same privilege was not allowed. Animals were tithed by being made to pass, one by one, out of some enclosure, before a person appointed to number them, who held in his hand a rod, with which he touched every tenth one as it came along in its order, and thus designated it for the Levites: hence the expression *to pass under the rod*, applied to cattle that underwent tithing. No animal thus designated might be changed for another; if a man was found guilty of making such an exchange, he forfeited both. (Lev. xxvii. 30—33, Jer. xxxiii. 13.) Religious tithes were in use long before the time of Moses; as we may learn from Abraham's homage to Melchisedek, and from Jacob's vow on his way to Padan-Aram. They were in use also among almost all nations, in those early times, as we are taught by ancient history.

We have already had occasion to state, that the law required a *tenth part* of every husbandman's agricultural produce, and a portion of its *first-fruits* also, together with the *firstlings* of his flock and herd, to be devoted to God as *peace-offerings*, and so turned into sacred feasts for the entertainment of the owner himself, with his family and others recommended to his hospi tality. This we are clearly taught in Deut. xii 17—19, xiv 22—26, and xv. 19—22. But how are we to reconcile this with the positive and explicit declarations found in other places, as we have just seen, that the tithes, firstlings and first-fruits, were to be given to the Levites and priests? Could they be thus appropriated, and yet feasted upon by those that presented them? There seems to be no way of getting clear of this difficulty, but by inferring that there was a *double* appropriation of each of these sorts of offerings—the *first* for the use of the priests and Levites, and the *second* for sacrifices of thanksgiving to be celebrated in the way that has been noticed, by the owners themselves. Thus we are to suppose, that the Jewish law required *second tithes*, *second firstlings*, (if we may be allowed the term,) and *second first-fruits*. That we are not told any thing expressly about the appointment of these, as distinct from those of the first class, but are made acquainted with their existence merely in the notice that is given of their nature and use, may be accounted for by supposing that they were in common use before the time of Moses, and did not need, therefore, to be formally distinguished. They are spoken of as being well known; and in no danger, accordingly, of being confounded at that time with the other sort, that were instituted for the support of religion, and so exalted to hold a rank of importance above them. What we are thus taught indirectly from the law itself, we find confirmed by later testimony more explicit. In the apocryphal book of Tobit, mention is made of two sacred tithes: "The first tenth part of all increase," says the writer, describing his own piety, "I gave to the sons of Aaron, who ministered at Jerusalem: another tenth part I sold away, and went and spent it every year at Jerusalem." (Tobit i. 7.) Jewish tradition, however, allows such a double tithe to have had place only in the case of the increase of the fields; while it affirms that the tithe of animals, which was single, was not given to the Levites at all for their use, but employed altogether in those peace-offering feasts that have been mentioned. And, indeed, there is no intimation in the law of more than a single tithe of cattle; but it seems most reasonable to suppose, that this, if it was the only one, was consecrated to the Levites, and that these offering-feasts found no victims in this way; especially, since in the enumeration of the offerings to be used for the feasts, we meet with no mention of such animal-tithes, where it would seem, if the Jewish notion on this subject were correct, they ought not to have been left without notice. It appears, that every third year the people might, instead of carrying their second tithes to the sanctuary, make a feast of them at their own houses; unless we suppose, with some, that the tithe which was required to be thus consumed at home, each third year, was really a third one, which on every such year was to be paid, over and above the two regular tenths that have just been noticed. In the latter part of the 26th chapter of Deuteronomy, we have an account of a particular solemnity that was to be observed on these occasions. The beautiful and impressive form with which the second sort of first-fruits was required to be presented before the Lord, is described in the first part of the same chapter.— In addition to the regular small portion of first-fruits which was consecrated in this way, to be used in the joyful peace-offering entertainments, the law directed that the whole produce of all manner of fruit-trees, after the three years during which it was considered uncircumcised, and might not be used at all, were over, should be in the fourth year devoted to religious use, in like manner. It was to be *holy*, it is said, " to praise the Lord withal." (Lev. xix. 23—25.)

4. VOW-GIFTS. A vow is a solemn voluntary promise to God, either to *do* or *abstain from doing* something, or to *give* something, for his service and honour. Such religious engagements were not rare among the Jews. Of the first sort, we have an instance in the vow of Nazaritism, an account of which may be found in the sixth chapter of Numbers. Those of the second sort, such as bound persons to make some kind of sacred *gift*, more particularly claim our attention at present. We have already seen, that one class of *peace-offerings*, noticed in the law, were such as men presented in consequence of vows made to the Lord in seasons of danger or distress. But these were only a part of what it was in some degree customary to consecrate to God in this general way. A man might thus sanctify to him at any time, not only common property of every sort, houses, lands, money, animals clean or unclean, &c., but servants also, and children, and even his own person. Animals so consecrated, that were fit for sacrifice, became victims for the altar; those that could not be so used were sold, if not redeemed by the original owners themselves. Human persons became servants about the tabernacle or temple; with the privilege of being redeemed, however, when it was desired to embrace it. Other things, in like manner, were rendered in this way holy to the Lord, to be employed for the support of religion, unless at any time recovered by redemption according to certain regulations. (Lev. xxvii. 1—27.) The vow of an unmarried daughter was not allowed to have force, if her father disapproved of it when it was made; so also that of

wife, if in like manner opposed by her husband. (Num. xxx 1—16.) In Matt. xv. 3—6, and Mark vii. 11, we have notice of a wretched abuse that was sometimes made of sacred vows in later times. An unprincipled man would say to his parents, "Be it Corban, or a consecrated gift, whatsoever you shall receive of me!" and then, the Pharisees taught, he was not only not required to give them any help, but could not do it without sin; because, after such a vow, any present that he might ever make them, although it was not holy or consecrated to the Lord before, immediately became so by the very act, and consequently would bring upon him the guilt of *sacrilege* as well as *perjury*, by being disposed of in this way. Such a manner of binding themselves in relation to certain things, by indirectly imprecating guilt of this sort upon their heads, if they failed to regard what they vowed, was not uncommon among the Jews, as we learn from other sources. Thus one would say, for instance, "Let all the wine I ever drink be consecrated!" or, "Consecrated be whatever of such a thing I ever taste!" and thus he laid himself under a curse, as it were, not to drink or taste in either case, because the moment he might do so the things became holy, and so unlawful to be so used. It was as if a man should say among us, "The Lord destroy me, if I do this or that!" So foolish and wicked was the imprecation with which a man insulted his father or mother, in the case which our Saviour notices, in direct opposition to God's holy law.

There was one sort of consecration, of an awful character, from which there could be no redemption in any case. It was called by the Jews *Cherem*. Enemies were in some cases *devoted*, as it has been termed, in this way; and when they were so, they were to be pursued with the most unrelenting destruction, and their property treated in most cases as an *accursed thing*, which it was not lawful to make common use of. (Num. xxi. 1—3, Josh. vi. 17—19, viii. 1.) From Lev. xxvii. 28, 29, we learn that a man might devote any sort of property that he owned with a vow of this nature, as well as with the more common one already noticed. What is there said about human beings thus devoted, viz. that they were to be put to death, is supposed to refer altogether to the case of such as were national enemies, which has just been stated; or such as drew upon themselves this curse by such guilt as is noticed in the 13th chapter of Deuteronomy. If Jephthah, therefore, in consequence of his rash vow, thought himself bound by this law to destroy his innocent daughter, as it seems to such extremity he actually did proceed, he must be considered to have misunderstood its meaning. (Judg. xi. 30—39.)

5. THE HALF-SHEKEL TAX. In Ex. xxx. 11—16, a statute is recorded, which required every male Israelite over the age of twenty, whether rich or poor, to pay at that time half a shekel for the service of the sanctuary. It is not clear, that it was intended this should ever again be contributed; much less that such a tax should be rendered to the sanctuary every year. Such, however, was the interpretation put upon the law after the captivity. Every Jew, it was taught, was bound to pay a yearly tribute of half a shekel for the use of the temple; and it was insisted upon, besides, that it should be paid in Jewish coin. Hence arose a regular system of care for the collection of this sacred revenue. The *money-changers*, of whom we read, that were accustomed to sit in the outer court of the temple, a short time each year before the Passover, were men whose business it was to receive this tribute, and to accommodate, at the same time, with Jewish half-shekels, such as wanted to exchange other money for them. (Matt. xxi. 12.) It seems to have been this same tribute that was demanded of our Saviour in Capernaum; which he intimated to Peter he was not properly under obligation to pay, inasmuch as he was the *Son* of that God to whom it was to be rendered. (Matt. xvii. 24—27.)

From the general survey of the various sacred offerings which has now been taken, it appears, that it was no small portion of their worldly substance which the Jews were required to consecrate to religious uses. Part of these offerings, indeed, were not altogether removed from the personal use of those that gave them; still, they were employed in a way that would not have been pursued if religion had not so ordered, and in a way that in a great measure deprived the offerers of all their real value in a worldly point of view, so that they had in them truly the nature of *gifts* presented to the Lord. But besides these, as we have seen, the Jew was called upon by his religion to render year by year a large tribute in the way of tithes, firstlings, &c. that went *altogether* to the support of the national worship; and was expected, moreover, to consecrate to God, in addition to all this, more or less of his property, in some way or other, of *free* and self-moving liberality. Thus the Lord reminded his people, that their earthly possessions were *His;* and that when his glory was to be promoted, they should be ready to part with them in any measure, having all assurance that no employment of wealth can be more reasonable or well-directed than that which is made in his service, according to his will, whatever may be the way in which it is appointed to be used, and whatever the degree of liberality that is called for.

Many who now call themselves the people of God would think it altogether unreasonable, if they were called upon to contribute such an amount of their property to religious purposes as was given in this way by the ancient Jews. And yet it is certainly not easy to find a satisfactory reason, why the Lord's people, at the present time, should be expected to be less ready and liberal in service of this sort for the advancement of his glory, than the Lord's people were required to be in former times. It cannot be said, that there is less room or less call for such liberality in his service, since the passing away of that worldly outward economy under which the ancient church was placed. For, although it be not wanted in fact for the support of a costly ceremonial worship, it is still needed, we all know, for the building up of Christ's spiritual kingdom in the earth. This latter was designed to be typically displayed in the Jewish state, and comprehends in it the substantial realities which the other but represented in airy shadow. How then can we suppose, that the church of old was bound to give more for the support of the Jewish religion —the way in which God *then* was pleased, in infinite wisdom, to have his name glorified and his truth honoured—than the church of these latter days is bound to give for the enlargement of her boundaries and the salvation of the world—the way in which God is *now* to be glorified, and which he has appointed for the accomplishment of that great work of mercy that he is carrying forward in the earth? The gospel has not, like the Jewish law, prescribed how much every individual shall contribute of his substance to the treasury of God, who giveth us all things richly to enjoy; but, while it urges the general duty, leaves every one to determine for himself his own particular measure. It seeks a spiritual service, such as is prompted by a willing heart, and not rendered with reluctance or by constraint: only, it reminds us, that "He which soweth sparingly shall reap also sparingly, and he which soweth bountifully shall reap also bountifully;" while it sets before us a dark, and lost, and dying world which our efforts may help, and then, with weeping look and hand directed towards distant Calvary, exclaims, "Ye know the grace of our Lord Jesus Christ, that, though he was RICH, yet for your sakes he became POOR, that ye through his poverty might be rich!" (2 Cor. viii. 9, ix. 6, 7, Acts xx. 35.)

SECTION II.

SACRIFICIAL RITES.

CERTAIN ceremonies and usages that were observed in the offering of sacrifices, claim a more particular notice than it was proper to bestow upon them in the general view of sacred offerings that has been taken in the preceding section.

1. Those who presented victims at the altar were accustomed, as we have seen, *to lay their hands upon their heads,* before they were slain. When offerings were required to make atonement for the sins of the whole congregation, this ceremony was performed by some of the elders or rulers as their representatives. By this symbolic act, the animal was *substituted* in the place of the offerer, and solemnly *devoted* to God as a sacrifice for his altar. Accordingly, it was the practice to accompany it with some sort of prayer or confession suited to this idea. In fact, the ceremony of laying on hands in *all* cases, as well when it was to commend its objects to the mercy of God, (Gen. xlviii. 14, Matt. xix. 15,) or to set them apart to some particular office, (Num. xxvii. 18—23, Acts xiii. 3,) as when it was to devote them to death, (Lev. xxiv. 14,) seems to have been as a matter of course associated with the notion of some address to the Most High; insomuch that when the first was enjoined or spoken of, the other was always understood to belong to it, even when it was not mentioned. In the case before us, when a sin-offering or trespass-offering was presented, the offender, with his hands between the horns of the victim and his eyes directed toward the front of the Sanctuary, made solemn confession of the particular transgression for which it was brought forward, and besought God, in his mercy, to receive its sacrifice as an atonement for his guilt, in room of that destruction which it was thus intimated might justly fall upon his own head. When a burnt-offering was presented, a more general confession of sinful short-coming in the obedience that God's law demanded, seems to have been common. It is probable also, though we are not so told explicitly, that the address to God had in it, on certain occasions, a supplication more especially for some other blessing than the forgiveness of sin, or a thankful acknowledgment for some goodness already experienced, according to the particular nature and design of the sacrifice that was offered. Especially may we suppose this would be the manner in the case of peace-offerings, which were often presented with a particular refer

ence to some single end of this sort. At the same time, however, even in such cases there might have been mention made of sin, with a petition for pardoning mercy, in view of the life that was going to be poured out in sacrifice to the Holy One According to Jewish tradition, confession was made over victims offered to make expiation for sin by individual offenders, in some such form as this: *"O Lord, I have sinned! I have transgressed! I have rebelled! This have I done:*—(and then he named the particular offence for which he sought forgiveness.) *But now I repent, and may this victim be my expiation!"*

2. Victims were *slain* immediately after the ceremony just noticed. Those that were presented for the whole congregation were required from the first to be killed by the priests or Levites. In other cases, it was originally the custom for the offerers themselves to perform the work; but afterwards, the Levites, being more expert at such business than others, had it yielded altogether into their hands. The animals, we are told by the Jews, were fastened by the neck or feet to certain strong rings, fixed firmly to the pavement of the temple-court, beside the altar, for convenient slaughter. Life was then taken by cutting the throat with a single stroke of the knife, so deep that all the blood might flow out of the body. This, as it streamed from the dying victim, was carefully received into a sacred vessel kept for the purpose, to be made use of according to law.

3. The *blood*, as we have seen, was differently disposed of in sacrifices of different kinds. In a few peculiarly solemn cases, some of it was carried within the Sanctuary, and sprinkled toward the mercy-seat, and placed upon the horns of the golden altar. In other instances, it was all employed about the altar of burnt-offering. From the bottom of this altar, in the temple, there was a subterraneous passage, it is said, by which it was carried away into the brook of Cedron.—The sprinkling and pouring out of the blood formed a most material and essential part of the sacrificial service. Because, as we are told, it was the blood, which is represented to be in an especial manner the seat of life, that made atonement for the soul; and this application of the blood to the altar, in any particular case, was that especially which had in it the virtue of expiation included in the sacrifice.

On account of its use in this respect, blood was made most solemnly sacred. Not only in the case of sacrifices, but in every other case also, it was prohibited with the greatest care from being tasted as food or regarded as a common thing; so that the most dreadful punishment was denounced against the man who should dare to transgress the Divine commandment respecting it. Nor was it merely with the establishment of the Jewish economy that this prohibition had place. It was spoken to Noah, the second father of the whole human race, immediately after the flood, when permission to use animal food at all was first granted; so that from the beginning of time man had not been allowed to eat blood. Nor does it appear to have been merely for a ceremonial reason that the statute was thus early clothed with obligation. The only reason assigned at first was that the *life* was in the blood. (Gen. ix. 4.) Hence many have, not without cause, adopted the conclusion, that the original prohibition was intended to have force among all men till the end of time, as a memorial that life, even in its humblest character, is *sacred*, and that man has no right to destroy it in *any* case except as God, the author of it, has been pleased to give him explicit permission. This idea is supposed to receive great confirmation from the celebrated decree of that Christian council, held in the earliest age of the gospel at Jerusalem, of which we have an account in the 15th chapter of Acts. Others, however, reject this notion, and consider the prohibition of blood to have had respect from the beginning only to the ceremonial use to which it was, on account of its vital nature, consecrated in the institution of sacrifices, and which accordingly was brought to an end, with other shadows of the ancient economy, in the death of Jesus Christ. Whether it is lawful for a Christian or any person at the present time to eat blood, is therefore a disputed question. In such a case, then, it is at any rate wise not to taste it. It *may* be that the use of it is not unlawful, but it is certainly safer on the whole to act as if it were clearly ascertained to be otherwise; especially, since the article is in itself so pernicious to health, and so uninviting naturally to a sound taste, that it is truly marvellous how, through a process of strange and artificial preparation, it should, in some parts of our country, have found toleration, and even right friendly reception in civilized entertainments.

4. The blood being disposed of, the animal was rapidly stripped of its skin, and cut in pieces, and as far as it was to be consumed upon the altar, made ready for the fire. In the second temple, there were tables of marble, and pillars with hooks fixed in them for hanging victims upon, which afforded every convenience for this business. The skins were all given to the priests. The animal was cut up, not carelessly, but neatly, and according to rule. Certain parts were required to

be carefully washed, that no sort of filth might be allowed to come upon the altar.

5. We read of particular parts of slain victims, as well as of whole offerings, at other times, both such as were bloody and such as were not, being presented to God with certain peculiar ceremonies, denominated *heaving* and *waving*. It is not clear what, precisely, these ceremonies were, or whether there was really any material difference between them. Some suppose, that the one was a *lifting up* of the offering, and the other merely a *letting down* of it again; so that every *heave-offering* necessarily became a *wave-offering*. The Jews tell us, that to *heave* an offering was to lift it upwards, and that *to wave* it was to pass it this way and that way toward the four quarters of the world; all which solemn ceremony was designed to signify that it was thus presented to Him who fills the universe with his presence—the Maker and Possessor of heaven and earth with all their fulness. In a few instances, animals were subjected to this rite before they were killed. (Lev. xiv. 24, xxiii. 20.) More commonly, it was performed with some particular parts, after they were cut up; especially, with the breast and right shoulder, in all cases of peace-offering sacrifices, which were appropriated for the use of the priests by a continual statute. Bloodless offerings, also, were at times presented with the same ceremony. (Ex. xxix. 22—28.)

6. All fat, in sacrifices of every sort, that could be conveniently separated from the flesh of victims, was required to be burned upon the altar. Thus, we find direction still given, however other parts of the victim might be disposed of, that those portions which were either altogether or principally composed of this substance, should be made an offering by fire unto the Lord. These being the richest portions, it was thus intimated, as it was in other requirements already noticed, that God ought to receive, in all our worship, the *best* service which it is in our power to render. Hence, fat became, in something of the same manner as blood, a sacred substance; so that it was declared unlawful to eat those parts that have been referred to, in the case of *any* animal of the different classes from which the altar derived its victims, even when it was killed at home for common use. (Lev. vii. 23—25.)

Destitute as it was, besides, of all the advantages of butter or pork in any shape, this prohibition of all manner of fat, whether of the flock or of the herd, would have left the Jewish cookery in a sad predicament, had it not all been more than compensated for by the excellent oil of olives which the country yielded in such rich abundance. In these latter days, many of the scattered family of Abraham, who dwell in other countries, where the olive of their ancient land is not known, have found themselves subjected to no inconsiderable inconvenience on this score. Butter, they maintain, was not only not in use among their ancestors for the preparation of food, as it was in Egypt and other countries, but actually *forbidden*, as much as hog's lard and the other fat that has been mentioned, by the Divine law. In this extremity, they have been compelled to put up altogether with such fat as can be procured from animals that were not reckoned in this prohibition, and are yet of that number that were considered clean; among which they number the *goose*, though its claim to the latter distinction is not entirely out of the reach of dispute, and have made it, accordingly, their most substantial resource for this purpose, using its fat in the room of butter, for want of the favourite oil of their fathers. The law that has been supposed to forbid the use of butter, it may be remarked here, by the way, is the following: *Thou shalt not seethe a kid in its mother's milk.* Nor is this interpretation without strong reason in its favour, however unnatural it may seem at first glance. It is not without countenance from the usage of eastern language, that the phrase, a *kid's mother*, is understood to mean, universally, a goat that gives milk, without reference to any particular case; or, that what is spoken particularly of *one* class of animals, is considered to include a general precept, having force in regard to OTHERS also, that gave similar room for its application. Thus, the *milk of a kid's mother* is interpreted to mean any sort of milk, and of course any thing produced from milk, as all butter is; while the flesh of a kid means any sort of flesh: so that, altogether, out of the sententious statute, *Thou shalt not seethe a kid in its mother's milk*, is derived this very practical signification, *Thou shalt not dress meat with butter.* However this interpretation may be received, it is clear, that the law gave no encouragement to the use of butter; but, by prescribing oil in all meat-offerings which were used in sacred entertainments, indirectly discountenanced it.

7. *With all thine offerings*, it was commanded in the law, *thou shalt offer salt.* (Lev. ii. 13.) This statute, the Jews tell us, was so strictly regarded, that nothing came unsalted to the altar, but the wine of the drink-offering, the blood sprinkled, and the wood that was used for the fire. Salt for this purpose used to be kept always at the temple, provided at the public charge, so that it was not expected to be furnished by those who presented the offerings. It was customary, we

are to.d, to salt the parts of victims that were to be burned, generally on the rise that went up to the altar, but, in some cases, on the top of it. To the usage of salting sacrifices, our Saviour refers in Mark ix. 49. Especially was it enjoined that this article should be found with every meat-offering. As it was the symbol of friendship, it was altogether fit that it should not be wanting in the sacred entertainments, where men were admitted, as it were, to participate with God on the most intimate terms. Because of its significance in this respect, it was denominated the *salt of the covenant*.

8. The wood was always placed in order, and set on fire *first*. Care having been taken to have it thus in readiness, the several parts of the sacrifice that were to be consumed, after the preparatory steps that have been noticed, were placed upon the burning pile. In the case of holocausts, or burnt-offerings, as we have seen, the *whole* victim, except the skin, was thus destroyed; in other cases, only certain portions of it.

9. The altar having received its share in those cases where the whole was not given to it, there were *three* different ways in which the remainder of the flesh, according to the nature of the sacrifice, was required to be disposed of. 1st. It was in some instances to be carried out of the camp, or out of Jerusalem, which, in the times of the temple, answered to the ancient camp in the wilderness, and burned as a polluted thing. The bodies of those beasts, whose blood was carried into the Sanctuary, were all borne forth, and destroyed in this way. 2d. It was, in certain cases, to be eaten by the priests. Thus, *all* was appointed to be used in the case of common sin-offerings, or trespass-offerings, in which the blood was not taken into the Sanctuary, and also in the case of the two lambs offered on the day of Pentecost, as peace-offerings for the whole congregation; and particular portions, viz. the breast and the right shoulder, in the case of all peace-offerings presented by individuals. In the cases first stated, it was considered especially *holy*, and might not be eaten anywhere out of the court of the Sanctuary, and only by such of the priestly family as were males. (Num. xviii. 9, 10.) But the flesh allotted to the priests from common peace-offerings, like that which fell to them in the way of *firstling* dues, might be eaten, it seems, anywhere in Jerusalem, and by all that properly belonged to their household, if only they were free, at the time, from ceremonial uncleanness—a thing that was required in every person that tasted, in any case, food that was made sacred by being presented at the altar. (Lev. xxii. 2—16, vii. 20, 21.) 3d. Whatever of the flesh of the sacrifices was not disposed of

in the ways that have been already mentioned, was appropriated to the use of the offerers themselves, and might be eaten in the sacred entertainments, in which it was expected to be all employed within less than two days, by all classes of persons that were clean, and in any part of Jerusalem. Thus, all the flesh not claimed by the altar, except the breast and right shoulder, which fell to the priests, was made use of in the case of every common peace-offering. In these offering-feasts, as already intimated, a sort of sacred communion was instituted between God and his worshippers. The entertainment was furnished by him from the provisions of his House; and as with men, social feasts are always indicative of friendly feeling among those who unite in them, and in ancient times, especially, were used as signs and pledges of mutual good-will and confidence between such as entered with each other into covenants of peace, (Gen. xxvi. 28—30, xxxi. 44—46, Josh. ix. 14, 15,) so those who were thus permitted to partake, as it were, of the Lord's table, in receiving entertainment from the altar, were supposed to enjoy the privilege of his friendship and peculiar favour, and to be, by this sign, in holy covenant with him, if not guilty of cold and false hypocrisy in their own hearts. (Mal. i. 7, 12.) The apostle argues with the Corinthians against the use of meat that had been consecrated in sacrifice to idols, from this well-known principle; showing, that, as under the Jewish law they who ate of the sacrifices were partakers of God's altar, so those who joined in the offering-feasts of the heathen around them might properly be said to have fellowship, in so doing, with devils. (1 Cor. x. 18, 20.)

SECTION III.

MEANING AND ORIGIN OF SACRIFICES.

It must be felt by every person who seriously thinks upon the subject, that the use of sacrifices, which entered so extensively into the whole system of religious worship in ancient times, had in it something strange and difficult to be understood on the principles of mere natural reason. Offerings of the *bloodless* sort, indeed, might be imagined, without much objection, to have taken their origin from the suggestion of nature itself, and to have been reasonable expressions of thankful piety, to which men would be led under its influence in the most direct and easy manner. Thus it might be considered not altogether wonderful or unnatural that they should have been moved solemnly to present to God, at times, some portion of the fruits of the earth secured by their labour, as Cain did, by way of acknowledging him to be the Author and Giver of all blessings, or to testify gratitude for special favours received from his hand. But, in the case of the Jews and of the pious patriarchs noticed in the Bible, offerings of this sort made but a small and secondary part of the general system of sacrifices All the more striking and distinguished features of that system were portrayed with *blood*. The slaying and consuming of animal victims entered essentially and primarily into its whole constitution, and formed both the basis and the principal body of all its peculiar structure. Here it is, that we are met with mystery in the institution, such as mere nature cannot help us to comprehend. What should lead men to suppose that God would be pleased with the slaughter of unoffending animals in his worship? What connection was there between this apparently cruel destruction of life and the Divine favour? or how could it express a pious temper in the person who thus sought to honour his Maker, or conciliate his friendship? And still more, how is it to be accounted for, that God did, in fact, approve of this bloody service, and make it an essential part of the only true religion, for so long a period of ages? Are we to imagine, that the Holy One could find satisfaction in the sufferings of his harmless creatures? Could he be pleased, in itself, with the blood of bullocks or of goats, or be soothed into complacency by the savour of their burning flesh?

To these last inquiries, all reason and natural sense answer, *No*. Nor can it be, with any propriety, imagined that men should ever, of their own accord, have taken up the notion, that such service could, in itself, seem agreeable to the Creator of heaven and earth. How, then, the question remains, did the notion of bloody sacrifices come into existence? and where shall we find a satisfactory reason for the fact, that such a strange and unnatural worship was really acceptable to the Most High? The Bible explains all this mystery. It teaches us the true *meaning* of this service, and so guides us to the discovery of its sacred *origin*. Let us attend to the instruction it imparts on these interesting points.

1. THE MEANING OF SACRIFICES. The Scriptures inform us, that the shedding of blood, in this ancient institution, had regard altogether to sin. Such a service was suited only to the worship of a *guilty* race, and never, in any case, left this consideration out of sight. Had men never fallen, it could never have had any meaning in their religious worship; and would never, accordingly, have found place in it. But the fall al

tered all their relation to God. It was no longer possible for the creature to come directly before the Creator, as when innocent and pure, with acceptable homage or supplication. Guilt hung a dark and impenetrable curtain between the soul and the favour of its God, and shut out the voice, alike of prayer and praise, in deep and hopeless despair. No worship of man could be accepted, until this awful hinderance was taken out of the way. God, however, in his mercy, devised a plan for its removal. The plan was to secure complete satisfaction to his holy law, by suffering its vengeance to fall somewhere else, (where it could be rightly received,) than upon the rebellious themselves—by *vicarious sacrifice*—by an adequate *atonement*, rendered through the shedding of blood, without which there could be no remission. Here, then, we have unfolded the general meaning of bloody sacrifices, and the general reason why the Most High regarded them with approbation, and required them from his worshippers. The whole system had reference to the guilt of sin, and its necessary expiation. Blood, the symbol of animal life, was consecrated, by a Divine appropriation, to this single holy use, and, in all its flowing at the altar, was expressive of *atonement for the soul.*

But could the blood of bulls and goats take away sin? Had it, in itself, the smallest efficacy to make atonement for guilt, and satisfy the holy law of God? The apostle assures us, that such a thing was not possible, (Heb. x. 1—4;) and, if he had not told us so, the smallest reflection might convince us, that such sacrifices, however multiplied, could never purge away the conscience of sin, and restore tranquillity or holy confidence to the guilty soul. We must not, for a moment, imagine, therefore, that an offering of this sort, in any case, did ever, of itself, make the smallest satisfaction for the offence of any sin, in the sight of the Most Holy. When we read of atonement being made in this way for particular sins, under the old dispensation, we are to understand, that while it *actually* availed, in consequence of the Divine appointment, to satisfy the requirement of the *ceremonial,* and in certain cases of the *civil* law, it answered the claim of the *moral* law only in *shadow,* having nothing whatever, in itself, suited to its nature, but merely setting forth, in typical representation, a far more excellent sacrifice to come. The Ceremonial system was altogether, as we have seen, a shadowy exhibition of the Great Gospel Reality; without substance, or value, or meaning, when looked upon wholly in itself, but full of expressive and instructive power when contemplated in its relation to this mystery of Grace. It had, accordingly, if we may be allowed the expression, a class of *shadowy sins*, among other things, for the more perfect illustration of its *shadowy atonement* The ceremonial law imposed an obligation of its own, distinct from that of the moral law, and might be violated, so as to bring its condemnation upon a man, while no true guilt, such as arises only from an offence against the latter, was contracted. This ceremonial guilt, as it may be termed, might be entirely taken away, by the ceremonial means appointed for the purpose. The guilt and the removal of it were alike symbolical; although, at the same time, not to make use of the means for this removal could not fail to bring upon the soul the stain of *real* guilt, inasmuch as it then became disobedience to God, and so a transgression of the moral law. So, in particular cases, the requirement of the *civil* law, viewed entirely apart from *moral* duty, was completely satisfied by the same sort of means. Thus, a representation was given of the true atonement, by which alone true sins were to be taken away. In some other cases, however, there was no claim of *any* law answered by these sacrificial offerings. They were presented altogether on account of moral transgressions, without regard to any of a merely ceremonial or civil sort: and then, of course, they accomplished nothing at all in themselves: only, they pointed to an all-sufficient sacrifice that was to be revealed; and when offered by the truly pious, were acceptable to God, as containing in them an acknowledgment of guilt, and a renunciation of every other ground of hope for pardon and righteousness, but the great provision which he himself had promised to make known in the latter days, for the purpose.

Such was the only value of the ancient sacrifices. They never purged the worshippers of God from the conscience of sins, and were therefore *continually* offered up, year after year, making continually new remembrance of guilt. To rely upon them, therefore, as taking away the guilt of sin, even when true repentance accompanied them, was to lean upon a broken reed; and still more presumptuous was it to do so, when no such repentance was felt at all. Yet to this degree of presumption were the Jews ever prone to be carried. They were apt to fall into the notion, that these sacrifices were *in themselves*, without regard to something else, highly acceptable to God, and that he could not refuse to be pleased with them, even when presented by the wicked. Hence we hear the Lord expostulating with them : " To what purpose is the multitude of your sacrifices unto me ? I am full of the burnt-offerings of rams, and the fat of fed beasts ; and I delight not in the blood of bullocks, or of lambs, or of he-goats," &c. (Isa. i. 11—

14, Ps. l. 7—14.) And all along it was taught, that to obey was better than sacrifice, and to hearken to the Lord's voice better than the fat of rams. (1 Sam. xv. 22, Hosea vi. 6.) Without such a disposition, it was not possible that the Lord could accept the service of any worshipper, though he appeared in his presence with thousands of rams, or ten thousands of rivers of oil; nor yet, at the same time, even with this disposition, could such expensive offerings, or the still more precious offering of a first-born son itself, have the smallest efficacy in their nature, to remove the guilt of transgression. (Micah vi. 6—8.) Just as now, to belong to the church and partake of the Lord's supper are things that can be of no avail without a heart ready to obey the will of God, and, even where there is such a readiness, cannot in themselves and on their own account procure saving benefit to the soul, but merely help to direct it to the Great Original Resource of Grace, and serve as channels through which its streams may be received.

What the ancient sacrifices only represented in empty shadow, Jesus Christ, by the *Sacrifice of Himself*, actually accomplished. This we are expressly taught in the epistle to the Hebrews. As the whole priestly office had respect to the mediatorial character of our Saviour, and never had any other than a shadowy, unsubstantial character, except in him, as has been before remarked; so also the entire scheme of sacrificial worship had reference to his atoning death, which was in fact the only true and efficacious sacrifice ever made; while all before it were mere pictures of its precious reality. Thus he was himself, at the same time, priest and victim. The typical priests before him stood "daily ministering, and offering oftentimes the same sacrifices, which could never take away sins; but this man, after he had offered one sacrifice for sins, for ever sat down on the right hand of God." (Heb. vii. 27, x. 11, 12.) In this sacrifice there was value enough to make full expiation for all the sins of the whole world; and to as many as embrace its advantage, by faith, it will be found, till the end of time, completely availing to remove the heaviest pressure of guilt, and to deliver them from its deepest condemnation, into a state of peace and reconciliation with a Holy God. Because the death of Jesus Christ was thus truly an atoning sacrifice, he is called the "Lamb of God which taketh away the sin of the world." (John i. 29.) And in vision he appeared to the beloved disciple, as "a Lamb that had been slain," (Rev. v. 6:) his blood also, which we are told "cleanseth from all sin," is represented to be like that of "a lamb without blemish and without spot." (1 Pet. i. 19, 1 John i. 7.)

We find his death, accordingly, all along spoken of as being on account of sin, and to make satisfaction for its guilt—sin that was not his own, but which he consented to bear in the room of his people, and to take away on their behalf, by becoming a *sin-offering* for them, and pouring out his soul beneath the awful pressure of infinite justice. Besides the 53d chapter of Isaiah, the following passages may be consulted on this point: viz. Matt. xx. 28, xxvi. 28, Rom. iii. 25, 26, viii. 3, 2 Cor. v. 21, Eph. v. 2, 1 Pet. ii. 24, iii. 18.

The death of atonement, then, which the Son of God died for our redemption, was that to which all sacrifices, from the earliest times, had respect as their great termination, and without which they would have been as destitute of reason as they were, in their very nature, of all actual value in the sight of Heaven. If holy men of old made an acceptable use of them, in drawing near to God, it was only by looking *through* them them to this all-perfect and sufficient sacrifice which they prefigured. This great sacrifice, accordingly, being offered up in due time, all that were before it were completely done away, and all that ancient sort of worship went for ever out of use.

2. THE ORIGIN OF SACRIFICES. Having thus discovered the true meaning of sacrifices, we cannot hesitate in deciding the question, whether they were of Divine, or of merely human origin. It is in fact decided already. For if the sacrifice of Jesus Christ was the only one that ever had any proper and substantial reality, and all others were entirely unmeaning, except as faint images and pictures of this, it is manifest that the whole system must have been derived altogether from the appointment of God. As the original idea of atonement by blood, which in the fulness of time became realized in the death of the Son of God, was conceived from the beginning in the Divine mind alone, so we are to trace back to the same source the entire plan of that preparatory representation by which it was held up for the encouragement and assistance of faith, in unsubstantial type, so many ages before its actual development. The great Pattern Sacrifice being altogether of heavenly device, and in its glorious nature a mystery, completely hidden from human knowledge till revealed in its own season, it would be absurd to suppose that other sacrifices before it, which answered so strikingly as shadows to its wonderful reality, and viewed in any other light, had no meaning or reason whatever, might have come into use notwithstanding, through mere human fancy, and without any regard at first to the end which afterwards they were made to respect.

However, therefore, some have imagined that the use of

sacrifices originated at first from men themselves, without any Divine direction, and have attempted to show how they might have been led to adopt the strange and unnatural service; it is clear, that as reason finds such a supposition attended with much difficulty, and feels dissatisfied with every explanation brought for its relief, so the whole representation of the Bible urges us to embrace a different sentiment. True, we are not told explicitly that God directed men in the beginning to worship him in this way: but the nature and design of the service are declared, and are found to be such as to forbid all thought of its having sprung from any other source than the express appointment of the Most High. And what is thus indirectly discovered, with almost irresistible evidence, is still farther confirmed by the historical account, so far as it reaches, which we have of ancient sacrifices. All along, before the age of Moses, we find them constantly employed by the people of God as an essential part of true religion, and honoured and accepted, and in certain cases *ordered*, of the Lord himself, as being not mere indifferent rites, but acts of piety of the first importance, and peculiarly well pleasing in his sight: all which would be strange indeed, if they had originally started out of human will-worship, and had no respect at all in their design at that time to the GREAT SACRIFICE to come, (as on such a supposition it must be believed,) but were used altogether according to some different view that led at first to the practice of them, which view must necessarily be considered at the same time to have been mistaken and false. But we are not left with the mere information that these early sacrifices were in use, to imagine that they might have been offered with a view altogether different from what was most particularly contemplated afterwards in those that were prescribed by the Jewish law. We have satisfactory evidence, that *before*, as well as *after*, the introduction of that law, the shedding of blood in sacrifice was regarded as an *expiatory* rite, having reference to guilt, and signifying that without atonement there could be no forgiveness or Divine favour bestowed upon the sinner. That such was the fact, is abundantly manifest from the notion found to have been entertained among heathen nations in every age, that the anger of Heaven was to be appeased by bloody sacrifices, and that they could avail to do away the offensive guilt of injury and crime; for these heathen sacrifices, that have been common in every quarter of the world, were not borrowed in any measure from those of the Jews, but had their origin much farther back from those that were in use in the earliest times, when the family of man was not yet multi

plied into different nations, or scattered over the face of the
earth. Besides all this, too, we are expressly informed that
the patriarch Job, who was accustomed to worship God with
these ancient sacrifices, offered them with a special reference
to sin; and that the Lord himself required burnt-offerings
from his three friends, to make expiation for their offence, and
to turn away his wrath, that was kindled against them. (Job
i. 5, xlii. 7—9.) It being clear, therefore, that while sacrifices, before the time of Moses, were held to be an essential
part of religious worship, they were regarded to be such, especially on account of their expiatory meaning, the same by
which they were so remarkably distinguished under the law,—
we are furnished with very conclusive evidence that they were
suggested and enjoined from the first, by no other than that
God who formed the design of the True Atonement, before the
foundation of the world, and employed them so extensively and
systematically, to shadow forth its mystery in the Ceremonial
system of the Jews.

This conclusion, so far it rests on historical grounds, becomes
still clearer when we go backward under the guidance of revelation, and find this service in use, not merely before the flood,
(as appears from the distinction of animals thus early into
clean and unclean, and also by Noah's sacrifice when he came
out of the ark, that was so acceptable to the Lord,) but in the
family of Adam himself, in the earliest age of the earth. We
read of Cain and Abel offering sacrifices; and it is so mentioned as to leave the impression that such worship was not a
new thing in this case: it had been practised undoubtedly before that, if not by these brothers themselves, yet at least by
their father. But can it for a moment be imagined, that
Adam should, of his own accord, have conceived the notion,
directly after the fall, that God would be pleased with having
the blood of peaceful animals poured out before him in solemn
offering, when, as yet, the liberty of using their flesh in any
way for food had not been granted? Are we not rather, in
order to account for his practice in this respect, *driven* to the
conclusion, that God himself, immediately after his ruin, when
He revealed even then the promise of the New Covenant, appointed sacrifice to be a standing pledge of its grace, and the
special means by which faith should be enabled to lay hold
upon its blessings, until the fulness of time should come for
the full manifestation of that great Real Atonement, on which
the whole plan of mercy was to be builded and secured? Thus,
while the institution became a continual monument of guilt
and death, introduced by sin, ever calling them into remem

brance, it was ordained to be at the same time a sure sign of salvation and life—a SACRAMENTAL MEMORIAL as one has expressed it, *showing forth the Lord's death until he came,* by the believing use of which, the full benefit of that death might be secured to the soul. In this way our first father, it seems, was instructed to exercise his faith and find spiritual encouragement, when there was yet none but himself and his guilty partner in the world. It has been supposed, with much probability, that the animals whose skins were employed at first to make garments for them, were slain and offered up as sacrifices by the direction of God. What was thus required to be observed by the first man, as a necessary part of acceptable religious worship, was appointed at the same time to be observed by his posterity, and it became his duty accordingly to acquaint his immediate descendants with its meaning and obligation, so as to have the use of it handed down from generation to generation. Thus it was made a solemn duty to worship the Lord by this method—to make penitent acknowledgment of sinfulness and desert of death in the symbolic substitution of an unoffending victim to bleed at the altar, and to show at the same time a believing confidence in the Divine plan for taking away guilt, though it was not yet understood, by looking in this way, with simple obedience, for reconciliation and acceptance.

To make use of sacrifice, then, according to the commandment of God, and with the temper that has just been mentioned, was in any case an evidence of piety and faith. Thus did Abel bring an offering of the best of his flock, and presented it as a bloody sacrifice to the Lord: and hence he is commended to our notice as an example of faith, by which, it is said, his sacrifice was more acceptable on this occasion than that of his brother Cain. (Heb. xi. 4.) This faith clearly supposes a Divine appointment, to which it had respect, and in the end of which it had full confidence, showing *both* by a simple obedience to the direction that had been given, in the whole manner of its service. Cain, on the other hand, evinced no such faith: he offered a sacrifice, but there was something in the service that was wrong—not in conformity with the Divine direction, and accordingly it was not accepted. Now if we inquire wherein this want of faith particularly was found, it seems by no means an unlikely answer that has been given, *that it was in refusing to offer a bloody sacrifice, as God had required, and thus disregarding all the high and solemn designs for which the institution was appointed.* He seems to have followed his own *reason,* rather than the *commandment of Heaven,* and, because he could discern no propriety in the slaying of an animal as an act of religious worship, to have persuaded himself that an offering without blood was the most suitable to be presented to a God who was infinitely merciful and good. Thus he made no account of his own sinfulness, and slighted the blood of atonement, presumptuously pretending to come before the Holy One, as if he had never offended, and the way had been free of all hinderance to the throne of mercy.

It has been generally believed, that the way in which God discovered his acceptance of Abel's sacrifice, was by causing fire to descend in a miraculous manner, and consume it, while that of Cain received no such mark of regard. It is clear that some open and striking sign of his approbation was given, that was easy to be understood; and it must be acknowledged altogether probable, that it was no other than this, which was in certain cases made such a token, we know, in later times. Thus the Lord *testified of his gifts*, and showed himself well pleased with the piety that presented them, while those of Cain were left without approbation and without notice. We find, in subsequent history, repeated instances in which the Divine acceptance of sacrifices was testified in this same way. Thus the Lord answered David and Elijah, and thus he furnished the altar with holy fire, directly after the consecration of the tabernacle first, and afterwards of the temple. (Lev. ix. 24, Judg. vi. 21, 1 Kings xviii. 38, 1 Chron. xxi. 26, 2 Chron. vii. 1.) Whence it is reasonable to suppose, that the same token was given also in other cases, where God is said to have accepted the service, though it is not expressly mentioned; and it is by no means unlikely, that all along from the beginning, such displays of heavenly approbation were often granted, for the encouragement of faith, and to put honour upon the Divine institution of Sacrifice.

As God's people are sometimes *figuratively*, not *properly*, represented to be *priests*, so the various kinds of spiritual service with which they honour him are not unfrequently, in the same figurative way, spoken of as *sacrifices*. As among the Jews, offerings of this sort entered so very extensively into their whole system of worship, and were in their nature expressive of different pious feelings, unaccompanied by which they had no worth, it was altogether natural, that the language of piety should borrow from their use a great number of images, and mingle in its habitual phraseology a great variety of terms derived from the altar and its solemn rites. Thus, accordingly, we find it all through the sacred volume. The Psalms, especially, and the writings of the prophets, abound with this sort of imagery and allusion. We meet with it also repeatedly in the New Testament: we are urged to present our bodies *a living sacrifice, holy and acceptable unto God*, to offer continually *the sacrifice of praise*, &c.; so we hear Paul speaking of his ministry among the Gentiles as a priestly work, and of their conversion as *an offering*, rendered through his instrumentality, to the Lord; and again, of his life being *poured out* as a drink-offering upon the *sacrifice and service of their faith*. (Rom. xii. 1, xv. 16, Phil. ii. 17, 2 Tim. iv. 6, Heb. xiii. 15, 16, 1 Pet. ii. 5.)

CHAPTER VI.

SACRED TIMES AND SOLEMNITIES.

As certain *places* were more holy than others in the Jewish economy, and were honoured with special regard, so there were certain *hours* and *days* and *seasons*, considered in like manner more sacred than other times, and distinguished accordingly by particular religious observances. These now call for our notice, and will lead us to contemplate in order the regular public worship of the sanctuary; as this, of course, was determined to such stated times from year to year.

SECTION I.

THE DAILY SERVICE.

There was a regular public service required to be performed every morning and every evening. Each altar was to smoke so often, at least, with its appropriate offering, presented in behalf of the whole nation. (Ex. xxix. 38—42, xxx. 7, 8.) The hours at which these sacrifices were regularly performed, came naturally to be considered as somewhat sacred and appropriate in a peculiar manner for the business of devotion.

The law prescribed no precise time for the service of the morning, but directed that the offering of the second lamb should take place *between the two evenings*. It is not clear, however, whether the first evening began originally, according to the way of reckoning that was used in later ages, some time *before* the going down of the sun, and with it, gave place to the second; or whether it only commenced itself at sunset and yielded to the other at dusk. Of the particular *manner*, moreover, of either service before the captivity, we have no account. In later times, though conformed as far as ther was knowledge to ancient usage, it was no doubt in man respects different from what it had originally been, especiall. by reason of various vain ceremonies added to it, such as wer so abundantly multiplied during the second temple, in every part of the national religion. The Daily Service, as it was thus found in the age of our Saviour, is described with sufficient fulness in the Jewish writings, according to the very ancient tradition of their ancestors. The following is a brief summary of the account of it that has been collected from this quarter.

The priests who were on duty at the temple had their chief place of residence, when not immediately engaged in their public work, in the north-west corner of the Court of Israel. Here was a very large building, having a great room in the middle of it, with four others of less size, that opened into this, and were placed around it, one at each corner. This central hall was styled the *House of burning*, because a fire was kept constantly in it, in cold weather, by which the priests might warm themselves during the day, when chilled in their work, and be kept comfortable through the night. Here the principal one of their three particular guards, or watches, was continually stationed. Such as were not required to continue awake in this service sought sleep for themselves on benches round about the room, or, if they were of the younger class, on the naked floor itself. Having thus passed the night, they were required to have themselves in readiness here, very early in the morning, for going forth, according to order, to engage in the business of the day. This readiness consisted in being *bathed* and *dressed* in their sacred garments. No one, it was held, might go into the Court where he was to serve, until he had washed his whole body in water; and, accordingly, they had several rooms fitted up as bathing-places for this purpose. After this first washing, it was not commonly necessary to wash again during the day, more than the hands and the feet: *that*, however, was to be done every time any one came into the Court of the priests, after having gone out, no matter how frequently this might be.

Thus ready, they waited till one styled the *President* came, according to his office, to lead them forth, and assign them their duties. When he was come, they all passed together out into the Court, with candles in their hands, and there, dividing themselves into two companies, began solemnly to move round the temple, half taking to the right, and the other half to the left. Having met on the opposite side, the inquiry was made, *Is all safe and well?* and the answer returned, *Yes, all is well;* and then immediately the pastry-man, who had his chamber in that quarter, was called upon to get ready the cakes for the high-priest's daily meat-offering. After this, they all withdrew to a particular room, in a building of considerable size, that stood at the south-east corner of the court, for the purpose of having it determined by lot, who should perform the first duties of the day. This was done by the president.

The first lot designated the one who should cleanse the altar of burnt-offering; and as soon as it was made known, he went out and set about his work. His particular part, however, was merely to make a beginning in this service, which was regarded as an honourable privilege, and not by himself to carry it through; as soon as he had so done, other priests came to his assistance, and separating any pieces that might be left of the last day's evening sacrifice to the one side, scraped together the ashes, and had them in a short time carried away, so as to leave the altar fit for new employment. These ashes were borne to a place without the city, where the wind could not easily scatter them, and no person might ever put them to any use whatever. The cleansing of the altar in this way was begun, on common days, at the dawn of day; but during the three great festivals, much sooner, and on the day of atonement, as early as midnight itself. The work was concluded by putting the fire in order, and placing in it any pieces that were left of the last offered victim, so as to have them completely consumed.

This first service over, the priests withdrew again to the room where the lot was given, and had a second class of duties distributed among thirteen of their number. One of these duties was *to kill the morning victim;* another, *to sprinkle its blood;* a third, *to dress the altar of incense,* &c. Half of them were merely to carry certain particular portions of the sacrifice, after the lamb was slain and cut up, to the rise of the altar, where it was usual to lay them down to be salted. There were two more lots, a little after this; one for the service of presenting the incense in the Holy Place, and the other for that of taking up the pieces of the sacrifice where they were first laid down, and bearing them to the top of the altar to be burned.

The lamb was slain as soon as it was fairly day. It was considered a matter of importance, however, that it should never be killed earlier than this, and care was taken to have it well ascertained beforehand, that day-light was truly come. *Go*, (the President was accustomed to say,) *and see whether it be time to kill the sacrifice*. Some one immediately went up to the top of one of the buildings about the court, and when he saw it to be decidedly day, gave the word aloud, *It is fair day.—But is the heaven bright all up to Hebron?* (the President would ask.) *Yes. Go then*, (he would say,) *and bring the lamb out of the lamb-room*. The lamb-room was one of those that were in the great building that has been mentioned, at the north-west corner of the court, in the middle hall of which, most of the priests were accustomed to pass the night. There were always as many as six lambs kept in it, ready for sacrifice. When the victim was brought to the altar, although it had been well examined before, it was again diligently searched all over with the light of candles, to be sure that it was perfectly free from imperfection and blemish. Those whose business it was, then proceeded to kill it, and dispose of it according to the common manner of sacrifice. In the mean time, the gates of the court had been thrown open, the trumpets sounded to call the Levites and others to their attendance, and the front door of the temple itself solemnly unfolded. It was just as this last thing was done, that the person who had to kill the victim, having every thing ready, applied the instrument of death to its throat. While the work of sprinkling the blood, cutting up the flesh, and carrying it to the altar then went rapidly forward without, the two men on whom it had fallen to dress the golden altar and the candlestick were found at their business in the Holy Place. All that he did who cleansed this altar was merely to brush off the ashes and coals that were on it into a golden dish kept for the purpose, which he then left standing by its side. The priest who dressed the lamps examined them, lighted such as were gone out, supplied them with oil, &c.

All these duties being accomplished, the whole company of priests betook themselves again to the room of lots, and there united in offering up a short prayer to God, rehearsing the ten commandments, and saying over the *Shema*, as it was styled—a religious form consisting of certain passages of the law, which was regarded as particularly sacred, and necessary to be repeated on a variety of occasions. The Shema was so called because that was the word with which it always began, meaning, in English, *Hear;* for the passage that was first said over was Deut. vi. 4—9, which begins, "Hear, O Israel," &c. And the other passages that belonged to it were Deut xi. 13—21, and Num. xv. 37—41. Not only were the pries in the temple required to say over this Shema, but every Jew, it was held, was bound to do the same thing, wherever he might be, every morning and every evening. This service over in the case before us, the lot was once more employed to determine the persons that should perform the next duties, when they immediately returned to the court of the sanctuary, to carry forward the morning work.

Then, while the pieces of the slaughtered lamb lay duly salted upon the rise of the altar, and ready to be carried to its top, the offering of incense was solemnly presented in the Holy Place. Two persons were always employed to perform the duty: one took in his hand a silver dish, in which was a censer full of frankincense, and the other carried, in a proper vessel, some burning coals from the summit of the brazen altar, and thus together they passed into the temple. Before they entered, however, they caused the great sounding instrument, that was provided for the purpose, to ring its loud note of warning, which directly brought the priests that might be out of the court, and any of the Levite musicians that happened to be away, to their proper places, and, at the same time, gave all the people notice, that they should be ready to put up their prayers with the incense that was to be offered. The two priests, also, who had been in a short time before to dress the candlestick and the altar, now went in a second time, just before the other two that have been mentioned: but they came out directly again, bringing with them their vessels of service, which they had the first time left standing in the Holy Place; and quickly after them, the one who took in the censer of coals, having placed them upon the altar, came out in like manner, leaving his companion, who had to offer the incense, alone in the sacred apartment. There he waited, till the President without called to him, with a loud voice, *Offer:* at which signal he caused the incense to kindle upon the golden hearth; when, all at once, the sanctuary was filled with its cloud, and its fragrant odour diffused itself all over the consecrated hill, while the multitude without united in solemn, silent prayer; and oftentimes, no doubt, there went up from hearts, like those of Simeon and Anna, the breathings of true and fervent devotion, more acceptable to the Almighty, far, than all the sweetest tribute of the altar.

So soon as this offering of incense and prayer was concluded, the person whose lot it was to lay the pieces of the lamb upon the altar top, with as much despatch as possible, committed them to the sacred fire. Then, while the dark smoke ascended toward heaven, some of the priests, especially those who had just been in the Holy Place, took their station upon the flight of steps that led up to the entrance of the Porch; and, lifting their hands on high, solemnly blessed the people; one of them (who, as it would seem from Luke i. 21, 22, was always the same that offered the incense,) taking the lead, and pronouncing the words first, and the others falling in and saying them over all along just after him, so as to make together one united benediction. The form of words which they used was the one, so beautiful and expressive, that is found in Num. vi. 24—26; and in answer to it, as soon as it was uttered, the people returned aloud, *Blessed be the Lord God, the God of Israel, from everlasting to everlasting!* After this blessing, the meat-offering of the whole congregation was presented, then that of the high-priest, and last of all, the regular drink-offering; when, immediately, the Levites lifted on high their song of sounding praise, after the manner that has been already described, and so concluded the morning worship It was not till about the third hour, or the middle of the forenoon, that the whole service was thus finished, and hence the Jews were not accustomed to eat or drink before that time of day, holding it improper to do so, until after this stated season of sacrifices and prayer was over. (Acts ii. 15.)

The Evening Service began about the ninth hour, or the middle of the afternoon. (Acts iii. 1.) It differed only in some few points, of no importance, from that of the morning, and needs not, therefore, any separate consideration. Generally, the particular duties were performed, severally, by the same persons that did them in the morning, so that no new casting of lots was required.

These were the stated services of every day; whatever other duties might be required on some other extraordinary days, these were not allowed in any case to be omitted. Between the sacred seasons of the morning and the evening worship, there was no particular regular course of employment in the temple: yet the interval was not unoccupied with acts of religion; it was then, that other common sacrifices, presented by individuals, were brought forward, from time to time, to the altar, of whatever sort they might be.

Ye shall reverence my sanctuary, was a holy commandment of the Lord himself, and all-reasonable it certainly was, that so solemn a place, especially in the time of public worship, should not be profaned by impious or thoughtless folly. The Jews did not, therefore, at any time, manifest a too careful regard to this point, however solicitous they showed themselves, in a certain way, to have it secured in the smallest things. But their zeal was not sound or consistent withal. It became, in some particulars, trifling and superstitious, while in others, it showed a marvellous indifference to the whole honour of God's House; here, as in many other cases, *it strained out a gnat, and swallowed a camel.* Thus, it was held unlawful to go out of the Court of Israel by the same gate that one came in by; or to retire, when their worship was over, any other way than walking backwards, lest it should seem disrespectful to the altar and the sanctuary, to turn the back upon them; while yet, all manner of worldly traffic was allowed to be carried on in the outer court, without scruple or shame. In their care, too, of outward forms, they lost, in general, all concern about the inward temper, which God especially regards. Still, much of this attention to outward carriage and appearance was altogether highly becoming, since true reverence toward God requires this, as well as a right spirit in the soul, and it is not to be doubted that the want of it must be truly offensive in his sight. No person was allowed to enter the ground of the temple with a staff in his hand, or with his scrip on, or with money in his purse, as if he were coming to a place of worldly business; neither might he go in with dust on his feet, but must wash or wipe them beforehand; nor might he spit upon the sacred pavement anywhere, nor might he pass *across* it, when going to some other place, because it happened to be the nearest way; all which things would have been disrespectful. Nor was any light or careless behaviour, such as laughing, scoffing, or idle talking, allowed to be indulged, as being unseemly and irreverent, in such a place: but those who came to worship were required to go to the proper place, with leisure and sober step, and there to stand during the service, each with his feet close together, his face turned toward the sanctuary, his eyes bended downward to the ground, and his hands laid one over the other upon his breast, having no liberty, in any case, to sit down, or lean, or throw his body into any careless posture whatever. What a pity it is that such a regard to reverence, in outward carriage, is found in so small a measure in most Christian churches! How little sense, alas! do the great multitude of those that visit the sanctuary now, seem to have of God's presence, even in his own house, as they come with light and careless movement into its solemn courts, and as they attend with all manner of outward indifference upon its sacred services—bearing on all their looks the image of a worldly spirit, and in their whole deportment showing more regard to themselves than to their Maker! Especially, what a spectacle of irreverence is often displayed in the time of prayer: what roving of the eye, indicative of roving thought within—what show of listless languor and weariness, that denotes a mind empty of all interest in the business of the place—what unseemliness of posture and manner, such as *sitting* without necessity, *leaning* this way and that way, *lolling* in every self-indulgent attitude, *changing* positions with continual impatience, &c., all evincing the little impression that is felt of the high solemnity and importance of the duty, and the little apprehension that is entertained of the presence and the majesty and the infinite glory of the Being that is worshipped, before whom the seraphim are represented as standing, with their faces and their feet covered, as they cry, in continual adoration, HOLY, HOLY, HOLY, IS THE LORD OF HOSTS.

SECTION II.

THE SABBATH.

The origin of the Sabbath is known to every one that has read the first three verses of the second chapter of Genesis, or learned to repeat the fourth commandment. It did not take its rise, like other sacred days and seasons, that are soon to be mentioned, with the Jewish system of worship, that was to pass away; nor was it instituted for any ceremonial reason, such as we have seen had place in the case of sacrifices, and of the priestly office, from their earliest appointment. Nay, so remote was its nature from any such character as this, that it was originally set apart for the use of beings altogether innocent and holy; for the seventh day was sanctified, or declared more holy than other days, *before* our first parents were become sinful and lost: even in paradise, where all days were so full of the worship of God, this of the Sabbath was to be distinguished as peculiarly sacred, and to be observed as a continual memorial of his goodness and power displayed in the great work of creation.

We have no express mention made of it again, in the history of the time that followed before and after the flood, till the age of Moses, (Ex. xvi. 22—30;) which is not to be wondered at, when we consider how very brief that history is There is, nevertheless, sufficient evidence, that it was not forgotten among the people of God, nor altogether among those that departed from the true religion. Noah, we find, reckoned time by periods of seven days, and from him some tradition of the Sabbath and of the week passed down among the various tribes and nations of his descendants, in every part of the world, as has been more particularly mentioned already, when taking notice of the ancient manner of dividing time, in a former part of this work.

When God formed his covenant with the Israelitish nation, the ancient appointment of the Sabbath was solemnly called to remembrance, and clothed with fresh authority. Jehovah himself, from the midst of the awful darkness, uttered the commandment, in the hearing of all the people. (Ex. xx. 8—11.) It was still uttered, too, as in the beginning, not as a precept designed for a single dispensation merely, but as a statute of universal and perpetual obligation: it was given as one of the *ten commandments*, which comprehended the whole *moral* law, and were proclaimed to the ancient church, as the original and fundamental rule of God's moral government, that was never to be lost sight of, while the world should stand.

At the same time, however, the Sabbath was made to bear something of a *peculiar* character, also, in the Jewish economy, such as it had not before, and was not designed to retain afterwards. It was invested with a certain *ceremonial* sacredness, in addition to that which it had of a purely *moral* sort. At least, it was required to be kept with a peculiar kind of outward observance, that belonged only to that system of carnal ordinances which was imposed on the Israelitish church till the time of reformation. Hence, the apostle reckons the Jewish Sabbath among other ceremonial institutions, that were, he says "a shadow of things to come." (Col. ii. 16, 17.) Still, the original and more essential nature of this institution was never suffered to pass out of sight; but may be found to have been, all along, distinctly recognised, in the peculiarly solemn *authority* with which its obligation was enforced, and in the moral and spiritual character of the *observance* with which it was enjoined to be kept, as well as of the *reasons* still assigned for its sacredness. (Ex. xxxi. 13—17, Lev. xix. 30. Isa. lviii. 13, Jer. xvii. 21—27.) To the Israelites it was urged as an additional *motive* for them to remember the rest of the Sabbath, according to its ancient appointment, that the Lord, whose day it was, had redeemed them, in his mercy and by his mighty power, from the bondage of Egypt. (Deut. v. 15.) And because it was given, from the beginning, to be a memorial of God's sovereignty, as the Creator and Governor of the world, and was designed to be religiously observed, in pious acknowledgment of this supreme dominion, it was regarded as a *sign of the covenant* that was formed between him and their nation, which had been taken out of the idolatrous world, to be his peculiar people; and hence, accordingly, when they neglected the Sabbath, it was considered to be a profane violation of the covenant itself, and a rejection of the original sovereign authority of God, that had in it the nature of idolatry outright. (Ex. xxxi. 13—17, Ezek. xx. 20.) The punishment for profaning the Sabbath day, like that of idolatry, was nothing less than death. (Ex. xxxv 2, Num. xv. 32—36.)

The law required a rigid observance of the sacred day. All the common employments of life, lawful on other days, were forbidden to be attended to on this. It was unlawful even to make a fire; and a man, on one occasion, was put to death for gathering sticks during its time of rest. The Jews, however, carried their regard to its outward observance, in this way, in later times, to a superstitious length. While they honoured it with little or no genuine regard in their spirits, they affected a most scrupulous care of offending against the letter of the commandment, in their actions: and yet, even in this case, they showed great inconsistency, sometimes *straining out a gnat*, and at other times *swallowing a camel*. The Pharisees, especially in the days of our Saviour, laid claim to great conscientiousness on this point, and often found fault with him for disregarding, according to their notion, the sacredness of God's day; though, all the while, it was not difficult to be perceived, that their hatred to Jesus, far more than their zeal for the Sabbath, called forth their censures and complaints. Our Lord exposed their malevolence and inconsistency, and taught the true nature of the sacred day. (Matt. xii. 1—15, Luke xiii. 10—17, John v. 16, vii. 22, 23, ix. 14, 16.)

In the sanctuary, there was no rest on the Sabbath from the labour of other days; but, on the contrary, an increase of work. Besides the daily offerings, two other victims were required still to smoke on that day upon the altar, (Num xxviii. 9, 10;) and regularly, as we have seen, the old shewbread was to be removed, and a new supply put in its place. Thus, *the priests in the temple profaned the Sabbath*, or spent it in work, and yet *were blameless*. (Matt. xii. 5.) It was meet that the public service of God should not be diminished, but increased upon his own day.

It was usual to make some preparation for the Sabbath toward the close of the sixth day. (Mark xv. 42.) According to the Jews, it was customary to cease from labour on that day at the time of the Evening Sacrifice; and from that hour till the sun went down, all busied themselves to get completely ready for the holy season that was at hand. Victuals were prepared, (for there might be no cooking on the Sabbath,) and all things attended to that were needful for orderly and decent appearance, such as washing the face, hands, and feet, trimming the beard, &c. that the day of rest might be entered upon without confusion, and in a manner of reverence and respect. A little before sunset, the *Sabbath candle* was lighted in each house, in token of gladness at the approach of God's day. At dark, they spread upon the table, from the provisions previously made ready, a supper, rather better than common; when the master of the family, taking a cup of wine in his hand, repeated the words in Gen. ii. 1—3, blessed God over the wine, said over a form of words to hallow the Sabbath, and raising the cup to his lips, drank off its contents; after which, the rest of the family did the same; and then, having washed their hands, they all joined in the domestic meal. Thus began the observance of the seventh day. On the next morning, they resorted to their synagogues: or, if they lived at Jerusalem, and felt an inclination to attend the temple, they might go and worship there. After breakfast, they either went to some school of divinity, to hear the traditions of the elders explained, or employed the time in religious duties at home, till the hour of taking dinner. About the middle of the afternoon, they again betook themselves to the synagogue or the temple, for worship. The day was afterwards closed with something of the same sort of ceremony with which it had been introduced. In this way, if we may believe Jewish tradition, the Sabbath was kept under the second temple.

How the Sabbath was spent before the captivity, when there were no synagogues, we are not informed. Those who lived nigh the Sanctuary might attend its worship. Parents might instruct their children in the knowledge of the law, as, no doubt, many did with care, regarding the Lord's repeated injunction. It seems, also, to have been common to visit the prophets on that day, to receive their instruction and counsel. (2 Kings iv. 23.)

Our Saviour, who was Lord of the Sabbath, caused it to be changed from the *seventh* to the *first* day of the week, that it might be, till the end of time, a memorial of his resurrection from the dead; while, being still unaltered in its essential nature, it should continue to answer, also, as before, all the purpose of its original institution.

SECTION III.

NEW MOONS AND FEAST OF TRUMPETS.

EVERY New Moon, or the first day of every month, was distinguished by a certain degree of sacredness from other ordinary days. From Amos viii. 5, we learn that it was not considered lawful to transact worldly business on such days. *When will the New Moon be gone*, the wicked are represented as saying, *that we may sell corn? and the Sabbath, that we may set forth wheat?* Like the Sabbath, also, they were deemed fit times for visiting the prophets to receive instruction, and these holy men, it seems, were accustomed to appropriate them regularly to the sacred employment of giving direction and counsel to all, of every class, that were disposed to seek it from their lips. (2 Kings iv. 23.) At the Sanctuary, the New Moons were observed with particular sacrifices, over and above the daily sacrifices; viz. two bullocks, a ram, and seven lambs, with their meat-offering and drink-offering, for a public holocaust or whole burnt-offering, and a goat, besides, for a sin-offering. (Num. xxviii. 11—15.) These sacrifices were attended with the blowing of the sacred silver trumpets. (Num. x. 10.)

There was one New Moon, however, distinguished in point of importance above all the rest. This was the first day of the seventh month, Tishri, and so, of course, the first day of the civil year, which always, as we have seen, commenced with that month. It was more sacred than other New Moons, being especially set apart as a Sabbath or day of rest from all common work; for the law did not forbid such work in the case of the others, although it was considered to have made it, to a certain extent at least, improper and wrong, as has just been stated, by the religious regard with which it distinguished them in other respects. The return of this day, which ushered in the ancient year, was required to be announced and proclaimed with a special blowing of trumpets; whence it was called "*the day of trumpet blowing*," and also "*the memorial of blowing of trumpets.*" It was honoured at the Sanctuary by peculiar offerings: the law prescribing for it, in addition to the sacrifices presented on other New Moons, a bullock, a ram, and seven lambs, for a burnt-offering, and a second goat, as it would seem, for a sin-offering. (Lev. xxiii. 25, Num. xxix 1—6.)

Thus, the months and the year were sanctified, as it were,

by having the *first-fruits* of their time still consecrated to the Lord: thus, the Israelite was continually reminded that his days, as well as his cattle and his crop, were all given to him from his Maker, and could not be employed too unreservedly in his service and for his glory. It were well, if the recollection of this fact could be habitually pressed upon the soul, in every age. It were well, if Christians could be brought to feel as they ought that they are, in every respect, but stewards for God, under obligations to use all that they have in the way that may be most for his praise, and for the advancement of his kingdom; and, that if they are not themselves their own, but are bound to glorify God with body and with spirit, as altogether his, it must be strangely inconsistent to look upon their property, or their time, as less absolutely sacred for his use, (even if these things were not essentially joined together,) or to waste or misapply them, or to withhold them from his service, without a feeling of responsibility, or a single serious thought of the reckoning that is surely to take place with every servant, for the manner in which he shall have improved each single talent given him to occupy—not for himself, but *for his Lord*. (Matt. xxv. 14—30.)

These New Moons differed from the Sabbath in having only a *ceremonial* sacredness, while that, as we have seen, was, in its original institution, altogether of *moral* character. With the close of the Jewish dispensation, accordingly, *they* lost all their distinction in this respect: (Gal. iv. 10, Col. ii. 16:) whereas the *Sabbath*, to this day, retains the whole of its essential nature, and the full measure of its earliest authority. Still, there can be no impropriety in setting apart such days, even now, for particular religious employment, as being naturally suited for profitable use in this way, if it be done voluntarily, for the sake of pious improvement, and not through any superstition. And certainly a special propriety there is, that the first day of the *year* should be observed publicly and privately after such a manner. How much more becoming and rational, thus to recognise the *flight of time*, so big with awful interest, than to celebrate its memorial with the shout of revelry, the boisterous laugh of folly, or the light extravagance of festivity and mirth!

SECTION IV.

THE THREE GREAT FESTIVALS.

THREE times every year, all the males of the Jewish nation who were of sufficient age were required to make their appearance at the Sanctuary, (the tabernacle at first, and afterwards the temple,) for the solemn worship of God. "Three times in a year," was the commandment, "shall all thy males appear before the Lord thy God, in the place which he shall choose; in *the feast of unleavened bread*, and in *the feast of weeks*, and in *the feast of tabernacles;* and they shall not appear before the Lord empty; every man shall give as he is able, according to the blessing of the Lord thy God, which he hath given thee." (Ex. xxiii. 14—17, Deut. xvi. 16, 17.) The feast of weeks lasted only for *one* day; the feast of unleavened bread continued as many as *seven*, and that of tabernacles, *eight*, though only the first and last, in each case, were considered especially sacred, being set apart from all common work, except such as was needed for the preparation of food. (Ex. xii. 16.)

It was on these occasions, that the second sort of first-fruits, firstlings, and tithes, noticed in the last chapter, were presented before the Lord, and then converted, according to his direction, into *offering-feasts* of sacred gratitude and joy. Free-will offerings, also, were presented more abundantly at these times than through all the year besides, and made use of in the same way; for those who lived at a distance still kept such offerings till they were called to attend some one of the festivals, and then brought all their different gifts together to the House of God. Thus, all came furnished with presents, and no one appeared before the Lord empty; so that the most liberal provision was secured for the religious entertainments with which the feasts were celebrated. These entertainments it is to be remembered, were required to be widely social, and to be made free, especially to the destitute and the unfortunate. In this way, the people rejoiced together in the presence of their God, acknowledging his wonderful mercies, and showing forth his praise; while, at the same time, they were drawn with kindly regard toward each other, and led to mingle their hearts in general benevolence and friendship, as forming, altogether, only a single happy family, and having all a common interest in the kind care of the same bountiful and compassionate Father. During these festivals, also, the *public* service of the Sanctuary was increased with additional offerings, over and above the daily sacrifices, presented each day, in the name of the whole congregation. Thus, with public and private sacrifices together, the altar found no rest, and the flowing of blood was not stayed from morning to night.

THE PASSOVER.

The feast of unleavened bread was so called because, while it lasted, no leaven whatever was allowed to be made use of, but unleavened bread alone was eaten by all the people. It was called, also, the *Passover*, because it was instituted in memory of that night of mercy, when the Lord *passed over* the families of his people, while he carried the terror of death into every household of Egypt. We have a full account of its original appointment, in Exod. xii. 1—28. In some circumstances, indeed, that first celebration which was required in Egypt was not imitated in those that were observed afterwards; but, in all essential points, the example of it was ever after followed. The festival lasted from the 15th to the 21st of the month *Abib* or *Nisan*, the first of the sacred year. It always fell, accordingly, in the time of our month April, though it came in some years several days sooner than it did in others, as we have seen, when considering the Jewish manner of reckoning time. Sometimes, the 14th of the month was termed the *first day of unleavened bread*, because on that day, before evening, all leaven was carefully removed from the houses, by way of preparation for the festival week.

The principal solemnity of the season was the sacred supper with which it was introduced; and this, more especially and properly, was that which had the name of the PASSOVER; the rest of the feast being called so from it, on account of its primary importance. This supper was required to be prepared by every family, unless in cases where they were small, when two might join and prepare it together. Nor were any who might be found unconnected with families allowed to neglect it; such had either to find admission into some domestic society for the occasion or to form themselves into companies of proper size, and so keep the feast by themselves. Each supper, it was directed, should consist of a whole lamb or kid, a male of the first year, without blemish, roasted whole, (that is, without being cut up after it was butchered and dressed) and served up with unleavened bread, and a salad of bitter herbs. The victims were to be selected on the 10th day of the month, and slain on the evening of the 14th, a short tim before the 15th began to be reckoned; with the commencement of which, at night, the passover suppers were made ready and eaten. In the case of the first celebration of the feast, the lamb of each family or company was killed at home, and its blood sprinkled upon the posts of the door; but afterwards, they were all required to be slain at the Sanctuary, and the blood and fat, as in the case of other sacrifices, appropriated to the altar. (Deut. xvi. 1—7.) The people were ordered to eat the first passover in haste, with their loins girded, and in a condition of full readiness for an immediate journey; this manner, however, which expressed the quick and sudden departure which they were compelled to make out of Egypt, seems not to have been observed in succeeding time, at least not in the latter age of the nation. If any of the flesh of these sacrifices was not eaten on the night of the feast, it was to be burned the next morning.

Various ceremonies were attached to the celebration of the Passover, in latter times, of which no mention is made in the ancient law. The following is a brief account of the manner in which it was observed in the time of our Saviour, according to the tradition of the Jews.

Individuals might bring their lambs with them to Jerusalem: but it was more common to purchase them at the temple itself, from the priests, who always had a large supply of suitable ones, ready to be disposed of on the occasion; being accustomed, it would seem, to select with care beforehand, (probably on the 10th day of the month,) from the general market which they encouraged to be held in the outer court at these seasons, such as were every way free from blemish, and to have them in readiness for as many as wanted to buy, so that they might have more security in getting their victims, that they were altogether sound and perfect, as the law required, than they could have, if left to look for them themselves in the market, after they had arrived at the city. It was a regulation, that no lamb should be used for less than ten persons: each family, therefore, or company, was required to have at least that number of members; generally they had more, and sometimes as many as twenty. They were all determined and fixed before the victims were brought to be slain.

Women were not *directly* bound to appear, as the males were, at any of the three Great Festivals; yet it was held, that *indirectly* the law made it their duty to attend, as far as circumstances might allow: especially were they under obligation, it was maintained, to be present at the Passover, inasmuch as it was written, "The *whole assembly* of the congregation of Israel shall kill it." (Ex. xii. 6.) They were accustomed, therefore, to come up to the feast regularly, in its season, with their husbands or fathers. Thus, whole families attended together, and most of the paschal societies were composed of one or more of them, husbands, wives, children, and servants, united to celebrate the sacred supper. In other cases, the companies were formed as convenience or inclination directed.

It is easy to conclude, that every room in Jerusalem that was large enough would be wanted on these occasions, to accommodate the vast multitude that assembled to keep the feast. The Jews have a tradition, that the houses of the city were all at such times regarded as common property, and were opened to admit as many as they could conveniently receive, without any charge whatever; so that strangers, when they came up from any part of the nation, might make use of any one they pleased that had room for them, free of all expense, and as a matter of right. Some have thought, that the inquiry of our Lord's disciples, "*Where* wilt thou that we prepare the passover?" proceeded upon the fact of such a usage; and intimates, that it might have been made ready *anywhere* he thought proper; and hence, also, it is to be accounted for, they imagine, that the man to whom they were directed, so readily gave them the use of his guest-chamber as soon as they asked for it. (Mark xiv. 12—16.) The tradition, however, like various other pretty stories that are told about the holy city, seems to have but a feeble claim to credit: and certainly it is not needed to explain the case now referred to; since the question of the disciples does not *necessarily* imply any such thing as it affirms; and it was as easy for our Saviour to control the mind of the man whose guest-chamber he wanted, even if we suppose him to have been altogether unacquainted with him, as it was for him to make the owners of the colt content when it was said to them, *The Master hath need of him*, or to rule the spirits of the powerful and the proud, as well as the affronted feelings of a company of unprincipled rogues, when twice he overturned the tables of the money changers, and drove from the temple those that profaned it with their worldly traffic.

Exceedingly great care was taken to have every particle of *leaven* cleared from the houses before the time of the passover began. The law on this subject was very strict, and to make sure a proper observance of it, the most diligent pains were considered necessary. As early as the beginning of the 14th day, that is, the night before the feast, there was a general search made all over every house with lighted candles, not leaving unexamined the smallest corner or hole where it was possible for leaven in any shape to be lodged. The next morning before noon, all that could be found was carefully burned, or thrown into the water, or scattered to the wind; and every one, as he thus put it away, was accustomed to repeat the established form of execration, "*All the leaven that is within my possession, which I have seen or which I have not seen, which I have cast out or which I have not cast out, be it as though it were not! be it as the dust of the earth!*" Thus was every house purged for the celebration of the passover; and after this it was not considered proper even so much as to make use of the word *leaven*, lest the thought of it should pollute the mind. The unleavened bread, which was now prepared for use, was baked in the form of thin cakes, full of holes, to keep them from the slightest fermentation, unseasoned with salt, and made only with water, without any sort of oil: in some cases, the higher class of the people had them enriched with sugar and eggs, though even such bread was not allowed on the first day of the feast, but only on those that followed.

The lambs were all slain, as other sacrifices, in the Court of the priests. It was a great work to kill and dress so many as were necessary for the occasion, and required a considerable part of the afternoon of the 14th day for its execution. The Evening Sacrifice accordingly, on that day, was offered before the middle of the afternoon, and the rest of the day, from that time to the end of it, was occupied altogether with this preparation for the passover. Though only one person of each family or society entered into the court with the lamb that belonged to it, it needs not to be remarked, that it was still impossible for all these to go in at once. They were accordingly divided into three large companies, which were admitted one at a time in succession. When one of these companies had entered, the gates were closed, and immediately the owners of the lambs, or those who brought them in, began to assist each other in killing them, taking off their skins, and removing the entrails and fat. The blood was handed to the priests, to be sprinkled on the altar and poured out at its bottom, and the common portions of fat to be burned upon its top; these standing all along in rows from the slaughtering places to the altar, and passing the articles from one to another continually to where it stood. Meanwhile, the Levites sang over, once, twice, or three times the 113th, 114th, 115th, 116th, 117th, and 118th Psalms. These were denominated, when taken together, the *Hallel*, or hymn of praise, and sometimes the *Lesser Hallel*, to distinguish it from another that was in use, styled the Greater Hallel. As soon as the first company had their work done, they went out, and the second took their place, going over the same business in the same style: so in their turn, the third one filled the court; after which it was all washed over with water, as we may well suppose it needed to be, after such an immense slaughter. (2 Chron. xxxv. 1—19.)

The lambs thus butchered were carried away to the several houses where they were to be eaten, and immediately made ready for roasting, by being thrust through from one end to the other, by a wooden spit or stake, and so placed before a large fire. According to the commandment, each was allowed to be thus exposed, till it was roasted in a perfectly thorough manner. Soon after it became dark, that is, with the commencement of the 15th day, the passover-table was spread, and surrounded by its little company, in all the houses of Jerusalem.

The supper commenced with the ceremony of drinking a small cup of wine mingled with water, after having given thanks over it to God the Giver of all blessings. Every one had a separate cup poured out, but only one uttered the thanksgiving in the name of all. This was the *first cup*. Then followed the *washing of hands*, after the manner of the purifying of the Jews, accompanied with another short form of thanksgiving to God. The table, having been till this time unfurnished, was now supplied with its provisions, viz. the cakes of unleavened bread, the bitter salad, the lamb roasted whole, with its legs, heart, liver, &c., and, besides, some other meat prepared from the flesh of common peace-offerings, that had been presented during the day, and a dish of thick sauce, composed of dates, figs, raisins, vinegar, &c.

The table thus furnished, the leading person, and all the rest after him, took a small quantity of the salad, with another thanksgiving, and ate it. After which, immediately, all the dishes were removed from the table, and a second cup of wine placed before each of the company, as at first. This strange way of beginning the meal was designed to excite the curiosity of the children, that they might be led to inquire what it meaned, according to what is said in Ex. xii. 26. When the inquiry was made, (for if there was no child present, the wife or some other person brought it forward,) the person who presided began, and told how their fathers had all been servants in Egypt, and how with many signs and wonders the Lord had redeemed them from their cruel bondage, and brought them forth from the place of their oppression, with a mighty hand and an outstretched arm. As he concluded the interesting story of Jehovah's mercies, the dishes that had been removed were again placed upon the table; whereupon he said, *This is the passover which we eat, because that the Lord passed over the houses of our fathers in Egypt;* and then holding up the salad, and after it the unleavened bread, he stated their design, viz. that the one represented the *bitterness* of the Egyptian bondage, and the other the *sudden* redemption which the Lord wrought on their behalf, when he smote the first-born of their oppressors, so that they urged his people to depart without delay. Then he repeated the 113th and 114th Psalms, and closed with this prayer: "*Blessed be thou, O Lord our God, King Everlasting! who hast redeemed us, and redeemed our fathers out of Egypt, and brought us to this night to eat unleavened bread and bitter herbs:*" which being uttered, all the company drank the wine that had been standing for some time before them. This was the *Second cup.*

Another washing of the hands now took place, when the person who presided, taking up the unleavened bread, brake one of the cakes in two, again gave thanks to God, and then, with the rest, began to eat; each first making use of a piece of the bread, with some of the salad, and the thick sauce, then partaking of the peace-offering meat, and last of all of the paschal lamb, with a separate thanksgiving still pronounced before each dish. Every one was required to eat at least as much of the lamb as was equal to the size of an olive. The meal thus over, they all washed again, according to the usage of common meals, and then united in drinking another cup of wine and water. This was the third cup, and was called, by way of distinction, "*the cup of blessing,*" because while it stood before them ready to be drunk, the leader was accustomed to return thanks over it in a particular manner, for the blessing of the sacred supper, and for all the goodness of the Lord. There was yet another cup made ready a little time after, just before the company rose from the table. It was denominated the cup of the Hallel; because it was the custom to repeat, in connection with it, the principal part of the hymn of Lesser Hallel: for as it was begun by the rehearsal of its first two psalms, the 113th and the 114th, over the second cup, (as we have seen,) so it was now finished by being carried on through the following four. In all common cases, this *fourth cup* closed the celebration of the feast. It was held to be a duty absolutely incumbent upon all who took part in the supper, men or women, old or young, rich or poor, to make use of all the four cups that have been mentioned.

In the account of the institution of the Lord's Supper, Luke xxii. 15—20, mention is made of two different cups.

which appear to have been the last two of the four that have now been noticed. Having given thanks over the third one, and refused to drink it himself, our Saviour took some of the bread that was left of the feast, and gave thanks, and brake it, in representation of his broken body, and then made use of the *cup after supper*, or the fourth one, to represent, in like manner, the shedding of his blood, after which, as Matthew tells us, they sang a hymn, and so finished the solemn entertainment. Others, however, suppose, that the *third* cup was the one which was used in the appointment of this holy sacrament; because they think it clear, from its being said that *while they were eating* Jesus took bread and brake it for this purpose, that it must have been done *before* the use of that cup, and not *after* it, as the other opinion presumes.

The day thus entered upon with the paschal supper was holy: till the going down of the next sun, it was not lawful to attend to any common work. At the same time it abounded with sacrifices: every male, the Jews tell us, was under obligation to appear in the temple-court, during the course of it, with a burnt-offering and a double peace-offering. These particular peace-offerings were called the *Hagigah*, and were considered to be altogether more important than the common peace-offerings that it was usual to present on other days of the festival. Hence the feast in which they were on that day employed, according to the manner of such sacrifices, seems to have been sometimes styled simply by itself, *the passover;* though that name properly belonged only to the paschal supper of the evening before. Thus, in John xviii. 28, we are told, that the Jews went not into Pilate's judgment-hall, lest they should be defiled; *but that they might eat the passover:* while, at the same time, it is clearly stated in the gospel history, that the celebration of the true passover supper had taken place the preceding night. In this way, also, John xix. 14 may be explained; unless it be supposed, that *the preparation of the Passover* mentioned there, means simply the *Passover preparation day*, or that particular preparation day, (as every Friday, or day before the Sabbath, was called,) which fell in the week of the Passover. It is certain, that from the first, other sacrifices, besides those of the paschal lambs, were required at the paschal solemnity, which are spoken of also, as making a part of *the Passover* with them. (Deut. xvi. 2, 2 Chron. xxxv. 7, 8.) These, according to the Jewish notion, were all along made use of as peace-offerings for the *Hagigah*, a sacred feast that took place on the morrow after the celebration of the paschal supper. It must be acknowledged, indeed, that there is no direct evidence that this Hagigah was ever denominated by itself *the Passover;* and that the most *natural* way of understanding the language of John in the passage just noticed, would be as referring to the supper commonly so called. Not a few, accordingly, and these not lightly learned, have maintained, that our Saviour celebrated the passover a day sooner than the usual time. But this notion whatever plausibility it may seem at first glance to derive from these passages and John xiii 1, inasmuch as it is confirmed by no other tolerable evidence whatever, and is accompanied with all manner of difficulty, ought not to be deemed worthy of much respect. The first day of the Passover was, it is true, a most unsuitable time for the confusion and care of a public trial and execution, having, in a good measure, the same holiness as the Sabbath itself; but envy and malice overleap every consideration of this sort; and it was not hard for Jewish zeal to forget all its affected rigour, when an opportunity was found to destroy the hated Prophet of Galilee.

On the second day of the Passover, or the morrow after the *Sabbath,* (as its first day was called,) a sheaf of barley was waved before the Lord, as an offering of the first-fruits of the harvest, in the name of the whole people: a ceremony which was required to be accompanied with a special sacrifice, and that was necessary to *introduce* the harvest of every year. (Lev. xxiii. 10—14.) On every day of the paschal week, besides all the peace-offerings and other sacrifices of individuals, there were regular public sacrifices peculiar to the festival, over and above the daily sacrifice. (Num. xxviii. 16—25.)

The Passover, it is plain, might begin on any day of the week, being regulated altogether by the moon. When the 14th day of the month happened to be the regular Sabbath, the great work of killing the lambs was still performed as if it had been a common day; for sanctuary work was held to be no profanation, in any case, of its sacred rest. In a case of this sort, however, it was not allowed to carry the lambs home till the Sabbath was over; the people waited with them in the courts of the temple until it gave place, toward dark, to the second day of the week. Presumptuously to neglect the passover, in its season, brought most dangerous guilt upon the soul; but if uncleanness or other unavoidable cause prevented any one from keeping it at the proper time, he might keep it in the month following, and be accepted. (Num. ix. 6—13.)

The sacrifice of the passover had a special reference to the death of Christ. This the gospel teaches us, when it says in the Scripture, "A bone of him shall not be broken," which was spoken so carefully concerning the paschal lamb, had its fulfilment when the soldiers brake not the legs of the Saviour upon the cross. (Ex. xii. 46, John xix. 36.) The same thing the Apostle Paul teaches, when he expressly calls Christ *our passover sacrificed for us*, and represents the happy condition into which Christians are brought by his death, as a passover *feast*, (not occasional and transient like those of the Jews, but of perpetual continuance,) which ought to be kept, not with "the leaven of malice and wickedness, but with the unleavened bread of sincerity and truth." (1 Cor. v. 7, 8.) The whole transaction of the first passover in Egypt strikingly prefigured the saving efficacy of the Redeemer's sufferings. The sprinkling of blood upon the door-posts was only a picture of the atoning blood of Jesus, the Lamb of God, applied to the sinner's soul: as *that* was made essential to deliverance and safety, when the angel of destruction passed through the land; so *this* is needed to secure a far greater redemption, availing, wherever it is found, to save from hell itself; while, where it is not found, there can be no escape from eternal wrath; it is only "the sprinkling of the blood of Jesus Christ," that can ever turn away the sword of infinite justice from the guilty spirit, or shield it from the touch of harm when the Lord arises to his holy and terrible judgment. (Heb. xii. 24, 1 Pet. i. 2.) In every succeeding Passover, there was a memorial of this same transaction in Egypt; and so, of course, an ultimate reference to the Great Redemption, of which that transaction was ordered to be so expressively an image and type: thus, while the institution looked *backward*, it looked at the same time yet more significantly *forward*, showing forth the Lord's death before it took place, as the Christian sacrament of the Supper has been appointed to do ever since. There was in it not only a symbolic prefiguration of the ransom secured by this death of the Saviour, but a signal also of all the living benefit which his people continually derive from him by faith, in consequence of his amazing sacrifice; inasmuch as while the *blood* of the paschal lamb was sprinkled to make atonement, its *flesh* was converted into a solemn peace-offering feast, in token of friendly covenant with God, and joyful participation of his grace, which are secured only by that believing reception of Christ which he himself speaks of when he says, "Except ye eat the flesh of the Son of man and drink his blood, ye have no life in you." (John vi 51—56.)

THE FEAST OF WEEKS.

The *feast of weeks* was celebrated at the close of harvest, as a festival of thanks for its blessings. It was required to be always observed at the end of seven weeks from the second day of the Passover, on which the sheaf of first-fruits was offered, as an introduction to the harvest, and lasted only for one day. It was because its return was determined by reckoning a week of *weeks* in this way, that it was denominated *the feast of weeks;* as it was called also *Pentecost*, or the *fiftieth day*, because this reckoning of weeks comprehended, of course, a period of forty-nine days. As it celebrated the goodness of God in giving the fruits of harvest, (whence it was named sometimes the *feast of harvest*,) it was distinguished by a first-fruit offering of two loaves of the new flour, presented in the name of the whole congregation. This offering was accompanied with several bloody sacrifices; and there was, besides, a great public offering of such sacrifices prescribed for the day, which had no connection with this, all over and above the regular daily service. (Lev. xxiii. 15—20, Num. xxviii. 26—31.) There were at the same time many private free-will offerings presented on the occasion, and converted into sacred entertainments. (Deut. xvi. 9—12.) During the public sacrifices that have been mentioned, it was usual, the Jews tell us, to sing over the Hallel.

As the Passover was instituted in commemoration of the wonderful night of redemption, in which the Israelites left Egypt, so it has been imagined that the Pentecost was designed to be a memorial of the giving of the law from Mount Sinai, which appears to have been just about fifty days later. Of such a design, however, we have no intimation in the Bible.

The day of Pentecost has been rendered especially memorable, in Christian history, by the remarkable event of which we have an account in the second chapter of Acts. By selecting such an occasion for the descent of the Holy Ghost upon his disciples, our Lord caused this unanswerable vindication of his truth and power to have the most extensive notoriety; for always, at that time, *there were dwelling at Jerusalem, Jews, devout men, out of every nation under heaven,* gathered for the celebration of the joyful solemnity.

THE FEAST OF TABERNACLES.

The third great annual festival prescribed by the law was called *the feast of Tabernacles;* because, during its solemnity, the people were required to dwell in booths, or temporary habitations, constructed of the boughs of trees, such as were made use of in the journey through the wilderness, in memory of which it was appointed to be kept. It was celebrated from the 15th to the 23d of the seventh month, *Tishri*, with which the civil year had its commencement; the first and the last, as in the case of the Passover, being considered more particularly sacred and important. Besides the design just noticed, viz. to be a memorial of the journey through the wilderness, its appointment had respect to the season of vintage and gathering of fruits, at the close of which it was observed; so that it was intended at the same time to be a festival of thanks for these, or rather for all the produce of the year now gathered from the field, as the feast of weeks was for harvest, which is spoken of as the first-fruits of all. Hence it is called the *feast of ingathering*. (Ex. xxiii. 16, Lev. xxiii. 34—44, Neh. viii. 14—18.)

A great number of public sacrifices were required to be offered during this festival; an account of which may be found in Num. xxix. 12—38. The season was also distinguished, as the other great festivals were, with private peace-offerings of various sorts, in daily abundance. (Deut. xvi. 13—15.)

Under the second temple, certain peculiar ceremonies were introduced into the celebration of the feast of tabernacles, in addition to those that belonged to it, originally, by Divine appointment. The Jews pretend, indeed, that intimations of their use, before the captivity, are found in the Old Testament; but what they show for such have no appearance of the sort, except by fanciful interpretation. Such were these that follow.

1. In the law it was commanded—"Ye shall take you, on the first day, the boughs of goodly trees, branches of palm trees, and the boughs of thick trees, and willows of the brook; and ye shall rejoice before the Lord your God seven days." (Lev. xxiii. 40.) These boughs, the Sadducees rightly maintained, were designed to be employed in making booths; but the Pharisees insisted they were designed to be carried by every individual, in his hand, in token of joy; and they farther asserted, that, by the expression translated, *the boughs of goodly trees,* (which means, literally, *the fruit of goodly trees,*) was to be understood nothing else than apples of the citron tree, which, accordingly, were appointed to be carried in the same manner. This was established, therefore, as the common usage. On the first day of the feast, every person provided himself with a small bunch of branches of palm and willow and myrtle, and was seen carrying it about, wherever he went all the day long On the follwing days it was not thus con

stantly carried, but only when individuals went up to the temple: each day, however, all were required to visit the temple, with their bunches in their right hands, and every one a citron in his left, and thus pass around the altar, crying aloud. *Hosanna*, (which means, *save now!*) and repeating also the whole 25th verse of Psalm cxviii., while all the time the sacred trumpets were sounding without restraint. On the seventh day this ceremony was repeated seven times, in memory of the conquest of Jericho.

2. There was a still more remarkable rite, which consisted in the *drawing of water, and solemnly pouring it out upon the altar*. Every morning, during the feast, when the parts of the morning sacrifice were laid upon the altar, one of the priests went to the fountain of Siloam, and filled a golden vessel, which he carried in his hand, with its water. This he then brought into the court, and, having first mingled it with some wine, poured it out, as a drink-offering, on the top of the altar. And still, as this ceremony was performed each day, the Levites began their music, and sung over the Hallel; while at times, especially when the 118th Psalm was sung, the people all shook the branches which they held in their hands, to express the warm assent of their feelings to the sentiments breathed in the sacred hymn. The meaning of the ceremony is not clear: some of those who mention it, say it was significant of the blessing of *rain*, which was thus invoked from God; others tell us, it was a sign merely of the *joy* that belonged to the occasion; others, that it was a symbol of the outpouring of the Holy Spirit, according to what is said in Isa. xii. 3, "With joy shall ye draw water out of the wells of salvation," which, it is pretended, was spoken in allusion to the usage in question, and so evinces, at once, its antiquity and its sense.

3. Every night, we are told, there was a most extraordinary exhibition of joy, styled *the rejoicing for the drawing of water*. When the water was offered, in the morning, the solemnity of the worship then on hand would not admit the extravagance of this ceremony; so it was put off till all the service of the day was over, when it began, without moderation, and occupied quite a considerable portion of the night. The scene of it was the Court of the Women, which, for the occasion, was furnished with great lights, mounted upon four huge candlesticks that overtopped all the surrounding walls in height. Here, while the women occupied the balconies round about, above, as spectators, the Levites, taking their station on the steps that led up into the Court of Israel, at the west end, began to unite their instruments and voices, in loud music, and a general

dance was started all over the square. It was, withal, a wild and tumultuous dance, without order, dignity, or grace; every one brandishing in his hand a flaming torch, leaping and capering with all his might, and measuring the worthiness of his service by its extravagance and excess. What made the exhibition still more extraordinary in its appearance, was the high and grave character of the persons that were accustomed to engage in it; for it was not the common people that joined in this dance, but only those that were of some rank and importance, such as the members of the Sanhedrim, rulers of the synagogues, doctors of the law, &c. It was not until the night was far spent, that the strange confusion came to an end; and then only to be renewed with like extravagance on the next evening, (unless when it was particularly holy, as the eve that began the Sabbath,) as long as the feast lasted. *He that never saw the rejoicing of the drawing of water*, runs a Jewish saying, *never saw rejoicing in all his life.*

Some have thought, that the whole manner in which our Saviour was met, the last time he came up to Jerusalem, was borrowed from the usage, that has been noticed, of carrying branches in the hand, and shouting *Hosanna*, in the temple, on the feast of tabernacles; and that the use of the ceremony, at this time, was designed to intimate, that what the prayer in Psalm cxviii. 25, then so much used, had respect to, viz. the coming of the Messiah, was now truly accomplished; and that Jesus of Nazareth was no other than this glorious personage, the Son of David, the Redeemer of Israel, that should come into the world: whence it was cried, at the same time, in the language that begins the next verse of the same Psalm— "Blessed is he that cometh in the name of the Lord!" (Matt. xxi. 8, 9, 15, John xii. 12, 13.) The use of palm branches on this occasion, as well as all the show of honour that was made, seems rather to have been taken from the general ancient manner of celebrating triumphs, or public entries of kings into cities; but there can be no doubt, that the minds of the people were carried, at the same time, by natural association, to the usage, so familiar, of their great feast, and that their acclamations, accordingly, were really derived from that quarter. A reference to the ceremony of drawing and pouring out water also, is discovered in the gospel history: our Lord, it seems evident, had allusion to it, when, on the last day of the feast, he stood in the temple, and cried, "If any man thirst, let him come unto me and drink! He that believeth on me, as the Scripture hath said, out of his belly shall flow rivers of living water." It was in this way, he was continually in the habit of taking advantage of earthly objects and circumstances around him, to draw attention to spiritual truths, and to convey the most salutary instruction in a clear and impressive manner; in the case before us, we are told, "that he spake of the Spirit, which they that believe on him should receive." (John vii. 37—39.)

SECTION V.

THE GREAT DAY OF ATONEMENT.

There was no day in all the year so important and solemn, in the Ceremonial System, as the 10th of Tishri, which fell, of course, not quite a week before the feast of tabernacles. This was the *Day of Atonement*, when guilt was called to remembrance in such a way as it was at no other time, and a service of expiation performed in behalf of the whole nation, altogether extraordinary and peculiar. It was required to be observed, therefore, not merely as a Sabbath of complete rest, but as a day of rigid fasting also, and general humiliation or *affliction of soul*, on account of sin. The atonement that was made had respect to all the sins of all the people, from the highest to the lowest, committed throughout the preceding year; and was designed to clear away, as it were, by one general expiation, the vast array of guilt that was still left, after all the ordinary offerings for sin, resting with awful weight upon the nation. It comprehended in itself, in fact, the vitality and chief essence of the whole system of ceremonial expiation, and required for its accomplishment, accordingly, the service of the high-priest himself, in whom was concentrated the virtue of the entire priesthood, and an entrance with blood into the Holy of Holies, where all the life and glory of the Sanctuary were appointed to reside.

We have a full account of the manner of this atonement in the 16th chapter of Leviticus. We are there told how the high-priest was required to make himself ready, by washing, and putting on his plain linen garments, in place of the richer apparel he usually wore; how he came before the Sanctuary with a bullock, as a sin-offering for himself and his family, and two goats for the whole congregation; how he selected one of the goats by lot, for a sin-offering, and set apart the other for a scape-goat into the wilderness; how he killed the bullock for himself, and afterwards the goat for the people; how he first carried a censer of coals, with some incense, into the Most

Holy Place, and there caused a fragrant cloud instantly to spread over the mercy-seat, and fill the apartment; how he then brought the blood of the bullock and the blood of the goat into the same awful place, and sprinkled them upon the mercy-seat, and seven times upon the floor in front of it; how, when he came out into the Holy Place, he applied them also to the horns of the golden altar, and sprinkled them upon it seven times; how he afterwards placed his hands upon the head of the living goat, confessed over it all the iniquities of the children of Israel, and all their transgressions in all their sins, and then sent it away, thus loaded, as it were, with the people's guilt, into the wilderness; and how, after all was over, he again washed himself in the Holy Place, put on his splendid dress, and offered a burnt-offering for himself and for the people, while the whole bodies of the bullock and the goat, whose blood had been carried into the Sanctuary, were sent away to be burned without the camp, as altogether polluted and unclean.

It was an awful thing to come before the throne of God as the high-priest did this day; and no doubt the duty was often performed with fear and trembling. The greatest care was needful to attend to every part of the service in a proper manner, and with becoming reverence, lest the anger of the Lord should suddenly display itself, to crush him with destruction. It was necessary that he should be free, at the time, from every sort of ceremonial defilement; and it became his duty, accordingly, to guard himself with the utmost diligence, from every kind of contamination, for some time beforehand. In later times, if the Jews are to be believed, he used to retire from his own house a whole week before the solemnity, taking up his residence, for that time, altogether in a chamber of the temple, that he might the better be in readiness for his great duty; for which he was accustomed to prepare himself by practice, in various ways, and by reading over, or having read to him, repeatedly, the order and manner of the service he would have to go through.

In the law, it is said, that the scape-goat should *be let go in the wilderness*, to carry clear away, as it were, the iniquity that was laid upon it, and it would seem that it was always allowed to escape with life; but under the second temple, a different interpretation of the direction gained place, and it came to be held essential that the animal should be destroyed. This was always done, accordingly, by precipitating it from a certain rock, about twelve miles off from Jerusalem, to which it was led away directly from the temple. The rock was very lofty and steep, so that when the unhappy beast came to the bottom, it was dashed to pieces.

There were particular public sacrifices prescribed for the day of atonement, besides those that were connected with the great expiation. (Num. xxix. 8—11.) These, the Jews say, were offered directly after the regular morning sacrifice, before that solemn service commenced. They tell us, too, that no one but the high-priest might do any of the priestly work that belonged to these or to any other offerings of this day; but that he was required to perform himself, in his rich dress, all the morning service, and all that was connected with these additional offerings; then to change his garments, and go through the work of atonement; and afterwards, in his common apparel again, having first offered the two burnt-offering rams, one for himself and the other for the people, to conclude all with the duties of the evening sacrifice.

The great *annual atonement*, embodying in itself, as we have seen, the essential virtue of the whole Jewish system of expiatory sacrifices, was, of course, the most perfect picture which the ceremonial dispensation had, of the *true Atonement* that was afterwards to appear. The whole institution of sacrifice was a shadowy representation of the Redeemer's death, and the whole priestly service had respect to his mediatorial work; they presented, in common cases, however, only some particular features of these mysteries in any single view, without bringing the scattered sketches at any time together, or supplying, even in this separate way, all that were wanting for filling up the general representation. But, in the case before us, there was, as it were, an orderly and complete concentration of typical images, into a single, full, and striking exhibition of the whole at once; such as, the more narrowly it is contemplated, cannot fail to excite the higher admiration, and to display the more convincingly, in all its colouring, the inimitable touches of a divine pencil.

Here was a symbolic representation of Christ's voluntary *sacrifice* for the sins of the world, and of his all-prevailing *intercession* in the presence of the Father, by which his people are made partakers of righteousness and eternal life. The Most Holy Place was a figure of heaven, where God dwells in eternal glory. As the high-priest entered into the one to intercede with incense for the Israelitish nation, so Jesus has ascended into the other to intercede for the whole congregation of his church, gathered out of all the kingdoms of the world. But as the intercession, in the first case, could not be admitted, except as it came recommended by blood of expiation, previously shed, so, also, without shedding of blood, there could be no such intercession of any avail, in the second; wherefore, our Lord appeared not before the infinite Majesty on high, for this purpose, till he had first offered an adequate sacrifice, on the merit of which he might found his mediation. He gave his blood for the remission of sins, and then presented himself in the presence of God, with the atonement as it were in his hands, to make reconciliation with it for guilt, and to plead its virtue in favour of all who apply to him for life. In the typical transaction, there was not, indeed, an entire correspondence throughout with the mystery it represented: it was not possible, in the nature of things, that it should be so. Thus, in the type, the high-priest and the victim were altogether distinct, while in the true transaction they were found in one and the same person; Christ was himself the sacrifice and the priest: he *offered* himself, of his own accord, as a victim for sin, (as he says in John x. 17, 18, and in that plea of his prayer for his disciples, "For their sakes *I sanctify myself;*") *endured*, in his own person, all the suffering of an expiatory death; and then passed, in the power of an all-sufficient High-Priest, into the Holy of Holies on high, to sprinkle the mercy-seat, as it were, with his own blood, and obtain eternal redemption for his church. In the type, moreover, there was, besides the offering for the people, a separate sacrifice for the high-priest and his family, inasmuch as he himself was encumbered with personal guilt, and needed atonement for his own sins, before he could come acceptably before God, to make intercession for the people: but the sacrifice of Christ was single, and had respect altogether to the sins of his people—he himself being holy, harmless, undefiled, and separate from sinners. In the type, at the same time, besides the sin-offering sacrifice, there was a scape-goat appointed to bear away, symbolically, the sins of the nation; both these figures, however, were answered at once in the death of Jesus Christ. They presented only two different aspects of the general nature of the atonement it accomplished; the one shadowing the transaction itself and its influence in heaven; while the other expressed, in significant emblem, its full efficacy to purge the conscience from all guilt, and to remove the transgressions of all that make application for its benefit, so that they shall not be remembered in the way of judgment any more for ever. The apostle Paul dwells upon this subject in his epistle to the Hebrews; representing the whole priestly office and the whole sacrificial system as typical of the mystery of redemption, but more particularly directing attention to the great service of the high-priest on the day of atonement, as

that which comprehended in itself, more especially, in ..t *
perfect and expressive image. "Christ being come," he tells
us, "a High-Priest of good things to come, by a greater and
more perfect tabernacle, not made with hands, that is to say.
not of this building; neither by the blood of goats and calves
but by his own blood, he entered in once into the holy place,
having obtained eternal redemption for us. For Christ," he
adds in another place, " is not entered into the holy places made
with hands, which are the figures of the true ; but into heaven
itself, now to appear in the presence of God for us : nor yet
that he should offer himself often, as the high-priest entereth
into the holy place every year with blood of others; for then
must he often have suffered since the foundation of the world :
but now once, in the end of the world, hath he appeared, to
put away sin by the sacrifice of himself." (Heb. ix. 11, 12,
24—26.)

SECTION VI.

SACRED YEARS.

THE SABBATIC YEAR. Still more to impress the minds of
his people with the great truth, that their time, as well as
their property, was not their own; and to carry out still more
completely the ceremonial scheme, God set apart every *seventh
year*, also, in addition to the *days* that have been already
noticed, to be, in some measure, sacred and free from the
labours of other years. It was not required, indeed, that it
should be all kept after the manner of a Sabbath, or solemn
festival, by a continual attendance upon religious duties. We
hear of no extraordinary public sacrifices appointed for it, and
the people seem to have been left to occupy the time in a
worldly or religious way, according to their own choice, about
as much as in ordinary years. The land, however, enjoyed a
complete rest: the fields were not allowed to be tilled, nor the
vineyards to be dressed; and whatever they yielded without
culture, was required to be regarded as common, for all to
make use of as they needed, without being reaped or gathered.
(Lev. xxv. 2—7, Ex. xxiii. 11.) The inquiry might naturally
suggest itself, how the nation could be secure from the distress
of poverty and famine, in the observance of such an institution;
but God himself silenced fear on this account: " If ye shall
say, What shall we eat the seventh year? behold, we shall not
sow, nor gather in our increase: Then I will command my

essing upon you in the sixth year, and it shall bring forth fruit for three years. And ye shall sow the eighth year, and eat yet of old fruit, until the ninth year." (Lev. xxv. 20—22.) As no produce was gathered from the soil, it was made a law, also, that no debts should be collected during the Sabbatical year; and it was, at the same time, solemnly enjoined, that no person should be moved by this consideration, to refuse lending to such as were in want, when it was at hand. The year was called, on this account, *the year of release.* Some have entertained the opinion, that this *release* required not merely, that debts should be allowed to *lie over*, without being exacted, till the eighth year, but that they should be altogether *cancelled* and never again called for: which, however, as it seems not easy in itself to be received, so it cannot be positively established from the language of the law. (Deut. xv. 1—11.) The Sabbatical year, we must believe, had its beginning with Tishri, the first month of the civil year, when the produce of the land was all gathered in, and before the time of sowing for another crop.

During the feast of tabernacles this year, the whole law was to be publicly read over at the Sanctuary. How important such a regulation was, when copies of the sacred writings were, of necessity, extremely scarce, needs not to be observed. (Deut. xxxi. 10—13.)

THE YEAR OF JUBILEE. There was another year of peculiar and extraordinary character, appointed to be observed, in the Jewish economy. Its return was still at the end of every seventh sabbatical year, that is, only once in 50 years. The law directed that it should commence on the great day of atonement, and that it should then be ushered in with the sounding of trumpets, through all the land.

This *Year of Jubilee,* as it was called, was to be, in all respects, as much as the common sabbatical years, a year of rest to the land, in which there might be neither seed-time, harvest, or vintage. It enjoyed, however, additional distinctions, exclusively its own. It was a *year of restitution,* when the whole state of society was to be, in some measure, re-organized, and brought back, as far as possible, to its original posture. It was ordained, that on every return of the Jubilee, all servants of Hebrew origin should obtain their freedom; and that inheritances, which had been sold or given up, in the way of mortgage or pledge for debts, and not previously redeemed, should return, all over the land, to the families to which they at first belonged. A particular account of these regulations, and of the manner in which they were to be understood and regarded, as well as of the institution of the year of Jubilee in general, is found in the 25th chapter of Leviticus.

We may well conceive, that the return of the Jubilee would be hailed through the land, not merely with the sound of trumpets, but with much gladness of heart and general manifestation of joy. It commenced, we may suppose, on the evening of the day of atonement, after its great solemnities were over; and so brought with it, as it were, a proclamation of peace and forgiveness, in answer to the deep humiliation, and the expiation so awful, with which the season had been distinguished. And truly, an interesting spectacle it must have been, and such as might well excite the most pleasant emotions, even in those who had no direct personal concern in the privileges of the time, to behold the gladsome change that was all at once accomplished throughout the nation; when the bond and the poor found themselves restored to freedom and a home; when the unfortunate were raised from distress, and brought back, each to his ancient patrimony and the dwelling-place of his fathers; when the obscure were seen suddenly rising into notice and importance; and when the whole face of the community, in short, was moulded by an almost instantaneous transformation into something of the same general semblance of order and arrangement that it carried fifty years before. The whole formed a lively emblem of the joyful blessings, holy and spiritual, that are brought to men by the gospel of Jesus Christ, wherever it is received by faith; and hence, accordingly, it is said of the Messiah in prophecy, with allusion to the proclamation of the Jubilee, that he should come *to preach* or *proclaim the acceptable year of the Lord.* (Isa. lxi. 2, Luke iv. 19.)

SECTION VII.

SACRED SEASONS OF HUMAN INSTITUTION.

To the sacred times which God himself appointed in the law, to be remembered and observed by his people, there were added, in later ages, some others, that rested, so far as we know any thing about them, on mere human authority. These remain to be briefly noticed.

ANNUAL FAST-DAYS. From the beginning, the Jewish nation was accustomed to observe public fasts on occasions of general calamity or danger; yet they had not, in the earlier periods of their history, any stated yearly day for fasting, ex cept the great day of atonement, that has been already considered. During the captivity, however, no less than *four* additional days of this sort were established, which continued to be observed in all subsequent times. These were, first, The fast of the fourth month, in memory of the capture of Jerusalem. (Jer. lii. 6, 7.) Second, The fast of the fifth month, in memory of the burning of the temple. (Jer. lii. 12, 13.) Third, The fast of the seventh month, in memory of the death of Gedaliah. (Jer. xli. 1—4.) Fourth, The fast of the tenth month, in memory of the commencement of the attack upon Jerusalem. (Jer. lii. 4.) Mention is made of all these in the book of Zechariah, vii. 3, 5, viii. 19.

THE FEAST OF PURIM. This festival, as we have the account of its origin in Esther ix. 17—32, was instituted to keep up the memory of that great deliverance which the Jews had from the wicked plot of Haman, in the days of Mordecai and Esther. It was celebrated about the middle of Adar, the twelfth, and regularly, the last month of the year, and had its name from the word *Pur*, which means a *lot*, because Haman had made use of the lot, in some way of idolatrous superstition, to determine the time when the massacre of the Jewish nation might be undertaken with the best success. (Esth. iii. 6, 7.) Two days, viz. the 14th and 15th of the month, were set apart to be observed; though it was usual to confine the principal celebration to the first, while it became the practice to keep a preparatory *fast* on the 13th, in memory of that in Shushan, on account of the decree that had gone forth for the destruction of the nation. The manner of celebrating this festival became, in time, very extravagant and licentious, and so it has continued to be down to this day. A principal service has been, to read over all the book of Esther, in the synagogues, and for all present, even the children, at every mention of the name of Haman, to clap with their hands, and stamp with their feet, and strike with mallets upon the benches, in token of deep abhorrence, crying out at the same time, *Let his memory perish!* The part of the time that is not required to be spent in the synagogue is occupied with all manner of festivity and mirth; which it has not been unusual to carry to a length not merely of ridiculous folly, but of downright intemperance, indecency, and outrageous revelry.

THE FEAST OF DEDICATION. This feast was instituted by Judas Maccabeus, not more than 164 years before Christ, to be a memorial of the new dedication of the Sanctuary, that then took place, after it had been profaned by that wicked wretch Antiochus Epiphanes This monarch had set himself, with all his might, to crush the Jewish religion, and introduce idola try in its room. He ordered the service of the temple to cease; Sabbaths and festivals to be entirely neglected; altars, groves, and chapels of idols to be set up through the land; sacrifices of swine and other unclean beasts to be offered, and incense to be burned at the doors of houses and in the streets; the whole law, in short, to be disregarded, and the whole Sanctuary polluted; thus requiring the people to "make their souls abominable, with all manner of uncleanness and profanation, to the end they might forget the law, and change all the ordinances." The Bible was hunted with diabolical persecution, to be torn in pieces and burned; and it was made an awful law, that whosoever was found with the sacred volume in his possession should be put to death. Among other things, the tyrant himself "entered proudly into the Sanctuary, and took away the golden altar, and the candlestick of light, and all the vessels thereof, and the table of shew-bread," with every precious vessel of the place, and carried them off into his own land; and afterwards he proceeded so far in his malice and profanity as to cause an image of Jupiter, the chief god of the heathen, to be placed in the temple, the Sanctuary itself, and its courts to be sprinkled with broth of swine's flesh, and a sow to be offered in sacrifice upon the altar of burnt-offering. At length, however, God gave his people deliverance. Judas Maccabeus prevailed over the oppressor in war; liberty was recovered to the land; the worship of God was rescued from restraint and persecution. Whereupon, immediately, it was held necessary to make a public purification of the Sanctuary, and to dedicate it anew, as having been stripped of its sanctity by the wickedness of the heathen. New holy vessels were made for its service, and a new altar also erected, in room of the old one, which it was thought best to pull down, lest it should be a reproach to them, because the heathen had defiled it. Then was it dedicated with appropriate sacrifices, and with songs, and with instruments of music, all the people rejoicing and praising the God of heaven. The solemnity was continued for eight days; and it was at the same time ordained, that a festival of so many days should afterwards be celebrated from year to year, with mirth and gladness, in commemoration of the interesting and joyful occasion. Ever since, accordingly, such a festival has been observed among the Jews. The dedication of the altar took place on the 25th of the ninth month, which answered in part to our December, and so the feast came to have its commencement ever after still with that day, falling of course in the season of winter. (John x. 22.) An account of the profanation of the temple may be found in the first chapter of the first book of the Maccabees; and in the latter part of the fourth chapter of the same is contained a history of the dedication now mentioned, and a notice withal, of the original institution of this festival to which it gave rise

CHAPTER VII.

MEMBERS OF THE JEWISH CHURCH.

HAVING considered the Sanctuary, its ministers, and its service, it now becomes us to take some notice of the church at large; to glance at the manner of its organization, and the principles that were appointed to unite and regulate its general system.

The Jewish church had its origin in the person of the patriarch Abraham. From the midst of a world rapidly falling into the deep darkness of idolatry, God called him to become the Head of a chosen people, with whom his truth and promises might be deposited and preserved, till the fulness of time should come for the introduction of the gospel; and entered, accordingly, into a gracious covenant with him, to be, not only his God, but the God also of his seed after him, and to take them for a peculiar nation, consecrated to himself, out of all the families of the earth. That it might be a continual sign and seal of this covenant, he instituted the rite of *circumcision*, and required it to be observed with the greatest care. It became, therefore, a perpetual regulation, never to be dispensed with, that every male child among the Jews, arrived at the age of eight days, whether born in an Israelitish house, or bought with money of any stranger, should be circumcised. (Gen. xvii. 7—14.) The covenant thus solemnly entered into with Abraham, was afterwards renewed with his posterity at Mount Sinai. (Ex. xix. 3—8.)

Every descendant of Abraham, then, was a member of the Jewish church: his *birth* made him heir to all its privileges, and subjected him to all its authority. He had no liberty ever to withdraw himself from the relation, if he might even have been inclined to do so. Hence, the whole nation was comprehended within the pale of the visible church, and was spoken of as a *holy people*—a *kingdom of priests*, in covenant with God, and interested in his special favour and care. The **whole** nation, accordingly, carried the sign of God's covenant **in** their flesh, and all its members were required to confirm their assent to it, year after year, by solemnly observing the passover supper, and the various other institutions which the law ordained; while they were, at the same time, considered equally partakers of all its earthly advantages, and equally concerned in all the public worship of the Sanctuary with which it was connected.

Still, there were certain qualifications of a ceremonial kind required, in order to a full and free participation, at any time, of the outward privileges of the church. When these were wanting, individuals were removed, in some measure, from the advantageous state which the rest of the community enjoyed in this respect: they were not at once excluded, indeed, from their relation to God, as members of his visible family, but only shut out for a time from the common liberty of its society; yet, if the disqualification under which they laboured was wilfully allowed to continue when it might be put out of the way, it caused them to be, in the end, entirely cut off from the sacred household and from the commonwealth of Israel, as transgressors of Jehovah's covenant and despisers of its glorious promises. To have part in the outward privileges of the church, or to engage acceptably in its outward worship, it was necessary, not only that a man should first of all have submitted to the rite of circumcision, but that he should be, at the time itself, ceremonially *clean*. Hereby, in that shadowy and symbolical system, it was signified, that moral purity is the first thing required for drawing near, acceptably, to the Most High, in any spiritual service, and that without holiness no one can ever see the Lord in peace, or find admission into the happy family of heaven.

Ceremonial uncleanness was contracted in a variety of ways, as may be seen by reading the 11th, 12th, 13th, 14th, and 15th chapters of Leviticus. Its necessary duration also varied in different cases; in some instances, continuing only till sunset; in others, for a whole week; and in a few others for a still longer period. While it lasted, it was attended with considerable inconvenience; for it not only shut out the subject of it from the privileges of the Sanctuary, but cut him off, at the same time, from all free intercourse with his friends and neighbours; since, for any other person to touch one that was thus defiled, was to make himself in like manner unclean; and he was bound, therefore, to let his condition be known, and to keep clear of his acquaintances. The most distressing of all defilements was that which the leprosy gave rise to. We have been called to notice already how the unhappy victim of this disease, in addition to all the sufferings directly occasioned by his malady, was required to separate himself from society altogether, and to live a solitary outcast in the midst of the community, (unless he found some like himself, with whom to associate in melancholy fellowship,) all the days that his plague lasted upon him.

Uncleanness, however, though in most cases made *necessary* only for a limited and short period, did not, in any case, pass away of itself, without some ceremony of purification, undergone by the persons on whom it rested. In most cases, all that was required of such a person was to bathe his body and wash his clothes in water. In other instances, when the degree of defilement was considered to be greater, a more solemn purification was demanded. Thus, when one had become unclean by the touch of a dead body, or a sepulchre, or a single bone of any dead person, in which case the defilement could not be removed till a week was past, it was necessary that he should get some person that was clean to sprinkle him, on the third and seventh days, by means of a bunch of hyssop, with the sacred *water of separation;* after which, on the last day, he bathed and washed his clothes, as in ordinary cases, and so became clean at evening. (Num. xix. 11—22.) The purification of persons recovered from the leprosy was accomplished with a form of rites altogether peculiar, of which we have an account in the 14th chapter of Leviticus.

The water of separation, just mentioned, was pure fresh water, mixed in a vessel with some of the ashes of a red heifer, burned with particular solemnity for the purpose. An account of the singular manner in which it was burned may be found in the first part of the 19th chapter of Numbers. A supply of these ashes was always kept on hand, for the use of such as might need them for purification; for still, as the quantity furnished by one victim came near to be exhausted, an additional stock was provided, by selecting a new one and destroying it in the appointed way. As very little of the ashes was needed to make the water of separation in any case, the quantity supplied by one heifer lasted a great number of years; so that, according to the Jews, there were only eight burned for the purpose during the whole time of the second temple. They tell us also, that the one burned in the time of Moses, without any other, served the people as long as till the captivity; but in this, their tradition is not entitled to any credit. As the service of burning the red heifer returned so seldom, it naturally came to be regarded as a solemnity of great interest; and, in later times, accordingly, was burned with no small share of the general encumbrance of unmeaning and superstitious ceremonies, which tradition then contrived to hang, with so much industry and zeal, about the whole ancient system of worship. In the first place, the most scrupulous care was employed in making choice of the animal; for it was held, that if only two hairs could be found upon it of white or black colour, it could not be fit for this use. Then the priest who was to burn it was shut up seven days beforehand, lest he might suffer some defilement by touching a grave or a dead body: for the purpose of preventing which, also, when he passed with a company of elders and other priests, from the temple to the place of killing the victim, a great causeway was raised upon arches, clear across the valley of Kidron, from the eastern gate of the outer court, in such a way that no grave could possibly hide in secret under the ground, and so pollute the procession, as it moved over it to the spot of its destination. This spot, which was arched underneath in like manner for the same purpose, was on the Mount of Olives, directly over against the front of the temple. When the company arrived there with the heifer, the person who had the principal service to perform was required to bathe himself in a chamber erected there for the purpose; while the other priests made ready the wood, tied the animal, and laid it upon the pile. The person just mentioned then came forward, applied the instrument of death to its throat with his right hand, received the blood into a vessel in his left, and immediately sprinkled it, with solemn silence, seven times, toward the front of the Sanctuary. The next thing was to set fire to the pile, and to throw into it, as it was burning, some cedar wood, some hyssop, and some scarlet wool; first showing each of the articles, however, to the company around, and saying of it three times over in succession, *This is cedar wood, or hyssop, or scarlet wool*, as the case might be; to which, in each case, they with great gravity replied, *Well, well, well*. After the burning was finished, the ashes were carefully collected, pounded, sifted, and laid up for use.

The red heifer, though not presented directly at the altar, had in it, notwithstanding, the nature of an offering for sin; as is manifest from the use that was required to be made of its blood, and from the fact that, like the bodies of those beasts whose blood was carried into the sanctuary, it polluted those who were concerned with the burning of it, as being itself a polluted thing, by reason of the guilt of the people that was supposed to be laid upon it. *Its ashes*, therefore, had a purifying efficacy, on the same principle that made *blood* to be regarded, in other cases, as making atonement for the soul. They comprehended, as it were, the essential virtues of the *expiatory death*, by which they had been procured; and, when applied to the unclean, were designed to signify, properly, an application of the merit of that death, as having, in its nature, power to cleanse them from defilement. Thus the whole institution pointed, with peculiar emphasis, to the death of Jesus Christ, and expressively represented its availing virtue to purge away the guilt of all sin from the conscience, as well as to procure complete deliverance from its pollution and power. The Apostle Paul, accordingly, teaches us, that its shadowy and symbolical efficacy, like that of the sin-offerings presented on the great day of atonement, found the actual reality, of which it was the figure, only in the blood of Calvary: for as the sprinkling of the water of separation upon such as were defiled rendered them ceremonially clean, and so fitted them to come before God in the solemn service of the sanctuary, from which they had been shut out; so this blood, wherever its virtue is applied, cleanses the soul from real guilt, and qualifies it to approach the living God, in an acceptable manner, with a service altogether spiritual, for which, until thus purged, it is found totally unfit, and can have no liberty whatever. "If the blood of bulls and of goats," the apostle argues, "and *the ashes of a heifer sprinkling the unclean*, sanctifieth to the purifying of the flesh, how much more shall the blood of Christ, who, through the eternal Spirit, offered himself without spot to God, *purge your conscience from dead works to serve the living God?*"

PROSELYTES.

To be descended regularly from Abraham, the father of the chosen race, was accounted a distinction of the highest sort, and such as elevated every person to whom it belonged far above all others of the human family. (John viii. 33—59, 2 Cor. xi. 22, Phil. iii. 5.) Still, the Gentiles, who were destitute of this advantage, were not utterly shut out from the possibility of becoming united with the Jewish church, and obtaining a part in its sacred privileges. By renouncing idolatry and every false religion, and consenting to embrace the faith and follow the worship of Israel, they might find admission into the holy family, and become adopted, with all their posterity, into the same highly favoured state that its other members enjoyed in virtue of their descent from its original head. Such as at any time made use of the opportunity thus afforded were called *proselytes*.

There were some Gentiles who became convinced that the Jewish religion was true, and renounced all idolatry for the wor ship of the one living and true God of the Bible, and yet were not willing to take upon themselves the rite of circumcision. These were not, of course, received as full members of the Israelitish church, and might not have part in its more important privileges; still they were regarded with considerable favour, and were spoken of as pious persons. They were accustomed to frequent the synagogues in company with circumcised Israelites, and used often to visit the temple also; they were not *bound*, of course, to bring their sacrifices there, when they wished to offer any; but as they were allowed to do so, they generally embraced the privilege, and had them presented at the altar of the sanctuary. They were not suffered, however, to offer sacrifices there of any other sort than *burnt-offerings;* and it scarce needs to be mentioned, that they could not accompany their victims into the court where the altar stood, but were under the necessity of having them presented altogether through the priests. This class of persons, we are told, were denominated *Proselytes of the Gate.*

Such as came fully into the Jewish commonwealth and church, by submitting to the rite of circumcision, and taking upon themselves the obligation of the whole ceremonial law, were called *Proselytes of righteousness.* These were completely grafted into the Israelitish stock, and mingled with the original branches, in the full and lasting participation of all its advantages. In latter times, the Jews, especially the Pharisees, exerted themselves with much zeal to bring other persons to embrace their religion; though, according to the declaration of our Saviour, it was to no good purpose.

CHAPTER VIII.

SYNAGOGUES.

SACRIFICES could be offered nowhere else than at the sanctuary, the great centre of the whole Ceremonial Service; but other exercises of religious worship might be performed in any place. The law, however, did not prescribe any other manner of public worship than that of the tabernacle and temple, and we are not informed that any regular meetings of the people for social prayer and praise, and for the purpose of receiving religious instruction, were in use, at any time, before the captivity. There were schools of the prophets, indeed, where young men were trained up with every advantage of this sort, for the

Jewish Synagogue. p. 403.

service of God; and it was not uncommon, it seems, for persons that desired such a benefit, to betake themselves, on Sabbaths and new moons, to places where prophets resided, that they might be instructed from their lips; but all this brought only a small portion of the community under the direct influence of such religious privileges, and fell far short of any thing like a general system of regular meetings through the nation, of the sort that has been mentioned. Some have been confident that such a system of regular weekly social worship was actually in use, and have pretended to bring evidence for their opinion from the Bible; but the evidence they produce is not satisfactory, and we are left at last to a mere conjecture, in support of the notion; that is, we find it, whether it be false or true, without historical notice. But of the state of things in this respect, under the second temple, we are not thus ignorant. After the captivity, social meetings, held weekly, for religious worship, became common all over the land. They were styled *Synagogues*.

Of the origin of synagogues, we have in history no account. They seem, however, to have come into use, if not at an earlier period, at least immediately after the nation returned from its captivity. One opinion on the subject is, that Ezra, acting under the direction of God, caused them to be established for the purpose of securing among the people generally a familiar acquaintance with the law, thus guarding them in the most effectual manner against the evil of idolatry; for Ezra had a commission from Heaven to restore the Jewish church, and re-organize its worship, after the confusion into which it had been thrown by the captivity, so that he has always been regarded by the Jews as another Moses, and styled, accordingly, *The second Founder of the Law*. There can be no doubt that the institution, in whatever way it originated, was admirably adapted to answer the end that has been mentioned, and that it did actually operate with the most salutary influence, in this way, during all the period of the second temple.

The word *Synagogue* means, properly, a *meeting* or *congregation*; it came naturally, however, to be used also as the name of the *place* or *house* where a congregation was wont to assemble. At first, synagogue-meetings appear to have been held either in the open air or in private houses; but after some time, the idea of erecting buildings of a public kind, expressly for such use, was conceived and carried into practice. These soon rose wherever, in any country, a settlement of Jews was found, as well as over all their own land. Originally, we are told, it was usual to erect them in fields, some distance off from other houses; but afterwards they were put up in cities; and it was required that they should always stand in the highest places, and should exceed in height all the houses about them. To build a synagogue was considered a deed of piety, greatly acceptable in the eye of God, as to build a church has often been esteemed in Christian countries. Hence it is not to be wondered at, that they were exceedingly multiplied in some places, far more than the necessity of the people called for. Jewish tradition assures us that there were no less than *four hundred and eighty* of them in the single city of Jerusalem: a lying statement, we may well suppose; but such as in its exaggeration leaves no room to doubt that the number must have been very great. Any person, a Gentile as well as a Jew, might build a synagogue; for the holiness of the place was supposed to result altogether from its consecration, after it was put up, without being affected at all by any previous circumstances. (Luke vii. 4, 5.) This consecration was merely by prayer, with very little ceremony or formality. We are told by Jewish tradition, that the general form of synagogues was always the same. They consisted, in some measure, of two parts: one of which was called *the temple*, and was designed to have some correspondence with the Most Holy Place of the Sanctuary, being, like it, retired in the back part of the building, and furnished also with an *ark* or chest, made after the model of the ark of the covenant, in which was kept a copy of the law for the service of the place; the other, which occupied the principal body of the house, was appropriated for the use of the people, when they assembled for worship, and was provided accordingly, with ranges of seats or pews, for their accommodation. Before the place where the ark was kept, and toward the middle of the synagogue, was erected a low pulpit or platform, with a desk in front, where the law was read and expounded before the congregation. A few seats were placed behind this pulpit, on which those that were called *elders* were accustomed to sit, with their backs turned toward the ark, and their faces directed toward the rest of the people, who were all arranged round about in front of the reader, facing the end of the building in which the sacred chest of the law had its retreat. Those seats which were farthest up toward the pulpit, and the place where the ark was deposited, particularly the seats on which the elders sat, seem to have been the *chief seats* of the synagogue, which it was considered honourable to occupy, and which, we are told, the hypocritical Pharisees were accustomed so much to covet on that account. (Matt. xxiii. 6.) The women, it is said, did not sit among the men, but in a sort of balcony or gallery that was raised along one side, from which they could see into the body of the house, and hear all the service of the place without being themselves much exposed to view There is a different plan of building synagogues in use, at the present day, in the East, more completely accommodated to the manner of the ancient temple at Jerusalem. They are made to consist of a *court* with *porches* round about; a *chapel* in the middle of it, (answering to the Sanctuary in the Court of the Israelites,) which is supported simply upon four columns, and has within it the desk on which the law is spread out and read; and a covered *hall* near this last, furnished with seats, for the people to occupy when the weather happens to be stormy or cold. It has been imagined by some, that the ancient synagogues were constructed upon this plan; but since the New Testament leaves us without any hint to determine the matter, it becomes us rather to acquiesce in the general tradition upon the subject, and to adopt as correct the representation already given. It was a rule, we are told, that no place might have a synagogue erected in it, unless it contained at least as many as ten persons of some learning and respectability, who were in such easy worldly circumstances that they could always have leisure to take care of its affairs and devote some attention to the study of the law. A congregation, it was supposed, might not consist of any number smaller than this; though there was no limit, other than convenience, to the greatness it might have; and in this way, accordingly, it was secured, that so many, at least, should be found in every assembly gathered for religious worship: for it was the duty of the ten men selected for the purpose to take care that their synagogue should never suffer a defect in its service in this respect. These select men seem always to have sustained the dignity of *elders*, (which title had respect not so much to their *age* as to their *gravity* and authority,) and to have had their place, accordingly, on the seats that were fixed behind the pulpit. There is another opinion, however, respecting these ten men of leisure, as they were called, not without considerable reason in its favour, which represents them to have been only common persons *hired* to be always present at the synagogue, when worship was to be performed, that there might be a certainty of having, at all times, a sufficient congregation for the purpose. It is a Jewish saying, that *the Divine Majesty will not dwell among less than ten*, that is, that God will not meet graciously with a less number assembled for public worship; and he is represented as turning away in anger from a synagogue that should happen to be found without that complement: but our Saviour inculcate a very different doctrine, for the encouragement of the pious in every age: "If two of you shall agree on earth as touching any thing that they shall ask, it shall be done for them of my Father which is in heaven: for where *two* or *three* are gathered together in my name, there am I in the midst of them." (Matt. xviii. 19, 20.)

Every synagogue had its *officers* appointed to manage its government and conduct its religious services. The supreme direction of its affairs was committed to the care of a *council of elders*, and one styled *the ruler of the synagogue*, who sustained among them the place of a president. These elders were persons of respectable and influential character in society, and such as had more than ordinary acquaintance with the law, so as to be qualified to take part with their president, and assist him with their counsel, in the government of the congregation. It seems, that, on account of their authority in this way, *they* also, at times, were called *rulers of the synagogue*, though the title properly belonged only to the officer just mentioned, who was placed at their head. (Acts xiii. 15.)—Then, besides its presiding ruler and its company of elders, each synagogue had its *deacons*, or collectors of alms, whose business it was to receive the charitable contributions of the congregation from week to week, and distribute them among the poor, as they might happen to be found in need of such assistance. It was usual, we are told, to have always three persons appointed to manage this business; who, although they acquired some considerable authority from the nature of their charge, were yet completely under the control of the superior officers just noticed, and could never dispose of the alms that were put into their hands in any way which these might refuse to sanction with their approbation.—There were also certain *ministers*, or attendants, of a still more subordinate character, who had particular employment assigned to them connected with the general care of the synagogue and its service; one, especially, whose business it was to take the book of the law out of the chest in which it was kept, and give it to the person who was called upon to read, and afterwards to receive it from him again and restore it to its place; who was intrusted, moreover, as it seems, with the charge of having the house in order for worship, took care that it should be swept, when necessary, and kept clean, and still opened the doors and closed them before and after the times of meeting. (Luke iv. 20.)

It was the duty of the ruler of the synagogue to preside in ll its meetings, and to superintend and direct the whole of its

worship. It was not considered necessary, however, that he
should himself, or that some one of the elders associated with
him, should always take the lead personally in every religious
exercise; though the whole right of doing this was vested
altogether in their body; and the exercise of it, accordingly,
as well as its responsibility, seemed naturally to devolve upon
them alone : it was held to be sufficient, notwithstanding, if it
proceeded merely under their immediate direction and oversight; so that other persons might, by their order or permission, perform such service with perfect propriety; and
hence it was actually the custom, to have it performed, to a
considerable extent, in this way altogether. Thus in every
meeting, different individuals, who had nothing to do with the
direction and government of the synagogue, used to take part
in conducting its public exercises of worship, under the eye
of the president and elders. One of these exercises was to
lead in the prayers of the congregation : another, to read a
particular portion of the Scriptures; another, to address the
people. The person who performed the first mentioned service used to be denominated *the angel of the synagogue*, that
is, its *delegate*, or *representative*, appointed to address the throne
of God in the name, and on the behalf, of the whole assembly.
It was usual to have some one appointed to officiate in this
character with regular and stated duty; and it was a maxim
at the same time, that the individual selected for the purpose
should be one of the greatest dignity and worth, eminent above
most others in the congregation for wisdom and virtue, and, if
possible, clothed with the venerable solemnity of age and the
experience of a multitude of days. In some cases, however,
the angel of the synagogue was constituted merely for a single
occasion, and the person chosen to officiate sustained the character no longer than the particular service lasted which he
was called upon to perform. The other exercises that have
been mentioned were not appropriated, in any case, as stated
services, to any particular individuals to the exclusion of others;
but different persons were in the habit of officiating on different
occasions, as they were invited to come forward by the president, either to read or to speak, or as they received his approbation when they presented themselves of their own accord for
the purpose, and he found no reason to deny them the liberty.
The privilege of addressing the people, however, was considered much more important than that of reading, and was,
accordingly, allowed with much less freedom : it was, in fact,
as it appears, confined in a considerable measure to those who
had the supreme direction, the president either exercising the

right himself, or yielding place only to some one of the company of elders of which he was the head; and, so far as it was not thus confined, (for it was still not uncommon to allow it to persons who held no office in the Synagogue,) it seems to have been a principle that no one should be suffered to teach in this way who was not in a more than ordinary degree versed in the knowledge of the law, and so entitled to rank among the *wise men*, as such used to be styled, by way of distinction from the common unlettered multitude.

As those who ruled the synagogue and superintended its regular service were called *presbyters* or *elders*, so they were denominated, (especially, as it would seem, the president and such of the others as were accustomed to take part in *teaching*,) by a figure familiar to the east, *pastors* or *shepherds;* and had the title also of *bishops*, or, to use a different word of the same meaning, *overseers*, in reference to the watchful care and authority which it was their duty to employ in the government of the congregation for its general welfare and the right order of its public worship.

We find no express mention in the New Testament of public worship in the synagogues, on any other day of the week than the Sabbath. Jewish tradition, however, asserts that it was common anciently, as well as in more modern times, to have it regularly celebrated also on the second and fifth days, (our Monday and Thursday,) and on all festival days besides, such as new moon, &c. We are told too, that it was usual to assemble on these days as many as three several times, viz. in the morning, in the afternoon, and at night: but on the week days the service was short, consisting chiefly of prayers, with the reading of only a small portion of the Scriptures; and on the Sabbath, the principal service was that of the morning, when there was a full reading of Scripture, and an address made to the congregation; while the afternoon and evening meetings were occupied more particularly with prayers and singing. Prayer, presented in public worship, was held to be more acceptable than prayer offered up in private; so that as many as made any pretensions to piety were still disposed to resort to the synagogues, on its meeting-days, for the performance of their morning and evening devotions, just as it was customary for serious persons who lived near the temple to go up to its courts at the times of the daily sacrifices. And it appears, that the synagogue was considered an advantageous place for individuals to present their stated prayers even on days when there was no public service to be attended; as we read that the Pharisees, to make an ostentatious show of religion loved to repeat their private prayers standing in these churches; which at other times they did not scruple to do even in the most public places of the streets, pretending that when the seasons for this duty arrived, their consciences would not allow them to neglect it a moment, wherever they might be found, but all, in fact, *to be seen of men*, and to obtain the praise of uncommon godliness among the multitude of the world. (Matt. vi. 5.)

When the congregation was collected together for worship on the morning of the Sabbath, the angel of the synagogue began the services of the occasion with an ascription of glory to God, and a regular address of prayer toward his holy throne. Then the portion of the *law* which belonged to that day was read, and the reading of it closed with another doxology chanted to the praise of the Most High; after which followed the reading of the appointed portion from the prophets. Next came the address to the people, and afterwards another prayer, which concluded the exercises of the meeting. Such appears to have been the general order observed in the ancient service of the synagogue, as well as it can be gathered from the occasional hints of the New Testament compared with the manifold traditions of the Jews; which, it is to be presumed, comprehend much correct information relative to the whole original manner of the institution, though it be so confounded with rubbish derived from more modern usage, as to be in no small degree difficult to be ascertained.

At the close of the prayers the whole congregation were accustomed to say, *Amen*, in token of their concurrence with him that uttered them, in the feelings of thankfulness or supplication which they expressed. So did they respond, also, when the priest pronounced the solemn *benediction*, according to the form in Num. vi. 24—26. It was usual, we are told, when this was to be pronounced, for all the priests that were in the house, if there happened to be more than one, to take their station on the pulpit, and repeat it after the manner that was practised in the daily service of the Sanctuary. If there was no priest present, the angel of the synagogue used to repeat it, still introducing it in some such way as this: *Our God and the God of our fathers bless us now with that three-fold benediction appointed in the law to be pronounced by the sons of Aaron, according as it is said,* "The Lord bless thee, &c." The people, however, were instructed to withhold in such a case their customary response of Amen. So goes the tradition; and it adds that this pronouncing of the benediction was toward the end of the principal prayer, though not altogether at the close of it.

It was the custom to have the whole law, that is, the five books of Moses, read over in the synagogues, every year. Hence, for the sake of convenience and certainty, it was all divided into fifty-four sections, as nearly equal in length as they could be made without serious injury to the sense, which were appointed to be read in regular succession, one every week, till the whole was gone over. It was thought proper to have as many as fifty-four, because the longest years consisted of that number of weeks, and it was desired to leave no Sabbath in such a case without its particular portion; but as the common years were made up of fewer weeks, they used in the course of these to join certain shorter sections, so as to make one out of two, in order to bring the reading regularly out with the end of year; for it was held absolutely necessary to have the whole read over without any omission, before it was commenced in course again, as it still was on the first Sabbath after the feast of tabernacles. The copy of the law used for this purpose, which, like all books of ancient time, was in the form of a roll, was written with great care, and generally with much elegance. It was not usual, we are told, for a single person to read over the whole section for any day, in the synagogue, but several individuals, according to the Jewish representation exactly *seven*, were called upon to read in succession; whence it became the practice to have each of the sections divided again into several smaller portions for their accommodation. Any male person, who was not a servant, a tatterdemalion, or a fool, and was able to read with ease and distinct utterance, might be invited to bear a part in the exercise: only it was the custom to call upon some of the more honourable individuals present in the congregation, to take the lead in reading the first two or three portions of the section, particularly it was thought proper to have the first portion read by a *priest*, if any was in the house, and the second by a *Levite*. It is not clear, however, that this particular manner, though found prevailing at a later period, was all observed in this part of the synagogue service in the time of our Saviour.

The reading of the *prophets*, which followed the reading of the *law*, was not practised in the synagogues from their first institution, but had the origin of its use in the time of Antiochus Epiphanes. We have already, not long since, had occasion to mention the persecution which that wicked monster waged against the worship and the truth of the God of Israel. The rolls of the sacred law of Moses, whenever they could be

BIBLICAL ANTIQUITIES. 409

discovered, were destroyed, and the punishment of death was denounced against every individual with whom a copy of it should be found. In this predicament, those of the nation who still adhered to the religion of their fathers were led to make choice of particular portions out of some of the other books of Scripture, (which, because they had not been in common use, like the books of Moses, in the public worship of the people, had not fallen under the same tyrannic condemnation,) and substitute them in room of the ordinary lessons from the law, in the service of the synagogue. In this way a new set of lessons was introduced, which ever afterwards continued in use; for although when the storm of that persecution had rolled away, the original reading of the law was restored as it had been in the beginning, it was still thought proper not to lay aside these other portions of Scripture, but to have them read also, in regular order as before, so that it became a perpetual rule to have TWO lessons, one out of the law, and one from the prophets, repeated in this way every Sabbath. The Jews reckoned, in that class of their sacred books which they denominated *the prophets*, not only such as are actually prophetical in their character, but the chief of those also which are merely historical, such as *Joshua*, *Judges*, *Samuel*, *Kings*, *and Chronicles:* whence the second series of lessons comprehended portions from these last, as well as from *Isaiah*, *Jeremiah*, *Ezekiel*, &c.: and these were not connected in any sort of order with each other, but had been selected independently, just as they were thought to have some particular correspondence with the sections of the law, to which they answered in the order of their course. As they were quite short, in comparison with the other lessons, they were not divided in the same way for several readers, but each used to be read altogether by a single person.

As the Jews, after the captivity, made use of a language materially different from that of their ancestors, in which their sacred books were written, it became necessary still to have the lessons of the synagogue *interpreted*, as they were read, into the common tongue. It seems that even in the time of Ezra, immediately on the return of the nation to their own country, something of this sort was found necessary, when that holy man caused the law to be publicly read in the hearing of the people. (Neh. viii. 8.) In later times, however, especially from the age of the Maccabees, it became still more needful, and was secured, as it appears, with more systematic arrangement. There is reason to believe, that the idea of distributing the Scriptures into *verses* was conceived, and put into practice, originally, for the sake of convenience and order in the interpretation of the synagogue lessons. As it was necessary for the reader to pause every few moments, till the interpreter beside him turned what he read into the common tongue, it was natural to think of breaking the whole into little portions of suitable length, so that he might not be at a loss where to stop, or so liable to interrupt and confound the sense by injudicious division, as he must have been, if left in every case to cut it up according to his own pleasure: and when verses were thus introduced into the sacred rolls of the synagogue, it was not strange that they should, in time, become established throughout the whole Jewish Bible, as we have them handed down to our own time, and still everywhere in use. The ancient tradition of the Jews is, that these, as well as the fifty-four greater sections into which the law was divided, had their origin from no less a source than the inspired authority of Ezra himself. The *chapters* into which we find all the Bible now distributed, it may be here remarked, were invented more than 1200 years after the time of our Saviour, and the *verses* of the New Testament at a period considerably later still. Nor was it again, until some time after the whole Bible was thus divided and sub-divided, that the plan of separating the verses into distinct little paragraphs, as they are now found in our common copies of the sacred volume, came into practice; the original plan having been, to let them still follow each other, like common sentences in other writings, in regular order according to the sense, (as all Hebrew Bibles are still printed,) and to place all the figures, when the practice of numbering them was adopted, down along the margin, altogether out of the text itself. And truly it is much to be lamented, that God's holy word should ever have been allowed to be so cut up and broken into pieces, as it has now come to be in our common Bibles, by having the chapters and verses all completely separated throughout; as it the Spirit that inspired it had given it for use in that style—whereas the whole has been the contrivance of man, and tends only to darken the meaning of the sacred page from beginning to end.

Much of our Saviour's teaching was performed in the synagogues. We are told that "he went about all the cities and villages, teaching *in their synagogues*, and preaching the gospel of the kingdom." It appears, that before he entered upon his public ministry, while he lived as a common man in the town of Nazareth, he regularly attended the synagogue of the place, as one of its members, and used often to bear part as a reader in its stated services: and we find him, directly after he had assumed his official character, clothed with the power of the Holy Ghost, addressing the same congregation as a *preacher;* in which capacity he continued afterwards to give instruction in these Jewish churches all over Galilee, and in other parts of Judea, wherever he came. (Luke iv. 14—44.) As it is not to be supposed that he taught in this way, in any case, without the consent of the rulers of the synagogues, if not by their express invitation, it has seemed strange to some, that a person so much disliked as he was, by the religious leaders of his country, should have been suffered, to such an extent, to enjoy this great advantage for the dissemination of his doctrine among the people: but we are to remember, that he was not only a Jew himself, of fair and unblemished character, and strictly attentive to all the requirements of the law, but a man at the same time of acknowledged wisdom and deep skill in the knowledge of religion, who had full claim to the title of *Rabbi* or *Doctor;* and that he was a prophet withal, "mighty in deed and word before God, and all the people," held in honour and *glorified* by the general multitude, notwithstanding the humble style in which he lived, and the weight of reproach that was flung upon him by the great and the learned of the land: so that there was no reason or room whatever to hinder him from speaking in the synagogues; and those who had the direction of them, even if they had been otherwise disposed in their own hearts, could not refuse to allow the *privilege*, where the *right* was so universally acknowledged, out of the respect which they were constrained to exercise toward popular sentiment. The apostles, who were also endowed with the highest ability to teach, made use of the same opportunity for preaching to the people; and for a time, the Gospel uttered its loudest sound, week after week, from the pulpit of the synagogue: but it soon became too offensive to Jewish prejudice and pride to be quietly endured, and was accordingly expelled, to seek for itself a separate accommodation, in some different quarter. We have on record a full exhortation delivered on one occasion by Paul in the synagogue of Antioch, in Pisidia, which may give us some idea of the style in which he was accustomed to improve such opportunity for proclaiming the glorious doctrines of the cross. (Acts xiii. 14—41.)

It has been already intimated, that it was the business of those who had the supreme direction of the synagogue, not only to superintend and direct its public worship, but to exercise some sort of *government*, also, over the congregation that belonged to it. They were invested with authority to take cognisance of particular offences, and inflict *discipline* upon such of their society as were found guilty of them. They might employ, it seems, *private reproof* and *public rebuke*, and when the offence was held particularly grievous, or these milder means proved unavailing to bring the offender to repentance and amendment, the more terrible penalty of *excommunication* was at their disposal. This, we are told, might be either *partial*, in which case the person on whom it fell was cut off from the liberty of free intercourse with every person out of his own family for the space of thirty days, though he was still allowed to enter the synagogue, provided he came not within four cubits of anybody that was in it; and this was the LESSER EXCOMMUNICATION : or it was *complete*, excluding him from all the privileges of the synagogues entirely, and cutting him off, as a heathen man, from the worshipping assemblies of his people; and then it was denominated the GREATER EXCOMMUNICATION. The design of each was, to produce in the offender humiliation and sorrow for his conduct, and to bring about a reformation of temper and practice, in whatever respect he had been found guilty; whence it was common to inflict the heavier sentence only after the other had been made use of once or twice without accomplishing its purpose. It is not clear that these two sorts of excommunication were so distinctly recognised in the time of our Saviour as they came to be at a later period; but we have sufficient notice that the punishment itself was in general use, and, as it seems, under its most severe form, so as to be held in universal dread by the people. The malice of our Saviour's enemies took advantage of the power which was thus lodged in their hands, to hinder the influence of his doctrine : they agreed, and caused it to be understood, that if any man did confess that he was Christ, he should *be put out of the synagogue;* and many, we are told, even such as stood high in society, were deterred, by this consideration, from making such a confession, though they were convinced of his true character; for they loved the praise of men more than the praise of God. (John ix. 22, 34, xii. 42, 43.) The rulers of the synagogue had power to inflict, also, when it was deemed proper, the punishment of *scourging*, which, as we have already seen, might consist of any number of stripes under forty, but was in no case allowed to exceed that amount. Though full enough of severity and shame, it was not reckoned so disgraceful or terrible, by any means, as excommunication. Our Saviour warned his disciples to expect the one as well as the other. (Matt. x. 17, John xvi. 2.)

The Jewish synagogue is entitled to our careful attention

on its own account, as an institution full of wisdom in all its general arrangement, to which the true religion has been greatly indebted in ancient time: but it derives a still stronger claim upon our interests and regard, from the consideration that our Lord was pleased to have it used as a model or pattern in the original constitution of the *Christian Church;* so that both in its service and in its government, as all who have thoroughly examined the matter are agreed, the latter became a lively image of the former; and though in certain respects altered, of course, to a somewhat different aspect, was made to exhibit, on the whole, the general outline of its features, with clear and striking resemblance. Hence, a familiar acquaintance with the order and usages of the synagogue cannot fail to contribute much to a right understanding of what we find written in the New Testament relative to the manner of the early churches; and even the most general information on the subject sheds light, in this way, on such points, and is adapted to guard the mind from error, and help it to a fair conception of truth, when it attempts to interpret the language of revelation concerning them. As the synagogues had their presidents, their companies of elders, and their deacons, so had the churches; and as an evidence that the officers of one were considered as corresponding in every respect with those of the other, we find the *names*, as well as the general *powers*, with which they were distinguished in the Jewish congregations, faithfully appropriated to them in the assemblies of the Christians. (Acts vi. 1—6, xx. 17, 28, Phil. i. 1, 1 Tim. iii. 1—13, v. 17, Tit. i. 5, 7, Heb. xiii. 7, 17, 1 Pet. v. 1—4.) We find, too, as far as we have any information on the subject, the same *mode* of worship, in a great degree, with that of the synagogues, practised in the early churches; only those who had the direction of it, in the latter case, were not accustomed to employ other persons to take the lead in religious exercises, under their eye, and in their stead, in the same way as the rulers of the synagogues used to do; but in almost all cases exercised, themselves, in this respect, the right, for the use of which they were responsible. Thus there was no such a person in the churches as the *angel of the synagogue*, who, without any official character, was employed to go before the congregation in their prayers: the presiding elder, or *bishop*, himself, discharged this duty, as well as that of addressing the people with religious instruction; on which account, as it seems, he was sometimes distinguished by the appellation of *the angel of the church*, as we find the bishops of the seven churches of Asia severally denominated in the second and third chapters of the book of Revelation.* It may be remarked, also, that the Lord's Supper, which was regularly celebrated in the Christian churches every week, was an institution altogether peculiar to their worship, to which there was nothing that corresponded, in any way whatever, in the services of the synagogue.

CHAPTER IX.

RELIGIOUS SECTS.

The Jews, before the time of Christ, had become very extensively dispersed. Various causes had contributed to scatter them into every country of the civilized world, and they did not fail to make proselytes to their religion wherever they happened to reside. Thus God was pleased, in his sovereign wisdom, to prepare the way for the dissemination of the light of the gospel among all nations; for, not only was some knowledge of the first principles of all true religion diffused abroad by this means, but an opening was secured for the introduction of Christianity into every part of the Roman empire; since, in every important place to which the apostles came, they found those that professed the Jewish religion; and being Jews themselves, were always allowed at first to preach in the synagogues. These Jews, *dispersed among the Gentiles*, (John vii. 35,) carefully preserved themselves, wherever they dwelt, separate from other people, and still continued to cherish, with religious fidelity, their connection with the temple of Jerusalem; not only paying for its use the yearly half-shekel tax, as regularly as their brethren in Palestine, but making it their practice, also, to visit it personally, for the celebration of their great festivals, as often as circumstances would allow; or, when this could not be done, to send gifts by the hands of others. (Acts ii. 5—11.) In Egypt, indeed, where a great number of them resided, they had erected, about 150 years before the time of our Saviour, a

---

* "The only question respecting these *angels*, or *bishops of the churches*, is, whether, they were *pastors of single churches*, or *diocesan bishops*, who superintended all the churches within a certain district, and who were superior, by their office, to presbyters. We are not disposed to enter into a discussion of this controverted point. It manifestly does not relate to the vital principles of Christianity. Let every man investigate this subject for himself, and be fully persuaded in his own mind. And 'et not the sweet bond of brotherly love be severed by differences of opinion respecting points of external order and government."

new temple, exactly after the plan of that which was at Jerusalem, and established in it a separate system of public worship, under the care of Levites and regular priests of the family of Aaron., justifying the measure by a wrong interpretation of Isaiah xix. 18, 19; but still the superiority of the temple at Jerusalem was acknowledged, and the privilege of being connected with it, by no means relinquished: so that the Jews of Palestine, although somewhat dissatisfied at first, were content in the end to wink at the irregularity, and keep up still a friendly correspondence with this important branch of their church. Such Jews as spoke the Greek language were called *Hellenists*, or Grecians. These were found not only in Greece, through Asia Minor, and in Egypt, but in various other countries of the Roman empire, (so extensive was the use of that language become,) and even to some extent, as we learn from Acts vi. 1, in Palestine itself. (Acts ix. 29, xi. 20.) The whole church, though joined together in general harmony as a single body when its relation to the rest of the world was in question, was, nevertheless, not free from sectarian divisions and disputes. Three regular sects arose under the second temple, and continued to flourish till the destruction of the state, which differed widely in their religious sentiments, and charged one another with the most serious errors—which, in each several case, no doubt was done not without reason. The precise time when they took their rise is not known; but we are assured that they were all flourishing in the age of the Maccabees, 150 years before Christ, and must refer their origin, therefore, to a more remote period. We will now proceed to give some account of the principles and character of each of them in order, after which it will be proper to notice, also, the *Samaritans*, whose religious faith and worship, being derived altogether from the Jewish church, give them a natural claim to our attention in connection with the Jewish sects.

SECTION I.

THE PHARISEES.

The Pharisees borrowed their name from a word which means *to separate*, because they affected to be more strictly religious than other people, and to be distinguished from the common multitude, not only for their superior acquaintance with the Divine will, but also by reason of their peculiar interest in the friendship and favour of God.

They believed, we are told, in the existence of angels and in the resurrection of the dead. (Acts xxiii. 8, 9.) At the same time, we learn, that they held the doctrine of the *transmigration* of souls, so important in certain systems of heathen philosophy, which pretends that they pass after death into other bodies, and so, completely forgetful of all their former condition, continue to act a part upon the theatre of life, while the frames in which they once resided lie mouldering in the dust. They held it not, however, in the same broad extent with which it has been received in these systems: they did not admit that a human soul might ever pass into the body of a dumb animal, so as to put any person in danger of destroying his grandfather when he might venture to kill a calf or a chicken; and they did not allow that *all* souls were appointed to re-appear in successive lives after this fashion. It was considered a privilege, it seems, which only the comparatively righteous were allowed to enjoy, after being rewarded for a time in their separate state, while the spirits of the wicked were doomed to go away into everlasting torments. It has been supposed, that there is a reference to this sentiment in that question which was put to our Saviour by his disciples, concerning the blind man of whom we have an account in the ninth chapter of the Gospel of John —*Master, who did sin, this man or his parents, that he was born blind?* for it is not easy to understand how the *birth* of any one could be imagined to be thus unfortunate on account of his own sinfulness, unless under the idea of a previous life enjoyed by the soul in some other body. How this doctrine of transmigration was made to accommodate itself to the doctrine of the resurrection, which it has just been intimated was entertained by the same sect, is not by any means clear. Some have thought, that they were not really different doctrines at all, but that the resurrection which the Pharisees taught was nothing more than this transmigration itself, which brought such as were not notoriously wicked once more back among the inhabitants of the earth. Perhaps there was some diversity of sentiment among themselves in relation to the future fate of souls; in which case it might be that opinions which were never held actually at the same time in all their length and breadth by the same persons, but were only different notions of different classes belonging to the general body, have been improperly joined together as entering alike into the common faith of the whole sect.

The Pharisees have been charged with holding the doctrine of *fate*. But the doctrine of fate is, that all things take place by such a continual and inflexible necessity as leaves no room for the action of free causes, and makes it certain that an event will come to pass, as it does in the end come to pass, whether preparatory means, which in fact bring about its result, be put into previous operation or not—an absurd doctrine that carries its destruction in its own bosom; whereas, the great Jewish historian assures us that this sect, while they held the absolute and unalterable certainty of all things according to the eternal determination of God, yet insisted that the will of man was free, and that its influence in the great machinery of action which fills the world, mighty and constant as it is, proceeds with unrestrained and continual liberty. On this point, therefore, though these notions of theirs have seemed to some as incompatible as the two doctrines of transmigration and the resurrection, the Pharisees appear to have entertained, in the main, the same sentiment that is taught in the New Testament, and the only one which sound reason can approve. Admitting the self-evident proposition, that nothing can occur except in accordance with the plan of Infinite Wisdom, which stretches *design* through all the system of creation, and explores at one glance, from beginning to end, the whole order of its innumerable changes, they embraced at the same time the clear dictate of universal consciousness, that every man chooses or refuses in all he does according to his own pleasure, without any other constraint whatever, so as to be altogether accountable for every thing that is wrong; rightly concluding, that it is as easy for God to make events certain which depend on human will without interfering with its freedom, as it is for him to make certain those that depend on the operations of the material world without hindering their regular and natural order; since we must allow, unless we would represent man to be the empty plaything of chance, that there is as much *order* and *law* in the manner of all the changes that take place in his mind as there is in the endless succession of changes which follow each other as causes and effects in the system of mere matter, though the nature of these laws and the way of their action be different in either case, according to the different quality of the subjects, viz. *mind* and *matter*, to which they respectively belong.

A primary article in the creed of the Pharisees, and one that became a most frightful source of evil in their character and conduct was, that in addition to the *written* law found in the Bible, and for the purpose of explaining and completing its otherwise dark and defective system, God had given also an *oral* law, to be handed down, without being committed to writing, by mere tradition, from generation to generation; and that this, accordingly, had full as much obligation upon men as the other, and was to be deemed in fact even more important, inasmuch as without it the whole law, it was maintained, would have been without light, without order, and comparatively without use. It is needless to say, that the traditions of which this law consisted were altogether of human authority, and that they had not all taken their rise at once, but were introduced gradually from the usages and opinions of different ages, still gathering new accession to their mass as it rolled forward, till it acquired that monstrous size which it had in the end. It seems to have been only about a hundred years before the time of Christ that they came to be regarded as of such high importance, that the written law itself was less in honour and regard; and the neglect of them was counted impious as the worst infidelity. The traditionary law, however, claimed for itself, of course, a far more honourable history, and since it aspired to equal authority with the true law of God given of old to Moses in the wilderness, referred its origin to the same antiquity, and to the same high and holy source. The Lord, it pretended, had uttered it all in the ear of his servant on Mount Sinai, that it might serve to interpret and explain the other law which was committed to writing. Then Moses, when he came down into his tent, had repeated it all over, first to Aaron alone, next to his two sons in his presence, then to the seventy elders, and lastly, while all these still listened, to the whole assembled congregation of Israel; so that when he went out, Aaron, having heard it four times recited, was able to say it over in his turn, then his sons, after he withdrew, could repeat it again; and on the departure of these, the seventy elders found no difficulty in rehearsing the whole still another time before the people—by which means everybody gave it four hearings, and was able to go home and repeat it tolerably well to his family, while the priests and elders had it so fixed in their minds that it was not possible for a particle of it to be lost. Afterwards, Moses again carefully said it over, just before he died, to Joshua. Joshua delivered it to the care of the elders. The elders handed it down to the prophets. The prophets left it finally to the charge of the wise doctors who flourished under the second temple; and so it came down in all the perfection of its original revelation to the latest period of the Jewish state. Thus the oral law made out its goodly title to respect and veneration, and presumptuously challenged for itself a right to control at pleasure the meaning of God's written word. The Pharisees discovered great zeal in the support of its claims, and employed it in many cases to countervail the true spirit of the Bible, actually making the word of God, as our Saviour said, of no effect by their traditions. (Mark vii. 1—13.) These traditions led them to observe a multitude of uncommanded ceremonies, as foolish oftentimes as they were useless, and loaded their religion with a weight of formality and superstition under which it was hardly possible for a single right principle of piety to avoid being crushed and destroyed ltogether.

Thus the *washing of hands* before meals, which had a very good reason for its practice in the manner that they were anciently made use of in eating, was converted at length into a solemn religious duty, and the omission of it was looked upon as a crime of the most offensive sort, that merited no less a punishment than death itself. So other washings, as of cups and pots and tables, came to be established as sacred duties. In similar style, they added other precepts, without end, to the divine law; and clothed indifferent or unmeaning practices with the highest solemnity of religion.

In all this zeal which they showed in favour of the traditions of the elders, the Pharisees affected a character of extraordinary piety; such as was not content to conform itself merely to the letter of the law, but sought, for its direction, a higher and more difficult rule. They measured the worth of their religion by the multitude of its outward observances, however empty and idle most of them might be, and fancied themselves more righteous than others in proportion as they outstripped them in the mere *show* of devotion; though beneath it might be nothing but hypocrisy and pride. It was not strange, accordingly, that hypocrisy and pride should actually characterize the sect, and that, since they looked upon mere external rites and appearances, such as strike the attention of the world, as having in themselves the nature of righteousness and highest merit, they should indulge the most selfish passions, always so congenial to the human heart, even while they seemed to others and to themselves to be continual patterns of the most rigorous piety. The religion which they used, though in many respects it was severe and hard to be complied with, had nevertheless *two* attractions which would have made it welcome to the carnal mind, if it had been attended with yet far more difficulty; it was in its whole nature *ostentatious*, and adapted to secure worldly admiration for the gratification of pride; and it was at the same time highly *self-righteous*, elevating the man to whom it belonged, according to its own representation, to the highest degree of earthly holiness; and giving him assurance, on account of his merit in this respect, of the most unbounded **favour** of God—all, too, without any restraint upon the inward man, which might still rankle with all manner of corruption like the cavern of a whited sepulchre, and without any regard to the weightier matters of the law, such as judgment, mercy, and faith, which might still be disregarded with contempt, and wantonly trampled under foot. It is not to be wondered at, therefore, that the Pharisees—though they distinguished themselves from others as more excellent and holy than they, and were looked upon by the world as the most righteous of the earth—though they made many long *prayers* in the synagogues and in the streets—though they *fasted* with a sad countenance on the second and fifth days of every week—though they *washed* with the most scrupulous care day after day, and were so afraid of being contaminated, that they would not so much as eat with *Gentiles* and those whom they counted *sinners*, such as publicans and harlots—though they paid *tithes* of all they possessed, so carefully that not even the smallest garden herbs, mint, anise, and cummin, were neglected—though they affected the most rigid respect to the Sabbath, and to every form of worship in the temple and the synagogue—though they made the *border-fringes* of their garments large and their *phylacteries* broad in token of their piety—and though they professed the greatest veneration for the ancient prophets, and builded the tombs and garnished the sepulchres of the righteous dead—it is not to be wondered at, I say, that the Pharisees, with all this show of religion, were full of the most worldly spirit, and under the dominion of the most shameful principles —that they prayed and fasted and did all their deeds of piety *to be seen of men*—that they courted every sort of distinction, the uppermost rooms at feasts, the chief seats in the synagogue, and respectful greetings and titles of honour in public places— that they neglected in a great measure altogether the practice of the highest moral virtues—and that many of them indulged all manner of secret iniquity in their hearts, and under the cloak of extraordinary piety were full of the vilest extortion and excess;—while yet, all the time, they were blinded to the hollow worthlessness of their character, and really imagined, that, on account of their multiplied duties of outward religion, and the strictness of their formality, they stood high in the favour of Heaven as truly as they procured for themselves the admiration and applause of men. (Matt. vi. 1, 2, 5, 16, xii. 1—14, xiii. 1—14, xxiii. 1—31, Luke xviii. 9—14.) We are not to suppose, however, that all who belonged to the sect were thus egregiously inconsistent and hypocritical; though the general body was undoubtedly corrupt, there were not wanting in it persons of truly excellent and upright character, whose principles of virtue were laid upon a deeper foundation, and whose morality acknowledged a more enlightened and comprehensive rule.

Though we are told that those of them who occupied the seat of Moses, and undertook to explain the duties of religion, used to inculcate a more difficult and laborious lesson than they were willing themselves to practise, binding heavy burdens on other men's shoulders, to which they refused to apply one of their own fingers, (Matt. xxiii. 2—4,) it is yet certain, that, according to their own system of righteousness, which made the reality and merit of religion to consist especially in outward observances, the Pharisees, as a sect, were remarkably strict and severe. They are styled by the apostle Paul *the most straitest sect* of the Jewish religion, (Acts xxvi. 5;) and the occasional notices, that are scattered through the Gospels, of their minute and careful attention to the wearisome and burdensome forms of their own superstition, are enough to convince us that the character which they had in this respect was not without reason in their general manner of life. That they had much of a certain sort of righteousness, which, though false and hollow in the eye of God, was nevertheless wrought out with exceedingly great care and pains, far surpassing the common diligence of men in this matter, is intimated also in that declaration of our Lord, "I say unto you, that except your righteousness shall exceed the righteousness of the Scribes and Pharisees, ye shall in no case enter into the kingdom of heaven." (Matt. v. 20.) The reputation and influence which they acquired by reason of this eminent character for religion was very great, and made them altogether the most powerful party in the state—an advantage which their pride and ambition were ever prone to abuse, and which was actually employed, from time to time, only to disturb the order and tranquillity of the country.

But while the religion of this sect professed to take for itself the strictest rule, and affected to do even more than the letter of the written law required, it not only gave indulgence to the worst feelings and passions of the heart, as we have already noticed, but proceeded also to pervert the true meaning of the word of God, and to erect a different standard of morality, less at variance with the natural temper of the human mind. Thus, as it added to the truth of Heaven in one quarter, it secretly took away from it in another; *loading* it with the dreams of a self-righteous superstition, while it sought to *strip* it of its native spirituality and power, in order that it might seem to accord completely with that defective and carnal, though highly imposing scheme of piety which they held up to the admiration of the world. In some cases, they perverted the spirit of Scripture, by exalting mere *civil statutes* into the place of *moral rules*, or insisting, that whatever the law of Moses allowed must needs be in its own nature right and safe, under all circumstances; not making a proper discrimination between principles of public government and principles of private morality; and forgetting that without a continual miracle exerted to control the minds of men, some things must be permitted, on account of the hardness of the people's hearts, in the constitution of every civil society, which are not in themselves proper, nor may at all be adopted as safe maxims for individual conduct. In this way, they derived some countenance from the Bible to maxims that were selfish and unjust, and contrary to the whole general tenor of the Scriptures. (Matt. v. 31—42, xix. 3—9.) At other times, they adhered too closely to the very letter of the law, or rather attached to the letter too narrow a sense, which was altogether at variance with its true spirit. Thus they limited the obligation of the law, which required them to love every man his neighbour, to the narrow compass of their own friends around them, or at least their own people, and considered themselves at liberty to despise others, and to hate their enemies, as much as they pleased. (Matt. v. 43, 44, Luke x. 29—37.) By attaching, also, an undue importance to *ceremonial* precepts and *outward* observances, or looking upon them as if they comprehended the greatest piety in their mere forms, they lost sight, in many cases, of true morality; and brought themselves to be indifferent about that spiritual service which the Lord requires in all who worship him, and without which the most diligent and laborious show of religion can have no worth whatever in his sight. In this way they verified, in a remarkable manner, the old proverb which we find applied to them by our Saviour: *Blind guides! which strain out a gnat, and swallow a camel!* They made clean the outside of the cup and the platter, but gave themselves no concern about the much more serious defilement that lodged within; so that, while it was counted a sin of dark enormity to neglect an appointed *washing* of the hands, anger and malice and every impure affection were allowed and indulged with little or no sense of their offensive nature; and it was even taught, that the commandments of God had respect only to the grosser forms of the evils they condemned, as if the secret workings of the soul came not equally under the eye of the Almighty, or the fountains of iniquity might have less odiousness in his sight than the streams that carried their pollution abroad. (Matt. v. 21—24, 27—30, xi. 7, xv. 1—14, Luke vi. 7—11.)

Though all the Pharisees maintained a general feeling of regard for each other, as members of one and the same sect, they were not at the same time without differences of sentiment and practice among themselves, such as divided them into various subordinate parties. Tradition tells us, that there were as many as seven regular classes of them, which were distinguished from each other with no inconsiderable unlikeness, and aimed at very various degrees of perfection. Mention has already been made, in a different part of this work, of the *Galileans*, who sprung, in a great measure, out of this sect about the twelfth year of our Saviour's life: they became a *separate* sect, distinguished more for their notions about government, or rather for their violence in urging into practice the general notion of the Pharisees on this subject, than for any thing else.

SECTION II.

THE SADDUCEES.

According to the common account of its origin, this sect took its rise between two and three hundred years before the birth of Jesus Christ. It derived its name, it is said, from one Sadoc, a disciple of one of the most celebrated teachers of the age, who fell into what became afterwards its principal error, by mistaking or abusing the sense of a particular doctrine inculcated by his master. That distinguished man had taught that the service of God and the practice of virtue ought to be *disinterested*, as being in their own nature excellent and reasonable in the highest degree; and that it was not proper, accordingly, to employ *mercenary* considerations, as he represented them, the fear of future punishment, or the hope of future reward, as motives to persuade men to a life of piety. He did not say, however, or mean at all, that rewards and punishments were not to be expected in a future state: but Sadoc and another of his scholars carried out his doctrine to the full point of this pernicious consequence, and publicly maintained, in their subsequent career, that the idea of a world to come was a dream, and that the soul was destined to sink into an eternal sleep with the ruin of the body—if *soul* it might be called, which was not allowed to have any independent existence, or to be capable of separation from the material organization to which it belonged. Contrary as the infidel sentiment was to the word of God, it did not fail to find some considerable reception, and to perpetuate itself as a principal article in the creed of a distinct and important sect, even while the Scriptures were as universally as ever acknowledged to be of Divine original and authority : for what inconsistency and extravagance will not the human mind, in its depravity, consent to, for the purpose of covering from its sight the awfulness of truth and shielding its impenitent slumbers from interruption within the dark and thickly embowered refuges of error? The wealthy, the honourable, and the fashionable of the world— who, in every age, are tempted to seek for themselves an easy and genteel religion, that will agree to tolerate with widest liberality the manners and spirit of the earth, and to administer withal encouragement and quiet to the unregenerate conscience gazing forward upon the future—were not displeased, of course, with the doctrine of Sadoc; and still as the number of his followers multiplied, and acquired to themselves some name and reputation among men, it assumed, in their eyes, a more reasonable and engaging aspect, and was found to bring upon their hearts arguments irresistible in its favour, till at length the wealthy, the great, and the fashionable of the land were, in a large measure, gathered into the sect of the Sadducees.

Because of the worldly importance, therefore, of most of its members, though in point of numbers it bore no comparison with that of the Pharisees, it was a sect of considerable influence in the state. It does not appear, however, that they took, generally, much part in the public affairs of the nation: the Pharisees had an influence among the people, which always secured to their sect the chief authority in the government, and against which it was vain to contend; and, at the same time, the Sadducees seem to have been, to a considerable extent, of the opinion that life might be enjoyed, on the whole, full as well, if not better, in the easy luxury of a private condition, crowded with all manner of worldly pleasures, as amid the cares of office and the drudgery of public service. Still, they were not excluded, by any means, nor did they withdraw themselves altogether, from places of trust and power: some of their number occupied, at times, the highest offices in the state; yea, more than once, the mitre of the high-priest itself was allowed to encircle the brow of an infidel Sadducee! In such cases, however, they were under the necessity of complying, in a great measure, with the views and wishes of the Pharisees, since they would not otherwise have been tolerated by the people.

We find the great error of the sect noticed in the New Testament; they maintained, we are told, "that there is no resurrection, neither angel nor spirit." (Matt. xxii. 23, Acts xxiii. 8.) From other authority we learn, that they erred also on the subject of the overruling providence of God: they thought that the doctrine of the Pharisees, which represented all events to be *certain*, as much before they come to pass as they are afterwards, according to the wise and eternal determination of Him who contrived, constructed, and continually sustains the vast machinery of the universe, was not compatible with that freedom of will and action of which every moral being is conscious; and they professed to believe, accordingly, that no such certainty exists; but that the affairs of the world, at least so far as they are connected directly or indirectly with the actions of men, proceed in a way of liberty so absolute as to be entirely uninfluenced by Divine will, and utterly independent of Divine direction. Thus, in their zeal to escape the dogma of *fatal necessity*, and while they attempted to commit the reins of every man's destiny as much as possible into his own hands, they thrust God, in their doctrine, from the throne of the universe, divested him in part of his glorious perfections, and delivered the whole order of the world to the government of chance—if *order* that might be called, which reason or rule could have none, but must, according to the idea of its highest perfection, unfold its series of events from day to day, altogether without determinate principle, and unconstrained by a single fixed or systematic influence.

If, in the points that have been mentioned, the creed of the Sadducees was sadly erroneous, when compared with that of the Pharisees, it was greatly to be preferred to it in the respect which it showed for the written word of God. It rejected altogether the authority of that *oral* law of which the Pharisees made so wicked a use, and rightly insisted that the Scriptures, of themselves, were abundantly sufficient to direct the faith and practice of men; that they ought to be received as the *only* infallible revelation of God's will; and that to allow any tradition whatever an equal sacredness, was presumptuous and profane. It has been suspected by some, that while it thus laudably trampled under foot the traditions of the elders, it covered the merit of that zeal with shame as great by proceeding yet farther to disclaim a large part of the Bible itself; refusing to acknowledge as the word of God any thing more than the pentateuch, or five books of Moses, after the manner of the Samaritans, with whom Sadoc, it is said, took refuge for a time, to escape the displeasure of his own countrymen, when he first began to publish his doctrine. This idea, it must be acknowledged, seems to have no small weight of probability in its favour, from the consideration that there is such clear contradiction to the leading sentiment of the Sadducee sect, in other parts of Scripture, as it is hard to see how they could get along with it at all, unless by rejecting the whole; and it appears, moreover, to derive indirect confirmation from the fact, that our Saviour, when he urged the authority of God's word against their doctrine, on a certain occasion, drew his argument only from the pentateuch, when he might have brought more direct and explicit testimony, as it would seem, from other portions of revelation, if all the Jewish Bible had been received by those whom he undertook to convince of error. (Matt. xxii. 31, 32.) Still, it is an idea unsupported by any positive evidence whatever; and, more than this, it is pretty clearly discovered to be erroneous, from the use that is found, out of the Jewish writings, to have been made in controversy with the Sadducees, of other books of the Old Testament, besides those of Moses, and even by the sect itself, in support of its own opinions, while no charge of rejecting any part of revelation is ever urged against them.

The Sadducees are represented to have been characterized, in general, by a selfish and unsociable spirit. Without much sectarian interest to knit them in friendly union among themselves, they felt still less regard for other members of the community; and as, according to their system, the man who secured for himself the greatest amount of personal enjoyment in this present world was supposed to make the best use of life, they appear to have contracted the sympathies of their nature within a narrow compass, and to have made it their great concern to fill their own houses with comfort and pleasure and to shut out from them the sound of sorrow, deliberately closing their hearts against all the gentle powers of charity, and leaving all the rest of the world to their fortune, evil or happy, with cold and careless indifference. The poor, and especially the unfortunate, were excluded from their favourable regard: they overlooked them with unfeeling neglect. It may be, however, that calumny has flung a darker colouring over the picture of the Sadducee character, in this respect, than the original ever gave reason for.

The sect of the Sadducees, it seems, did not retain much of its importance long after the destruction of the temple and the state. It shrunk at last into insignificance, and expired; while that of the Pharisees continually diffused and strengthened the authority of its creed, till in the end, though its *name* has passed out of use, its *sentiments* have become the almost unanimous faith of the whole Jewish people. There is still, however, a little sect—a very little one—that dares to dissent from the general body, and reject, like the Sadducees of old, the whole system of *traditions*, acknowledging only the *written word* to be of supreme and Divine authority, in every question of religious faith or practice. It has been imagined by some, that it ought to be regarded as the feeble remnant of the ancient sect of Sadoc itself, still struggling to sustain itself after so many centuries, amid the triumphs of its rival; but since it disclaims altogether the Sadducee infidelity, admitting the existence of angels, and allowing the reality of a future state, there seems to be no good reason to derive it from so foul an original. The sect of the *Caraites* (for so they are called) has been in existence more than a thousand years, all along bearing witness for the true word of God, against the overwhelming influence of the *Rabbinists*, as the party that embraces the Pharisee doctrine of traditions has come to be denominated, and endeavouring to retain, in their little body, some image of the ancient faith of Israel, amid the melancholy rubbish of superstition and corruption that is gathered upon the ruins of their national religion.

SECTION III.

THE ESSENES.

The *Essenes* are not noticed in the New Testament: for although their sect was in as flourishing a state in the days of our Saviour as it ever was at any time, yet their manner of life separated them in a great measure from the scenes of his ministry, and cut them off from all connection with the interesting events of his history. All our knowledge of this remarkable class of Jews, accordingly, is derived from other sources; not, however, through the streams of uncertain tradition, as in some other cases we are compelled to derive information from the distant region of antiquity, but by the testimony of authentic history, conveyed in sure and regular channels over all the intervening waste of time.

The Essenes lived together in separate societies of their own, withdrawing themselves altogether from public cares, refusing to participate in the general employments and interests of the world, and adopting for their habitual use a system of principles and manners so utterly diverse from all the common plan of life around them, that it became completely impracticable for them to mingle in any free intercourse with the rest of the nation: they constituted, in short, an order of *monks;* were led, by religious feeling, to tear themselves away from the whirlpool of society, so full of danger to the soul, and so fatal to almost all that move within its sweep, and to work out in retirement, with rigorous diligence, the great and arduous preparation for a world to come, for which, supremely, the trial of human life is allowed to every child of Adam. They considered the business of piety so important, that it called for the *continual,* and as far as possible for the *exclusive,* care of every person that hoped to secure its blessings; and they looked upon the world, at the same time, as so contrary, in all its influence, to the spirit of devotion—and upon the constitution of the human heart, as so disposed through moral derangement to yield to this influence, and so almost inevitably liable to lead to ruin and death, when allowed to proceed in any measure according to its natural operation,—that it seemed to them the wisest and the only safe course to seek security by *flying,* as far as it was in their power, from the vantage-ground of the enemy, and by making it the painful toil of life to *extinguish* or *eradicate,* by self-denial and mortification of the body, the treacherous principles of evil that lodged in their own bosoms. It was the same way of thinking, which, in later times, carried many a Christian *hermit* away from the tumult of society, to take up his lonely dwelling in the wilderness or the mountain cave, and in the end erected the *monastery* and the *nunnery* in every district of the church.

It has been conjectured, that this third Jewish sect had its origin in Egypt, where so large a body of the nation came to be settled under the second temple: an idea that gathers some plausibility from the consideration, that the climate of that country has always been peculiarly adapted to create and cherish such a temper of mind as disposes persons to the sort of feeling and the manner of life that monkery requires. At any rate, a very considerable proportion of the sect, which altogether, of course, was quite small, was found in Egypt; and it was that part of it, too, which carried to the most rigorous extreme the principles of its constitution. They had some little societies also in other countries, into which the Jews were dispersed: but still their chief strength was at last in Palestine itself, where, we are told, about four thousand of them resided, principally upon the western shore of the Dead Sea. These last were in several respects less rigid than their brethren of Egypt, not thinking it necessary to retire so completely from the midst of ordinary life, and not caring to cut themselves off, to the same extent, from its common pursuits. Hence the sect consisted properly of two classes of members, viz. the *practical* Essenes, who were found for the most part in Palestine; and the *contemplative* Essenes, who had their residence especially in Egypt. The name *Essenes* was appropriated, in a great measure, altogether to the practical class in Judea, while those in Egypt were styled *Therapeutæ;* the last name, however, is only the first one translated into Greek, and both mean *Physicians;* a title which the sect assumed, not so much on account of any acquaintance with the art of healing *bodily* diseases, which some of them might have had, as because they made the health of the *soul* their great care, and professed to cure its infinitely more dangerous maladies.

The Essenes of Palestine, although they deemed it advisable to keep at a distance from large cities, had no objection to living in towns and villages, and were accustomed not only to pay some attention to agriculture, but to practise certain arts also, taking care only to avoid such as contribute in any way to the purposes of war and mischief. They held all their property in common, living, wherever they were found, in societies by themselves, uniting the fruits of their labour in one stock, and all receiving out of it whatever they needed for the support and comfort of life. Their wants, at the same time, were not such as were very difficult to be supplied: their clothing was all of the plainest kind, and no one thought of having more than a single suit at once, which he wore till it was worn out: their food was at all times simple in the extreme, a piece of bread and a plate of soup being the ordinary portion of every individual, at their principal meal: their houses were humble, and altogether without ornament: their whole manner of life, in short, was after the most frugal and unrefined style; for it was their opinion, that only the real wants of nature should be regarded in the provision that is made for the accommodation of our bodies in this world; and that every sort of luxury and pleasure of mere sense, being suited only to strengthen the baser principles of our nature, and to hinder the soul in its attempt to emancipate itself from the dominion of the flesh, ought to be dreaded and avoided with the most anxious care. Commerce, accordingly, as designed to minister only to the unnatural and unreasonable appetites of men, they considered altogether an unlawful employment. They made no use of wine: they held war to be in all cases sinful, and every art also that was designed to be subservient to its interests; yet when they travelled, they thought it not improper to carry weapons, in order to protect themselves from the robbers that abounded through the country: they held slavery under any form to be contrary to nature and reason; they did not approve of oaths, and made no use of them, except when they became members of the society; on which occasion, having previously lived on trial for the space of two years, every one who joined them was required to bind himself in the most solemn manner to love and worship God, to deal justly with all men, to abstain from doing harm to any creature, &c.; and yet they were remarkable for their strict regard to truth in all the concerns of life; insomuch that the *word* of an Essene was allowed by all that had any knowledge of them, to be worth full as much as the *oath* of another man. They did not think it wrong to marry, and some of them, accordingly, consented to make the experiment of wedlock; but it was considered to have so much hazard in it that a single state was esteemed to be more desirable. In their religious duties they were remarkably strict and regular: in the morning, they never uttered a word about common business before the rising of the sun, (the sun never found any of them in bed of course,) but occupied themselves till that time with their prayers: after this duty of devotion, they all went to their several employments: about eleven o'clock, they left their work, washed themselves with cold water, retired for a while to their several cells, or apartments, and then assembled in their dining room to partake of their plain meal of bread and soup; the afternoon called them again to their work, and when it was over, brought them a second time round their common table, spread with a supper of the most frugal sort, after which each withdrew to attend to his evening prayers: at the commencement and the close of every meal a short prayer was addressed to God, as the author of the blessing. The Sabbath they kept so carefully that they would not so much as move a dish in the house during the whole of it, lest it should be a violation of its holy rest; and besides attending to private religious duties, they regularly met on that day for public worship in synagogues, which they had of their own, where the Scriptures were read, and explained by such among them as by reason of age and understanding were best qualified for the task. When any member was found guilty of gross crime, or unfaithful to his profession, they cut him off entirely from their society.

The Therapeutæ of Egypt differed from the Essenes of Palestine only in being more rigidly severe in their manner of life. They withdrew from the midst of the common world altogether, and gave themselves up almost entirely to solitude and contemplation Those who joined them did not bring their property along with them and put it into the common stock, as was usual with the Essenes, but leaving it all to their friends whom they felt it their duty utterly to forsake, they came into the society unburdened with a particle of its care. Marriage was not in use among them at all. Their diet was merely coarse bread and salt, accompanied sometimes with a little hyssop, and the only drink they allowed themselves was water; nor did they indulge themselves with even this scanty fare, except in the most sparing manner, making it their daily practice not to taste any food before sunset, because they thought the day should all be appropriated to the cultivation of the soul by meditation and study, and that the night alone ought to be employed in satisfying the necessities of the body—and little enough even of that was needed for this purpose in their self-denying and abstemious manner of life; some of them, it is said, used to become so absorbed in their contemplations, and so engrossed with their pursuit of wisdom, that they forgot to take their food even at the close of the day, and at times for as much as three whole days together—yea, in some instances, a whole week was passed almost without eating at all—so wonderfully did the entertainment with which the mind was fed in the banqueting house of Philosophy, enable them to dispense with the grosser aliment that is appointed to invigorate and sustain our animal nature! The women—for there were such belonging to the society—never came into company with the men, (who themselves, in fact, lived every one separate from the rest almost all the week,) except on the Sabbath, when they assembled with them in the synagogue, though in a distinct part of the house, cut off by a wall of some height from that which the rest of the congregation occupied; and also at the common table which it was the custom to spread on the evening of that sacred day for their whole company to partake together. In their worship, they made much of hymns, and on certain occasions joined in sacred dances.

The whole sect agreed with the Pharisees in their belief of the existence of spirits and the immortality of the human soul, and seem also to have entertained the same general idea of God's sovereign providence in the government of the world. They denied, however, the resurrection of the body; and as they looked upon it as the chief hinderance to virtue and wisdom in this present state, and made it, accordingly, their great care to mortify all its natural appetites while lodged in its fleshly prison, it did not seem to them desirable at all to have it recovered from its ruins; or rather the thought of shutting up the emancipated spirit a second time within its walls was utterly at variance with their whole notion of the blessedness of that future state to which they looked forward. They did not receive, it seems, the *traditionary* law of the Pharisees; but, while they acknowledged the *written* word of God to be the only infallible rule of religion, they made use of a fanciful sort of interpretation in explaining it, which subjected it, after all, to the authority of human opinions, and opened a door for the introduction of all manner of error: they held that the Scriptures, besides the direct and natural sense of their language, have a deeper and more important meaning, mystically buried in that first one, which alone constitutes the true heavenly wisdom of their pages, and merits the continual study of all that aspire after the perfection to which they are appointed to guide the soul; and this meaning, accordingly, their teachers pretended to search out and bring forward, in their use of the sacred volume, turning it all into *allegory*, and so constraining it to speak, under the powerful control of fancy, whatever mystic sense they pleased. They did not bring *sacrifices* to the temple, as the law required; and the Therapeutæ, it seems, disapproved of bloody sacrifices altogether; the Essenes of Palestine, however, admitted the propriety of such offerings, and used to present them from time to time, in a solemn manner, among themselves; but with peculiar rites, altogether different from those which the law appointed. They were presented, it appears, on the occasions of their great solemnities, *in the night*, after the day had first been observed as a *fast*, and were always *wholly* burned, together with much *honey* and *wine*. It is not improbable that the strange rites which they made use of occasioned their separation from the temple; since, even if they had been disposed to offer sacrifices in their way at that place, it would have been wrong for the priests to give them permission.

SECTION IV.

THE SAMARITANS.

THE SAMARITANS, though accounted as little better than idolaters outright by the Jews, and though actually cut off from the sacred commonwealth of Israel, may, nevertheless, be looked upon as, in some sense, a *Jewish sect;* since they not only had their origin, in some degree, from the holy stock, but received the law of Moses as the rule of all their religion, and looked forward to the hopes of the Jewish church with all the confidence that was cherished by any of its tribes.

We have an account of their origin in the 17th chapter of the second book of Kings. The king of Assyria, according to the cruel policy of that ancient age, carried the great body of the ten tribes away into a distant land, and settled their country with a colony of heathen strangers—a mixed multitude from Cuthah, Ava, Hamath, and Sepharvaim, on the other side of the Euphrates. These gradually amalgamated with each other, and with such of the Israelites as were still left in the land, so as to form a single people, who came to be called, from the name of their principal city, *Samaritans*. At first, they worshipped only the false gods of their native countries, but being chastised by the Lord in a remarkable way, they were led to desire some knowledge of the God of Israel and the manner of his worship, and gladly received to instruct them one of the captive priests of Israel whom the Assyrian king sent back from Babylon for the purpose: but they had no idea still of giving up entirely their old idols; they foolishly thought that every country had its particular gods; that the God of Israel was only one of the multitude among whom the earth was divided; and that, although it was unsafe to neglect him altogether in his own territory, there could be no impropriety, having now learned the manner of his worship, and being careful to show him respect and fear according to his appointed way, in showing honour, at the same time, to other deities, and in mingling with their new religion, as they might please, the miserable idolatry of their fathers; so they *feared the Lord* after their own notion, and served their idol gods at the same time. In time, however, a more correct notion of religion began to gain ground; and at length, after the Jewish captivity, idolatry disappeared from among them altogether.

When the Jews, on their return, began to rebuild their temple, the Samaritans sought to associate themselves with them in the work; but that people would not consent at all to the proposal, perceiving that they were actuated by no good motives in urging it, and that, notwithstanding their fair professions, they had still little regard for the true religion, and were still in love with their idolatry. This refusal filled the Samaritans with rage, and led them to use every means in their power to hinder the building of the temple; in which attempts they were so successful, that the work was interrupted directly after its commencement, with a delay of full fifteen years. (Ezra. 4th, 5th, and 6th chapters.) The minds of the Jews were, of course, greatly embittered against them by this opposition, and the enmity was still more increased by the malicious arts which they afterwards employed to prevent Nehemiah from restoring the walls of Jerusalem. (Neh. 4th and 6th chapters.)

When Nehemiah undertook to reform the abuses that existed among the Jews, and among other things, required them to put away their strange wives, Manasseh, the son of the highpriest who had married a daughter of Sanballat, prince of the Samaritans, refused to comply with the order, and being compelled to quit his own people, sought refuge with his father-in-law. (Neh. xiii. 28.) Sanballat, taking that advantage of the circumstances which he thought would be most offensive to the Jews, obtained permission from the Persian monarch, erected a NEW TEMPLE on mount Gerizim, and constituted his son-in-law the father of its priesthood. Thus a regular system of national worship, corresponding in all respects to that of the true people of God, was established, and every vestige of the former idolatry became obliterated from the land. After this, it was usual for such Jews as became exposed to punishment in their own country for violating its laws, or were excommunicated for their offences from religious and social privileges, to betake themselves, for security or relief, to the Samaritans, among whom they were received without difficulty In this way, the jealousy and enmity of the two people, instead of wearing away with time, gathered continually fresh encouragement and renewed vigour. During the persecution of Antiochus Epiphanes—that enemy of all righteousness and truth—the Samaritans, caring more for their worldly advantage than for their religion, secured themselves from the desolating storm, by abandoning altogether their national worship; they complied with all the wishes of the tyrant, consecrated their temple to Jupiter, the chief of the heathen gods, and lent their aid in the war that was carried on against the Jews, to reduce them to the same apostasy. (1 Maccabees iii. 10.) After the persecution was over, they returned again to the religion of Moses; but their polluted sanctuary was not allowed to stand much longer: John Hyrcanus, the triumphant Jewish prince, about 130 years before the time of Christ, turned his arms against their country, subdued it completely, and destroyed, in anger, that proud temple of Sanballat.

All this, of course, had no tendency to remove the old hatred which each of the countries cherished for the other; it struck its root still deeper, and flourished in yet greater and more active luxuriance. So bitter and rancorous did the mutual enmity become, that all intercourse between the two nations was brought to an end—*the Jews had no dealings with the Samaritans*—and it was even counted somewhat unsafe for persons of either country to travel through the territories of the other; or at least it was found so extremely inconvenient, by reason of the inhospitable treatment they were sure to meet with, that it was generally preferred to avoid it, though at the expense of making a considerable circuit out of the direct way; whence it was usual for the Jews, in going from Galilee to Jerusalem, on the contrary, to cross the Jordan, and pass along through Gilead, on the east side, rather than go through Samaria, which lay directly between. We ought not to be surprised, therefore, at the question of the Samaritan woman, whom our Lord, oppressed with weariness and thirst, asked to give him some water at Jacob's well: " How is it that thou, being a Jew, askest drink of me, which am a woman of Samaria?" (John iv. 4—9.) Nor should it seem strange, that, when Jesus, on another occasion, passing through that country, sent messengers before him to a certain village, to secure entertainment for the night, the inhabitants utterly refused to receive him, " because his face was as though he would go to Jerusalem." (Luke ix. 51—56.) It appears, however, that the same prejudice was not cherished to such an extent among all the Samaritans; for we are told that he went to another village, where the people seem to have made no objection to his presence; and it was the common custom of our Saviour to pass through their country with his disciples, in his journeys to and from Jerusalem; so that he must have still been able to procure among them such accommodations as his humble style of life required. There is reason to believe, in fact, that there was, at this time, altogether more of bitterness and malignity on the part of the Jews than on that of the Samaritans in the mutual hatred of the two people, (John viii. 48,) and that the Samaritan enmity, though it was deeply settled, did not, nevertheless, so thoroughly as the Jewish, crush every sentiment of generous humanity under its weight: this our Lord seems to intimate in that parable which he employed, on a certain occasion, to answer the inquiry, " Who is my neighbour?" (Luke x 31—37) The readiness with which the inhabitants of Sychar, as we have account in the 4th chapter of John, laid aside all prejudice, honestly attended to the doctrine of Christ, and yielded to the evidence with which it was accompanied, is truly worthy of our admiration: and it ought to be remembered, that, when ten lepers were, on one occasion, all healed at once, while obeying the direction of the Saviour, the only one of all their number who came back with an overflowing heart, to express his gratitude, and to give glory to God for the amazing benefit, was a Samaritan (Luke xvii. 12—19.)

The Samaritans still continued, after the destruction of their temple, to worship on Mount Gerizim, and to insist as strenuously as ever, that no other place in the world had so good a claim to this distinction. For they had been accustomed, since the days of Sanballat, to challenge for the place of their sanctuary, the highest measure of sacredness: they were not content to sustain its title to reverence on any thing short of a divine consecration, nor disposed at all to seek any compromise with the pretensions of Moriah; but allowing with the Jews themselves, that God had made choice of only one place for his public worship, and that no other, accordingly, ought ever to be acknowledged, they boldly maintained that their own Gerizim had been, from the first, distinguished with the honour of this choice, and that the contrary claim which Jerusalem urged in favour of her celebrated hill was altogether unfounded and false. Here, they contended, altars were erected, and sacrifices offered by Abraham and Jacob, (Gen. xii. 6, 7, xxxiii. 18—20,) and on this account, they said, the hill was afterwards appointed by God himself, to be the place of blessing, when the Israelites entered the promised land, and they were required to build an altar upon it, and to present burnt-offerings and peace-offerings there, before the Lord—by which direction, it was affirmed, God clearly signified that he had chosen Mount Gerizim to be the place where, according to his promise, he would set his name, and actually consecrated it by a solemn appointment, to be the seat of his worship in all future time. The great objection to this argument is, that when we consult the 27th chapter of Deuteronomy, in which we have the Divine direction relative to this matter recorded, we find the altar was ordered to be set up, *not* on Gerizim, but on Mount *Ebal*, which stood directly over against it, (with the city of *Shechem, Sichem,* or *Sychar,* in the valley between,) and was appointed to be on the same occasion the hill of cursing. But in the Samaritan Bible—and they maintain their argument, of course, on no other authority—the difficulty is not found; for instead of the word *Ebal*, in the fourth verse, it reads *Gerizim*, and thus at once alters the whole case. It seems, that the controversy about the place of worship was never allowed to sleep, but was that which, at all times, most naturally presented itself, when the quarrel that existed between the two nations came under consideration; and we find, accordingly, that the woman of Sychar, when she perceived that Jesus was a prophet, and then wished to give the conversation a turn that might seem to be religious, while it should not continue the disturbance which she began to feel in her conscience, without ceremony brought forward this subject of dispute: *Our fathers worshipped in this mountain*, said she, pointing to Gerizim close at hand, *and ye say that in Jerusalem is the place where men ought to worship*. Our Saviour, while he assured her that the true church and worship of God were found among the Jews, directed her attention to that new dispensation which he was about to introduce, in which the pomp and form of the ceremonial system should pass altogether away, and worship would be deemed acceptable, not at all as it should rise from Jerusalem, or the summit of Gerizim, or any other particular place, but only as it should carry on high the spiritual service of the heart, in whatever part of the world it might be found.

It may seem strange to some, that the Samaritans should have considered the whole controversy about the place of worship decided in the single passage of Deuteronomy just mentioned, and should have not felt themselves confounded at all by various other passages of Scripture that clearly decide the question in favour of the Jews: but it is to be recollected that their Bible comprehended no more than the five books of Moses, and they paid no respect, accordingly, to any testimony whatever that might be brought forward from other parts of the sacred volume.

There is still a very small remnant of the Samaritan race found in their ancient country. Their principal residence is in that same valley, at the foot of the sacred mountain, in which, of old, the city of Shechem or Sichem, denominated in later times *Sychar*, (by the Jews, perhaps, in malignant derision— for Sychar means *drunken*,) had its beautiful retreat; and in that same city, too, though greatly altered for the worse, like the whole face of Palestine, from its ancient state, and divested entirely of its original appellation, instead of which it now bears the name of *Napolose* or *Nablous*. Though reduced to insignificance, for their whole number, it is said, does not exceed forty, they still preserve themselves separate from the rest of the world around them, and adhere with the greatest constancy and zeal to the faith of their fathers; inveterate as ever in their opposition to the Jews, and jealous, as of old, for the honour of Gerizim, on which they have a synagogue, or rather a sort of a temple, of long standing, and which they still insist is the place where men ought to worship; though they have not themselves been allowed, of late years, by their Turkish masters, to visit its summit for that purpose.

APPENDIX.

List of the Principal Writers who have treated on the Antiquities of the Scriptures.

The Antiquities of the Hebrew Republic. By Thomas Lewis, M. A. 8vo, 4 vols. London, 1724–5.

This is a laborious compilation, from the most distinguished writers, whether Jews or Christians, on the manners and laws of the Hebrews.

Jewish, Oriental, and Classical Antiquities; containing Illustrations of the Scriptures and Classical Records, from Oriental Sources. By the Rev. Daniel Guildford Wait, LL. B., F. A. S. Vol. I. Cambridge, 1823. 8vo.

The object of this elaborate work is to illustrate Biblical and Classical Antiquities from the oriental writings. This first volume is exclusively devoted to a demonstration of the coincidence which subsists between these different departments of study; and that coincidence the author has satisfactorily shown by various examples. The subsequent volumes are announced to contain disquisitions on detached subjects, and elucidations of the text, and assertions of those Greek writers who have treated of Eastern History, or alluded to eastern customs. Mr. Wait has long been known to biblical students as the author of numerous valuable articles on sacred criticism, which have appeared in different volumes of the Classical Journal.

Various treatises on Sacred Antiquities have been written by different authors: of these the following are the most valuable.

The Manners of the Ancient Israelites, containing an account of their peculiar Customs, Ceremonies, Laws, Polity Religion, Sects, Arts, and Trades, &c. &c By Claude Fleury 8vo. London, 1809.

For this third and best edition, the public are indebted to Dr. Adam Clarke, who has enlarged the original work with much valuable information, from the principal writers on Jewish Antiquities. The Abbé Fleury's work was translated many years since by Mr. Farnworth. The late excellent bishop of Norwich, (Dr. Horne,) has recommended it in the following terms: "This little book contains a concise, pleasing, and just account of the manners, customs, laws, policy, and religion of the Israelites. It is an excellent introduction to the reading of the Old Testament and should be put into the hands of every young person."

Jewish Antiquities, or a Course of Lectures on the Three first books of Godwin's Moses and Aaron. To which is annexed a Dissertation on the Hebrew Language. By David Jennings, D. D. 8vo. 2 vols. London, 1766; Perth, 1808; and London, 1823, in one volume, 8vo.

This work has long held a distinguished character for its accuracy and learning, and has been often reprinted. "The Treatises of Mr. Lowman on the *Ritual* (8vo. London, 1748,) and on the *Civil Government of the Hebrews*, (8vo. London, 1740,) may properly accompany these works."

The most elaborate system of Jewish antiquities, perhaps, that is extant, is Godwin's *Moses* and *Aaron;* a small quarto volume, now rather scarce: it was formerly in great request as a text book, and passed through many editions: the latest, we believe, is that of 1678. Numerous other treatises on Hebrew antiquities are to be found in the 34th volume of Ugolini's Thesaurus Antiquitatum Hebræarum.

Jahn's Biblical Archæology: An elaborate compendium of biblical antiquities, abridged from the author's larger work, on the same subject, in the German language, (in four large 8vo volumes,) and arranged under the three divisions of domestic, political, and ecclesiastical antiquities. At the end of the volume are upwards of sixty pages of questions, framed upon the preceding part of the work; the answers to which are to be given by students. A faithful English translation of "Jahn's Biblical Archæology, was published at Andover, (Massachusetts,) in 1823, by T. C. Upham, (assistant teacher of Hebrew and Greek in the Theological Seminary at that place,) with valuable additions and corrections, partly the result of a collation of Jahn's Latin work with the original German **treatise**, **and partly** derived from other sources.

APPENDIX. 441

The Antiquities of the Jews, carefully compiled from authentic sources, and their Customs illustrated, by Modern Travels. By W. Brown, D. D. London, 1820, 2 vols. 8vo Also, Philadelphia, W. W. Woodward, 1823.

This work is exceedingly rich in one department—viz. that of Jewish and Rabbinical traditions. No book is more full in regard to the whole routine of the temple service, as understood by the Jews. It is also remarkably adapted to continuous perusal, though it must be owned the texture of the work is careless, and the style homely.

Calmet's Dictionary of the Holy Bible—Historical, Critical, Geographical, and Etymological—in five vols. quarto.
The same, abridged by Rev. E. Robinson, D. D. 1 vol. royal 8vo.

A Cyclopædia of Biblical Literature, edited by John Kitto, D. D., F. S. A., &c. Illustrated with numerous engravings. New York. Mark H. Newman. 2 vols. 8vo, 1846.

This work is at once learned, convenient, and interesting—especially rich in embellishments. It is, however, the work of many hands, in Great Britain and some even in Germany; and of these, some are very loose in their opinions. The work is, therefore, to be used with great discrimination

Illustrations of the Holy Scriptures, in three parts. By the Rev. George Paxton. Edinburgh, 1819, 2 vols. 8vo. Reprinted at Philadelphia, 1821, 2 vols. 8vo.

Scripture Costume, exhibited in a series of Engravings, representing the principal Personages mentioned in the Sacred Writings. Drawn under the superintendence of the late Benjamin West, Esq., P. R. A., by R. Satchwell; with Biographical Sketches and Historical Remarks on the Manners and Customs of Eastern Nations. London, 1819. Elephant 4to.

Observations on divers Passages of Scripture, placing many of them in a light altogether new, ... by means of circumstances mentioned in Books of Voyages and Travels into the East. By the Rev. Thomas Harmer. London, 1816, 4 vols. 8vo, best edition.

As books of voyages and travels are, for the most part, vo luminous, the late reverend and learned Thomas Harmer formed the design, which he happily executed, of perusing the works of oriental travellers, with the view of extracting from them whatever might illustrate the rites and customs mentioned in the Scriptures. His researches form four volumes in 8vo, and were published at different times towards the close of the last century. The best edition is that above noticed, and is edited by Dr. Adam Clarke, who has newly arranged the whole, and made many important additions and corrections. In this work numerous passages of Scripture are placed in a light altogether new; the meanings of others, which are not discoverable by the methods commonly used by interpreters, are satisfactorily ascertained; and many probable conjectures are offered to the biblical student.

The Oriental Guide to the Interpretation of the Holy Scriptures. Two Discourses preached at Christ Church, Newgate street, with Illustrative Notes, and an Appendix, containing a general and descriptive catalogue of the best writers on the subject. By the Rev. Samuel Burder, A. M. London, 1823, 8vo.

Oriental Customs; or, an Illustration of the Sacred Scriptures, by an explanatory application of the Customs and Manners of the Eastern Nations. By the Rev. S. Burder, 6th edition, 1822. 2 vols. 8vo.

This is a useful abridgment of Harmer's Observations, with many valuable additions from recent voyagers and travellers, arranged in the order of the books, chapters, and verses of the Bible. It was translated into German by Dr. E. F. C. Rosenmüller, (5 vols. 8vo, Leipsic, 1819,) with material corrections, and much new matter. Such of these as were additions to the articles contained in the "Oriental Customs," have been translated and inserted in the sixth edition above noticed. But those articles which are entirely new, being founded on texts not before brought under Mr. Burder's consideration, are translated and inserted in—

Oriental Literature applied to the Illustration of the Sacred Scriptures; especially with reference to Antiquities, Traditions, and Manners, collected from the most celebrated Writers and Travellers, both ancient and modern; designed as a Sequel to Oriental Customs. By the Rev. Samuel Burder, A. M. London, 1822, 2 vols. 8vo.

The Eastern Mirror; an Illustration of the Sacred Scriptures, in which the Customs of Oriental Nations are clearly developed by the Writings of the most celebrated Travellers. By the Rev. W. Fowler. 8vo. Exeter, 1814

APPENDIX. 443

An Abridgment of Harmer's Observations, and the earlier editions of Burder's Oriental Customs, with a few unimportant additions.

⁎ The mode of illustrating Scripture from oriental voyages and travels, first applied by Harmer, has been successfully followed by the laborious editor of the "Fragments," annexed to the quarto editions of Calmet's Dictionary of the Bible, and also by Mr. Vansittart in his "Observations on Select Places of the Old Testament, founded on a perusal of Parsons's Travels from Aleppo to Bagdad." 8vo. Oxford and London, 1812.

Josephus's Antiquities of the Jews. 1 vol. 8vo.

Introduction to the Critical Study and Knowledge of the Holy Scriptures. By Thomas Hartwell Horne. 4 vols. 8vo. Various editions.

Popular Introduction to the Study of the Holy Scriptures. By William Carpenter. 1 vol. 8vo.

The Union Bible Dictionary; or, Complete Biblical Cyclopædia. With maps and several hundred illustrations. Containing an explanation of all the words used in the Bible which are not self-explained, or the force and meaning of which may not be learned from a common Dictionary. American Sunday-school Union. 1 vol. 8vo, and 18mo.

The Natural History of the Bible. By Francis A. Ewing, M. D. American Sunday-school Union. 1 vol. 18mo, with numerous illustrations.

Scripture Illustrations—of the Agriculture, Dwellings, Meals, Books, Tents, Sacred Utensils, Altars, Customs of War, Worship, &c. 4 vols. 18mo. American Sunday-school Union.

Hebrew Customs. 18mo. American Sunday-school Union

Evening Recreations. A series of dialogues, embracing:—The Geography and General Description of Palestine.—History of the Patriarchs and their Families.—History of the Israelites in Egypt; their deliverance from bondage; and an account of their laws.—The Jewish Service; the Conquest of Canaan; and its Division among the Tribes. 4 vols. 18mo American Sunday-school Union.

ON THE DIVISIONS OCCURRING IN THE BIBLE.

The Old Testament resolves itself into two grand divisions—the *Canonical* and *Apocryphal* books: the former were written under the guidance of Divine inspiration; are part of the rule of faith and conduct of Christians; and have ever been undisputed as regards their authority: the latter are of no Divine authority, and are only useful as historical documents. The books of the Maccabees are of considerable value, as helping to fill up the history of that interval of time which elapsed between the ceasing of prophecy and the advent of the Messiah. It is to be regretted that some of the Apocryphal books contain gross and palpable perversions of truth, and some details of an indelicate nature.

The Jewish church divided the canonical books into three classes, under which form they were generally referred to and quoted. These were denominated THE LAW, THE PROPHETS, and the HAGIOGRAPHA, or holy writings. THE LAW contained the five books of Moses, frequently called *the Pentateuch*, i. e. *the five books*. THE PROPHETS comprised the whole of the writings now termed *prophetical*—from Isaiah to Malachi inclusively—and also the books of Job, Joshua, Judges, Ruth, Samuel, Kings, Chronicles, Ezra, Nehemiah, and Esther; these books having been either written or revised by prophets—probably the former. THE HAGIOGRAPHA included the Psalms, Proverbs, Ecclesiastes, and the Song of Solomon. It is probable that our Saviour alluded to this division of the Old Testament when he said, "All things must be fulfilled which are written in the law of Moses, and in the Prophets, and in the Psalms, concerning me," (Luke xxiv. 44;) for *the Psalms* standing first in this collection of books, gave its name to the division.

Since the completion of the canon of the entire Scriptures, the general or principal division adopted is that of the *Old and New Testament*. The books included under each of these divisions are too familiar to every reader to need repetition here. It must be observed, however, that the order of the books, as placed in our translation, is not according to the times in which they were written, or the course of the history to which they relate. The several books stand as unconnected and independent documents.

The division into chapter and verse is a modern invention which it is to be regretted should ever have assumed a higher character than convenient divisions for the purposes of reference and quotation. They should be totally disregarded in reading the Bible.

APPENDIX.

OF THE BOOKS OF THE NEW TESTAMENT.

The books of the New Testament are divisible into three classes—HISTORICAL, DOCTRINAL, and PROPHETICAL. The first embraces the four Gospels and the Acts of the Apostles; the second includes the Apostolic Epistles; and the last, the book of Revelation. We do not mean, however, that either of these classes excludes the subjects of the other: like all the other sacred books, those of the *New Testament* are of a mixed nature, and contain *history, prophecy,* and *doctrine.*

In the second and third centuries the New Testament was divided into two parts—the *Gospels* and the *Epistles,* or *Gospels* and *Apostles.* Other divisions have obtained in subsequent ages, with which it is unnecessary to trouble the reader.

THE NEW TESTAMENT is called in the Greek, H KAINH ΔIAΘHKH, (*e Kaine Diatheke,*) *the New Testament* or *Covenant,* a title which was early borrowed by the Church from the Scriptures, (Matt. xxvi. 28, Gal. iii. 17, Heb. viii. 8, ix. 15, 20,) and authorized by the apostle Paul, 2 Cor. iii. 14. The word $διαθηκη$, in these passages, denotes a *covenant;* and in this view THE NEW COVENANT signifies, "A book containing the terms of the new covenant between God and man." But, according to the meaning of the primitive church, which adopted this title, it is not altogether improperly rendered NEW TESTAMENT; as being that wherein the Christian's inheritance is sealed to him as a son and heir of God, and wherein the death of Christ as a testator (Heb. ix. 16, 17) is related at large and applied to our benefit. As this title implies that in the gospel unspeakable gifts are bequeathed to us, antecedent to all conditions required of us, the title of TESTAMENT may be retained, though that of COVENANT is more exact and proper.

The term GOSPEL, which is more generally applied to the writings of the four Evangelists, comprising a history of the transactions of our Lord Jesus Christ, is not unfrequently used in a more extended sense, as including the whole of the New Testament scriptures, and also that system of grace and mercy which they unfold. This word, which exactly answers to the Greek term Ευαγγελιον, is derived from the Saxon word, *God,* (Good,) and *spel,* (speech or tidings,) and is evidently intended to denote the good message, or the "glad tidings of great joy" which God has sent to all mankind, "preaching peace by Jesus Christ, who is Lord of all," Acts x. 36.

Concerning the order of the New Testament books, biblical writers are by no means agreed. The following table is compiled from Mr. Townsend's Chronological Arrangement, where the conflicting opinions of chronologists have been considered and decided upon with great care and judgment:—

APPENDIX.

Book.	Author.	Place at which it was written.	For whose use primarily intended.	A. D.
Gospel of Matthew	Matthew	Judea	Jews in Judea	37
——— Mark	Mark	Rome and Jerusalem	Gentile Christians	44
Acts of the Apostles	Luke			—
Epistle to the Galatians	Paul	Thessalonica		51
First to the Thessalonians	———	Corinth		—
Second to the Thessalonians	———	———		52
Epistle to Titus	———	Nicopolis		53
First to the Cor.	———	Ephesus		56
First Epistle to Timothy	———	Macedonia		56 or 57
Second Epistle to the Corinth.	———	Philippi		58
Epistle to the Romans	———	Corinth		—
— to the Ephes.	———	Rome		61
— to the Philip.	———			62
— to the Colos.	———	———		—
— to Philemon	———			—
— of James	James	Jerusalem	Jewish Christians	—
Epistle to the Hebrews	Paul	Italy	Jews	—
Gospel of St. Luke	Luke	Achaia	Gentile converts	64
Second Epistle to Timothy	Paul	———		65 or 66
First Epistle of Peter	Peter		Jews and Gentile converts	—
Second Epistle of Peter	———	Italy or Rome	Jewish & Gentile Christians of the Dispersion	
Epistle to Jude	Jude	Probably Syria	General	66
Book of Revelation	John	Asia Minor	———	96
Three Epistles of John	———	———	———	96 to 100
Gospel according to John	———	———	———	—

APPENDIX.

That all the books which convey to us the history of events under the New Testament, were written and immediately published by persons contemporary with the events, is fully proved by the testimony or an unbroken series of authors, reaching from the days of the Evangelists to the present times; by the concurrent belief of Christians of all denominations, and by the unreserved confession of avowed enemies to the gospel. In this point of view the writings of the ancient Fathers of the Christian Church are invaluable. They contain not only frequent references and allusions to the books of the New Testament, but also such numerous professed quotations from them, that it is demonstrably certain, that these books existed in their present state a few years after the conclusion of our Saviour's ministry. No unbeliever in the Apostolic age, in the age immediately subsequent to it, or indeed in any age whatever, was ever able to disprove the facts recorded in these books; and it does not appear that in the early times any such attempt was made. The facts therefore related in the New Testament, must be admitted to have really happened; and these abundantly prove the divine mission of Christ, and the sacred origin and authority of the Christian religion.

www.ingramcontent.com/pod-product-compliance
Lightning Source LLC
Chambersburg PA
CBHW070748020526
44115CB00032B/1413